RENEWALS 458-457-

D0772986

WITHDRAWN
UTSA Libraries

Votaries of Apollo

THE CAROLINA LOWCOUNTRY AND THE ATLANTIC WORLD
*Sponsored by the Carolina Lowcountry and
Atlantic World Program of the College of Charleston*

Votaries of Apollo

The St. Cecilia Society and the
Patronage of Concert Music in
Charleston, South Carolina,
1766–1820

Nicholas Michael Butler

The University of South Carolina Press

Library
University of Texas
at San Antonio

© 2007 University of South Carolina

Published by the University of South Carolina Press
Columbia, South Carolina 29208

www.sc.edu/uscpress

Manufactured in the United States of America

16 15 14 13 12 11 10 09 08 07   10 9 8 7 6 5 4 3 2 1

Library of Congress Cataloging-in-Publication Data

Butler, Nicholas Michael.
  Votaries of Apollo : the St. Cecilia Society and the patronage of concert music in
Charleston, South Carolina, 1766–1820 / Nicholas Michael Butler.
      p. cm. — (The Carolina lowcountry and the Atlantic world)
  Includes bibliographical references (p.   ) and index.
  ISBN-13: 978-1-57003-705-4 (cloth : alk. paper)
  ISBN-10: 1-57003-705-1 (cloth : alk. paper)
      1. Music patronage—South Carolina—Charleston—History. 2. Music—South Carolina
Charleston—History and criticism. 3. St. Cecilia Society (Charleston, S.C.)—History.
I. Title.
  ML200.8.C454B87 2007
  780.79'757915—dc22   2007015524

This book was printed on Glatfelter Natures, a recycled paper with 50 percent
postconsumer waste content.

For Wendy

Contents

Illustrations

Preface

THE ST. CECILIA SOCIETY of Charleston, South Carolina, was formed in 1766 as a subscription concert organization, a mode of private music patronage inspired by many similar groups in contemporary Britain. Named for the traditional patron saint of music, the society served as the local arbiter of musical taste, and for more than five decades its annual concert series formed the backbone of the city's rich musical life. Its membership was limited to the gentlemen of Charleston's elite, who were encouraged to bring the ladies of their families and invited guests to the concerts. The sounds of the most modern and fashionable European music, performed by the society's orchestra of amateur and professional musicians, served as an elegant accompaniment to the audience's polite conversation and to the formal dancing that followed each concert. Intermingling the practices and values of the Old and the New Worlds, St. Cecilia Society events formed an exclusive social stage on which the patronage, performance, and appreciation of contemporary European concert music asserted the cultural and political authority of its participants. The convergence of several local and international circumstances induced the society to abandon its concert series in 1820 and to withdraw into a more private existence, but it continues to exist today as a venerable and highly exclusive social organization. Since its corporate property and records were lost during the Civil War, however, the details of the society's early history have long since faded from local memory.

Over the past century stories of the society's elegant antebellum entertainments have become part of the mythology and romance of Charleston. The highly romanticized descriptions of the society that have appeared in print heretofore focus almost exclusively on its social activities, however, and only occasionally mention its origins as a musical organization. Most twentieth-century surveys of American music history at least mention the society's existence, and a handful of music dissertations have included brief sketches of its activities.[1] This entire pool of historical literature is, however, clouded by inaccurate data and misunderstandings that have prevented historians from properly recognizing the significance of this important organization. This book seeks to remedy these faults by reconstructing, as fully as presently possible, the activities of the St. Cecilia Society between the years 1766 and 1820, during which time the society was simultaneously the premier social organization in the American South and the most significant musical organization in North America. In the absence of the St. Cecilia Society's manuscript journals and other records of its first century of operation, a minutely detailed narrative of its musical activities is not possible. Rather than presenting the surviving data in a strictly chronological fashion, therefore, the ensuing chapters are arranged topically and focus on the most significant aspects of the society's activity.

The goal of this study is not merely to depict one narrow historical view of a community's musical heritage, but rather to present this era of the St. Cecilia Society's activities as a means for exploring the intersection of local, national, and international cultural forces. Examining the society's origins and prosperity in the late colonial era, its perseverance through changing economic and social conditions, and its eventual withdrawal from musical patronage is a means through which we can study the evolving cultural atmosphere of the southern seaport city of Charleston. The fifty-four-year trajectory of the St. Cecilia Society's musical activity epitomizes the contemporary transformation of Charleston's cultural life from the confident cosmopolitanism and ambitious expansion of the late colonial era to the onset of economic decline and isolationist attitudes at the advent of the antebellum era.

Simultaneously this project bolsters our understanding of the impact contemporary European musical models had on the nascent musical culture of the United States. While previous scholars of this topic have characterized early American concert life as a "feeble imitation" of European practices, this reconstruction of the St. Cecilia Society's activities demonstrates the existence of a robust and long-term effort to replicate Old World models.[2] The details of the society's sustained concert series, which was fully commensurate with the content, form, and character of those in the urban centers of contemporary Great Britain, greatly enhance our understanding of the vitality of early American concert life and thus provoke a reappraisal of established historiographic conclusions.

Many scholars have convincingly argued that the accumulation of material luxury—such as art, furnishings, and architectural fashions—in colonial and early federal America was part of an attempt to demonstrate sociopolitical legitimacy by emulating European, and more specifically British, cultural patterns. Musical performance, although a sibling to material wealth, has been far less thoroughly examined by historians of early American culture. Because of its re-creative and temporal nature, this aural phenomenon defies traditional materialist approaches. Nevertheless, the performance of imported music in eighteenth- and early-nineteenth-century British America followed precisely the same cultural impulses as the accumulation of London fashions, books, and furnishings. By identifying the music performed at the St. Cecilia Society concerts and the social contexts and physical environments in which this music was heard, we can begin to explore the aural history of early Charleston. That is, we can use this information as a tool for imagining how these auditory sensations, cultural sensibilities, and intellectual pursuits coalesced to shape a segment of Charleston's early population.

The primary musical significance of the St. Cecilia Society's first half century was its sustained patronage of sophisticated European musical culture during an era when the nascent United States was just beginning to develop its own national identity. Organized performances of imported concert music took place in other American cities during the eighteenth and early-nineteenth centuries, of course, but no contemporary musical phenomenon in this country matched the continuity or the level of organization demonstrated by the St. Cecilia Society's long-standing series. From around 1730 onward, for example, concerts began to be performed with varying frequency in a number of colonial American cities from Boston to Charleston. Most of these early performances appear to be isolated, sporadic events organized by professional musicians for their own benefit. Later, professional musicians were responsible for inaugurating the subscription concert series that commenced nearly simultaneously in Boston, New York, and Philadelphia in the wake of the Treaty of Paris in 1763. None of these series was established under the auspices of a society or self-perpetuating organization, however, and none appears to have survived the Revolution. Using the parlance of contemporary Britain, these series were "commercial" rather than "polite" concerts; that is, they were designed to advance the careers of the performers who directed the events and depended on the mercurial patronage of the public (specifically the gentry) in order to continue.[3] In contrast, Charleston's St. Cecilia Society is the earliest known example of a "polite" musical society in British America—an organization formed and managed by amateur musicians specifically for the purpose of sponsoring an ongoing series of cosmopolitan concerts open only to a select, mixed-sex audience. The endurance of this society's concert activities for more than a half century represents a unique chapter in this nation's musical heritage, one that might inspire a new and clearer understanding of our musical roots.

Despite the precedence of the St. Cecilia Society and similar concert activity in other colonial cities, very little scholarly attention has been paid the to the presentation of concert music in early America in general. Recent historical models for the establishment of "highbrow" European (principally orchestral) music in this country have passed over evidence of eighteenth- and early-nineteenth-century concert life and focused instead on the later Romantic idealism that was "sired by Puritanism and born of evangelical-ism."[4] The rise of the romantically imagined morality of music occurred to some extent in Charleston too but only in the decades after the St. Cecilia Society had withdrawn from its musical endeavors. The musical era that pre-ceded that change—as illustrated by the nearly four hundred concerts the society presented over more than five decades—is a separate aesthetic period that deserves a thorough investigation informed by larger, international issues.[5] As the evidence demonstrates, the concert patronage of Charleston's St. Cecilia Society was as much an Enlightenment phenomenon as the rise of the Boston Symphony in the mid–nineteenth century was a Romantic one. By examining the musical epoch of the St. Cecilia Society, we see not a puri-tanical, conditional acceptance of European concert music, but an early and passionate attachment to music sired by British cosmopolitanism, born of colonial pretensions, and eventually obscured by overwhelming cultural and economic changes.

Editorial Notes

Since a great deal of the primary source data presented in this book is taken from Charleston newspapers of the late eighteenth and early nineteenth cen-turies, a few words about these sources is appropriate. From the first issue of the *South-Carolina Gazette* in 1732 through the 1760s, Charleston's newspa-pers were generally weekly publications. By the end of 1768, however, some of city's papers began to appear two and then three times a week. This trend con-tinued through the 1770s and was resumed in 1783 after numerous interrup-tions caused by the Revolutionary War. Daily papers (Sundays always excepted) began to appear in December 1784, and by the end of that decade this schedule became standard in Charleston. Properly identifying the daily newspapers is a simple task, for each has a unique date, but the same is not nec-essarily true for the other papers. Some of the weekly and semiweekly newspa-pers used a date span (for example, *Royal Gazette,* 10–14 November 1781) to identify the period of coverage, while others used only the date on which they were published. When referring to specific issues of newspapers, therefore, I give the date of the paper in the same form as it appears in the original source.

Many of the newspaper advertisements and notices cited in the following chapters were published repeatedly over a period of days or weeks, often appearing simultaneously in two or three competing papers. In providing ref-erences to specific announcements—such as meeting notices and subscrip-tion arrears—I have elected to cite the earliest appearance of the item in question. Except for unique advertisements or early advertisements found in secondary papers, I cite the dominant paper of the day. The Charleston *City Gazette and Daily Advertiser,* for example, was the main newspaper of the 1790s and early 1800s. By about 1810, however, the *Charleston Courier* had emerged as the dominant paper. For references to published concert programs (as found in chapter 9), I cite the date of performance, even if the program was advertised in the days or weeks leading up to the event. Advertised commercial concerts for which a program (if one was provided at all) did not appear in the newspaper on the day of performance were very rare. Thus by citing the newspaper on the date of performance the reader is apprised of both the performance date and the location of the accompanying program. Deviations from this method are noted as they appear.

As a general rule throughout this book, material quoted from primary sources, whether from a newspaper or a manuscript, is reproduced with the original spelling, punctuation, and emphasis. Any editorial modifications of this material are noted in square brackets. This policy also includes references to the city in which this study is set. From the late seventeenth century through early August 1783, the capital of South Carolina was known as Charles Town, or, in the late colonial era, Charlestown. Since its incorporation on 13 August 1783, however, the city has been called Charleston. In this study, therefore, primary source references to the city's name will be given without alteration, while, for the sake of consistency, I use the current spelling in my prose.

Similarly three different spellings of the name of the society's patron saint were used interchangeably in late-eighteenth- and early-nineteenth-century Charleston: "Cæcilia," "Cœcilia," and "Cecilia." The use of an "a-e" (æ) ligature in "Cæcilia" reflects the classical Latin form of the name. The "o-e" (œ) ligature in "Cœcilia," which was used much more frequently in Charleston, is an incorrect adaptation. The use of a simple "e" in "Cecilia," which was commonly used throughout Europe by the eighteenth century, represents the typical medieval flattening of the "æ" sound.[6] This spelling was used occasionally in eighteenth-century Charleston, and by the early years of the nineteenth century it became the standard form used in printed advertisements.

The cultural clout of the early St. Cecilia Society might seem to be undermined by its frequent use of the inaccurate spelling "Cœcilia." After all, how could a group of ostensibly well-educated, sophisticated gentlemen, most or all of whom had studied Latin, overlook the proper spelling of their titular saint? The answer to this question lies not in the intellectual merits of the society's members (at least not entirely), but rather in the typographical practices of the day.

The use of the inaccurate spelling "Cœcilia" occurs much more frequently in print rather than in manuscript sources. From its very first newspaper advertisement in 1766, this organization was identified with the spelling "St. CÆCILIA." In the months and years following, the three above-mentioned spellings were used interchangeably (in both uppercase and lowercase letters). In early 1774, when the society had its rules of operation printed, the spelling "Cœcilia" appeared prominently on the title page. By the mid-1770s this spelling was well established in the Charleston press and became the most common form of the name.

The confusion between the "æ" and "œ" ligatures occurred in the transcription of handwritten text into typeset print. Handwriting was an important part of formal education in the eighteenth century, for it gave visual evidence of one's refinement and intellect. The standard lettering style for handwriting was italic, which is characterized by a steep slant from the baseline to the right. In contrast to the upright roman type most commonly used in printing, the slanting italic style requires the alteration of some letter shapes to render them more legible. Hence, the roman letter "a" becomes "*a*" in Italic script. When an "æ" ligature is written in italic script (*æ*), it closely resembles the roman "œ" ligature, and could easily be mistaken as such by a less-educated typesetter.

Although the spelling "Cecilia" was in use from the earliest days of this Charleston society's existence, it did not totally replace the other two forms in printed sources until the early nineteenth century. The spelling "Cæcilia" disappeared from the Charleston newspapers after 1798, and "Cœcilia" made its final appearance in the local press in November 1803. Long after these classical, ligated spellings disappeared from newspaper advertisements, however, a number of extant manuscript sources (such as the manuscript records of the lawsuits brought by the St. Cecilia Society against various members in arrears, 1800–29) demonstrate a continuation of the italic form *Cæcilia*. In light of these variations, quotations from or citations of primary sources in this book will therefore reproduce the spelling as given in the original, while I use the more modern spelling *Cecilia* in my own prose.

This study contains a number of references to monetary sums, which may be difficult to grasp because of the effects of inflation over the past two centuries. In an effort to make such references more meaningful, monetary figures given in historical denominations—such as South Carolina currency, eighteenth-century British sterling, Spanish dollars, and early-nineteenth-century U.S. dollars—are supplemented with approximate U.S. dollar equivalents for the year 2005. The conversion of these figures is based on the methods described by John J. McCusker in *How Much Is That in Real Money? A Historical Commodity Price Index for Use as a Deflator of Money Values in the Economy of the United States.*[7] Like other colonies in British America, South Carolina rendered its own provincial currency in pounds, shillings, and pence in conformity with the old British system: one pound (£1) is equal to twenty shillings (20s.); one shilling is equal to twelve pence (12d.); one guinea (1gn.) is equal to £1 1s. From the 1730s through the mid-1770s, the period of greatest economic stability in colonial South Carolina, a South Carolina pound was was worth roughly one-seventh of a British pound sterling. From 1783 through 1802, monetary transactions in Charleston were still rendered in pounds, shillings, and pence, but in a South Carolina state currency that was valued just below British sterling. Although a national currency system employing dollar, cents, and mils was created in the mid-1790s and was officially adopted by the state of South Carolina in 1795 (and by the city government of Charleston in 1796), many individuals and corporations continued to use South Carolina currency for private business transactions.[8] By 1803, however, monetary sums in Charleston, including those concerning the St. Cecilia Society, were consistently rendered in U.S. dollars.

Acknowledgments

AT THE CULMINATION OF this long project I would like to acknowledge at least a few of the many people who played a role in its completion. At the University of South Carolina, Christopher Berg, Georgia Cowart, and Jerry Curry provided early encouragement for my interest in musicology. At Indiana University the original version of this work was shaped by J. Peter Burkholder, Jeffrey Magee, Austin Caswell, and Steven Stowe, while Donna Ritter provided valuable off-campus encouragement.

The long hours of discovering and compiling this data passed quickly thanks to the assistance and camaraderie of many archivists and librarians in South Carolina. The complete list of their names would constitute a chapter unto itself, so I will briefly and humbly extend my thanks to the entire staffs of the Charleston County Public Library, the Charleston Library Society, the Charleston Museum, Drayton Hall, the Historic Charleston Foundation, the Middleton Place Foundation, the South Carolina Department of Archives and History (especially Charles Lesser), the South Carolina Historical Society (especially Mike Coker), and the South Caroliniana Library. Rick Rhodes made excellent photographic copies of the materials from the Charleston Library Society and of my print of Mrs. Sheridan.

I was fortunate during the course of this research to make the acquaintance of a number of Charlestonians whose insight and experience were of invaluable assistance. For their welcome encouragement, I thank them all, especially Robert Cuthbert, Dr. Charlton deSaussure and his family, Richard Hutson Jr., Elise Pinckney, Henry Buist Smythe, and George W. Williams.

The music faculty at the College of Charleston has been a constant source of encouragement over the past several years. So too has the faculty of the college's Carolina Lowcountry and Atlantic World Program, who awarded this work the Hines Prize in September 2005. For their active support in bringing this work to publication, I am indebted to Samuel Hines, David Gleeson, Simon Lewis, and W. Scott Poole, as well as Alexander Moore of the University of South Carolina Press.

The greatest praise is, of course, reserved for my family, who made the fulfillment of this goal a reality. To my parents, Stephen and Sarah Butler, I owe a great debt of gratitude for their support, encouragement, and patience. In particular I owe a special thanks to my late maternal grandmother, Edythe Kenney Powers, who took me to Colonial Williamsburg, Virginia, during the festive summer of 1976 and opened my imagination to the field of early American history. In recent years, however, the greatest source of encouragement in my life has been my wife, Wendy Kanako-Oki Tahara. Without her patient support, unwavering confidence, tireless sense of humor, and inspiring musical sensibility, this project could not have been completed.

Votaries of Apollo

Economic and Cultural Background, 1670–1820

THE DURATION OF THE ST. CECILIA SOCIETY'S concert activity coincided with the most significant and influential period of early Charleston history. From the end of the seventeenth century to the middle of the nineteenth, Charleston was one of the principal cities of North America and the cultural heart of the American Southeast. For a time this port city was renowned for its extravagant wealth, cosmopolitan tastes, and generous hospitality. Beginning in the 1730s and continuing for nearly a century, the city enjoyed what historian George C. Rogers Jr. aptly described as a "golden age of commerce," during which "the rise, flourishing, and decline of Charleston's greatness all took place."[1] The numerous architectural, intellectual, and artistic endeavors of this prosperous era, which crested in the early 1770s and again in the mid-1790s, left an enduring stamp on the city's character, but the collapse of Charleston's fortunes at the end of the second decade of the nineteenth century sapped the city's original vitality. Not the least of its golden-age endeavors was the St. Cecilia Society, whose long-standing concert series was at the apex of the city's early musical brilliance. The original identity and purpose of this musical organization—formed amid a host of other faintly remembered cultural phenomena—are deeply rooted in this golden age. From the height of South Carolina's late colonial prosperity to the great depression of the 1820s, the prevailing economic conditions in Charleston played a crucial role in shaping the concert patronage of the St. Cecilia Society. To understand the context in which the society thrived as a musical organization, therefore, we must first understand some of the early history of this southern seaport.

The area now known as South Carolina was the site of some of the earliest European attempts to settle in mainland North America. Part of the attraction to this particular spot was the area's proximity to the West Indies, which from the beginning of the sixteenth century were bustling with colonial activity.

Although not as close to those islands as modern Florida, the Carolina coast-line is in a strategic position, for it marks the point at which the Gulf Stream—a powerful surge of warm water flowing northward from the Caribbean Sea—makes a sudden eastward turn toward Europe. Regardless of their national origin or final destination, all shipping convoys traveling from the West Indies back to Europe skirted the Carolina coastline to follow the hinge of this strong ocean current.

In the 1560s both France and Spain sponsored settlements near present-day Beaufort, South Carolina (just south of Charleston). The short-lived French outpost of Charlesfort ended disastrously, but the subsequent Spanish town of Santa Elena endured for years as the northernmost outpost of the Spanish colony La Florida. Although the settlement was not unsuccessful, the Spanish government ordered the abandonment of Santa Elena in 1587 and withdrew to St. Augustine in modern Florida.[2] In the ensuing century, Euro-pean efforts to establish North American colonies were concentrated farther north of modern South Carolina. With the founding of settlements from Jamestown, Virginia, to Plymouth, Massachusetts, the eastern seaboard of North America was claimed as the colonial territory of England.

On his restoration to the English throne in 1660, Charles II began rewarding those who had assisted him in his return from exile. In 1663, in consideration for their loyalty to the Crown, Charles granted to a group of eight petitioners a charter for a colony between Virginia and Spanish Florida, to be called Carolina. The eight petitioners, now Lords Proprietors, were free to run the colony not only as an extension of the British realm but also as a business venture for their own profit. Its Fundamental Constitutions were partly written by philosopher John Locke, secretary to the chief proprietor, Sir Anthony Ashley Cooper (later the first Earl of Shaftesbury). The constitutions contained the necessary laws to establish a civil community while also laying the foundation for a social structure that had profound effects on the later his-tory of the colony.[3] In contrast to the later democratic ethos of the United States, this early document specified that the colony should "avoid erecting a numerous democracy" and created the aristocratic titles of *landgrave* and *cas-sique* to distinguish those in possession of multiple baronies, representing twelve thousand acres each.[4] By emphasizing large-scale landholding and the profits arising therefrom, the Carolina colony was stamped with the tradi-tional English social stratification based on the supremacy of the landed gentry. During its colonial history—and even well after the American Revolution—this new territory was governed by a landed oligarchy that began to emerge in the earliest generations of its existence.

The distribution of land was a major issue in the management of early Carolina. The quantity and quality of land available for profitable cultivation quickly attracted the attention of English colonists already in the New World. The island of Barbados, which by the middle of the seventeenth century had achieved an English-speaking population density surpassed only by London, served as the main "culture hearth" and prototype for the other British island colonies of Jamaica, Antigua, St. Christopher (St. Kitts), Grenada, and Nevis.[5] While these colonies yielded a great deal of agricultural wealth during the seventeenth century, they were constrained by a growing population and a limited supply of arable land. Thus between 1670, when the first settlers arrived in Carolina, and 1690 the majority of Carolina colonists came from Barbados, and many others arrived from the remaining British island colonies. In effect, then, Carolina began as a "colony of a colony." These early settlers were not necessarily the idealistic, puritanical refugees seeking to create a new paradise who are depicted in mainstream of American history texts. Rather, many were experienced colonial adventurers attempting to amass fortunes and then return home to the mother country.[6]

Soon after permanent settlement began in 1670, the proprietors of Carolina began referring to their colony as comprising of two distinct regions, to the north and to the south of Cape Fear. At times the young province had two governors, at times just one. By the turn of the eighteenth century the terms *North Carolina* and *South Carolina* were in common use, but Carolina was not officially divided until its proprietors sold the entire venture to the British Crown in 1729.[7]

Well into the early eighteenth century South Carolina functioned as an adjunct to the Barbadian economy by supplying provisions and naval stores for the lucrative Atlantic shipping trade. Even after it developed its own plantation economy, based primarily on rice cultivation but supplemented by the production of indigo, Carolina continued to have more in common culturally and economically with the Caribbean colonies than with the other English colonies to the north.[8] Although Virginia was also a commercial colony with a plantation-based economy, it differed from Carolina in one important aspect: it lacked a substantial urban center. Early Virginia had a number of port towns, of course, but none developed into a social and commercial hub comparable to Charleston. The slightly inland town of Williamsburg, Virginia, served as the main colonial capital, but its significance was more political than economic. From the beginning of Carolina, however, the port city of Charleston (known as Charles Town or Charlestown until mid-August 1783) served as the political, economic, and social capital of the colony. Established on the peninsula where the Ashley and Cooper rivers meet and empty into the Atlantic Ocean, Charleston served as the nexus of a vast network of plantations, the point at which most of the colony's commerce was transacted. Even as the growing population spread inland, Charleston remained the cultural center in which colonial success was displayed and celebrated. In effect, the city developed into what might be described as "a miniature London."[9]

Historians of early America have suggested that music and the arts in general prospered in the southern colonies because of the absence of the restrictive puritanical mores that held sway to the north. While it is true that such puritanical attitudes were less prominent in early South Carolina, the province was not without a substantial religious influence. Between 1706 and 1778 the Church of England was the official, or established, church of the South Carolina, meaning the public treasury funded its buildings, its clergy, and its music. As in Barbados, colonial South Carolina was divided into parishes—many of which had the same names as those on Barbados—for which the various Anglican church vestries served as the local civil governments. The Church of England was not the only religious presence in Carolina, however. Although not in a position of dominance, there were still significant numbers of dissenters, such as Baptists, Presbyterians, Quakers, Independent Congregationalists, and Lutherans. Most of these groups had migrated southward from New England and Pennsylvania, bringing with them the traditions and attitudes characteristic of those regions. Nevertheless, conformist Anglican attitudes clearly held sway in the South Carolina low-country, for while the English preacher George Whitefield caused a great stir in the northern colonies during his American tours in the 1730s and 1740s, his message of a more personal, "enthusiastic" approach to Anglicanism found little support in Charleston during his three visits to the city.[10]

Also contributing a significant influence on the culture of early South Carolina were the French Protestants, or Huguenots, who began arriving in 1680. Their numbers increased after Louis XIV revoked the Edict of Nantes in 1685, and during the colonial era these French immigrants formed a larger percentage of the local population than in any other British colony.[11] The descendants of Huguenot immigrants assimilated well into the Anglocentric community, and their commercial and planting interests prospered. Many of the family names associated with the early years of the St. Cecilia Society reflect this French-speaking heritage, and most retained their French pronunciation: Bacot, Bonneau, deSaussure, Fayssoux, Gaillard, Gourdin, Hörrÿ, Hüger, Izard, Laurens, Manigault, Mazÿck, Motte, Ogier, Peronneau, Porcher, Prioleau, and Ravenel, for example.[12]

Charleston also hosted a small yet significant Jewish population. Composed mostly of Sephardic Jews, originally from Portugal and Spain, this small community was still the largest of its kind in America through the first quarter of the nineteenth century.[13] The only major religious denomination actively suppressed in colonial Charleston was Catholicism, owing to fears of spies in the employ of Britain's enemies, France and Spain. After the

South Carolina constitution of 1778 ensured freedom to all religious groups, a Catholic congregation, St. Mary's, was finally established in Charleston in 1789. In the years following the revolutions in France and its West Indian colony, St. Domingo (now Haiti), most of the French musicians who immigrated to Charleston were members of this church.[14]

One of the most basic and enduring cultural features of early South Carolina—much more than religion—was the focus on land ownership and wealth emanating from agricultural products. The availability of vast tracts of arable land was the chief attraction for most of the early settlers, and land quickly became the main source and form of wealth. From its beginning the colony's proprietors awarded large grants to favored individuals, and by the early eighteenth century the best lands were in hands of a small group of planters. Up to the eve of the Revolution, the headright system enabled poor Protestant immigrants to receive free land (usually located well inland, away from Charleston) on their arrival in South Carolina. Although they did not receive much land or the choicest locations, an immigrant's landgrant was increased for each additional member in the settler's household, including slaves. Thus a small investment in agricultural production could quickly result in dramatic yields, which could be reinvested to create a cycle of spiraling wealth. With the help of British markets and trade protection, as one colonial observer noted, "frugal planters, every three or four years, doubled their capital, and their progress towards independence and opulence was rapid."[15]

In its early decades the young colony of South Carolina acquired wealth by exporting deerskins and naval stores (including tar, pitch, turpentine, and lumber). The colony's remarkable rise to wealth, however, was made possible by its primary agricultural export: rice. Pierced by rivers and creeks, the low, swampy lands of the coastal plain (referred to locally as the *lowcountry*) proved suitable to the intensive water requirements of this crop (see figure 1.1). The work required to bring what became known as "Carolina Gold" to market, however, was intense and dangerous. The extreme heat and humidity of the subtropical lowcountry, combined with the constant threat of mosquito-born diseases, were considered too severe for European laborers. The solution was to import slaves from the rice-growing coastal regions of West Africa, who not only understood rice cultivation but also possessed some immunity to the malarial fevers common to the swampy climate. The system of chattel slavery, introduced from the West Indies at the outset of the Carolina colony, proved to be the engine of liberating wealth for the plantation owners and a lucrative trade for merchants. "*Negroes* may be said to be the Bait proper for catching a *Carolina* Planter," observed the *South-Carolina Gazette* in 1738, "as certain as Beef to catch a Shark."[16] From the beginning of the eighteenth century until the Revolution, Charleston was the principal

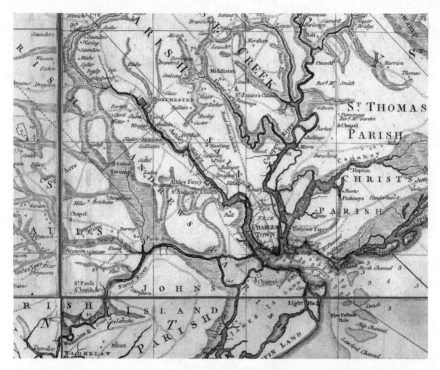

1.1. Detail of Charleston and the surrounding the lowcountry, from *A Map of South Carolina and Part of Georgia* (London: William Faden, 1780). From the collections of the South Carolina Historical Society

port of entry for the American slave trade, receiving about 40 percent of all Africans brought into North America.[17]

Within the first decade of the eighteenth century, the African population of South Carolina achieved a majority status, which endured for most of the next two centuries.[18] Most slaves were imported to work on the plantations, but many lived and worked in the urban environment of the capital city. Writing in England during the American Revolution, Alexander Hewatt recalled that in 1765 the population of Charleston included between five and six thousand white inhabitants and between seven and eight thousand slaves. Another former Charleston resident, George Milligen-Johnston, similarly estimated the total city population in 1775 at fourteen thousand.[19] In terms of population, Charleston was the fourth largest city in the American colonies and about one third the size of the largest, Philadelphia. Despite its smaller size, the port city of Charleston—as the focal point of all the Carolina colony's wealth—was by far the wealthiest city in North America. By 1774 the mean aggregate wealth per inventoried estate in the Charleston

District was £2,337 7s. sterling (about $250,000 in 2005)—approximately four times that of the Chesapeake region and six to eight times that of Philadelphia, New England, and New York. Of the ten wealthiest men in North America at that moment, nine lived in the lowcountry of coastal South Carolina.[20] The number of rich inhabitants in the province was not great, however, as Alexander Hewatt described in 1779, "most of them being in what we call easy and independent circumstances."[21] The economic prosperity of early South Carolina was not lost on the mother country. Marveling at the quantity of rice and indigo exported from Charleston, an English visitor in the early 1780s commented that during its final years as a British colony, "South Carolina met with infinitely more attention from [the British] government than the other provinces."[22] South Carolina's exports for the year 1771 alone, reported Hewatt, amounted "to a sum not less than £756,000 sterling" (roughly $81,713,000 in 2005).[23]

The cumulative result of all these factors—the landscape, the dependence on slave labor, and the profitability of rice and other crops—was the concentration of great wealth within a community that was relatively small, young, and remote from its cultural roots. Plantation agriculture was a very lucrative business, and the reliance on slave labor allowed the wealthiest planters to divorce themselves from the rigors of production and to embark on an intense pursuit of refinement.[24] The quotidian business of plantation administration was largely entrusted to overseers and drivers, while the commercial aspects of selling and shipping the agricultural products were dispatched by factors in Charleston. Emulating the genteel landed families of the English countryside, the proprietors of large estates in South Carolina cultivated conspicuous emblems of refinement to demonstrate their success and their distance from physical labor. "For, with the exception of the learned professions," lawyer Charles Fraser recalled of this era, "no pursuit which yielded income, from personal effort or employment, was properly respected."[25]

By the middle of the eighteenth century South Carolina—and especially its capital, Charleston—had achieved a level of prosperity and refinement that often surprised visitors from the northern colonies and from abroad. The Reverend George Whitefield, visiting Charleston in 1740, was shocked by what he observed and questioned "whether the court-end of London could exceed them in affected finery, gaiety of dress, and deportment."[26] "An European at his first arrival," wrote Hector St. John de Crèvecœur in the 1780s, "must be greatly surprised when he sees the elegance of their houses, their sumptuous furniture, as well as the magnificence of their tables. Can he imagine himself in a country, the establishment of which is so recent?" Having lived among the American colonists for several years, St. John de Crèvecœur pronounced Charleston "the centre of our beau monde" and its inhabitants "the gayest in

America."[27] Moving from New Jersey to Charleston in 1785, Timothy Ford voiced a similar reaction. He observed that the industrial arts of his new home were at an early stage of development, but "with regard to manners and customs they have reached their climactric."[28] Likewise, Massachusetts native Ebenezer Smith Thomas, who moved to Charleston in 1795, found his new home "so totally different from Boston, that I could scarcely realize the idea, that it was a part of the American Union, and under the same government." Remarking on the city's architecture and its crowded wharves, Thomas noted that Charleston "presents to the New Englander, or the European, a spectacle new and interesting, so totally unlike their father land, that their curiosity cannot fail to be excited by it."[29] The city's refinement was proudly touted by local residents too, as in 1772 when the English-born Reverend Robert Smith informed his dinner guest, William Dillwyn of Philadelphia, "that Persons coming from the Northward and England received a Polish at Charles Town which they all wanted at first coming there."[30]

For many eighteenth-century South Carolinians, England still represented their spiritual home. After visiting Charleston in 1765 and mingling with the local elite, Lord Adam Gordon wrote that the residents, "almost all of them, first or last, have made a trip to the Mother Country. It is the fashion indeed to send home all their Children for education." Gordon went so far as to state "I am of opinion the most opulent planters would prefer a home life"—that is, a life in England. His observation was apparently not unique, for he added that "it is in general believed, that they are more attached to the Mother Country, than those Provinces which lie to the Northward."[31] David Ramsay, a Philadelphia physician who settled in Charleston prior to the Revolution, noted that the inhabitants of his adopted city were "fond of British manners even to excess" and often "spoke of that country under the endearing appellation of Home."[32]

Conscious of their provincial status, many Carolinians sought to demonstrate their success by emulating the familiar cultural patterns of the Old World. Alexander Hewatt noted that because South Carolina enjoyed "easy and frequent" communication with Britain during the last years of colonial rule, "all novelties in fashion, dress and ornament are quickly introduced; and even the spirit of luxury and extravagance, too common in England, was beginning to creep into Carolina." As a result, he added, "they discover no bad taste for the polite arts, such as music, drawing, fencing and dancing."[33] The members of Charleston's exclusive Library Society, founded in 1748, sought to establish a local repository in order to stay abreast of contemporary literature and scholarship. By their own description, they were "ambitious of approving themselves worthy of their Mother-Country, by imitating her Humanity, as well as her Industry, and by transporting from her the Improvements in the finer as well as in the inferior Arts."[34] Looking back at the years before the American Revolution, Governor John Drayton acknowledged in 1802 that South Carolinians had been "too much prejudiced in favour of British manners, customs, and knowledge, to imagine that elsewhere, than in England, any thing of advantage could be obtained."[35]

Although the American colonies had no true aristocracy, there was a clear sense of social stratification in South Carolina. "The Men and Women who have a Right to the Class of Gentry," remarked one English immigrant in the early 1760s, "are more numerous here than in any other Colony in North-America."[36] Despite its small population, Hewatt found Charleston genteel enough to sponsor "assemblies, balls, concerts and plays, which were attended by companies almost equally brilliant as those of any town in Europe of the same size."[37] The drive toward social refinement was an upward race fueled by inflated social ambition in which—the local press wryly observed in 1773—"every Tradesman is a Merchant, every Merchant is a Gentleman, and every Gentleman one of the Noblesse."[38] In this pursuit Charleston outdistanced other America cities. "The manners of the inhabitants of Charleston are as different from those of the other North American cities as are the products of their soil," wrote visiting German physician Johann David Schoepf in 1784. Plantation agriculture had created vast fortunes for numerous families, "who therefore give themselves to the enjoyment of every pleasure and convenience to which their warmer climate and better circumstances invite them." Having made a tour of all the North American colonies, Schoepf observed that in the absence of the "particular religious principles" he had witnessed among the Presbyterians of New England and the Quakers of Pennsylvania, Charleston fostered a more cosmopolitan lifestyle. As a result, he surmised, "luxury in Carolina has made the greatest advance, and their manner of life, dress, equipages, furniture, everything denotes a higher degree of taste and love of show, and less frugality than in the northern provinces."[39] This state of opulence was beyond the range of experience for some eighteenth-century travelers, who looked farther afield for a comparison. "The rich planters of the State," Elkanah Watson wrote in 1778, "live in almost Asiatic luxury."[40]

Not everyone was pleased with the "improvements" that accompanied South Carolina's economic prosperity. Sophia Hume, a Charleston native who became an outspoken Quaker, in 1747 chastised the city's elite who "fail not to give your attendance at every occasion of Mirth and Jollity" and strive to "mimic *Great Britain* in every Foppery, Luxury and Recreation, within your reach."[41] In a sermon first delivered in the 1750s and then published in 1778, Baptist minister Oliver Hart scorned the licentiousness of Charleston's wealthy citizens. Rather than leading a reverential and pious lifestyle, Hart complained, they frequently attend "balls, assemblies and the play-house, where they take the timbrel and harp, and such like instruments of musick, with which they play, and their children dance."[42] A generation later, on the eve of the Revolutionary War, other Americans complained of the same pre-occupation with luxury in Charleston. Boston statesman Josiah Quincy Jr. reflected on his 1773 visit to the city that "state, magnificence and ostentation, the natural attendants of riches, are conspicuous among this people. . . . Cards, dice, the bottle and horses engross prodigious proportions of time and atten-tion; the gentlemen (planters and merchants) are mostly men of the turf and gamesters."[43] Philadelphia merchant Ebenezer Hazard noted during his 1778 visit to Charleston that its inhabitants possessed "liberal sentiments and polite manners," but he chided "a learned education has been much neglected among them. Gentlemen of fortune usually sent their children to Europe for education, but they generally attended more to fashions while there than to learning."[44] The attachment to fashion and leisure was an outgrowth of the colonial drive toward rapid improvement and the desire to emulate the gentry of England. "We are a Country of Gentry," a correspondent complained to the *South-Carolina Gazette* in 1773. "We have no such thing as a com-mon People among us: Between Vanity and Fashion the species is utterly destroyed."[45] While working as a tutor in Charleston in 1778, Benjamin West was both fascinated and repelled by the dissipative lifestyle of rich Charlesto-nians. He wrote to his brother in New England that "you have no idea of their extravagant mode of living here, nor would it be of any service to you if you had."[46] For better or worse, Charleston's reputation for fostering voluptuous lifestyles continued for generations to come. "The people of Charleston live rapidly," Dr. Schoepf lamented, "not willing letting go untasted any of the pleasures of this life."[47]

As the political, religious, social, and commercial center of an over-whelmingly rural landscape, Charleston became the primary locus of con-spicuous cultural displays—the stage on which the local gentry displayed their wealth, education, and sophistication. "In short," Alexander Hewatt reflected, "the people are not only blessed with plenty, but with a disposition to share it among friends and neighbors; and many will bear me witness, when I say, that travelers could scarcely go into any city where they could meet with a society of people more agreeable, intelligent and hospitable than at Charlestown."[48] Hewatt's countryman Edmund Burke concurred, noting that in Charleston "every thing conspires to make this the liveliest, the pleas-antest, and the politest place, as it is one of the richest too, in all America."[49]

But Charleston's economic and cultural success did not last forever. The American Revolutionary War (1775–83), caused a dramatic reversal in Charleston's fortunes. Although the port remained open until the British army captured the city in May 1780, the final years of the war were especially destructive in the South Carolina lowcountry. While the colony's great wealth induced some to remain loyal to the British, many prominent South Carolinians stepped forward to become among the most ardent patriots of the new nation. Because of this internal division, the Revolution in South Carolina took on the character of a civil war. This fact, combined with more than two years of occupation by the British army, turned the state into a very active theater of military action. In the course of nearly eight years of warfare, more than two hundred battles and skirmishes took place in South Carolina— perhaps more than in any of the other original thirteen states.[50] Britain's hold on its former colonies may have been dashed at the Battle of Yorktown in October 1781, but the war was not yet over. Fighting with the British continued in South Carolina long after Yorktown, until the occupying forces finally evacuated Charleston and the surrounding lowcountry in mid-December 1782.

In the wake of the Revolution, a long period of recovery began in South Carolina. Timothy Ford, who settled in Charleston in 1785 and joined the St. Cecilia Society, recorded in his diary that "the planter who had been accustomed to live at his ease found himself much distressed at the conclusion of the war; involved in debt, his plantation torn to pieces, his stock of negroes gone, & his creditors pushing for payment."[51] In order to administer its civic needs better, the city was incorporated on 13 August 1783, and its name officially changed from Charlestown to Charleston. Throughout the 1780s the export of rice and other agricultural products gradually resumed, but the limited supply of specie and paper money slowed the recovery. "To bring order out of confusion was no easy matter," remembered David Ramsay in 1809, "the eight years of war in Carolina were followed by eight years of disorganization."[52]

In addition to this postwar economic stress, the state also encountered a new political crisis. The westward expansion of South Carolina, once predominantly a coastal colony, required its leaders to admit greater representation from the newer settlements to state government. In a move to promote the equality of political representation and to sustain the spirit of republicanism that had won the Revolution, the South Carolina legislature voted in 1786 to move its capital from Charleston to the newly created inland city of Columbia. Although the relocation did not formally occur until early 1790, the first major blow had been struck to Charleston's monopoly on the state's political, economic, and cultural life.[53]

Despite the removal of state government from the coast, economic conditions in Charleston improved greatly in 1789, after the ratification of the U.S. Constitution. This act not only provided legal protection of American trade and capital but also brought in a much-needed infusion of nearly $1.5 million (roughly $30 million in 2005) in federal compensation for South Carolina's losses during the Revolution.[54] The rapid increase of Charleston's shipping trade during the 1790s, as in the late colonial era, was owed in large part to the city's status as an important American entrepôt: a large quantity of European merchandise on its way to the West Indies was shipped through Charleston, as were West Indian agricultural products destined for Europe. The outbreak of war between Britain and France in the spring of 1793 was a boon to American shipping in general, which supplied materials to both sides. Despite harassment by West Indian privateers sailing under the warring flags, the increased shipping trade in and out of Charleston meant a ready market for the agricultural exports that had been so reduced during the late war. Innovations in tidal rice cultivation enhanced the productivity of South Carolina's traditional plantation cash crop, and Eli Whitney's refinement of the cotton gin in 1792 paved the way for the advent of large-scale cotton production. As a result of these important advances, South Carolina's agricultural exports more than tripled in the decade between 1791 and 1801.[55]

The labor of this expanded agricultural activity was, of course, borne on the backs of African and African American slaves. The Revolutionary War had interrupted the importation of slaves from Africa, however, and the U.S. Confederation Congress of the mid-1780s sought to end this commerce permanently. While South Carolina delegates did succeed in postponing the Constitutional end of the foreign slave trade until 1808, between March 1787 and December 1803 the state legislature prohibited the importation of slaves. On the passage of a new law allowing the resumption of such imports in late December 1803, however, Charleston planters and merchants went into a four-year buying frenzy. "A great change at once took place in everything," recalled Charleston bookseller and newspaper editor Ebenezer Smith Thomas. "Vessels were fitted out in numbers for the coast of Africa, and as fast as they returned, their cargoes were bought up with avidity." The voracious appetite for new slaves exhausted both cash reserves and credit lines, to the extent that planters began to mortgage their slaves in order to acquire more. "So completely absorbed were the funds of the agriculturalists," Thomas noted, "that those who had been in the habit of indulging in every luxury, and paying for it at the moment, took credit for a bundle of quills and a ream of paper."[56] Even after a hurricane decimated crops on many of the coastal plantations in August 1806, Charleston's appetite for pleasure continued unabated. "*No Money* is already the general complaint," reported Margaret Bowen that season to her family in Boston. "I know not however that even this can cause any abatement of the extravagance of the people. Debts may not be paid, but Dinners and parties & balls must go on as usual."[57]

The economic difficulties caused by storms and the temporary renewal of the foreign slave trade were compounded by the onset of naval hostilities between the United States and Great Britain. In the months following the unprovoked attack of the British frigate *Leopard* on the U.S. frigate *Chesapeake* off the coast of Virginia on 22 June 1807, Charleston received the news "like an electric shock" and joined the rest of the nation in making frantic preparations for another war with the former mother country.[58] A national policy prohibiting the importation of British goods was adopted in December 1807, and, as David Ramsay observed the following year, the port of Charleston's foreign trade was "completely arrested" almost at a moment. When Congress subsequently halted all commercial intercourse with Britain, South Carolina lost a major market for its agricultural produce. Crop prices fell precipitously in 1808, and the activities of wharfingers and factors "suddenly passed over from the full tide of employment to listless inactivity."[59] By the time the U.S. Congress formally declared war against Britain in June 1812, Charleston's golden era of commerce was clearly slipping into decline.

Since South Carolina had developed almost no domestic industry besides agriculture, the years of suspended trade with Britain were particularly hard on the state. In contrast the citizens of New England avoided economic stagnation in the years preceding and during the War of 1812 by shifting their commercial energies to manufacturing in order to supply their own needs. By the time peace returned in 1815, New England had emerged as a burgeoning manufacturing area and was lobbying the federal government to win protection for its growing industrial economy. Editorial discussions of such federal tariffs to protect American trade filled the Charleston newspapers of the immediate postwar period too. Contrary to the views held by later generations of southern politicians, many South Carolinians initially supported the protective measures as a means of avoiding future dependence on foreign markets.[60]

Prospects for South Carolina's economic recovery immediately after the war were initially sanguine. Prices for the state's agricultural products were rising, and speculation in shipping and internal improvements was reawakened.[61] Such changes had a direct and immediate impact on Charleston's cultural life. Speaking of the reopening of the Charleston Theatre after three years of silence, the *City Gazette* proclaimed in October 1815, "From the rapid and prosperous increase or every kind of business, and the great number of strangers who spend the season in our city, we presume the enterprise and labor of the manager and the company will be richly rewarded."[62] But the resumption of trade after the War of 1812 was accompanied by an important difference for South Carolina. The merchants who amassed shipping fortunes between the 1760s and the 1790s, a class of men that included many members of the St. Cecilia Society, had by 1815 either retired from trade or were dead. In their place arose a new generation of merchants whose primary commercial connections were with northern ports rather than with those in Europe.[63]

Economically and culturally Charleston was quickly evolving from an outpost of the British Empire into a satellite of larger domestic cities.

In addition to these difficulties, the advent of steam navigation in the early nineteenth century began to erode the status of Charleston's port. Under steam power, commercial shipping could break from the ocean currents and wind patterns that had once dictated transatlantic shipping routes. Charleston's prominence as an entrepôt was founded on its proximity to the Gulf Stream, the conveyor of wind-powered ship traffic. As dependence on this natural phenomenon decreased, so did the city's share of the Atlantic trade.[64] A Frenchman visiting Charleston in the spring of 1817 observed the dissonance between the city's cultural desires and its economic realities. "One might think that he perceives a tendency towards the taste for pleasures which is more pronounced here than in the north," he wrote, echoing the observations of earlier tourists, "but the nature of the country, the force of custom and the temper of the national character repress the development of this happy inclination. They complain here, as elsewhere, of the stagnation of trade and the bad state of business."[65]

Charleston's economy was indeed in decline, but it was not alone in this condition. Both in Europe and in the United States the years 1815 through 1818 were characterized by an abnormal inflation of prices and currency. A postwar boom in the extension of credit and bank speculation led to the establishment in 1816 of the Bank of the United States, which was founded to keep these conditions in check. Speculation in this national institution only fueled the inflation, however, and in August 1818 the bank's management initiated a policy of credit and monetary contraction. This action set in motion an "unbroken chain of economic circumstances and political agitation": a national shortage of specie, the suspension of payments, and ultimately the failure of many banks, including the Bank of the United States itself. The economic and social shock that resulted from this collapse, known as the Panic of 1819, affected the United States as well as its European trading partners.[66]

When the postwar economic bubble burst at the end of 1818, the prices of agricultural staples plummeted. This drop affected the economies of all American states, but the presence of domestic manufacturing in the American northeast allowed that region to avoid a serious depression. The economies of southern states such as South Carolina, which had resisted the development of such domestic industries, experienced a much greater commercial decline.[67] American cotton, the steady supply of which had become an economic "drug" to the international market, fell by 50 percent between January and June 1819.[68] As early as December 1818, Charleston's *Southern Patriot* reported that the "distress of the mercantile part of this community is, we believe, without a parallel in times of peace and prosperity. The scarcity of money is the loud and general cry, and the grand theme of complaint, the Banks, which have contracted their issues, owing to the extraordinary demand for specie, and caused, in consequence, a stagnation of trade which is almost unexampled."[69] In the autumn of 1819 the "commercial and pecuniary embarrassments of the people" in Charleston were exacerbated by the "unusual celerity" of the proceedings at the local Court of Common Pleas. In the prevailing economic climate, reported the *Charleston Courier,* many "unfortunate debtors" were being ruthlessly "driven to jail and despair."[70]

The economic opportunities available in coastal South Carolina during the first half of the nineteenth century could not compare to those experienced a century earlier, and the region's reputation for cultural sophistication quietly lapsed. In the early 1770s Charleston had been the fourth largest city in British America, but by 1820 its urban population of 24,711 (57 percent of which was black) made it the sixth largest in the young United States. In the intervening years the growth of the city's white population—the potential audience for private and public concerts—lagged far behind that of the larger cities to the north.[71] In October 1821 the *Southern Patriot* took note of the city's "spiritless, listless, sparse population" and lamented that Charleston, once a cosmopolitan arena of ostentatious social display, had become "a mere winter town." The recent collapse of economic prosperity, the paper noted, had brought an end to a cultural era. "The fine arts are the fruits of wealth and leisure. But no arts can thrive where man cannot live."[72] A decade later, in 1832, visitor Timothy Green aptly summarized Charleston's general decline for a former resident living in New York: "Charleston has for some time appeared to live upon the remnants of its former prosperity—the continued habits which had been formed in better days."[73]

The cultural climate of eighteenth-century Charleston was a distinctly American phenomenon. As with other colonial cities, its early years were marked by hardship and toil; its early settlers were required to live with a sense of adventure. At the end of its first century, the dramatic expansion of economic prosperity that accompanied the final decades of the colonial era produced a community of wealthy, leisured individuals who cultivated pleasurable social platforms for the display of their affluence, education, and sophistication. The small, provincial capital of South Carolina thus became the ideal environment for the emergence of a musical institution whose central activity, the patronage and performance of concerts, provided sensual gratification and reinforced its patrons' social position. Turbulent economic and political conditions marked the early decades of Charleston's independence from Great Britain, however, and by 1820 the city was in "full economic decline."[74] This historical background provides an indispensable frame for viewing the musical activities of the St. Cecilia Society, for the vitality of the

St. Cecilia Society from its founding in 1766 to its withdrawal from concert patronage in 1820 was intimately tied to the ebb and flow of its community's fortunes. Just as the union of economic prosperity and social desires facilitated the birth of the society in the late colonial era, the broken economy and changing cultural patterns in the decade after the War of 1812 played a major role in disrupting the city's tradition of musical patronage.

British Subscription Concerts and
the Meaning of St. Cecilia

CHARLESTON'S ST. CECILIA SOCIETY MAY HAVE been the first concert organization in British America, but it was hardly unique. Like the musicians who
immigrated to America and the imported repertoire they performed, the
mechanisms of private concert patronage were part of the cultural heritage
transplanted from the Old World. Concert societies, specifically those founded
on a subscription basis, were widespread in eighteenth-century Britain. Sponsoring performances in multipurpose, semiprivate rooms, these societies
provided gentlemen amateurs a forum for exercising their musical talents
alongside their friends and even hired professionals. The motivations sustaining such endeavors went beyond the simple enjoyment of music, however. By
establishing exclusive barriers to membership and by admitting ladies into
their audiences, subscription concert organizations became a valuable medium
for the display of cultural and political legitimacy and an important stage for
the enactment of rituals of gendered sociability. Through their personal, family, and business connections with Britain, the gentlemen of late colonial
South Carolina were certainly aware of such societies and their manifold benefits. Their commitment to replicating this cultural practice in Charleston
marks a significant moment in the maturity of their community, for the formation of the St. Cecilia Society represents more than the simple emulation
of a specific British musical model. The creation of a subscription concert
society, especially one invoking St. Cecilia as its titular figure, reflects the
colonial desire to employ the private patronage of music as a means of
demonstrating cultural achievement, specifically refinement and virtue, in a
very public and conspicuous manner.

When orchestral music in the modern sense came into being in the late
seventeenth century, only wealthy institutions such as royal or ecclesiastical

courts were capable of supporting this luxury. By the early eighteenth century, music lovers throughout Europe began to seek alternative schemes for sponsoring concert performances outside the courts. Musical salons, usually sponsored by aristocratic patrons, for example, flourished in Continental cities such as Paris and Vienna. In post-Restoration London, Charles II established the King's Band of twenty-four violins (that is, mixed string instruments of the violin family) in imitation of the French court, but otherwise a general decline in royal and aristocratic music patronage created a vacuum that induced private individuals to pool their resources into independent concert organizations.[1] The basis of this alternative scheme was the subscription, by which a group of gentlemen, frequently organized as a club or society for the purpose, each contributed a predetermined amount of money to cover the expenses for a series of concerts. Performers were normally drawn from among the members of the organization, but the subscription money could be used to hire professional musicians to round out the ensemble. A number of these subscription concert series appeared in London and throughout the provincial cities of the new United Kingdom in the early eighteenth century, but the arrival of famed Italian violinist Felice Giardini in London in 1751 inspired an explosion of concert activity that lasted for several decades.[2] Such was the breadth of this musical phenomenon that subscription concert series in eighteenth-century Britain ran the gamut from humble affairs composed exclusively of amateurs to elegant assemblies patronized by the nobility or aristocracy.[3]

Most eighteenth-century subscription concert series in the United Kingdom took place not in purpose-built concert halls, but in discrete rooms within taverns or coffeehouses. With the rising independence of the urban merchant class in the decades after the Restoration, the nation's traditional taverns and recently established coffeehouses became important social arenas. Here businessmen met with suppliers and customers, merchants negotiated with ship captains, travelers found room and board, and people of different social status conversed. In addition to beverages, food of varying sophistication was available, as were the latest newspapers and magazines. In port cities many houses advertised that they kept a ship registry and a wide selection of newspapers from abroad. A common feature of these establishments was their lack of "respectable" women, though ladies were allowed to attend special events such as concerts or dancing assemblies within the house when escorted by gentlemen. The respectability of a house depended on several factors, such as its proprietor, clientele, location, size, and furnishings, but in general coffeehouses, a novelty in late-seventeenth-century Britain, were considered more genteel than taverns. For the price of a drink, a meal, or a pipe of tobacco, men could enter these "penny universities" to learn and practice the public manners necessary for commerce. So important to the growth of

Britain's commercial interests were such institutions that they quickly spread to British colonies, from India to the Caribbean and North America.[4]

The growing importance of taverns and coffeehouses in British culture during the late seventeenth and early eighteenth centuries also fostered the rise of voluntary associations within this homosocial environment. As men began to spend more of their business and leisure time in these institutions, their informal conversations and activities coalesced into a wide variety of new social organizations, clubs, and societies. Taking advantage of the multi-purpose rooms, kitchens, and wine cellars found at taverns and coffeehouses, private associations—such as Masonic lodges, smoking clubs, beef-steak societies, and a panoply of other themed organizations—used such venues as their public headquarters.[5] Private rooms within taverns and coffeehouses also served as the perfect venue for the musical recreation of gentlemen amateurs. Without the pressures of a more public situation, amateurs could put their skills into practice with friends, and sometimes even side by side with professional musicians. Such gentlemen's recreation frequently included the singing of popular songs—airs, catches, canons, and glees—written specifically for this sociable environment. Contemporary with the rise of tavern and coffee-house culture in post-Restoration Britain, these genres of vocal music gave voice to the masculine, convivial gentlemen's clubs, using wit and humor to celebrate the pleasures of wine, women, and various bodily functions.[6] From this environment emerged musical organizations that presented concerts to private or semiprivate audiences. While some of these groups were composed purely of gentlemen amateurs who organized concerts for small audiences, some included celebrated professionals and attracted larger and more fashionable crowds. In either case the earliest concert societies in eighteenth-century London were deeply influenced by the overtly masculine environment of the tavern and coffeehouse.[7]

Examples of the early interdependence of subscription concert societies and taverns abound. During the first quarter of the eighteenth century, the respectable Devil's Tavern at Temple Bar served as one of the most common sites for concerts in London.[8] The enigmatic Philo-Musicae et Architecturae Societas, which flourished briefly between 1725 and 1727, consisted of about twenty merchants and musicians (including famed violinist Francesco Geminiani) and met primarily at the Queen's Head Lodge.[9] Between 1726 and 1784 the Academy of Ancient Music, one of the best-known examples of an eighteenth-century concert society, met fortnightly at the Crown and Anchor Tavern in the Strand (in the fashionable West End of London). During the last eight years of its existence (1784–92), the academy's performances were held in the larger (and newer) Freemasons' Hall. Like other subscription series, these concerts were open only to members of the society, which included both aristocratic gentlemen and eminent musicians, and their invited guests.[10] The Apollo Society—founded in 1731 when Maurice Greene, William Boyce, and others defected from the Academy of Ancient Music—performed their musical concerts at the Devil's Tavern. The Noblemen and Gentlemen's Catch Club, founded in 1761 at Almack's Tavern, later met at St. Alban's Tavern and at the Thatched House Tavern in St. James Street. This organization included many professional musicians, such as Carl Friedrich Abel, Johann Christian Bach, and Thomas Arne; its principal patron and leader was a nobleman, John Montagu, the third Earl of Sandwich.[11]

With the participation of gentlemen amateurs, professional musicians, and aristocratic patrons, a great deal of time and money was invested in subscription concert societies in eighteenth-century Britain. In spite of this fact, most of these concert series were not intended to be moneymaking ventures. The subscription plan was designed to facilitate a projected series of concerts by securing a list of patrons in advance, in much the same way as eighteenth-century authors and composers gathered a list of subscribers before attempting to publish a book or musical work. This method not only ensured financial solvency but also allowed the series organizers to predetermine their audience, for while the eighteenth-century subscription concert laid the foundation for the modern orchestral concert, it was by no means a public event.[12] Establishing the concert series under the auspices of a club or society created social boundaries that effectively controlled access to the performances. Membership or participation was not only subject to the approval of other members but also contingent on one's economic status. The expense of the subscription itself helped to define the prestige of the organization and thus effected a strong measure of social screening.[13] Although not as exclusive as performances at a royal court, eighteenth-century subscription concerts did not provide democratic access to music. Lacking the appropriate social connections or sufficient disposable income, many people were denied the opportunity to hear certain performers or certain repertoire.

The insular character of the subscription concert society allowed it to become one of the many eighteenth-century sociability rituals—such as balls, formal dinners, and polite conversation—that were intended to promote the cultural and political authority of the gentry. These rituals facilitated the exhibition of cultural accomplishments—such as the possession of manners, physical grace, and the appreciation of music, wine, and fashionable clothing, all of which implied wealth and cosmopolitanism—and thus were regarded as the hallmarks of legitimate social rank and leadership.[14] Membership in concert societies that cultivated sanctioned musical tastes (those approved by qualified authorities) within an exclusive sphere thus allowed men to bolster their claims of social status.[15] The performances of all-male private musical societies within the masculine atmosphere of eighteenth-century taverns no doubt provided a great deal of fraternal conviviality to the participants, but this gender monopoly could also be a liability. In such an environment, echo-ing with the sound of bawdy songs and drunken laughter, the private concert society was essentially a gentlemen's club with a musical focus and, as such, carried the risk of being viewed as a disorderly and dissipating event. By admitting women into the audience, however, the social character of sub-scription concerts could be tempered.

Ladies were not allowed to subscribe to early concert series, but by the middle of the eighteenth century most musical societies welcomed them as guests. In fact, members were frequently permitted or even expected to bring several ladies with them.[16] At a time when moral philosophers and novelists were increasingly investing women with the qualities of idealized feminine virtue and grace, the introduction of women into the concert audience shifted the focus from masculine conviviality to gendered sociability. Like the theater, the opera house, and dancing assemblies, subscription concerts became part of the rising culture of "sensibility," in which women were regarded as the arbiters of proper behavior and taste in mixed company. The contemporary definition of taste—the rational distinction between vulgarity and morality—was held to be a feminine virtue and an essential expression of woman's sen-timental culture. The male proprietors of mixed-sex concerts encouraged the cultivation of feminized taste, therefore, as a means of publicly tempering the potential for overstimulation and licentiousness.[17]

Music was ostensibly the central focus of these events, but the social con-tact they provided was also a powerful attraction. Audiences patronized con-certs not simply to hear the music but also to engage in polite conversation, to make new acquaintances, and to form alliances. In her novels *Evelina* (1778) and *Cecilia* (1782) Fanny Burney—daughter of the famous chronicler of London's musical life, Charles Burney—articulated the necessity for young ladies of fashion to attend the most prestigious musical assemblies in London in order to enhance their reputations. Rather than sitting in attentive silence, a characteristic of a later aesthetic era, audiences in Burney's day carried on their social business during the performance. In *Evelina*, for example, the heroine expresses dismay at the noise heard during a large concert in London: "There was an exceeding good concert, but too much talking to hear it well. Indeed I am quite astonished to find how little music is attended in silence; for though everybody seems to admire, hardly anybody listens."[18]

While modern audiences might find it difficult to imagine tolerating such distractions during a concert, music and polite sociability once enjoyed an interdependent, "natural" relationship. It would be an anachronistic mis-take to view this relationship as a flaw, for it represents a manifestation of eighteenth-century cultural ideology. Attitudes toward concert music were not yet imbued with the qualities of reverence and morality that contributed to the "sacralization" of music in the Romantic period. Rather, eighteenth-century concerts reflected an ideology that has been called the "sociable aesthetic," in which the socialization that accompanied musical activity was valued as much as the music itself, if not more. In this aesthetic, talking and moving about during the performance did not necessarily indicate a lack of appreciation for the music. These practices were an accepted and familiar part of the eighteenth-century concert experience.[19]

A natural extension of this aesthetic of sociability was the frequent pairing of concerts and balls. In the Age of Reason, this pairing seemed a logical choice because music and dance served a common purpose: they provided sensual pleasure and promoted harmonious social interaction. On a more practical level, both activities required the presence of instrumental musicians, and a rational sense of economy encouraged their comingling. Furthermore both concerts and balls frequently took place in the same venues: large, multipurpose rooms with seating that could be removed to create space for dancing. The standard measure of the success of each of these events was not necessarily the skill of the performers' execution, however, but rather the quantity and appearance of the company. The more ladies present at such heterosocial gatherings—and the more elegant and refined their countenances—the greater the perceived sensibility, or feminine virtue, embodied in the event. A band of musicians in a multipurpose room, attended by an exclusive crowd of fashionable ladies and gentlemen, thus invited a long-standing interdependence between these two social arts.[20]

By the middle of the eighteenth century, the subscription concert society was well established in Britain. Its pleasant mixture of sophisticated music, dancing, and an exclusive social network reinforced class identities, promoted the aesthetic of sentimentality, and provided a sanctioned arena for mixed-sex interaction. As social rituals subscription society concerts demonstrated accomplishment and success to those included and to those left outside. In colonial South Carolina, especially in the economic and social climate of Charleston in the mid-1760s, the desire to replicate such a social and cultural milieu must have been very powerful. Considering the proliferation of subscription concert societies in the United Kingdom, it seems unlikely that any one of these organizations served as a specific model for Charleston's St. Cecilia Society. Nevertheless two potential candidates for this role appear worthy of mention.

In London from at least 1753 through 1759 there was an active concert series sponsored by a "St. Cæcilian Society." Directed by the organist and composer Thomas Arne from 1756, this St. Cæcilian Society met at the

Crown Tavern and was dedicated specifically to the cultivation of English music rather than the more fashionable Italian and Austro-Germanic repertoire.[21] Such a circumscribed, nationalistic scope is not consistent with what is known of the early repertoire of Charleston's St. Cecilia Society, however. Nevertheless, the similarity between the names of this London society and Charleston's St. Cecilia Society may be more than a coincidence. Both societies focused on secular instrumental music, and both were named in honor of a saint who is usually associated with the performance of sacred vocal music. The literary construction of the saint's identity in eighteenth-century Britain may have been a factor linking these two societies.

Several factors also suggest a possible link between Charleston's St. Cecilia Society and the Edinburgh Musical Society, the most prominent subscription concert organization in eighteenth-century Scotland. Most of the administrative records of this organization have survived, and thus its activities are better known than those of most of its contemporaries. Founded by gentlemen amateurs in 1728, the Edinburgh Musical Society at first limited its subscription list to seventy gentlemen, but the list gradually increased to a total of two hundred subscribers by the 1780s. This society's regular Friday concerts were open only to members, but occasional oratorios and "Ladies Concerts" provided opportunities for mixed-sex gatherings.[22] During its existence, this society employed some of the finest instrumental and vocal performers in Europe. Among these were Alexander Reinagle (1749–1809), who later immigrated to Philadelphia, and William McGibbon (ca. 1690–1756), a native of Edinburgh who served for twenty years as the society's principal violinist and is regarded as the leading Scottish composer of the late Baroque era.[23] By 1762 the Edinburgh Musical Society was successful enough to construct its own concert venue, which it named St. Cecilia's Hall. After some years of decline, the society disbanded in 1798. The causes for this collapse were manifold: ineffectual administration, rising performers' salaries, and changing fashions that induced the audience to spend their evenings and money on other forms of entertainment.[24]

Following the political and economic union of England and Scotland in 1707, the Scottish population of South Carolina grew dramatically. Charleston's St. Andrew's Society, founded in 1729 by Scottish immigrants as a social and charitable society, was the first organization of its kind outside Scotland. Before the end of the colonial era, Scots dominated the local merchant community.[25] A number of the early members of Charleston's St. Cecilia Society also belonged to the town's Union Kilwinning Lodge of Freemasons. This club was formed in 1755 as the Union Lodge (no doubt in reference to the union of 1707), but added the name *Kilwinning* after it received an honorary charter from the Grand Lodge of Scotland around 1760.[26] The first president of the St. Cecilia Society, Dr. John Moultrie, studied medicine in Edinburgh and was also president of Charleston's St. Andrew's Society when the musical organization was founded in Charleston.[27] In the second half of the eighteenth century, the officers of the St. Cecilia Society included men with such Scottish family names as Gordon, Inglis, Kinloch, Olyphant, Pringle, Ramsay, and Swinton, all of which appear on a 1775 membership list of the Edinburgh society.[28] Coincidentally a book of sonatas for German flute and violin by the Edinburgh musician William McGibbon was among the many music books in the library of Dr. William Pillans, a Scottish-born Charleston apothecary and founding member of the St. Cecilia Society.[29]

Considering this evidence, it is possible that the Edinburgh Musical Society served as a primary model for Charleston's St. Cecilia Society. Without more substantial proof, however, such a claim would be imprudent.[30] Despite the prominence of the Scottish element in the social and economic life of mid-eighteenth-century Charleston, there are several compelling reasons to allow for a broader group of influences. First, a large number of the founding members of the St. Cecilia Society were young men with stronger connections to London than to Edinburgh. Some were natives of England, some were Carolina born but English educated, and some were merchants who traded primarily with English ports. Second, although concert societies could be found throughout Great Britain by the middle of the eighteenth century, their highest concentration was always in London. Third, the professional musicians who contributed to the establishment of the St. Cecilia Society—Benjamin Yarnold, Peter Valton, Thomas Pike, and Anthony L'Abbé—had no known personal or professional connection to Scotland. Benjamin Yarnold (ca. 1728–1787) served for two years as organist at St. Mildred Bread Street in London before immigrating to Charleston in 1753.[31] Peter Valton (ca. 1740–1784) received his musical education at the King's Chapel, or Chapel Royal, the choir of which is known to have performed occasionally at the subscription concerts of the Academy of Ancient Music.[32] The agents who hired Valton in 1764 noted that the young man "came highly recommended to us," having "for some years acted as deputy organist to Dr. [William] Boyce, Dr. [James] Nares, and Mr. [John] Keeble, at the King's Chapel Westminster Abbey and St. George's Hanover Square."[33] Anthony L'Abbé (ca. 1729–1798) may have been related to another man of that name who was active on the London stage and at the courts of George I and George II during the first half of the eighteenth century. Although a native of Tournais, L'Abbé arrived in Charleston via London "under the protection of the government" in 1764, bearing "particular recommendations" from an unknown source forwarded by the Lords Commissioners for Trade and Plantations at Whitehall.[34]

The formation of Charleston's St. Cecilia Society, therefore, was the result of numerous intersecting influences accumulating from the varied backgrounds and experiences of its founding members. As a result of this heterogeneity, the distinctive, identifiable characteristics of any one specific precedent were obscured, and the operations of this society mirror those of subscription concert societies in general rather than one particular model. Although the St. Cecilia Society may have been a unique phenomenon in colonial British America, subscription concert societies were so abundant in eighteenth-century Britain that it would have been more remarkable if the Charleston society's founders had indeed attempted to replicate a specific example.

IF THE MODELS for the formation of Charleston's first musical organization were profuse and widely known, the same may also be said about the saint chosen for the society's name. Cecilia, an early Christian martyr, has been regarded as the patron saint of music and musicians for many centuries, and her name was quite well known in eighteenth-century England and America. That a fledgling musical society in colonial South Carolina should name itself in her honor, therefore, seems a simple choice. By the turn of the nineteenth century there were St. Cecilia societies in several other American cities, such as New York, Boston, and Providence. By the turn of the twentieth century, musical societies named for this venerable saint could be found far into the western regions of the United States. In contrast with the Charleston organization, which was devoted to fashionable secular music (both vocal and instrumental), however, each of these later Cecilian societies cultivated sacred vocal music.[35] The choice of Cecilia as the titular saint of this secular music society, therefore, stems from a cultural perspective quite different from that of later societies devoted to sacred music. The existing historical literature on St. Cecilia's relationship to music dwells exclusively on sacred music in Catholic nations, and thus does not address this dichotomy. Why, then, would a gentlemen's club in eighteenth-century Charleston's strongly Anglican community name their secular music society after a female Roman martyr traditionally associated with sacred music? The answer to this question has less to do with the roots of St. Cecilia's legend than it does with the distinct cultural meaning she acquired in eighteenth-century Britain and, by extension, in colonial South Carolina.

In the hagiographical literature of the early Middle Ages, when her legend first appeared, St. Cecilia was not associated with music. She was known as a beautiful young Roman virgin of noble birth whose devotion to the Christian God drew nightly visits from a protective angel in the form of a young man. After becoming betrothed to a pagan nobleman, Valerianus, Cecilia warned her husband on their wedding night that the angelic visitor, whom he could see only if he converted to Christianity, would not permit him to violate her vow of chastity. Valerianus was then converted and even convinced his brother, Tibernius, to do the same. For their involvement in the Christian community in Rome and for refusing to offer sacrifices to the Roman gods, the brothers were beheaded. After surviving various forms of Roman torture, Cecilia was similarly martyred.

Although there is some debate about precisely when and why Cecilia became connected with music, her legend had acquired musical significance by the time of the European Renaissance. Paintings from this era frequently depict a beautiful, young Cecilia playing an organ (or occasionally a lyre, harp, or lute) and attended by a number of angels. This tradition continued well into the nineteenth century, with each age depicting the saint in the fashions of the day. The St. Cæcilia painted by English artist Joshua Reynolds in 1775, for example, depicts a young Elizabeth Linley Sheridan (1754–1792) in an elegant state of late-eighteenth-century dishabille (see figure 2.1). The daughter of musician Thomas Linley Sr., Elizabeth made her vocal debut in London in 1767 and quickly became one of the most celebrated sopranos of her time. Although she retired from public performances after her marriage to playwright Richard Sheridan in 1773, Reynolds's famous depiction of the former Miss Linley, as well as the music she popularized, enjoyed wide circulation throughout the English-speaking world. For that brief moment in British history, the talented Mrs. Sheridan was celebrated as the embodiment of the qualities of beauty, musicality, and virtue that have been associated with St. Cecilia for more than a millennium.

Commenting on the sparseness of real evidence connecting Cecilia to music, English music historian John Hawkins wrote in 1776, "there is a tradition of St. Cecilia, that she excelled in music, and that the angel, who was thus enamoured of her, was drawn down from the celestial mansions by the charms of her melody; this has been deemed authority sufficient for making her the patroness of music and musicians."[36] Once her association with music became generally accepted, musicians adopted Cecilia as the patron saint of their profession and celebrated her feast day, 22 November, with special musical events. In England this practice appears to have commenced in the 1680s, shortly after the return of Charles II and his court from exile in the predominantly Catholic nation of France. Well into the eighteenth century, St. Cecilia's Day was observed in Britain with performances of semisacred concerted vocal music; that is, music for one or more solo voices, chorus, and instruments. Although these performances were usually held in secular venues, such as Stationers' Hall in London, they were often preceded by an Anglican service that included a sermon on the value of music in religious worship. Henry Purcell's Welcome to all the Pleasures and Hail, Bright Cecilia, and George Frideric Handel's Ode for St. Cecilia's Day and Alexander's Feast may represent the best known examples of this tradition, but many lesser-known English composers, such as John Blow, Daniel Purcell, Nicola Matteis, and Giovanni Baptista Draghi, also made contributions to the genre.

Cecilian music produced in Catholic nations during the sixteenth and seventeenth centuries is largely written in a conservative style influenced by a centuries-old tradition of liturgical vocal music. By contrast, the Cecilian

2.1. *St. Cæcilia*, by Joshua Reynolds, 1775; mezzotint by William Dickinson, London, 1776. From the collection of the author

music from post-Restoration England exhibits a "modern" secular style, joy-fully combining voices and instruments and interweaving vocal solos and choruses with orchestral interludes. This idiom, established by such com-posers as Blow and Henry Purcell and continued by Handel and his contem-poraries in England, has more in common with the increasingly secular spirit of early modern Britain than with the European tradition of Cecilian music. The same can be said for the texts of these vocal compositions, which were written by many of the leading English poets of the day. Rather than praising Cecilia's virtues in the conservative language of medieval hagiography, as was traditional in Roman Catholic celebrations, the composers and poets of Augustan England invoked Cecilia in the Neoclassical language of the Age of Enlightenment. Just as Greek and Roman imagery were absorbed into the arts of eighteenth-century England to depict the spirit of the age, Cecilia, the vir-tuous Roman martyr, was appropriated as an emblem of modern cultural refinement and sensibility. And while musical compositions written in her honor were performed only on St. Cecilia's Day, the texts associated with these works were widely published and thus enjoyed greater currency than the music. By examining a sample of the textual evocations of the patron saint of music, therefore, we can begin to understand the meaning she had for English-speaking audiences of the eighteenth century.

Many of the Cecilian odes written in late-seventeenth- and eighteenth-century Britain follow a similar pattern of juxtaposing and comparing the musical skills of Cecilia with those of various Classical figures. Since these works were created specifically to celebrate the young virgin martyr, it is hardly surprising that Cecilia is invariably judged supreme. The nine muses of Greek mythology, for example, representing the inspiration of the arts, sci-ences, and literature, are frequently called on to proclaim Cecilia's musical superiority. In the opening of his *Ode for Musick, on St. Cecilia's Day* (set to music by Maurice Greene in 1730 and by William Walond in 1757), Alexan-der Pope commanded the muses to bear witness to Cecilia's prowess by exclaiming "Descend ye Nine! descend and sing."[37] Likewise the "sons of all the learned Nine" admire "bright Cecilia" from Mt. Parnassus in Thomas D'Urfey's 1691 ode *The Glorious Day is Come* (set to music by John Blow), for she is the "aweful goddess that informs their brains."[38] Praised by the muses, Cecilia's talents are also placed in direct comparison with those of other myth-ical figures of antiquity. The musical accomplishments of Orpheus, while powerful enough to free his wife, Eurydice, from the bonds of death, pall in contrast to those of the Roman martyr. Noting the reputation of his musician-ship, John Dryden's 1687 *Song for St. Cecilia's Day* (with music originally com-posed by Giovanni Baptista Draghi and later reset by Handel), refers to Cecilia's Christian legend to explain her triumph over Orpheus:

> Orpheus could lead the savage race;
> And trees uprooted left their place,
> Sequacious of the lyre.
> But bright Cecilia rais'd the wonder high'r;
> When to her organ vocal breath was giv'n,
> An Angel heard, and straight appear'd,
> Mistaking Earth for Heav'n.[39]

Similarly Pope's *Ode for Musick, on St. Cecilia's Day* succinctly weighs the respective accomplishments of these two figures and again judges Cecilia's Christian virtue superior:

> Of Orpheus now no more let poets tell,
> To bright Cecilia greater pow'r is giv'n;
> His numbers rais'd a shade from Hell,
> Hers lift the soul to Heav'n.[40]

Timotheus, the Greek musician praised in Dryden's 1697 ode *Alexander's Feast, or the Power of Music* (set to music by Jeremiah Clark and later reset by Handel), is forced to yield his musical prize on the sudden, somewhat incongruous arrival of "Divine Cecilia, Inventress of the vocal frame," in the final stanza. While he had "raised a mortal to the sky," Cecilia's musical skill, fortified by "Nature's mother-wit and arts unknown before," had drawn an angel down from heaven.[41]

Of all the ancient literary figures associated with music, however, none outranks Apollo (also known as Phoebus Apollo), the Greek god of light, music, and prophecy. Representing the ideal personification of masculinity, Apollo has been invoked for centuries as the symbol of gentlemanly music making (witness the 1731 Apollo Society). But even this Olympian deity, who is often depicted with a harp or lyre, must abdicate his throne in favor of the mortal Cecilia. Although it does not articulate a specific reason, William Congreve's *Hymn to Harmony*, written for the St. Cecilia's Day celebration of 1701 and set to music by John Eccles, proclaims Cecilia's triumph over Phoebus Apollo:

> Cecilia, more than all the Muses skill'd!
> Phoebus himself to her must yield,
> And at her Feet lay down
> His Golden Harp and Lawrel Crown.[42]

The lack of explanation for Cecilia's superiority over Apollo in Congreve's poem is not unusual among this body of literature, for the two figures are rarely placed in direct rhetorical competition. In fact, the Christian saint and the Greek god seem to occupy a common plane of symbolic value in late-seventeenth- and eighteenth-century British verse. In Congreve's hymn, unlike the above-mentioned examples, Apollo's mythological powers are not swept aside or outmatched by Cecilia. Rather the Greek god yields his position to the maiden, as any gentleman of the poet's era would have done for a young lady, as an expression of respect. This deferential act simultaneously preserves Apollo's symbolic meaning for masculine music making and reveals another important facet of Cecilia's appeal to eighteenth-century British audiences: more than just a skilled musician, Cecilia embodies both the physical and spiritual aspects of idealized femininity.

The union of music and physical beauty in the Cecilian literature of Augustan England is as commonplace as the well-known expressions of music's power to soothe the savage breast and to calm the troubled mind. While she is traditionally depicted as young and attractive in the visual arts, Cecilia's physical appearance is not the object of veneration here, however. Instead the fair young woman is invoked to preside over the rhetorical marriage of music and beauty, an interdependent bond that is frequently expressed in very sensual, earthly terms. In Theophilus Parsons's ode for St. Cecilia's Day of 1693 (set to music by Gottfried Finger), for example, the appreciation of physical beauty is activated by the sensations of music, and the presence of female beauty heightens the enjoyment of music:

> Beauty may wound th' unguarded eyes,
> And slowly creep into the heart:
> But Music quick as lightning flies;
> The pleasure dances with the smart,
> And melts and trills through ev'ry part.
> Without the magic of the fair,
> We love, we sigh, and we despair,
> We catch at sounds, and grasp the fleeting air.[43]

Transposing the language used to describe physical beauty and music, William Thompson's Cecilian ode *Beauty and Musick* explains how the saint's harmonious powers can calm those struck by Cupid's arrow:

> Beauty, silent Harmony!
> Softly stealing through the Eye
> Smiles into the Breast a Dart.
> Musick, fine-proportion'd sounds!
> Pours Balm upon the Lover's Wounds
> Through the Ear into the Heart.[44]

The sensual appreciation of music and beauty is superficial and fleeting, however, and the fervent pursuit of such mortal pleasure, especially in the moral climate of the eighteenth century, could easily be perceived as impious and dissipating. Cecilia's godly virtue dispels any hint of impropriety from this union, and under her influence the celebration of music and beauty is raised to a higher plane of devotion. This transformation forms the conclusion in most of this Cecilian literature, which after all was written to celebrate the saint's sacred day. After acknowledging the amorous nature of such worldly pleasures, for example, Thompson's *Beauty and Musick* immediately turns to Cecilia's power to transform the corporeal into the spiritual:

> Harmony, the Soul refining!
> Beauty, Sense, and Virtue joining
> In a Form and Mind like Thine,
> Nobly raise a mortal Creature
> To a more exalted Nature;
> We alone are more Divine![45]

Similarly John Oldham's 1685 ode *For an Anniversary of Musick kept upon St. Cecilia's Day* extols the power of music to link the pleasures of the mortal realm with those of the eternal:

> Music does all our Joys refine,
> 'Tis that gives Relish to our Wine,
> 'Tis that gives Rapture to our Love,
> It wings Devotion to a pitch Divine,
> 'Tis our chief Bliss on Earth, and half our Heav'n above.[46]

After praising all the instruments sounded in her honor, John Lockman's *Ode for St. Cecilia's Day* (set to music by William Boyce for the Apollo Society in 1739) counsels the audience to follow Cecilia's lead by turning away from worldly cares, represented by Classical figures, to embrace the spiritual:

> Now the ætherial lyrist sweeps her strings,
> And thus, responsive to her harp, she sings.
> Mortals, scorn the boasted Nine,
> Sing of Love, but Love Divine."[47]

Cecilia's musical devotion, renowned for having drawn angels down from heaven, served as a potent example of music's power to elevate the pleasures of human experience to a more spiritual plane. Musical harmony, under her influence, became synonymous with reason, godliness, and refinement—the opposite of chaos and vulgarity. Peter Anthony Motteaux's 1695 Cecilian ode, set to music by John Blow, encapsulates the full spectrum of Cecilia's constructive influence:

> Cecilia taught new Graces to the Choir,
> And made all Instruments in one conspire.
> By Music taught, in her harmonious Mind,
> All Vertues in full Concert join'd.
> Faith, Hope, and Love the Trebles were:
> Reason the Tenor still was there;
> And, ev'ry Part to grace,
> Humility the Basse.[48]

In short the portrayal of Cecilia in this eighteenth-century English literature suggests an ideal symbol to preside over mixed-sex concerts of secular music. As the personification of idealized youthful femininity, she provides an attractive alternative to the austere musical icons of the Classical world, especially the masculine image of Apollo. The angelic rapture inspired by her grace and musical skill validates the sensual enjoyment of performing and listening to music. Devoting her body and music to a virtuous, Christian purpose, Cecilia sanctifies the intermingling of beauty, music, and love. These literary texts were originally created for the religious observation of the saint's feast day, but the image they created endured well beyond this narrow framework. As the patron saint of music and musicians, Cecilia was also venerated in secular contexts such as songs, paintings, and, of course, musical societies named in her honor. We must remember that while membership in eighteenth-century concert organizations such as Charleston's St. Cecilia Society was open only to men, the presence of women at their concerts was an integral part of their purpose. As demonstrated by many remarks in Charleston's newspapers over the years, in fact, the number of fashionable, vivacious women present at these concerts was to a large degree the measure of their success. By choosing Cecilia as their symbolic patron, therefore, the organizers of such concerts invoked the saint's virtuous reputation to project a spirit of refined sensual enjoyment within the bounds of respectable decorum.

In the decades after the first known musical celebration of her feast day in Britain in the early 1680s, St. Cecilia, or at least the rhetorically constructed image of her, became a fixture in English literature and musical compositions. Like the books, furniture, and other material commodities imported into colonial South Carolina from Britain, Cecilia's symbolic importance to the world of music could not have escaped the notice of the affluent gentlemen of Charleston who sought to surround themselves with the trappings of genteel refinement. Conjecture about this point is unnecessary, however, for evidence confirming the currency of Cecilia's cultural meaning in late colonial Charleston has survived in the works of two men directly connected with the beginnings of the St. Cecilia Society: South Carolina merchant Henry Laurens and London-trained musician Peter Valton. As their words demonstrate, Cecilia's emblematic power was just as meaningful and useful in the New World as in the Old.

Following the unlawful seizure of one of his merchant ships in 1768, Henry Laurens (1724–1792, see figure 2.2), a wealthy Charleston merchant, planter, and early St. Cecilia Society member, published in November 1768 a polemical pamphlet titled *Extracts from the Proceedings of the High Court of Vice Admiralty, in Charles-Town, South-Carolina*. Laurens's goal in having this work printed was not only to lay the groundwork for legal redress but also to expose the dubious practices of Sir Egerton Leigh (ca. 1732–1781), master of the South Carolina Court of Vice-Admiralty.[49] As a placeman, a politician appointed to office by the British government because of his family's social status rather than elected by local constituents, Leigh was distrusted and resented by many Charlestonians.[50] In the early spring of 1769 Leigh published his response, a pamphlet titled *The Man Unmask'd*, in which he questioned the motives behind Laurens's accusations and attacked his rival's character. Laurens countered Leigh's use of "personal Invective, Chicanery, and Falsehood" by publishing a second, expanded edition of his *Extracts,* complete with further examples of Leigh's official misdeeds. In an advertisement for this new work, Laurens confessed to having personal shortcomings and invited Leigh to "bring forth all the Errors of my private Life that *he knows of*," to which Laurens offered to "add some Faults that *he does not know of.*" From this nadir of rhetorical humility Laurens then catapulted himself to the moral high ground of the argument by inserting a brief quotation from Shakespeare's *Merchant of Venice* into his advertisement to denigrate poetically Leigh's character:

> The Motions of his spirit are dull as night;
> And his affections dark as Erebus.
> Let no such man be trusted.

> Those Lines are applied by *Shakespeare* to Men whose Souls are not
> attuned to Music.—The Author of the Extracts &c. delights in Music,
> he has been one of the Votaries of *Apollo,* and his Name is written in
> St. *Cæcilia*'s Roll.[51]

Laurens's own words allude to the lines immediately preceding those he quoted: "The man that hath no music in himself / Nor is moved with the concord of sweet sounds / Is fit for treasons, stratagems, and spoils."[52] Thus employing his knowledge of Shakespeare, a knowledge undoubtedly shared by his affluent peers, Laurens invoked his membership in the St. Cecilia Society as part of a literary defense against Leigh's attempts at character assassination. By identifying himself as one of the gentlemen "Votaries of Apollo" who sponsored the respectable St. Cecilia concerts in Charleston, Laurens, a nouveau-riche colonial, offered proof that his soul was "attuned to Music" and testified to the vitality of his spirit, the clarity of his affections, and the fidelity of his character.

2.2. *Henry Laurens Esqr. President of the American Congress, 1778*, by John Singleton Copley; mezzotint by V. Green, London, 1782. This portrait was painted shortly after Laurens, the highest-ranking American prisoner of war during the Revolution, was released from the Tower of London. From the collections of the South Carolina Historical Society

For his alleged lack of sensitivity to music, Leigh, a wealthy British aristocrat, was portrayed (rather accurately, it turns out) as a selfish, dishonest rogue.[53]

An even more direct link between the characterization of St. Cecilia in Britain and in colonial Charleston 'appears in a three-voice catch (a kind of round) by Peter Valton, *Divine Cecilia,* which was published under the auspices of the Noblemen and Gentlemen's Catch Club of London in 1770 (see figure 2.3).[54] The details of Valton's connection to this exclusive musical organization are not known, but his affiliation with the Chapel Royal in the late 1750s must have facilitated his entry in to London's more fashionable musical circles. In fact Valton published a number of vocal compositions in London during the 1760s and 1770s. *The Reprisal,* for example, a song performed at Marylebone Gardens in 1765, is set to a text by John Lockman, who had also provided the text for William Boyce's *Ode for St. Cecilia's Day* in 1739. Other vocal works by Valton were published in London during the early 1770s, suggesting that he maintained ties to London's musical life well after settling in Charleston in late 1764.[55] As the text of his brief *Divine Cecilia* demonstrates, Valton (or the unknown author of this verse) was clearly familiar with the traditional Cecilian imagery of Augustan England.

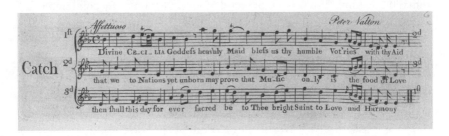

2.3. *Divine Cecilia,* by Peter Valton. From Thomas Warren, comp., *A Ninth Collection of Catches Canons and Glees for Three Four and Five Voices* (London, 1770). Courtesy of the British Library

For several decades after its formation in 1761, the Noblemen and Gentlemen's Catch Club sponsored an annual collection of unaccompanied vocal catches, glees, and canons selected from among those submitted to the prestigious club for its consideration. Composed by both professional musicians and gentlemen amateurs, these works are often humorous and occasionally quite crude, but a portion of the vocal pieces in the Catch Club's annual collections has a more serious and even religious tone. Valton's *Divine Cecilia* falls into this latter category, pairing a regal, marchlike musical setting with a text steeped in religious sentiment:

> Divine Cecilia Goddess heav'nly Maid
> Bless us thy humble Vot'ries with thy Aid
> That we to Nations yet unborn may prove
> That Music only is the food of Love
> Then shall this day for ever sacred be to Thee
> Bright Saint to Love and Harmony.

As in the literary examples mentioned above, the text of Valton's catch intertwines Neoclassical imagery with Christian sentiment, for Cecilia is at once both a goddess beseeched by votaries and a divine, heavenly saint. Her feast day (implied by the phrase "this day") is declared sacred not in a generally religious sense but specifically to the celebration of the power of love and harmony. Cecilia's influence is not solely religious, however, for while she represents the divine marriage of music and idealized love, she is also invoked to sanction more earthly affections. Speaking, no doubt, on behalf of Charleston's St. Cecilia Society, Valton seeks Cecilia's aid to prove Shakespeare's well-known romantic dictum: "If music be the food of love, play on."[56] By combining elements both sacred and secular, Neoclassical and Christian, Valton's catch demonstrates that the spirit of Charleston's newly formed St. Cecilia Society was modeled after established British conventions and celebrates the society's intermingling of music and sociability. Although it was published in London, this piece was undoubtedly first sung by Cecilia's votaries in Charleston, gentlemen who combined their collective resources and experiences to display the power of music to a New World—"to Nations yet unborn."

As the titular saint of a secular concert society in colonial South Carolina, therefore, St. Cecilia was a logical and meaningful choice because she embodied the most desirable elements of two contrasting worlds. On one hand, as a remote, semimythological figure, she represented a link to the Neoclassical aesthetic that characterized much of eighteenth-century Augustan England. On the other hand, her reputation as a chaste and devout Christian served as a moral shield to defend an activity that could potentially be construed as overly luxurious and dissipating. By invoking her name as its patron figure, the sponsors of mixed-sex concerts—especially those in a remote provincial town such as eighteenth-century Charleston—could feel assured that their activities would be perceived as refined, orderly, and dignified events. In the words of the great English critic of their day, Samuel Johnson, Cecilia personified the contemporary definition of music as "the art that unites corporeal with intellectual pleasure, by a species of enjoyment which gratifies sense, without weakening reason."[57]

FROM THE CONSTRUCTION and administration of their own concert organization to the cultural and political motivations underlying its activities, the musical world of eighteenth-century Britain provided significant and multi-layered models for the elite gentlemen of late colonial Charleston. The financial practicality of the subscription concert system encouraged the mutually beneficial collaboration of amateur and professional musicians. The construction of a conscientiously exclusive and fashionable musical organization offered members the opportunity to demonstrate their sophistication and rank. The admission of women into the audience broadened the appeal of the subscription concert society by transforming an otherwise mundane musical performance into a ritual of gendered sociability. That the full breadth of this cultural model was embraced in late colonial South Carolina is demonstrated by the choice of St. Cecilia as their figurehead, for she offered a powerful moral symbol to those desirous of projecting an appearance of virtue and refinement. To the founders of Charleston's St. Cecilia Society and to their observers, the adoption of the semiprivate subscription concert mechanism thus provided conspicuous proof of the continuity between the avowedly refined cultural practices of the Old World and those of an emerging provincial capital.

3

The Rise and Fall of the Concerts

THROUGH PEACE AND WARTIME, prosperity and depression, the concert activities of the St. Cecilia Society flourished during a truly vibrant and dramatic era of early American history. Because of the loss of its records in 1865, however, historians have achieved little success in situating the society's career of concert patronage within a proper historical framework. Published accounts of the society consistently repeat inaccuracies regarding the founding of the society and the termination of its concert series that were introduced in the late nineteenth century. Descriptions of the society's musical era have heretofore focused on its activities during the late colonial era, declaring this era the society's heyday. Taking a cue from a mid-nineteenth-century memoir, many historians then skip ahead to note, with nearly uniform vagueness, the end of the society's concerts "about the year 1822." The decades between these landmarks, a period forming the bulk of the society's musical activity, thus remain unexamined. While the loss of the society's own records precludes the writing of a detailed linear narrative, there is plenty of evidence to create a robust and meaningful overview of the St. Cecilia Society's entire concert-giving era. A thorough search of surviving primary sources and newspapers shows that the society's fortunes, particularly the details of its inception and its withdrawal from concert patronage, are intimately connected to the larger socioeconomic history of Charleston. Founded in 1766 amid a burst of late colonial cultural expansion, the St. Cecilia Society waxed and waned in harmony with the fortunes of its host city, with its activities peaking in the mid-1790s and the turn of the new century. In the years after the War of 1812, the confluence of factors such as the weakened local economy and the sudden decline of the city's population of orchestral musicians, disrupted the society's traditional practices and led to the cessation of its concert series in 1820. As the focal point of the social aspirations of the region's elite, therefore, the rise and fall of the society's concert series between 1766 and 1820 can be seen as the cultural epitome of Charleston's golden age.

In his *Reminiscences of Charleston,* published in 1854 and venerated by generations of local historians ever since, the lawyer, painter, and musician Charles Fraser (1782–1860, see figure 3.1) devoted a few brief paragraphs to the musical heritage of his native city. "The love of music was an early characteristic of the people of Charleston," he recalled, "and very generally cultivated by them as an accomplishment." Certainly by the last decade of the colonial era (1765–75), the musically inclined gentlemen of Charleston—including Fraser's Scottish-born father, Alexander—possessed both the economic resources and the knowledge of British precedents to create a subscription concert society in their community. "Out of this grew the St. Cecilia Society," remembered Fraser, "originally an association of gentlemen amateurs, who met together to indulge a common taste and to pass an agreeable hour."[1] Alexander Fraser was, in fact, among the society's founding members, and his son Alexander Jr., Charles's favorite older brother, was an active participant in its musical activities the 1790s. Fraser's brief description of Charleston's early musical life, which dwells exclusively on the St. Cecilia Society, was thus based on his own family's credible, firsthand knowledge. Despite his close connection to information about the society's early days, however, Fraser's reminiscences do not specify the founding date of this musical organization. At the time of his writing, its records were still intact, and the details of the society's founding may not have held particular interest for Fraser and his audience. Since the destruction of its records in the 1860s, however, the St. Cecilia Society's founding date has been the subject of much confusion among historians and locals alike. Various publications have ascribed its establishment to a wide range of dates, from as early as 1735 to as late as 1782. Most commonly its founding is placed in the year 1762, though no evidence has ever been produced to support that date. There is copious evidence, however, to place the founding of the St. Cecilia Society securely in the year 1766. The loss of the society's records precludes a simple solution to this issue, but the matter can be confidently settled by a survey of the historical evidence.

The earliest evidence of concerts in Charleston dates from the first issues of the city's first newspaper in 1732, though there was probably some concert activity preceding these advertisements. The wording of several concert notices in the early 1730s suggest that the musical performances they advertised were part of an annual subscription series—most likely the earliest of its kind in British America.[2] Amid this early concert activity, Charles Theodore Pachelbel (1690–1750), soon to be organist at St. Philip's Church, advertised a St. Cecilia's Day concert in November 1737, featuring "a Cantata suitable to the Occasion."[3] No evidence has been found, however, to suggest that this performance arose from or led to the establishment of a musical society. Pachelbel's public concert celebrating this feast day may have indeed been a first for the city, but we should be wary of assuming a connection between that 1737 concert and a later society simply because they honor the same saint. Other concert advertisements over the next several decades confirm

3.1. *Self-Portrait,* 1823, by Charles Fraser (1782–1860). Watercolor on ivory, Gibbes Museum of Art / Carolina Art Association, 1920.02.01

that gentlemen amateurs collaborated with professional musicians in presenting concerts in Charleston, but such performance notices do not convey a
sense of regularity or continuity.[4] While it is clear that musical activity in
Charleston became increasingly common toward the middle of the eighteenth
century, the critical mass of resources and stability necessary to create a formal musical organization did not occur for several more years.

Even if the gentlemen of Charleston had wished to create an annual series
of concerts after Pachelbel's 1737 St. Cecilia event, there were a number of
obstacles to discourage such an endeavor. Although South Carolina had
reached a point of calm prosperity by the early 1730s, after its transformation
from a proprietary to a royal colony, a series of crises in the next several
decades disrupted the local social scene. Epidemics of yellow fever and small
pox ravaged the capital city in 1738–39. The Stono uprising—a bloody slave
revolt described as the largest incident of its kind in British North America—
took place just south of Charleston in September 1739, terrifying the planters
and shattering the young colony's tenuous sense of domestic security. A great
fire in November 1740 consumed half of urban Charleston's buildings and
bankrupted many local merchants. King George's War (1744–48), the American phase of the War of the Austrian Succession (1740–48), disrupted South
Carolina's shipping during the 1740s and caused the rice market to collapse. A
severe hurricane in September 1752 caused extensive damage to the fabric of
Charleston that took years to repair. Finally between 1759 and 1763 the local
campaigns of the larger French and Indian War proved to be a serious distrac-
tion. Soldiers returning from combat against the Cherokee Indians in 1760
brought an epidemic of smallpox back to Charleston, which effectively curtailed the city's social life for several seasons. By the mid-1760s, however, the
long-lingering threats posed by disease, Native Americans, the French, and
the Spanish suddenly receded, and the province of South Carolina was able to
rest more securely than at any time in its nearly one-hundred-year history.

Britain's military triumph over the French and their Native American
allies in 1763 ushered in a period of unprecedented calm in North America
and at home as well. The stability and optimism of the postwar era caused a
surge in the British economy, which in turn led to a dramatic increase in
musical concerts in London during the 1760s.[5] A similar scene unfolded on
the opposite site of the Atlantic, in coastal South Carolina. As Charleston
physician David Ramsay observed immediately after the Revolution, "few
countries have at any time exhibited so striking an instance of publick and
private prosperity as appeared in South-Carolina between the years 1763 and
1775. . . . Wealth poured in upon [the inhabitants] from a thousand channels
. . . and [they] were secure in their persons and prosperity."[6] After nearly a
century of growing pains, opportunities for expansion in South Carolina

reached unprecedented levels, and Charleston was primed for the establishment of more permanent cultural institutions.

A number of sources demonstrate conclusively that the St. Cecilia Society was established in 1766. The society is not among the many "Publick Societies" (private clubs), such as the St. Andrew's Society and the St. George's Society, listed in the *South-Carolina Almanack* of 1763 or 1765.[7] The St. Cecilia Society does appear in a similar list of Charleston's social and benevolent organizations in the 1793 *South Carolina and Georgia Almanack,* which states that it was "formed in 1766."[8] Later in the nineteenth century, newspaper notices for the society's anniversary meetings occasionally referred to its date of origin. Advertisements for the society's meetings in November 1853 and November 1860, for example, announced the celebration of its eighty-seventh and ninety-fourth anniversaries, respectively.[9] Calculating back from these dates yields, of course, the year 1766. Since these notices appeared several years before the society's records were destroyed, we can assume its members were familiar with the details of its history. Even after the loss of the society's records in 1865, however, its first meeting after the conclusion of the Civil War, held at the hall of the South Carolina Society on 22 November 1866, was announced as "The Centennial Anniversary Meeting of this Society."[10]

An anonymous article published in the *Charleston Courier* in October 1868 contains a number of intriguing details about the early history of the St. Cecilia Society. Appearing as part of "Charleston in Olden Times," a series of nostalgic recollections of Charleston's past, the article states that the St. Cecilia Society was formed on 28 April 1766 and provides the names of thirty-seven founding members.[11] The unnamed author was probably Wilmot Gibbes deSaussure (1822–1886), for among his personal papers at the Charleston Library Society is a manuscript containing much of the information that appeared in this nostalgic newspaper series—including data about the founding of the St. Cecilia Society.[12] Although deSaussure did not name his source for this information, his reputation as a knowledgeable local historian and his experience as an officer of the St. Cecilia Society lend a great deal of credibility to his words. He was, after all, known by his contemporaries as one who "has given more time and study to Old Charleston than any man now living."[13]

Considering the strength of this evidence, one might justifiably wonder how the confusion over the founding date ever began. The solution to this mystery appears in the earliest surviving volume of the St. Cecilia Society's minutes. After a brief period of inactivity at the end of the Civil War, the society gathered for a reorganizational meeting on 22 November 1866. With Wilmot Gibbes deSaussure presiding, the surviving members took stock of the society's heavy losses during the war and sedately celebrated the organization's centennial anniversary. As the society gradually recovered in the years after 1866, its meeting minutes record the correct ordinal number of each anniversary: 101st, 102d, 103d, and so on. In November 1874, however, the society's anniversary is suddenly designated the 112th instead of the 108th. A marginal note, penned by the society's secretary at that time, Thomas Pinckney Lowndes (1839–1899), explains this nonsequential leap by stating simply "it was discovered that the numbers of the previous anniversaries were incorrect."[14] The inspiration for this alteration probably came from Robert Mills's *Statistics of South Carolina,* published in 1826. In a brief survey of the arts in South Carolina, Mills (1781–1855), a Charleston-born architect of national prominence, stated simply that the St. Cecilia Society was established "some time in 1762."[15] Although Mills spent most of his career outside Charleston, most notably in Washington, D.C., where his designs include the U.S. Patent Office and the Washington Monument, he was employed by the state during the 1820s to produce an *Atlas of the State of South Carolina* (1825) and the *Statistics.* Mills may have been invited to some St. Cecilia Society events during his return to South Carolina, but it seems unlikely that he was a member, much less that he ever had occasion to examine the society's records. In the absence of any documentation, then, it would seem that Mills's statement was based on hearsay rather than on any documented proof. Aside from Mills's *Statistics,* no other references to the supposed 1762 founding date of this society are found until the 1874 alteration of the minute books. We can only surmise that the extra four years added to the society's age may have seemed plausible to its newer, younger members at that moment, and the loss of their early records during the war may have given the older members cause to question their memories.

Thus it can be stated definitively that the St. Cecilia Society was established in 1766. This is not to say that other concerts, or perhaps even concert series, did not take place in Charleston for many years prior to this date, for it is certain they did. Rather, the year 1766 marks the beginning of a musical organization whose members may have collaborated on many prior occasions but only now coordinated their efforts into a formal society.

What, then, can be said about Wilmot Gibbes deSaussure's very specific assertion that the St. Cecilia Society was founded on 28 April 1766? How and why did this group of thirty-seven gentlemen come together at that moment? A conjectural answer to both of these questions may be drawn from a brief look at the general cultural scene in Charleston in the several years leading up to April 1766.

Four of the society's founding members, Benjamin Yarnold, Thomas Pike, Peter Valton, and Anthony L'Abbé, were professional musicians—the last three having arrived in Charleston in late 1764. Between October 1765 and February 1766, each of these three recent arrivals held a subscription concert for his own benefit, which probably included the assistance of gentlemen amateurs.[16] These performances were all held at the city's theater in Queen Street—a venue constructed (or refurbished) in late 1763 on the site of Charleston's first Dock-Street Theatre, opened in 1736. Between December 1763 and April 1764, David Douglass's American Company of Comedians presented a season of dramatic entertainments at this venue, accompanied by an orchestra of unknown size. Pike's concert of 16 October 1765 included only instrumental music, but after members of Douglass's troupe returned to Charleston from London several weeks later, Valton's benefit on 13 November featured the vocal talents of two young actresses. L'Abbé's concert on 3 February 1766 occurred during Douglass's brief theatrical season of January through April 1766 and likewise included a mix of vocal and instrumental selections.[17] At the conclusion of the performance season, another benefit concert was held on 1 April 1766 to augment the fund for a new organ at St. Michael's Church. Although the performers and repertoire were not announced, this event probably included the same professionals and amateurs as the earlier benefit performances. The wardens and vestrymen of the church who organized the organ-fund concert later reported that it had brought in £702 5s. in the current money of South Carolina, or about £100 sterling (roughly $10,700 in 2005). Two years later this sum, twice the organist's annual salary, formed one-fifth of the purchase price of an organ from the London workshop of Johann Snetzler.[18] Two days after the concert to benefit the organ fund, an actress, a Miss Hallam, presented her own benefit performance at the theater. Underscoring the collaboration among the theatrical troupe, professional musicians, and gentlemen amateurs, her benefit was advertised to conclude with "an Ode set to musick, call'd, Gratitude and Love, Written by a Gentleman in this Province. The Musick composed by Mr. Valton."[19]

Furthermore, during the first decade of the society's existence, there was only one other perennial opportunity for professional musicians in Charleston: an exclusive annual series of subscription dancing assemblies during the customary autumn-to-spring social season. Antedating the St. Cecilia Society by several years, the "city dancing assemblies" ran a parallel course with this concert organization. After the founding of the society, these twin events were held in alternate weeks and took place in the same venues. In fact Charleston's early subscription dancing assemblies may have served as a sort of launching vehicle for the St. Cecilia Society by demonstrating the local feasibility of the subscription scheme and providing a ready-made social network in which to circulate the subscription papers for a new concert series.[20]

By mid-April 1766, then, one can imagine that both the professional musicians and gentlemen amateurs of Charleston recognized that a mutually beneficial opportunity was at hand. By collaborating more regularly with the

professionals, the amateurs could provide a more expansive musical entertainment for their social circle. Perhaps the substantial profits from the organ
fund benefit concert were enough to convince them that the local taste for
music was strong enough to support such a series. Reciprocally the establishment of a more formal organization would give the professionals a new source
of regular income. Their increased association with the wealthiest families in
the region would certainly enhance their social status and hence their salaries
as music teachers.

It seems unlikely that there was a mass meeting of the thirty-seven founding members on 28 April 1766. The surviving local newspapers mention no
social events scheduled for that day, though the South Carolina General
Assembly, in which a number of the founding members served, was in session
in Charleston at the time.[21] Barnard Elliott, who is named among the founding members in deSaussure's notes, was married on 27 April and was probably
not available for a mass meeting on the twenty-eighth.[22] Similarly the young
Charles Cotesworth Pinckney, who is also listed among the founding members, was still in school in London at that time and did not return to Charleston until 1769. Perhaps his friends wrote to him to inquire if he were interested
in supporting the establishment of a musical society in his hometown. If so, he
would have been a "corresponding member" until his return to Charleston. It
seems more likely that instead of a formal meeting, a subscription list was
drawn up and passed among the eligible gentlemen of Charleston or posted in
a conspicuous location. For either possibility, the site of such activity would
have been the most popular meeting place for Charleston gentlemen in 1766:
Robert Dillon's Tavern at the northeast corner of Broad and Church streets,
which later hosted ten seasons of St. Cecilia Society concerts. In addition to
serving food and drink, this house was the hub of conversation among gentlemen as they gathered to smoke their pipes, read domestic and imported newspapers, and discuss business and politics. The date 28 April most likely
represents the date on which a subscription list was first drafted, for it was
apparently not regarded with any special significance. In all subsequent years
the society celebrated its anniversary on 22 November, the traditional feast day
of St. Cecilia. Regardless of the precise circumstances of its founding, however,
the commencement of the society's concerts in the autumn of 1766 signaled
the beginning of a new stage in Charleston's musical life.

The first notice for the society's music series, known as the "St. Cæcilia
Concert," appeared in Charleston newspapers in early October 1766 (see figure 3.2). From this advertised beginning through February 1773, the first
seven seasons of the society's existence, there is little direct evidence regarding the number and frequency of its concerts. This paucity of St. Cecilia Society advertisements might seem to suggest infrequent performances, but other

evidence demonstrates that most of the society's early concerts were not advertised at all. In the society's first season, 1766–67, there were four, or perhaps seven, advertised concerts; in the second, two; and during the next four seasons, no advertisements at all (see appendix 1). It seems safe to say, however, that while there may not have been a fixed schedule during these early years, performances probably took place every few weeks during the social season, which lasted roughly from October through April. In spite of these historical uncertainties, it is clear that during these early years the society was flourishing. From a founding group of thirty-seven gentlemen, including wealthy planters, prosperous merchants, and members of the Anglican clergy, its membership rapidly expanded. Inclusion in the society's roster soon became a social necessity for the elite gentlemen of the South Carolina low-country, including politicians, lawyers, physicians, planters, and transatlantic

THE St. CÆCILIA CON-
CERT will be opened to the
ſcribers on tueſday evening next,
ſix o'clock, at the houſe of Mr.
Robert Dillon, before which time
the ſubſcribers are deſired to ſend to
the treaſurer of the ſociety for their
tickets of admittance, who is impowered to receive the ſubſcription
money.
By order of the Preſident,
ISAAC MOTTE, Treaſurer.
October 8, 1766.

3.2. The first known advertisement for a St. Cecilia concert, from the *South-Carolina and American General Gazette,* Friday, 3–10 October 1766. Courtesy of the Charleston Library Society merchants. In the years immediately after its establishment, Charles Fraser recalled, the society "increased in numbers and resources. On its roll were inscribed the names of our most respectable citizens; and amongst its officers were always found some of the first men even of the State."[23] In order to maintain a sense of exclusivity, however, its membership was set in the early 1770s to consist of no more than 120 men.

Men were not the only participants at the St. Cecilia Society events. Imitating the practice of many other subscription concert series in eighteenth-century Britain, the society admitted ladies to its performances from the very beginning. Many of its advertisements during the initial 1766–67 season, in fact, concern the distribution of tickets to admit ladies to the concerts. Continuing in the mold of British precedents, the St. Cecilia Society, from its beginning in 1766, probably followed each of its concerts with social dancing.[24] Evidence to support this assertion did not appear until many years later, however. During his visit to Charleston in December 1783, the young Italian Count Francesco Dal Verme attended a "subscription concert with good music in the evening"—undoubtedly a St. Cecilia Society event. With unequivocal plainness, he added to his travel journal, "this was followed by a ball."[25] Despite this delay in confirmation, dancing clearly formed an important part of the society's activities and contributed to its rapid expansion.

By April of 1771 the society was successful enough that it advertised in the newspapers of Charleston and cities as far north as Boston for supplemental musicians—specifically a first and second violin, two oboes, and a bassoon —and offered contracts of one to three years as encouragement.[26] Similarly in the summer of 1772, when the vestry of St. Michael's Church was trying to entice George Harland Hartley to come from Barbados to serve as their organist, they mentioned that "the Plan of Our St. Cecilia Society has been lately extended" and forwarded a proposition from the society's president.[27] Responding to such sanguine prospects, Hartley and a number of other international musicians set sail for Charleston. Near the end of the 1772–73 concert season, the society announced that beginning on Tuesday, 16 March, its concerts were "to be continued every other Tuesday, of which the Members are desired to take Notice."[28] This new plan introduced a regular schedule of eight to twelve concerts per year that remained in effect for the next five decades.[29] At its anniversary meeting later that year, the society "agreed upon and Finally Confirmed" a set of rules that had already been in use for several years (see appendix 2).

A contemporary description of a St. Cecilia Society event demonstrates that its concerts had reached a level of great opulence. The travel diary of Josiah Quincy Jr. (1744–1775), who visited Charleston in the spring of 1773, has been quoted in many texts for its colorful glimpse into social life in late colonial Charleston. Quincy, a young but frail Boston lawyer, ostensibly traveled to Charleston for the benefit of his health, but his reputation as a vocal opponent of British colonial policies suggests that at least part of his mission was to measure the political temperature of this wealthy southern seaport.[30]

On the evening of Sunday, 28 February 1773, Quincy landed near Charleston's newly finished Exchange Building, facing the Cooper River, and proceeded directly to the Coffee House on East Bay Street to meet his local contacts and secure accommodations.[31] Quincy's initial impression of his new surroundings was similar to that of many other visitors to eighteenth-century Charleston. "The number of shipping far surpassed all I had ever seen in Boston. I was told there were then not so many as common at this season, tho' about 350 sail lay off the town. The town struck me very agreeably; but the New Exchange which fronted the place of my landing made a most noble appearance." He spent the next day in viewing the city and socializing with the gentlemen of Charleston who summered in Boston and in Newport, Rhode Island. On Tuesday, 2 March, two days after his arrival, Quincy recorded that he had "received a ticket from David Deis [Deas], Esquire, for the St. Cecilia Concert, and now quit my journal to go." The following day he returned to his journal to describe the event in detail:

> March 3. The Concert-house is a large inelegant building situated down a yard at the entrance of which I was met by *a Constable with his staff.* I offered him my ticket, which was *subscribed by the name of the person giving it,* and directing admission of me *by name,* the officer told me to proceed. I did and was next met by a white waiter, who directs me to a third to whom I delivered my ticket, and was conducted in. The Hall is preposterously and out of all proportion large, no orchestra for the performers, though a kind of loft for fiddlers at the Assembly. The performers were all at one end of the hall and the company in front and on each side. The musick was good. The two bass-viols and French horns were grand. One Abbercrombie, a Frenchman just arrived, played a first fiddle and solo incomparably, better than any I ever had heard: I have several times heard John Turner and Morgan play a solo. Abbercrombie can't speak a word of English and has a salary of 500 guineas a year from the St. Cecilia Society. Hartley was here, and played as I thought badly on the harpsichord. The capital defect of this concert was want of an organ.[32]

After taking notice of the society's concert space and its orchestra, Quincy then turned his attention to the quantity and character of the company in attendance that evening. The evening of 2 March 1773 provided a clear demonstration of how the rules allowed gentlemen subscribers to bring as many ladies as they thought proper to the concerts. According to Quincy:

"Here was upwards of two hundred and fifty ladies, and it was called no great show. . . . In loftiness of head-dress these ladies stoop to the daughters of the North: in richness of dress surpass them: in health and floridity of countenance veil to them: in taciturnity during the performances greatly before [surpass] our ladies: in noise and flirtations after the music is over pretty much on par. If our Women have any advantage it is in white and red, vivacity and fire."[33] Turning to the gentlemen, Quincy recorded a succinct comparison between those present and those of his native Boston: "The gentlemen many of them dressed with richness and elegance uncommon with us—many with swords on. We had two Macaronis present—just arrived from London. This character I found real, and not fictitious. 'See the Macaroni,' was common phrase in the hall. One may well be stiled the Bag—and the other the Cue-Macaroni."[34]

This particular evening was indeed a special event, as the royal governor of South Carolina, Lord Charles Greville Montagu, was, as Quincy noted, about to return to London. Governor Montagu (1741–1784) was the second son of Robert Montagu, third Duke of Manchester. The governor and his lady were personally well liked in Charleston, but, after several political confrontations with the South Carolina Commons House of Assembly, he resigned his position and prepared to return to London. Montagu's presence at the St. Cecilia concert of 2 March 1773 marked his farewell social appearance in Charleston. On meeting the governor and his retinue, Quincy felt no regret for the departure of George III's chief representative in South Carolina: "Mr. Deis [Deas] was very polite: he introduced me to most of the first characters. Among the rest to Lord Charles G[reville] Montagu, the Governor (who was to sail next day to London), and to the Ch[ief]: Justice [Irishborn Thomas Knox Gordon] and two of the Assistant Judges, and several of the [Royal] Council. Nothing that I now saw raised my conception of the mental abilities of this people: but my wrath enkindled when I considered the King's Governor."[35]

Quincy's invaluable description illustrates that by the conclusion of its seventh concert season Charleston's St. Cecilia Society had reached a level of musical and social success that compared favorably with similar institutions in the major cities of Great Britain. During the following two seasons the society continued to accumulate musicians and to enjoy the patronage of the South Carolina elite. Quincy's disparaging view of South Carolina's royal governor and his political entourage, however, foreshadowed the growing resentment toward monarchical control. By late 1774 political tensions with Britain began to cast an increasingly hostile shadow over American freedom and the cultural life to which Charleston's elite had grown accustomed. The editor of the *South-Carolina Gazette* summed up the situation by comparing the city's recent achievements with the prospects of future entanglements with Britain, noting that "a grand *Assembly-Room* has been built; and within Six Months past, an elegant Theatre established . . . and great attention is also paid to the fine *Arts,*—the St. Cœcilia Society has warmly patronized *Music;* while many Gentlemen of Taste and Fortune, are giving the utmost Encouragement to Architecture, Portrait Painting, and the ingenious Performances of the *first* capital *Landscape-Painter* that has visited America, whose Works will do him Honour.—And shall it be said, that such a People, will suffer themselves to sink into Slavery?"[36]

In September of 1774 the Continental Congress, with representatives from each of the colonies, was convened in Pennsylvania to discuss a plan of action. On 20 October the congress formally adopted and signed a set of resolutions that became known as the Articles of Association. The eighth of these articles asserts that the representatives and the inhabitants of their respective colonies will "encourage frugality, economy, and industry, and promote agriculture, arts and the manufactures of this country, especially that of wool; and will discountenance and discourage every species of extravagance and dissipation, especially all horse racing, and all kinds of gaming, cock-fighting, exhibition of shews, plays, and other expensive diversion and entertainments.[37] The South Carolina signers of this document—Henry Middleton (president of the Congress at the time), Thomas Lynch, Christopher Gadsden, John Rutledge, and Edward Rutledge—also represented the elite members of the St. Cecilia Society, to which most if not all of these men belonged. Despite their oath to the cause at hand, the society's 1774–75 concert season proceeded as usual, for the new South Carolina Provincial Congress did not begin to consider the Articles of Association until mid-January. By season's end the increasing hostility toward England brought political tensions to a head, and many of those loyal to the British Crown or at least ambivalent to the issues, including many musicians, made a quiet exodus from Charleston.

After its quarterly meeting in May 1775, the society entered a period of musical dormancy. South Carolina's last royal governor, William Campbell, arrived in Charleston a month later to a cool reception; by mid-September, the heated political climate forced him to make a quiet nocturnal exodus from the city. Tensions continued to simmer for months and finally came to a head on 28 June 1776, when an under-equipped force of Americans within a small, unfinished fort on Sullivan's Island at the mouth of Charleston's harbor repulsed an attack by a strong British naval force. As the might of the British military turned its energies toward more northern campaigns, this victory ushered in a period of relative calm and, perhaps, overconfidence on the part of Charleston's military forces. Speaking of the years immediately after the victory of June 1776, David Ramsay recalled a very prosperous era: "During this period South-Carolina felt very few of the inconveniences which were then grinding their brethren to the northward. They were in possession of a lucrative commerce, and comparatively happy. . . . At no period of peace were fortunes more easily or more rapidly acquired."[38]

Despite the hardships endured by the northern states, many of the members of the St. Cecilia Society enjoyed a measure of freedom in their activities over the next several years. A standing order recorded in the 1778 order book of John Faucheraud Grimké, an officer of the St. Cecilia Society, stipulated that officers of the Continental Army who were also members of the South Carolina General Assembly (the new state legislature) were "exempt from duty during their attendance upon the assembly . . . unless the necessity of their service should make their Presence absolutely requisite at their Posts or with their Detachments or Corps."[39] Since most of the state legislators were also members of the St. Cecilia Society, they enjoyed a number of opportunities for leisurely music making. In the autumn of 1777 the society requested its members to attend the anniversary meeting on 22 November, "as some matters of the greatest importance to the Society will be debated."[40] The matter, of course, was the fate of the society itself. The members were asked to assemble "in order to determine on the propriety of either reviving or abolishing the said society, and to devise some means of discharging the debts of the society, either by applying part of the society's stock to that purpose, or enforcing the payment of the long arrears due to the society. Gentlemen will be pleased to consider that the honour of the society is concerned in paying those who have administered to their amusement, who have already been too long kept out of their due, and will therefore, it is hoped, make a point of giving their attendance, in order to prevent the continuance of so great a hardship."[41] Perhaps too few members attended this anniversary meeting to achieve a quorum, as the matter was deferred to the next quarterly meeting, in February 1778, "when the members are requested to attend, as the society will certainly resolve either to abolish or revive the concerts."[42] By applying part of its stocks or by some other method, the society must have by this time settled its accounts with the musicians, as that same notice mentions that it would "excuse those who have too long neglected to pay their arrears."

In February 1778 the members apparently resolved to continue the society's musical mission, for they gathered again for a regular quarterly meeting on 20 August 1778.[43] The next day, the society purchased a bond for £2,250 South Carolina currency from the newly formed state government.[44] An "extraordinary" meeting was then announced for early September 1778, at which "the Managers for the present year are to report 'on the practicability of reviving and continuing the Concert,' and other matters equally interesting to the Society."[45] Again the mood was positive, as the society announced that its customary anniversary dinner and concert would be held on Monday, 23

November (St. Cecilia's Day falling on a Sunday that year).[46] Beyond the fact that this event was held during the midst of the military struggle for independence, this concert is especially significant because it represents the only St. Cecilia concert for which a handbill is known to have survived. As the British army began a siege of Savannah, Georgia, one hundred miles to the south, the votaries of St. Cecilia enjoyed the orchestral music of such British favorites as Handel, Johann Anton Filtz, Friedrich Schwindl, Franz Xavier Richter, and Lord Kelly (Thomas Erskine, Earl of Kelly).

The British capture of nearby Savannah just one month after this anniversary concert undoubtedly precluded the continuation of the concert season. A year later, the society announced that it would observe its anniversary in November 1779, but this public notice did not mention whether or not a concert would take place in the evening after the usual business meeting.[47] Despite the near certainty of a British attack on the city within the coming months, many residents of Charleston continued to conduct their lives with a degree of normalcy. In addition to the St. Cecilia Society, other social clubs continued to hold their regular meetings, and the managers of the city's subscription dancing assembly announced that the fortnightly balls would commence in early January 1780.[48] The final weeks of Charleston's traditional social season were accompanied by a forty-two day siege by the British army and navy, however, and the city surrendered on 12 May.

During the British occupation of Charleston, from 12 May 1780 to 14 December 1782, all activities of the St. Cecilia Society were suspended. Many of its members had remained loyal to the Crown, and some had returned to England early in the conflict. The majority, however, were active in the struggle for American independence. In August and November 1780 a number of South Carolina's leading military and political officials were arrested and imprisoned at St. Augustine and then exiled to Philadelphia in late 1781 for the remainder of the occupation. Men remaining in Charleston were paroled and allowed to resume relatively normal, though circumscribed, lives. Some, believing the war to be lost, renewed their allegiance to the Crown and were allowed more social and commercial liberties. A number of loyalists—including some musicians—who had earlier fled or were forced out of Charleston, now returned to reconstruct their careers.

While the St. Cecilia Society was dormant during the British military occupation of Charleston, a similar fortnightly schedule of concerts emerged under new management. For two full seasons, December 1780 through May 1781 and October 1781 through May 1782, the "Gentlemen of the Army, Navy, and most respectable parts of the loyal Inhabitants" were treated to the "Musick of the best and most modern Authors" at the South Carolina Statehouse.[49] According to a letter from a German officer garrisoned in Charleston at the time, these concerts were performed by an orchestra of twenty instrumentalists—probably a combination of amateurs, professionals, and regimental musicians.

Though it dashed Britain's hopes of regaining control over its former American colonies, the British surrender at Yorktown, Virginia, in October 1781 did not bring the war to a close. While peace negotiations began in Europe, armed skirmishes continued in South Carolina, and British and German forces held Charleston for more than a year after Yorktown. The bulk of the garrison, including many loyalist citizens, evacuated the city on 14 December 1782. By March of 1783, the St. Cecilia Society was moving to reinstate its musical activities. Its officers called a general meeting and announced that "all persons indebted to the Society for interest on their bonds, are hereby requested to pay the same immediately; and those who have in possession any of the instruments or other effects belonging to the Society, to give notice thereof to the Treasurer."[50] In the fall of that year, eight years after its last regular season, the society resumed its schedule of fortnightly concerts, though now on Thursday evenings rather than Tuesdays as before the war. Despite occasional postponements and special events, the St. Cecilia concerts remained a fixture of Charleston's social calendar for nearly four more decades.

In the spring of 1784, just one year after the return of peace to Charleston, the society petitioned for and received formal recognition as a corporate entity from the state of South Carolina. This act took advantage of both a newly established system of political home rule and the society's intimate relationship with the local government, for the roster of the St. Cecilia Society was nearly the same as the membership of the South Carolina Senate, House of Representatives, Privy Council, and other civic offices. Reflecting the simplicity favored in the Age of Enlightenment, the preamble to the act of incorporation succinctly articulates the purpose of the society, noting that "several persons, inhabitants of this State, have associated themselves together . . . with the laudable intention of encouraging the liberal science of music."[51]

The incorporation of the St. Cecilia Society was a major step toward ensuring the long-term financial stability of this musical organization. In the aftermath of the Revolution, however, the society was not immune from the economic hardships that plagued the new nation. The general scarcity of British sterling and Spanish dollars, the limited supply of depreciated South Carolina paper money, and the burden of large wartime debts all came together to dampen Charleston's economic and cultural recovery in the 1780s. As a result of this gloomy economic climate, many of the society's members fell behind in their annual subscription payments. By October 1788 the society's managers were forced to announce that if the debts of every member in arrears were not promptly satisfied, "it will be impossible to continue the concerts the ensuing season."[52] The response to this appeal was not sufficient to meet the society's financial obligations. Only five years after its concert series had recommenced, the St. Cecilia Society was again forced to suspend its musical activities for two full seasons, until November 1790.

In 1791 an extraordinary meeting of the society was called for 9 April, "as business of a particular nature is to be submitted to their consideration."[53] The topics to be discussed were undoubtedly the upcoming visit of President George Washington and the preparations for a special concert in his honor. On Monday, 2 May, Washington crossed the Cooper River into Charleston, accompanied by a flotilla of well-wishers. "During the passage on the water," reported the City Gazette, "the gentlemen of the Amateur Society, assisted by Mr. [Job] Palmer, Mr. James Badger, Mr. Jonathan Badger, Mr. Harris, with the choir of St. Philip's church, performed a concert, vocal and instrumental, composed of pieces of music and choruses suited to the joyous occasion." On Thursday evening the president was entertained by a concert in the city hall (then in the Exchange Building), given by the St. Cecilia Society with the assistance of the Amateur Society.[54] Together, these two ensembles formed "an excellent band of music" and were accompanied "in the vocal strain" by the choir of St. Philip's Church.[55] At the concert, Washington recorded in his diary, "there were at least 400 lad[ie]s—the Number & appearances of w[hi]ch exceeded any thing of the kind I had ever seen."[56]

A quarter century after its formation, the St. Cecilia Society was a flourishing, fashionable enterprise, the success of which was evident even to the community beyond its narrow membership. After reporting on the elections held at the society's 1792 anniversary meeting, for example, the Charleston City Gazette noted "the evening concluded with a concert, at which upwards of seventy ladies dressed with great taste and elegance, and a number of gentlemen strangers, were present. It must be pleasing to every well wisher to Carolina, to witness the prosperity of this Society, which, in the gratification of its amusement, and liberality of its institution is equaled by none on this continent."[57] The society was, in fact, just entering its most prosperous and brilliant era, sparked by the confluence of several factors in the early 1790s: the renewed prosperity of Charleston's agricultural market, the construction of the Charleston Theatre in Broad Street, and the influx of a large number of refugees from the French island colony of St. Domingo.

In contrast to the sporadic theatrical seasons of colonial Charleston, the opening of the Charleston Theatre in early 1793 marked the beginning of a permanent institution. The musical component of this establishment, including an orchestra and theatrical singers, provided a significant boost to the city's musical population. Rather than relying on a fixed, settled company, the theater insured that a steady supply of theatrical musicians appeared in

Charleston each season through frequent communication and exchange with theaters in northern cities and in England. The Charleston Theatre and the St. Cecilia Society did not compete for musical talent, however. From the very beginning of this new era, the society took advantage of the increased musical population by contracting with theatrical performers. The establishment of a permanent theater with active connections to a larger network of professional talent actually relieved the society's burden of recruitment. For the next quarter century the St. Cecilia Society settled into a relatively passive reliance on the local theater to staff its concerts.

Contemporary with the opening of the new theater, a series of violent slave revolts in the French West Indian colony of St. Domingo forced tens of thousands of refugees to seek shelter in the United States. Many settled in Charleston and were absorbed into the social fabric of the city. A number of these refugees, formerly wealthy gentlemen amateurs, possessed considerable musical talents from which they earned a living by teaching and performing at the theater, concerts, and balls. Cognizant of the distress of their fellow planters in St. Domingo, a number of gentlemen in Charleston formed a Benevolent Society in July 1793, "for the purpose of raising a fund to be applied to the relief of the necessitous of every country, who may come amongst us."[58] The St. Cecilia Society, at its quarterly meeting that August, resolved to convene an extra meeting in early September 1793 "to take into consideration the propriety of bestowing the funds of the society to the encrease of the Benevolent Society."[59] From that time until the end of its concert-giving era, it is estimated that the professional contingent of the St. Cecilia Society's orchestra was composed principally of French musicians who arrived during this wave of West Indian immigration.

While concert life in Boston, New York, and Philadelphia appears to have been at a low ebb during the mid to late 1790s, Charleston experienced a sudden surge of economic and cultural expansion that raised the musical activity of the St. Cecilia Society to unprecedented heights.[60] Riding this wave of prosperity, the society advertised its desire to extend its concert series, and evidence suggests that the customary fortnightly concerts were performed without interruption from September 1793 through the spring of 1796. In addition to having a bounty of performers and a robust concert schedule, the society was also blessed with a membership whose passion for music was very strong. Not the least among them was the English-born Reverend Dr. Henry Purcell (1742–1802), who, in his joint capacity as an officer of the society and as rector of St. Michael's Episcopal Church, "invited the St. Cæcilia Society band to perform sacred music, at St. Michaels," on Sunday, 14 October 1798. On account of "it being new and uncustomary, and knowing it to be disagreeable to a part of the congregation to have a band of music in the church on a

Sabbath day," however, the church's vestry, composed of other St. Cecilia men, "declared *their* disapprobation of the same" and withdrew the invitation.[61] Despite this aborted foray into the realm of sacred music, the society continued to dominate secular musical activities in Charleston into the early nineteenth century.

Charles Fraser, who reached his majority in August 1803 and thus became eligible for membership, remembered this era of the St. Cecilia Society's activity with great affection. "My earliest recollection of the concerts was about the year 1803," he later recalled, "when the Society was in very successful action."[62] The society's continued success in the early years of the nineteenth century is further demonstrated in the diary of Jonathan Mason (1756–1831). Much like Josiah Quincy nearly forty years before him, Mason, a Federalist lawyer and legislator from Boston, kept a travel journal of his visit to Charleston in the spring of 1805. Mason was invited to a concert of the St. Cecilia Society, as were many wealthy gentlemen, including Quincy, who visited Charleston over the years. Although Mason was not as loquacious a diarist as Quincy, his entry for 14 February 1805 demonstrates that the society's musical evenings had changed little in the intervening years: "*Thursday.* Dined this day with Mr. Frederick Rutledge, and passed the evening at a subscription concert, and ball afterwards. A handsome display of ninety and upwards of ladies, many of them [with] strong pretensions to beauty, and all of them handsome in appearance and agreeable and refined in manners. The music excellent, and everything conducted with much propriety."[63]

But the early years of the new century also brought ominous signs of coming difficulties. After decades of pleading with members to pay their sizeable arrears in a timely and responsible manner, the society at last resorted to litigation. Despite the unpleasantness of filing suit against amicable companions, the society resolved that such action was necessary to maintain its honor and to discharge its financial obligations. These suits, a total of forty in all, commenced in the summer of 1800 and continued through 1829. The majority of the society's legal proceedings concerned arrears accumulated in the first decade of the new century, a period marked by the appearance of two draining economic conditions that were likely connected to the concentration of arrearages accumulated during these years: the brief reopening of the foreign slave trade in America and the onset of naval hostilities between the United States and Britain. The quantity of South Carolina funds invested in the importation of new African slaves resulted in a great shortage of cash and the liberal extension of commercial credit in Charleston. The addition of a trade embargo with South Carolina's leading commercial partner brought further hardships to the local economy. Maritime commerce was the lifeblood of Charleston, essential for the disposal of agricultural products and the importation of manufactured goods, luxuries, and chattel. In the light of these economic and political difficulties, the St. Cecilia Society's long wave of prosperity was about to end.

Although in retrospect it is clear that the political and economic friction with Britain during the years 1807–11 was a prelude to the War of 1812, Charleston's social scene remained relatively active and sanguine during this brief antebellum period. In addition to the concert seasons of the St. Cecilia Society, which continued with normal frequency through the spring of 1812, dancing assemblies hosted by such new organizations as the Charleston Assemblies, Cotillion Parties, and Amicable Assemblies appeared with growing frequency. Trying to capitalize on the city's optimistic spirit during this period of economic strain, French dancing master and violinist Peter Fayolle even advertised in the autumn of 1808 that he was willing to receive tuition payments in "produce of any kind, or to wait until the present embarrassing times are over."[64]

The society's 1811–12 season featured an average number of performances (nine) and followed a rather normal schedule, but the interference of Mother Nature caused a further reduction in concert attendance that spring. A series of strong earthquakes centered near New Madrid, Missouri, between mid-December and early February shook the South Carolina lowcountry, some eight hundred miles distant, and terrified its residents. Stricken with fear of imminent disaster, many Charlestonians kept close to their homes and abstained from social events for several months. Margaret Izard Manigault and her teenage daughter observed this phenomenon among their social peers in Charleston, and in mid-February 1812 described the scene to Alice Izard in Philadelphia: "Charlotte & I went [to] the [St. Cecilia] Concert the other night, with my Aunt Manigault. The Earthquakes have frightened all the people so, that they are afraid of going out. There were only fourteen Ladies, & about twice as many Gentlemen, however we danced a great deal, & found it very pleasant, in spite of little Doctor [Charles] Drayton, who tried very hard to make us believe that the Earth was quaking while we were there."[65]

Following the formal declaration of war with Britain in June 1812, the St. Cecilia Society's concert season for 1812–13 got off to an unusually late start, at the end of November, but otherwise proceeded in a normal fashion. The society's concert season of 1813–14 began typically enough in early November, but then concluded at the end of February rather than at the end of March or in early April. By the autumn of 1814, however, the exigencies of war began to take a more serious toll on the society's activities. Beginning in late August, news of British naval attacks along the southeastern coast of the United States—especially the burning of Washington, D.C.—caused great alarm in Charleston. All available labor was immediately focused on the construction of defensive works around this peninsular city, and all the money from each of its banks was loaded onto wagons and taken inland to Columbia.[66] The St. Cecilia Society published the customary notices for its general meetings in August, November, and February, but, owing to the general preoccupation with military affairs, its concerts were suspended for the remainder of the war.

News of the December 1814 peace treaty with Britain did not reach Charleston until mid-February 1815. With appropriate military and musical pomp, the official declaration of peace was then celebrated "in form throughout this city, by the Sheriff of Charleston District, accompanied by a full band of Military Music in a carriage, with the star-spangled banner of the Union and the red cross of Britain united."[67] Days later, the St. Cecilia Society notified its members of a single concert to take place on 9 March.[68] A number of celebratory balls and concerts filled the remainder of the social season, including "a Splendid National Ball, In Commemoration of Peace," which featured "two Select Bands of Music, one for the dance, and the other to fill up the intervals with favorite Martial Tunes."[69]

In the autumn of 1815 the St. Cecilia Society moved to resume its normal schedule of concerts. That season was far less brilliant than in the years prior to the war, however, comprising only two concerts before the usual holiday recess and only two in the spring of 1816. The following season, marking the society's fiftieth anniversary, had a more vigorous schedule of eight concerts, including three before the New Year's holiday and five in the spring of 1817. From a contemporary's point of view, it may have seemed as if the shadows of war had finally passed and that the society had regained its former vitality. Because of several circumstances, however, the performances of 1816–17 proved to be the St. Cecilia Society's last "normal" season of concerts. Beginning abruptly in the autumn of 1817 and continuing over the next three years, the society's musical activities were significantly diminished.

Since the publication of his *Reminiscences* in 1854, Charles Fraser's brief comments on the St. Cecilia Society's decline in the years around 1820 have been quoted and paraphrased as the definitive, if not the only, explanation for the society's withdrawal from concert patronage.[70] As a talented artist specializing in miniature portraits, Fraser has long been remembered as a significant figure in Charleston's cultural heritage, but his intimate connection to the St. Cecilia Society has been long forgotten. Following in the footsteps of his father and older brothers, Fraser joined the society in 1803, and by 1810 he had been elected one of its concert managers. Not only did he help to shepherd the organization through the difficult years after the War of 1812, but as a practicing lawyer he also represented the society on several occasions throughout that decade in suits against members in arrears. In short Fraser's credentials as a reliable source of information about the termination of the society's concerts are beyond question. In his *Reminiscences* Fraser laconically referred to a wide range of circumstances that contributed to the society's transformation from a subscription concert society into a primarily social organization, but he focused on two circumstances in particular: changing tastes and difficulties in "procuring" an orchestra.

Around the year 1820, Fraser wrote, "the purposes of the Society seemed to have been accomplished, and its destinies fulfilled." Since the society's purpose, as stated in the 1784 act of incorporation, was to encourage the "liberal science of music," it could justly rest on the fact that the aim had been accomplished. But Fraser also noted that "musical entertainment could be enjoyed elsewhere"—referring ostensibly to the city's Philharmonic Society.[71] It seems more likely that Fraser was remembering the Union Harmonic Society, which emerged in 1816 and became the most vital musical organization in Charleston before fading in the late 1820s. Like Boston's Handel and Haydn Society (founded in 1815), this mostly volunteer organization was devoted to the performance of sacred vocal and choral music. Its concerts were neither as frequent nor as exclusive as those of the St. Cecilia Society or the Philharmonic Society, but they clearly represented the newer democratic ethos of concert music that emerged in America and abroad in the years around 1820. The rising members of the fifty-year-old St. Cecilia Society were the grandsons of the youngest founding members. Their attachment to the Enlightenment ideology of concert music was not as strong as that of the two previous generations. Times had changed, and, as Fraser succinctly noted, "new tastes were formed—new habits came into fashion."

In Fraser's explanation for the society's transformation, however, the appearance of "new tastes" and rival organizations are but a prelude to his chief reason—the inability to procure musicians—to which he devoted several sentences: "At length, viz. in [on] February 7, 1819, the board of managers reported that they had found it impracticable to procure an orchestra for the society, and therefore ordered a ball to be given. After that, one more effort was made to obtain performers, when the committee reported to the society that they could only procure a quintette [*sic*]. Finally, about the year 1822, the concerts were given up, and the society substituted dancing assemblies, which have been regularly continued, every season, with great elegance."[72] While Fraser is correct in stating that the society's concerts suffered from a want of professional musicians during that period, the chronology and implications of his statements are not completely accurate. A more contextual explanation of this crisis can be discovered in the St. Cecilia Society's well-established dependence on the Charleston Theatre for its supply of professional musicians.

In the autumn of 1817, the management of the Charleston Theatre embarked on a scheme to divide the company's performance season among several southeastern cities. Over the next several seasons, the activity at the Charleston Theatre evolved from a fixture of the city's social season into a mere transient entertainment. As a result of this change, the St. Cecilia Society was left with a dual handicap: a diminished supply of professional talent and an atrophied familiarity with the process of recruiting musicians. After several months of difficulty caused by the theater's new traveling schedule, the society published a notice on 6 February 1818 (note Fraser's error) substituting a ball in place of a scheduled concert, "it being found impracticable to procure an Orchestra for the Society for the present season."[73] From this moment on, the society began to present balls occasionally in lieu of concerts, and over the next two years the number of balls increased while the number of concerts gradually declined. The brief residence of the theater company in the late spring of 1819 enabled the society to present a "splendid Concert and Ball" for President James Monroe on 1 May, "which was attended by a very large assemblage of Ladies, to whom the President had the pleasure of paying his respects."[74] During the following season, however, the number of balls eclipsed musical events, and on 20 January 1820 the St. Cecilia Society gave its last regular concert performance. In subsequent years the dancing assemblies of the St. Cecilia Society continued, as Charles Fraser recalled, with "great elegance," but also with a noticeably diminished frequency. Over the course of the next decade the society mustered the resources to present two further concerts, one in the summer of 1827 and another in February 1831, but these were clearly irregular events, disassociated from the continuity of its former concert series.[75]

Thus, the termination of the St. Cecilia Society's concert series was brought about by a number of factors, some of which had been developing for several years. The staffing crisis that began in the autumn of 1817 was a trigger, bringing latent uncertainties to the surface and forcing the society to act. Its attachment to concert music—which apparently had been waning for a decade because of "changing tastes"—was not strong enough to sustain the society's series through the crisis by perhaps employing a smaller band or presenting a shorter season. Even if the society had wished to continue its concert series in some form, however, its ability to sidestep its long-term relationship with the local theater and recruit musicians independently was severely weakened by the economic depression known as the Panic of 1819. By 1820 Charleston's general cultural vitality—not simply that of the St. Cecilia Society—was in rapid decline. In April 1820 Sarah Rutledge reported to her sister in Washington, D.C., "Charleston has been unusually dull, even during the gayest season, & at present there are few parties of any kind."[76] In February 1825 the *Charleston Courier* complained that the annual horse races, the apex of the city's social season for the past several decades, were "not so well attended, by any means, as in former years." In light of changing cultural and economic conditions, the *Courier* surmised, "the season of splendor, is resolved into the season of convenience."[77]

In Charles Fraser's often-cited *Reminiscences of Charleston,* the author's recollection of musical life in his hometown from the 1780s to the midpoint of the nineteenth century focused solely on the St. Cecilia Society. Other musical organizations, personalities, and events also formed part of this cultural era, but in Fraser's mind (or at least in his memoir) the society's activities dominated the musical experiences of his life. To historians straining to see the details of lives and incidents long forgotten, Fraser's focus on the rise and fall of the St. Cecilia Society's concert series may seem overly narrow and exclusive. When viewed through the historical lens of the foregoing survey, however, Fraser's motivation for focusing on this one organization becomes clear and offers an instructive hint. In any description of the cultural character of early Charleston, specifically that of its so-called golden age from the 1760s to the 1820s, there are few organizations, events, or individuals whose sustained activities encapsulate the character of this era as well as the St. Cecilia Society. The society arose from the bountiful economic climate of the late colonial era, when the desire to replicate the social and cultural practices of England was at its apex in South Carolina. Its recovery after the Revolutionary War and flowering at the turn of the nineteenth century were built on evolving cultural patterns that, while linked to British precedents, represented new, distinctively American phenomena. The demise of the society's concert series was caused by the confluence of factors that not only affected this musical organization but also brought profound changes to the city of Charleston and South Carolina in general. The St. Cecilia Society was so clearly a product of its era, therefore, that the outline of its half century of concert patronage serves as a colorful epitome of Charleston's golden age.

The Management

THE CONTINUATION OF THE ST. CECILIA SOCIETY's concert series for more than a half century testifies to the solidity of its foundation and the strength of its management. By adopting a protodemocratic method of governance, the society's early members created a self-perpetuating organization stable enough to carry on for many generations and yet sufficiently dynamic to adapt to changing circumstances. Were it organized as an informal confederation, or dominated by the energies of a few zealous individuals, the society could not have weathered the storms of war, economic depression, and evolving cultural ideologies that assailed it over the years. Although the loss of the society's early records makes it impossible to know the full details of its administrative practices, a robust outline can be assembled from information found in scattered external resources and supplemented by comparisons with contemporary practices abroad.

The evidence relating to the management of the St. Cecilia Society and its concert series can be grouped into seven topics that fall into two general categories. The first category concerns the society's self-governance: the adoption and evolution of its rules, the regularity of its annual elections, the number, sort, and duration of its business meetings, and the titles and duties of its officers. The second category embraces several administrative practices employed by the society to address more mundane matters: the use of public advertising to announce its concerts, the customs surrounding its concert schedules, and its use of tickets to control the admission of members and guests to its events. Considered as a whole, this material forms a valuable body of evidence from which we can begin to understand the quotidian matters of the St. Cecilia Society's early history and gain unprecedented insight into the operations of a private musical society in early America.

Rules

During its first half century of existence, the St. Cecilia Society published only one complete set of its rules: those adopted in November 1773 and printed in early 1774 (see appendix 2).[1] Its newspaper advertisements from the subsequent forty-six years in which the society operated as a musical organization, however, suggest that there were many unpublished alterations and additions to these rules. An extensive revision of the rules took place by the anniversary meeting in 1792, following which several notices articulated changes in the numbering and content of specific regulations.[2] In February 1794 the members were requested to attend the society's general meeting "to take into their consideration the digest made of the rules of the society."[3] During the 1802–3 season, a number of advertisements mentioned a complete revision of the society's rules, which were read over at three consecutive general meetings and finally confirmed in February 1803.[4] Small changes to specific rules were noted in advertisements in 1808 and 1809, but it was not until 1831 that the St. Cecilia Society again published a complete set (see appendix 3). Although these 1831 rules postdate the society's musical era by eleven years, they reveal that the governance of the society had changed little since the cessation of regular concerts, and thus they provide some insight into the alterations made after 1773.[5]

A later set of rules, approved and published in 1843, reflects the society's consolidation into a purely social organization in which the number of meetings and annual events were substantially curtailed.[6] In is interesting to note, however, that the rules published in 1831 and 1843 both contain several references to concerts, or, more precisely, "concerts or balls." Furthermore, rule 2, section 6, of the 1831 and 1843 editions also repeats a phrase from the regulations adopted in 1773, empowering the managers "to fix the number and times of the Concerts." The vestigial presence of such vocabulary does not necessarily imply that concerts were actually taking place, of course. Rather, it seems that the term *concert* simply lingered in the rules through force of habit or custom long after the society's regular concert series had in fact ceased. Alternatively, however, one could speculate that the society's reluctance to banish the term *concert* from its vocabulary might suggest a tacit desire to resume its musical activity at a future date.

Like the rules of most voluntary organizations, fraternal clubs, and benevolent societies, those of the St. Cecilia Society tersely articulate its general structure. They describe, for example, the election of officers and their duties, the calendar of meetings, and the admission and expulsion of members. Basic financial matters such as subscription fees, miscellaneous fines, and the management of the society's capital are also discussed. Subsequent revisions of the 1773 rules may be divided into two categories: alterations and clarifications. The most publicized of these revisions fall into the latter category and reflect the society's attempts to deal with two contentious issues not adequately addressed in 1773: the admission of nonmembers to its concerts and the handling of members in arrears. Only briefly mentioned in the 1773 rules, these issues dominated the society's public advertisements over the ensuing five decades and form the greater part of the rules adopted in 1831.

In addition to its administrative rules, the society apparently also devised regulations to govern the behavior of its concert audience. Little evidence of these "rules of the Concert Room" has survived, but it appears that they originated as a set of resolutions adopted by the managers. A notice published in March 1800, for example, informed St. Cecilia members that, "under a resolution of the Managers, no gentleman can be admitted into the concert, who is booted."[7] The meaning of this curt warning was clarified three years later, when a matter concerning the rules of postconcert dancing required the society to articulate the matter more plainly: "At a monthly meeting of the managers, on the 7th March, 1803—On motion, Resolved, that as the following rule of the Concert Room hath not been duly observed by *members* and *others* attending the Concerts, the same be published for information, and that it be *strictly enforced* in future. Rule 8th. None but *military* gentlemen can be permitted to *appear* in boots, and *no person* whosoever can be permitted to *dance* in boots."[8] Another notice published in 1808 mentioned that the "rules for the Concert Room" had been "lately revised by the Managers," indicating that their ratification did not require the approval of the full membership. Unlike the regulation about boots, which does not appear in any later source, however, the 1808 rule concerning the proper admission of guests is included among the rules adopted by the society in 1831. Nothing is known of the other rules of the concert room, but the fusion of the rules governing the management of the society and those controlling the decorum at its concerts in the early nineteenth century is suggestive. Once the internal management of the society had been settled, its administrative energies focused increasingly on controlling access to its exclusive events and monitoring the behavior of its guests.

Meetings

In addition to their fortnightly concert performances, the gentlemen of the St. Cecilia Society also gathered regularly for business meetings. The society's rules describe two distinct kinds of meetings: general meetings of the full membership and meetings of the managers only. The numerous published notices for these meetings, which appeared regularly throughout most of the society's concert era, provide many important clues regarding the management and stability of the organization.

The society's first set of rules specifies that there should be four general meetings of the society each year, "namely, on St. Coecilia's Day, which shall be the Anniversary of the Society," and on the third Thursday in February, May, and August. Prior to the adoption of these rules, the first mention of a meeting of the St. Cecilia Society appeared in November 1767, when the *South-Carolina Gazette* named the gentlemen recently chosen as officers at its first anniversary meeting.[9] The first published advance notice of a meeting of "the Members of the St. Cæcilia Concert" appeared in June 1768, but this seems to have been an extraordinary gathering—probably to discuss Benjamin Yarnold's sudden return to London—rather than a regular meeting.[10] Beginning in August 1772, more than a year before the formal adoption of its first set of rules, the society consistently advertised each of its general meetings in the Charleston newspapers.[11] Following the adoption of a new set of rules in February 1803, the May meeting was eliminated. The motivation behind this choice was probably twofold: the desire to wrap up the society's business before its members fled to cooler climes for the summer and the lack of pressing business at the end of the concert season. From that point onward, these gatherings are consistently described as "general" rather than "quarterly" meetings.[12]

In addition to regular meetings, the 1773 rules empowered the managers to call extraordinary general meetings of the society "in Case of the Death, Resignation, or Removal from Charlestown, of any of the Officers . . . and, on every other emergency." The few such meetings of the society that were advertised appear to concern issues other than its officers, however. Most of these gatherings were called to discuss the state of the society's finances, which were perpetually dogged by the arrears of its members.[13]

The 1773 rules specify that the general meetings should begin at 11:00 A.M. and break up at 6:00 P.M. The anniversary meeting, however, was to end at 5:00 P.M.—no doubt to allow members a brief respite before the beginning of the anniversary concert on that evening.[14] Fines were levied against anyone not attending these meetings punctually, with the officers paying a far greater penalty than regular members for such offenses.[15] Following the discussion of a "digest" of the society's rules in February 1794, however, the opening of the general meetings vacillated between noon and 1:00 P.M. through 1801. During the years 1802–4 the general meetings regularly started at 1:00 P.M. From February 1805 to the end of the St. Cecilia Society's concert-giving era, however, its general meetings proceeded to business at two in the afternoon.[16]

The general meetings were always held at a coffeehouse or tavern, so that after the transaction of business the members could partake in food and drink. Rule 2 of those adopted in 1773 directs that "Every Member shall be charged Twenty Shillings currency [roughly $15 in 2005] towards defraying the Expense of the Dinner; and in Case of any Deficiency, the same shall be paid by the Members present at the said Meetings." Like the annual subscription, the expense for dinner was altered over the years as the form and value of local currency changed. During the society's first two decades, dinner—eighteenth-century Charleston's main meal—was served at three in the afternoon. Beginning with the general meeting held in May 1788, however, the dinner hour began to vacillate between 3:00 and 3:30 P.M.[17] From August 1799 through the 1820s, the standard dinner time was half-past three.

In examining these details, the gradual decrease in the frequency and duration of the St. Cecilia Society's general meetings during its concert-giving era becomes apparent. While no definitive explanation for this trend exists, several hypotheses can be advanced. It is possible, for example, that the expanding social and commercial life of early-nineteenth-century Charleston gave the society's members ample opportunities to socialize with each other beyond the context of the St. Cecilia Society, and subsequently they chose not to linger at such meetings. It is also likely that the increasing pressures of day-to-day business consumed more of the members' leisure time than in the society's early years. More important, the decreasing vigor of the society's general meetings may have been linked to a decline in the musical pursuits of its members. Like the gatherings of similar gentlemen's clubs in eighteenth-century Britain, the seven-hour meetings of the society's early years probably included much informal music making. Besides eating, drinking, and singing, these long meetings may have also included the rehearsal of instrumental music for upcoming concerts. Concerts in eighteenth-century Britain were frequently performed with little or no advance rehearsal, and the same was probably true for those of Charleston's St. Cecilia Society.[18] This seemingly important topic is not mentioned in any known source—a fact that may reflect the more relaxed attitude toward "perfection" in musical execution prevalent during that time. If rehearsals of some sort did occur at the society's general meetings, the gradual shortening of such gatherings would surely indicate a decline in its collective commitment to music. In the absence of more conclusive evidence, however, we may reasonably conclude that the shrinking frequency and duration of these meetings was likely the result of a combination of all these factors.

The society's second kind of meeting involved only the society's managers, who—according to their earliest rules—gathered in the evening of the first Thursday of every month during the calendar year. Although evidence is limited, it appears that these meetings took place at the same coffeehouses or taverns where the general meetings were held. Since they were restricted to a small group of members and convened on a fixed schedule, the managers' regular meetings were not advertised in advance.[19] Over the years, however, the society published a number of notices regarding issues resolved at the recent meeting of the managers—thus confirming that they did in fact take place. The first such postmeeting notice, appearing in October 1791, concerned a change of venue for the society's upcoming concerts.[20] Later resolutions of the managers principally addressed the chronic issue of members with long-standing arrears. On a few occasions an extra meeting of the managers was called, and appropriate notice of the event was published.[21]

Elections

After the inception of the St. Cecilia Society in April 1766, at which time its first officers were apparently chosen, the subsequent annual elections of officers and managers took place at the anniversary meeting on the feast day of St. Cecilia. The first published results of these elections appeared in November 1767, and similar returns were published intermittently in the following decades.[22] The elections continued to be held in November for nearly thirty years, through 1794, after which a change occurred. The election that should have taken place in November 1795 was deferred to the society's next quarterly meeting in February 1796. Although no explanation for this change was published, the annual elections continued to take place at the February meetings for the next thirteen years. Accordingly in February 1810 the St. Cecilia Society requested its members to attend the regular general meeting, in order "to elect officers and transact the other business of the society."[23] A few days after the meeting, the local papers carried the news that all the society's sitting officers had been reelected.[24] The advertisement for its next general meeting in August 1810 (the number of such meetings having been reduced from four to three in 1803), however, requested members "to attend at 2 o'clock, to elect officers for the ensuing year, in conformity to the new Rule."[25] Confirming that another shift in the election calendar had taken place and that the reelection of officers in February 1810 had been a temporary measure, a new slate of officers was announced in the days following this August meeting.[26] For its remaining years as a concert organization, the St. Cecilia Society continued to hold the election of officers and managers at its August general meeting. By 1824, however, the annual elections had returned to the society's anniversary meeting on 22 November.[27]

　　　The 1796 and 1810 changes in the calendar of the St. Cecilia Society's annual elections were probably motivated by the same force: the increasing importance of the South Carolina Jockey Club's Race Week, which was held in Charleston each February. Gentlemen's horse racing had been an important part of Charleston's social life since the first half of the eighteenth century, but the formal organization of the South Carolina Jockey Club after the Revolutionary War placed the sport on a more stable, institutional footing. A great number of people, both residents and visitors, gathered in Charleston for these equestrian festivities, which were accompanied by a plethora of fashionable social events.[28] It is conceivable that the St. Cecilia Society initially moved its elections because the coincidence of Race Week, and the society's February meeting may have insured the attendance of a larger percentage of members than at the anniversary meeting in November. By the early nineteenth century, however, it seems that the festivities surrounding the Jockey Club's Race Week, which embraced a larger social community, began to eclipse the more narrowly exclusive events of the St. Cecilia Society. This theory is supported by the increasingly common practice of rescheduling the society's February concerts. The events of Race Week—including its social climax, the Jockey Club Ball— became so important during this time that when the St. Cecilia Society's regularly scheduled concert fell during Race Week, it was either moved to another weekday, postponed, or skipped altogether.[29] As early as February 1797, the society notified its members that "this being the Race Week, the Concert which ought to be performed on Thursday evening next, is postponed to Thursday evening, the 16th instant."[30] In the ensuing years the schedules of the St. Cecilia Society's concerts and of Race Week occasionally overlapped, and the concerts invariably deferred to the races. After the customary holiday recess in the season of 1802–3, the society forestalled such a conflict by announcing that its concerts would recommence and continue once a fortnight, "except in race week, during which there will not be a Concert."[31]

Officers

During its half century of concert patronage, the St. Cecilia Society annually elected officers to administer the various aspects of its operations: president, vice president, treasurer, steward (later changed to secretary), librarian, and eleven other "managers" who acted in a more general capacity. The copious advertisements published by the society provided not only the names of the men who served in these roles but also some insight into their duties.

Wilmot Gibbes deSaussure's notes on the founding of the St. Cecilia Society name only three officers chosen in 1766: president, vice president, and treasurer. The duties of these officers were consistent with other eighteenth-century voluntary organizations in Britain and in Charleston, such as the South Carolina Society, the St. Andrew's Society, the German Friendly Society, and many others. The president, for example, served as the chief executive of the society and the chairman of its meetings. In his absence the vice president was empowered to perform his duties.[32] The treasurer, as stipulated in the St. Cecilia Society's 1773 rules, "shall immediately, upon his Election into Office, take Charge of all the Ready Monies, Bonds, Securities, and other Effects, belonging to the society." In addition to these stated duties, the treasurer may have been the most active and influential agent of the society. As with many subscription concert organizations in contemporary Britain, he was probably responsible for keeping the accounts, collecting the subscriptions, pursuing arrears, regulating the elections, enforcing discipline and attendance, and recruiting and negotiating with musicians and venues.[33]

The first public notice of the existence of the society's steward appeared in an ad for the general meeting in August 1772, thus indicating that an election for this office had been held in November 1771, if not earlier.[34] The society's 1773 rules include the office of steward, and state that his principal duty was, at the conclusion of the general meetings, to "call for and settle the Bill." The steward may have served a similar function for the society's concerts, supervising the provision of refreshments for the members and their guests. In one intriguing coincidence James Miller, the St. Cecilia Society's steward in November 1788, was a wine and liquor merchant whose business was located next door to McCrady's Tavern, the site of the society's performances and meetings at that time.[35] Although not all the stewards elected by the St. Cecilia Society represented such a convenient business match, the office was continued through the society's first four decades. In the early nineteenth century, however, it was gradually phased out and replaced by the office of secretary.

The St. Cecilia Society's 1773 rules do not mention the office of secretary, but other evidence suggests that the position did exist, at least informally, from the society's early years. Jervis Henry Stevens was elected "Librarian and Sec'ry" at the anniversary meeting in 1772, but neither of these titles is mentioned again for many years. In the society's 1784 act of incorporation, John Splatt Cripps is listed as "Treasurer and Secretary," suggesting a combination of these duties in the title of the former.[36] By the turn of the nineteenth century, however, evidence suggests that the steward doubled as the secretary of the society. John Stevens Cogdell was elected steward in February 1805, for example, but his name was appended to subsequent advertisements as the society's "secretary."[37] The notices of the society's annual elections in February 1808 and 1809 state that Daniel Cannon Webb was chosen "Secretary & Steward," though after these announcements the title of steward appears to have been dropped from the offices of the St. Cecilia Society and that of secretary continued in its stead.[38]

The society's rules adopted in November 1773 further specify that "Eleven other Members, Residents of Charlestown," should be annually chosen to act as "managers."[39] Interpreting this criterion literally, we can surmise that members of the society who resided principally on plantations in the countryside, but journeyed into town periodically for concerts, were not eligible to serve as managers. Similarly members who kept a townhouse in Charleston for use during the social season but removed to the country during the recess of the society's concerts were likewise ineligible. The 1773 rules further stipulate that these eleven gentlemen, "with the fore-named Officers, shall be consti-tuted Managers for the current Year." Including the president, vice president, treasurer, and steward (later secretary), therefore, the St. Cecilia Society's managers technically included all fifteen elected representatives of the society.

According to the 1773 rules, the managers were "impowered to fix the Number and Times of the Concerts" and "to regulate every other Matter relat-ing thereto, as well as every other Business of the society, during the Recess of the Society." Despite this rather general description of their roles, many adver-tisements over the years provide further details of the managers' duties. In addition to scheduling the number and times of the performances, the man-agers were also responsible for contracting with professional musicians, han-dling the expenses of the concerts, securing the venues, and calling extra meetings of the society. A single advertisement in April 1792 alluded to the existence of a suborganization of the managers, a "committee on musical mat-ters."[40] Considering their responsibility for attending to the various logistical concerns of the society's concert series, it seems likely that this was a stand-ing committee of managers who played a significant, if not principal, role in determining the musical repertoire. This conclusion is strengthened by the fact that the officers of other eighteenth-century subscription concert series— such as those in Edinburgh, Manchester, Oxford, and Dublin—were usually drawn from their performing members and were charged with the responsi-bility of handling such "musical matters."[41]

Early in its history, the St. Cecilia Society earned a reputation—one that endures to the present day—for the propriety and decorum observed at its gatherings. During its years as a musical society, this legendary etiquette was regulated by the "rules of the Concert Room," which the managers were responsible for composing and enforcing. Rather than all managers being on duty at each concert, however, it seems that pairs of "acting managers" took turns chaperoning the concerts.[42] As in many other eighteenth- and nine-teenth-century social organizations, the managers of the St. Cecilia Society (including its officers) could be identified at their gatherings by an emblem-atic badge.[43] Thomas Waring of Charleston, for example, left behind a small white silk rosette that he described as "a Quondam badge of Distinction" (see figure 4.1). Fixed to the back of the rosette is a short silk band fitted with matching pairs of metal clasps, suggesting that this badge may have been worn around the arm or wrist.[44] An attached note, written by Waring in 1830, states "the Enclosed Rose was once my badge of distinction as Secretary and Manager of the St. Cecilia Society in Charleston;—it was politely made for me by Miss Keppely of Philadelphia." Although the dates of Waring's tenure as secretary are unknown, the practice of wearing such official emblems was probably established in the early days of the St. Cecilia Society's existence.

Between the mid-1790s and 1820, a number of advertisements for benefit concerts in Charleston list the managers of the events—which always included a ball after the musical performance. Invariably the two to four gentlemen named in such advertisements were also managers of the St. Cecilia Society.[45] The society's reputation for propriety extended beyond its own events, therefore, and the presence of its representatives at other entertainments undoubtedly assured prospective audiences that strict etiquette would prevail. A pair of benefit performances (each followed by a ball) in the winter of 1803–4 went so far as to specify that "the rules and decorum observed at the St. Cecilia Society, will be strictly adhered to."[46]

The final office of the St. Cecilia Society's management is also the most intriguing from a musical point of view. Jervis Henry Stevens was elected "Librarian and Sec'ry" of the St. Cecilia Society at the 1772 anniversary meeting.[47] As with modern orchestras that retain a librarian to manage their collection of printed music, the society undoubtedly elected Stevens to collect, organize, and distribute the music performed at its concerts. Stevens may have also been responsible for copying instrumental parts by hand and perhaps even orchestrating music from grand-staff notation. While he is known

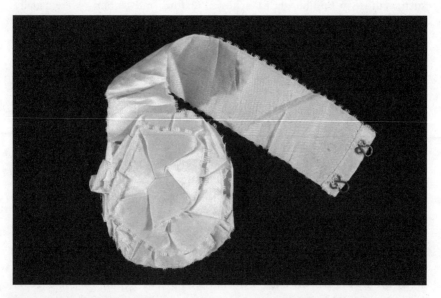

4.1. A white silk "badge of distinction" worn by Thomas Waring to identify him as an officer at St. Cecilia Society events. From the collections of the South Carolina Historical Society

to have been a performer, teacher, and composer of music, Stevens's general level of expertise is not known. If his training did not equip him to perform such tasks, he may have supervised other professional musicians in copying and orchestrating music. The reduction of orchestral music to grand-staff notation (two staves, treble and bass clefs) was a common cost-saving measure in eighteenth-century music publishing. Purchasers of such publications who wished to perform the music in its original form then had to reorchestrate, or expand the instrumentation, in order to provide written parts for a larger ensemble. While this was a fairly specialized skill, many professional musicians of the day had experience in this practice and could readily provide such a service to an orchestra.

The extant records of the Edinburgh Musical Society, a subscription concert organization contemporary with Charleston's St. Cecilia, include a manuscript index to that society's collection of several hundred volumes of printed music—no doubt the work of that society's librarian.[48] Two eighteenth-century advertisements demonstrate that the St. Cecilia Society had a similar collection of music. In December 1773, the society advertised for the "Tenor [viola] and thorough Bass Parts" (that is, bass parts with numerical figures to guide improvised chordal accompaniment) of a number of works, which, having been "bound up together, and mark'd No. 1. belonging to the St. COECILIA Society, have been for some Time missing, supposed to have been borrowed."[49] Rather than directing the guilty party to return the volume to the society's librarian, however, the advertisement asked that the music be returned to the treasurer. Similarly in September 1788 the society published a request stating "if any gentlemen of the society have in their possession any music, the property of the Society, they are requested to leave it with either [any] of the managers as soon as possible, for the purpose of being bound up."[50] The reasoning of this direction probably relates to the society's assessment of its music books as property and thus part of its "stocks." As such they would fall under the purview of the treasurer, who was responsible for keeping track of the society's assets. The fact that these advertisements fail to mention the society's librarian, therefore, does not rule out the continued existence of this position.

Jervis Henry Stevens (1750–1828) was the son of John Stevens, an English-born professional musician who arrived in Charleston around 1768 from London by way of Savannah, Georgia. Although he may have been enticed to leave Savannah by the St. Cecilia Society's recently founded concert series, John Stevens also served as deputy postmaster in Charleston and as interim organist at St. Michael's Church. Shortly after Benjamin Yarnold's return to England in June of 1768, Stevens was hired to occupy this position while the church recruited a suitable replacement directly from England. When Stevens petitioned that his temporary status be made permanent in

1769, his employment was continued for several more years, but his request was denied.[51] It appears that the church vestry, composed of men within the circle of the St. Cecilia Society, retained Stevens on a yearly contract, for in 1772 they resolved to continue his employment "for one year from the 22d November last." The fact that his employment contract coincided with the feast day of St. Cecilia suggests that Stevens was also employed by the St. Cecilia Society, perhaps as its librarian.[52]

When John Stevens died in June of 1772, his twenty-two-year-old son, Jervis Henry, continued his duties as deputy postmaster and auditioned for his father's post at St. Michael's. After careful consideration, the vestry awarded the organist's position to Ann Windsor, a local harpsichord teacher and wife of another musician, Shadrach Windsor.[53] Five months later the St. Cecilia Society elected the young Stevens to be its librarian—thus raising the question of whether he had been already serving in that capacity since his father's death.

Over the next several years young Jervis Henry Stevens garnered praise for the industry he exhibited in caring for his distressed family. His mother, the widow Mary Stevens, operated the city's main coffeehouse on East Bay Street (visited by Josiah Quincy in 1773), which also housed the city's post office. During the Revolutionary War, Stevens served as an officer in the South Carolina militia. After the war he spent many years as a merchant, Charleston's city sheriff, city coroner, and as a justice of the quorum. At the same time he maintained a part-time career as a musician and music teacher until 1815, when he retired after thirty years of service as the organist of St. Philip's Church. Two of his hymn tunes, "Hackney" and "Church Street," are preserved in an 1809 manuscript organ book from St. Michael's.[54] Throughout his career Stevens had much professional and social contact with members of Charleston's elite, especially through his enduring and conspicuous presence in the local Masonic community and other voluntary associations.[55] His friends, neighbors, and business partners were invariably connected with the St. Cecilia Society, and his nephew, John Stevens Cogdell (1778–1847), was a long-time officer of the society. Considering these facts, it is possible that Stevens continued to act as the society's music librarian during the forty-eight years between his election in 1772 and the cessation of the society's concert series in 1820.[56] Despite this intriguing possibility, the tenure of the St. Cecilia Society's librarian remains a matter of conjecture, as no further mention of this position appeared in any of the society's published notices after the announcement of Stevens's election.

Concert Advertising

Only a small number of notices for St. Cecilia concerts are found in extant newspapers from the first twenty-five years of the society's existence. Despite the dearth of information about the society's early concert schedule, there is evidence to suggest that these events were performed with some degree of regularity. On many occasions in eighteenth-century Charleston, postponement notices for otherwise unadvertised concerts serve as the only clue of an active, yet low-profile, concert life. Occasionally information about concerts appeared in newspapers after the performances had taken place, thus demonstrating that advertising was not necessarily required or even expected for the event to succeed. Considering the intimate size of the city and the relatively small pool of potential patrons, Charleston in its first century had little need for regular concert advertising. Between 1738 and 1765, for example, only four concerts were advertised in the local newspapers, but other evidence suggests that musical performances were occurring much more frequently. In February 1753, the vestry of St. Philip's Church asked one of its "Carolina Friends in London" to recruit a new organist for the parish. The agent was instructed to "honestly assure" candidates for the position that—in addition to earning a salary of at least £50 sterling (roughly $6,200 in 2005) and about £150 from teaching harpsichord in Charleston—"the Benefit of Concerts of Musick, which on his obliging Behaviour to the Gentlemen & Ladies of the Place, may amount to 30 or 40 Guineas P. Ann. more."[57] This estimate demonstrates not only that prospects for the professional musician in Charleston were encouraging but also that concerts were a regular part of the city's social life—regardless of sparse published advertising.

As subscription events, the St. Cecilia Society's concerts were open only to a narrow group of members and their invited guests. Information about this concert schedule would most likely have been conveyed through private channels of communication, such as word of mouth or personal message. Printed broadsides—a common form of public advertising in eighteenth-century Europe and America—were used to promote concerts and theatrical events in early Charleston, but probably not those of the St. Cecilia Society. It is possible to imagine, however, that informal notices posted at a common gathering place, such as the tavern hosting the society's early meetings and concerts, could have been sufficient to remind its members of the schedule. Given the relatively small area and population of eighteenth-century Charleston —and the frequency of social and business contact among the society's members—information about private or semiprivate musical gatherings could travel quickly and efficiently. Even in eighteenth-century London, which supported a far greater population spread across a much larger geographic area, exclusive musical societies did not publicly advertise their concerts.[58] It was understood that subscription events scheduled to take place at predetermined intervals required no advertisement, unless there was some deviation from the normal routine.

The St. Cecilia Society first announced in March 1773 that its concerts would be performed every other week during the season. After an eight-year interruption caused by the Revolutionary War, the society resumed this schedule of fortnightly concerts in the autumn of 1783. During his visit to Charleston in December 1783, Count Francesco Dal Verme attended an unadvertised concert of the St. Cecilia Society and reported in a letter to his father that "a ball or concert is held on alternate Thursdays during this season."[59] In the Decembers of 1784 and 1785 the society gave notices of changes in the regular starting time of the concerts.[60] Following the anniversary concert in November 1786, the managers reminded members that the concerts "will be continued once a fortnight as usual."[61] Starting in the autumn of 1791, the St. Cecilia Society began to advertise individual concerts with increasing regularity, though general reminders of the concert schedule, such as "once a fortnight" and "every second Thursday," also continued to appear. From 1803 onward, each of the society's concerts was individually advertised in the city's newspapers. Rather than suggesting that its concerts were becoming less exclusive, this increase in advertising after 1791 was probably related to the contemporary increase in the population of Charleston. As the community expanded and the social calendar of its members grew busier, the publication of regular reminders of the society's concerts began to serve a more practical purpose.

The Concert Season

For the most part the concerts of the St. Cecilia Society did not take place on a continuous schedule throughout the calendar year. Rather, they were performed during a portion of the year known as the social season, or simply "the season." Mirroring the annual migration to the city by the landed gentry of post-Restoration England, the Charleston social season generally began in the autumn and continued through the spring.[62] The society's concert seasons varied from year to year—some beginning as early as 16 August, others as late as the society's anniversary, 22 November. Some seasons continued as late as May, while others concluded in early March. There is also evidence of concerts performed during the summer months and, during at least a few seasons, the strong suggestion that concerts were performed every other week throughout the entire year.

The St. Cecilia Society's concert season, like other social activities in Charleston, followed the seasonal residence patterns of the landed elite of the South Carolina lowcountry, which were determined by matters of temperature and local health conditions. While its mild winters encouraged an active social season for many English natives, the extremity of the summer heat stood in sharp contrast to the coolness of that season in the mother country. In the early 1760s the Englishman George Milligen-Johnston noted in his description of Charleston that "the Weather is much too hot in Summer, for any kind of Diversion or Exercise, except Riding on Horseback, or in Chaises, (which few are without) in the Evenings and Mornings; and this is much practiced." Alexander Hewatt offered a sterner warning in 1779: "During the summer months the climate is so sultry, that no European, without hazard, can endure the fatigues of laboring in the open air." Perhaps repeating a phrase he picked up during his stay in Charleston during the spring of 1784, Johann Schoepf recorded in his journal that "Carolina is in the spring a paradise, in the summer a hell, and in the autumn a hospital."[63]

In general those who could afford to leave Charleston and the lowcountry during the hottest months did so. From the middle of the eighteenth century, the most popular destination was Newport, Rhode Island, to which such numbers of wealthy lowcountry planters traveled for their health that it was known as "the Carolina hospital." In early June 1770 the *South-Carolina and American General Gazette* reported, as it did each summer, the departure of numerous Charleston families who were to pass the summer in Newport and other northern destinations. On this specific occasion, however, the paper noted with an air of frustration, "these annual Migrations drain this Province of a great Deal of money." Those who did not venture northward during the summer either remained in Charleston, where cooling ocean breezes brought some relief, or sojourned on their estates in the country.[64]

By midautumn those families who had left the city but had not departed the province began to return to Charleston. As Lord Adam Gordon noted during his visit to the city in the mid-1760s, "almost every family of Note has a Town residence, to which they repair on publick occasions, and generally for the three sickly Months in the fall, it being a certainty, that the Town of Charles Town, is at present the most healt[h]y spot in the Province."[65] "Time and experience had now taught the planters," Alexander Hewatt concurred, "that during the autumnal months, their living among the low rice plantations subjected them to many disorders, from which the inhabitants of the capital were entirely exempted. This induced the richer part to retreat to town during this unhealthy season."[66] Charleston physician David Ramsay, himself a native of Pennsylvania, advised strangers to the southern climate to arrive "about the beginning of November, that their constitutions may have time to become accommodated to the climate before the commencement of the sickly season."[67] Those who migrated northward for the summer months also returned to South Carolina at the beginning of the social season. As the ship passenger notices in the local newspapers demonstrate, however, many of Charleston's leading citizens returned from their summer migrations only after the St. Cecilia Society's concerts and other social events had commenced. This conspicuous tardiness was then a common occurrence, as it is at many modern social events. As late as 1830, the British consul to Charleston, William Ogilby, noted that his first experience at a St. Cecilia event "was a complete failure as there were not twenty Ladies in the room[,] but I am told this is always the case at the first ball of the season."[68]

In mid-December the concert season was interrupted by a break of several weeks while much of Charleston's social elite repaired to their country homes for the holidays. During the winter of 1785 Timothy Ford observed this migration, noting in his diary "it is almost vulgar to spend the Christmas holidays in the city; and of course the gay part of its inhabitants pour into the country."[69] A number of advertisements in the 1790s announced that the society's concert schedule would be suspended during the holiday season, and then recommence in January. The exact dates for these actions varied from year to year, but several notices mention the resumption of the fortnightly schedule on the "second Thursday in January next."[70] Although the annual suspension during the Christmas and New Year's holidays was probably an early feature of the society's concert schedule, the first published notice of this holiday suspension appeared in December 1793. In the decade following the St. Cecilia Society regularly published notices specifying the dates of the holiday suspension and resumption of its concert schedule. The last notice of this phenomenon appeared in December 1803.[71] The consistent advertisement of each of the society's concerts in subsequent seasons rendered such notices unnecessary, but the holiday suspensions continued. In 1830, nearly a half a century after Timothy Ford's comments, William Ogilby testified to the persistence of this tradition, noting in his diary that "as it is all the fashion here to go to the country for the xmas holidays I accepted an invitation from Mr. Milne of Johns Island."[72]

Each year the St. Cecilia concerts continued into early spring until the managers announced the end of the season. The timing of this conclusion may have been determined in part by the finances of the society—the managers terminating the season relatively early, for example, if the liquid assets of the society were low. In addition the conclusion of the concert season was determined in part by the weather. The prospect of spending an evening of music and dancing in a confined space lighted by burning candles surely induced a cessation of the concerts before—as a Vauxhall advertisement put it in 1795—"the great heats commence."[73] In their restrictive and elaborate clothing, the ladies were undoubtedly more aware of this necessity than their gentlemen escorts. In early March 1809, for example, Margaret Izard Manigault complained to her mother, Alice Delancy Izard, in New York that "the proper temperature for dancing is past—but the balls are not over."[74]

Sultry weather notwithstanding, there is intriguing evidence that during some seasons the St. Cecilia concerts were continued as late as July and perhaps even throughout the calendar year. The English vocalist Maria Storer performed at St. Cecilia concerts during the summer of 1785 (May through August), but this exception to the society's normal season probably had more to do with the rarity of Miss Storer's presence in Charleston than with a premeditated extension by the society.[75] In April 1792, however, the society addressed the extension of the concert season directly, when the managers called an extraordinary general meeting to consider "the report of the committee on musical matters, and particularly *as to continuing the concerts during the summer season.*" Although no further mention of this plan was published, the society's fortnightly concerts in the following autumn commenced on 22 November 1792—a very late start for that active era. Perhaps the concerts were indeed continued through the summer, but then suspended in the early autumn to allow a brief respite before the start of the 1792–93 season. No summer concerts appear to have taken place the following year, as the last concert for that season was announced for 16 May 1793, and the first concert of the following season was scheduled for the very early date of 5 September 1793. In mid-March 1794, however, at what should have been the end of the performance season, the society announced, "The concerts will commence on Thursday next, the 20th instant, and to continue every other Thursday for one year certain."[76] Owing to the so-called certainty of this extended schedule, the society published no further notice of its concerts until its anniversary in November 1794, and we are left to assume that the fortnightly performances did take place. Two pieces of evidence appear to support such a conclusion. On 5 March 1795, a few days short of a year after the society announced its decision the continue the concerts for "one year certain," it held an extra meeting "to transact business of much consequence to the society." The topic at hand was probably the further continuation of the concerts through the summer months, but the outcome of the meeting was not published. At a meeting on 6 October 1795, however, the managers "resolved, that the Concerts do continue until Monday, the 23d of November, (the 22d St. Cœcilia's day falling on Sunday) on which evening there will be a Concert." The wording of this notice, combined with our knowledge of the several seasons immediately preceding it, suggest that the society's concerts continued on a fortnightly schedule from 5 September 1793 through March or April of 1796 (excluding the regular breaks for Christmas and New Year's). By the autumn of 1796 the society's concert advertisements indicated the return to a less ambitious schedule, commencing in mid-September of that year and continuing into the early spring of the following.[77]

There are no further suggestions that the society performed regular concerts during the summer months after 1795, but there is evidence that it may have occasionally performed concerts more frequently than once a fortnight.

At the beginning of the 1800–1801 season, for example, the society announced that the concerts would commence on 30 October, "and will be continued every Thursday until St. Cecilia's Day."[78] When the season recommenced in January 1801, however, the concerts were again performed on a fortnightly schedule. While it is possible that this advertisement may have inadvertently omitted the word *other* between the words *every* and *Thursday,* another piece of evidence appears to support this weekly schedule. When the St. Cecilia Society began to pursue legal action against members in arrears at the turn of the nineteenth century, twelve of the earliest lawsuits specify that the defendants had neglected to pay for their subscription to the society's "weekly concerts."[79] These suits concerned arrears accrued in the 1790s, a fact consistent with the other evidence for a more robust concert schedule during that period. Regardless of the myriad possibilities suggested by these clues, it is clear that the concert season of the St. Cecilia Society varied from year to year and that the vitality of the society was subject to a variety of conditions, be they social, economic, political, or health related.

Commenting on the regularity of the St. Cecilia's calendar, Charleston historian Harriott Ravenel wrote in 1906 that "its times and seasons are as fixed as if ordered by the heavenly bodies. Lent alone disturbs its dates! Saturday is unheard of! That would hardly be a St. Cecilia which did not begin on a Thursday at 9 P.M."[80] Mrs. Ravenel's comments, though based on first-hand experience of such events, describe practices adopted in the years after the cessation of the society's concert activity. The surviving evidence of the society's concert seasons prior to its transformation in 1820 contradicts the bulk of her assertions. Although the society did take care to avoid performing concerts during Passion Week, it allowed more flexibility in its concert schedule than Mrs. Ravenel witnessed. The society's 22 November anniversary and its attendant anniversary concert, for example, were usually observed on the appropriate day of the week for that date, though never on Sunday. Even after the society switched its regular fortnightly concerts from Tuesdays to Thursdays after the Revolution, performances were occasionally held on other days of the week as circumstances required.[81]

Mrs. Ravenel's assertion that the St. Cecilia Society's nineteenth-century balls commenced at 9 P.M. may in fact be a vestige of its pre-1820 practices, and thus provides a hint at the duration of the society's concerts. During its early years the St. Cecilia Society began its concerts at six o'clock in the evening.[82] Both immediately before and after the Revolution, however, the society's concerts occasionally started at 7 P.M.[83] In early 1784 it announced that the concerts would "begin at half past Seven o'Clock until further Notice." By December of that year, this hour was again revised and notice was given that "the Concerts will begin precisely at SIX o'clock until farther notice." A

year later, in December 1785, the society's managers resolved "that the CON-
CERTS in future will begin at seven o'clock precisely."[84] Advertisements published in subsequent decades confirm that from this point on, the St. Cecilia
concerts regularly started at 7 P.M.[85] In all likelihood the society's concerts
lasted about two hours, with the dancing commencing at 9 P.M. In December
1799, for example, newspaper advertisements for the benefit concert of Isadore
Labatut articulated a similar plan. Labatut, a professional musician in the society's employ, announced that "the Concert will begin at half past six o'clock,
and the Ball at nine."[86] The dancing after the St. Cecilia Society's concerts continued for about three hours, for in the early years of the nineteenth century
the society's musical evenings are known to have concluded at midnight.[87]

Tickets

The audience at the St. Cecilia Society's concerts was not limited to members
of the organization. Like subscription concert societies in eighteenth-century
Britain, the St. Cecilia Society made provisions for the admission of both
ladies and "gentlemen strangers." During its five decades of concert activity,
the society published a number of notices regarding its admission policies,
which provide valuable insight into the social milieu of its musical evenings.
This evidence demonstrates that the society's policies regarding the composition of its audience were shaped by the cultural ideology of eighteenth-century British and European concerts, revealing a struggle to find a balance
between exclusivity and hospitality and confirming that the cultivation of
polite sociability at the society's concert series was nearly as important to its
success at the performance of music.

As in contemporary Britain and Europe, most concerts in eighteenth-
and early-nineteenth-century Charleston were exclusive events to which one
usually gained access through a subscription list circulated in advance of the
performance. In an age of pronounced social stratification, this conscientious
exclusivity was designed to exclude persons whose political, social, or economic status did not endow them with the requisite cultural legitimacy to
attend. Confirmation of the importance placed on this rationale in Charleston is provided by the criticisms of "Sylvanus," a correspondent to the *City
Gazette* in February 1794. One year after the opening of the new Charleston
Theatre, Sylvanus railed against all such entertainments "open to the community at large" because they "draw together a promiscuous multitude, without
any laws to confine them within the bounds of decency and good manners."
In contrast to this decadence, argued Sylvanus, musical performances and
other amusements attended by "select parties and assemblies" were "rational
and useful," because "they recreate and improve, [and] serve also to promote
friendship and refinement of manners."[88] Attempting to maintain a rational

and refined environment, the St. Cecilia Society went to great lengths to regulate the composition of its audience.

The published rules and advertisements of the St. Cecilia Society identify
four kinds of tickets for its concert series: season tickets for members, tickets
for ladies, single tickets for gentlemen strangers, and season tickets for
strangers. The one feature common to each of these categories was that the
tickets had to be procured in advance of the performances. Even the advertisements for many non–St. Cecilia performances in Charleston, which lacked
the society's rigid organization, observed this practice. The distribution of
tickets at the door, the last line of defense in maintaining social exclusivity,
would have rendered the evening's entertainment too vulnerable to the
admission of "improper" guests. The advance distribution of tickets and the
regulations surrounding them, therefore, was more of a social-screening
mechanism than a matter of simple logistics.[89]

As a subscription concert organization, the St. Cecilia Society was able to
plan an entire season of musical performances in advance. Rather than charg-
ing members for individual tickets at each concert, a flat subscription rate was
charged to members annually for entrance to all concerts during the season.
With a predetermined schedule in place, tickets did not need to be printed or
distributed for each individual event when one, reusable season ticket could
be issued to each member. Many advertisements for the society's concerts
direct the members to pick up their tickets from the treasurer. These notices
invariably appear at the beginning of the season rather than before each concert, confirming the use of semipermanent season tickets.[90]

The Charleston Library Society possesses a St. Cecilia Society ticket that
appears to have been used for an entire season rather than for a single concert. Printed on heavy card stock and measuring three inches by four and a
half inches, this ticket is decorated with intricately engraved floral swags,
music books, and clusters of instruments—lyre, flute, violin, valveless horns
and trumpets, and English guitar (see figure 4.2). Also printed on the ticket
are blank spaces for the names of the bearer, treasurer, and president, while
the date ("1831") and number of the ticket ("No. 11") are written on the card
by hand.[91] Despite the fact that this ticket postdates the end of the society's
concert activity by eleven years, "St. Cecilia Concert" is elaborately printed in
the center of the card. In addition to this curious anachronism, the ornamen-
tation, instruments, and typeface of the ticket reveal another inconsistency.
All are strikingly Classical in design—a style that would have been out of date
by 1831. The solution to these apparent contradictions lies at the lower edge
of the ticket, in the engraver's mark: "Abernethie Sculpt. Charleston." Thomas
Abernethie, a Scottish surveyor and engraver, came to Charleston around the
time of the American Revolution and died in the city in August 1795. The

printing plate for this ticket, therefore, was engraved sometime between 13 August 1783—when the city's name was officially changed from Charlestown to Charleston—and Abernethie's death. In 1831, while the St. Cecilia Society did not have a regular concert series, it either continued to print season tickets from a plate engraved some four decades earlier or was still using an existing cache of ready-made eighteenth-century tickets.[92] The sets of rules adopted by the society in February 1831 and January 1843 confirm the continuation of this practice by directing each member to obtain his "ticket for the season" from the treasurer, though it is unclear how long the use of Abernethie's engraving persisted.

Although the membership of the St. Cecilia Society was limited to 120 gentlemen in its early years, the audience at its concerts may have been largely female, for the 1773 rules stipulate that "every Member is allowed to introduce to the Concert as many Ladies as he thinks proper." According to contemporary custom, the "proper" number of female guests was usually two ladies for every gentleman, a ratio that is confirmed by a number of advertisements for other concerts in eighteenth- and early-nineteenth-century Charleston.[93] The rationale for this indirect admission of ladies is tied to the social mores of the

4.2. A member's season ticket for the St. Cecilia concerts, engraved ca. 1784–95 by Thomas Abernethie, whose name appears at bottom center. Courtesy of the Charleston Library Society

era. In order to maintain their reputation for propriety, a lady simply did not appear at St. Cecilia concerts—or even other less exclusive social events—without an escort, whether it be her husband, father, brother, uncle, cousin, brother-in-law, or a friend of the family. The memoirs of Josiah Quincy, George Washington, and Jonathan Mason all confirm the fact that the number and vivacity of the ladies present of these musical events were the measure of their social success. As a further example, the *Charleston Evening Gazette* noted an improvement in the society's concert of 11 August 1785, owing in part to the presence of "the most shining beauties in Charleston."[94] A review of a special St. Cecilia Society concert on 26 February 1805, given for the benefit of refugees from St. Domingo, noted that the event "was more numerously attended, we believe, than any other that has heretofore been given; the rooms were literally crowded, and prepared to view a display of elegance and beauty that is not often witnessed."[95]

Many of the St. Cecilia Society's earliest advertisements concern the distribution of tickets to admit ladies to its concerts. In the early stages of the society's existence the resolution of this matter was clearly of crucial importance to its success. From these early notices for ladies' tickets, published chiefly in 1766–67, it appears that while a gentleman received a single ticket for the entire season of concerts, his female guests were required to present a separate ticket for each performance.[96] This fact is substantiated by the rules adopted in 1773, which state that ladies "are to be admitted by Tickets, signed by a Member, and expressing the Name of the Lady to whom each Ticket is Presented." A reminder of this regulation, published in December 1792, demonstrates that the admission of ladies had remained constant over the years, except for the fact that their tickets now had to be "dated and signed by a member."[97]

The subscription concerts of the St. Cecilia Society were exclusive events, but provisions were made to allow gentlemen visitors, or "strangers," as non-residents of the South Carolina lowcountry were called, to attend as the guests of members. Like many other eighteenth-century descriptions of Charleston, Alexander Hewatt's 1779 *Observations* boasts, "the Carolineans in general are affable and easy in their manners, and exceedingly kind and hospitable to all strangers."[98] As evidence of this trait, the St. Cecilia Society made provisions for the admission of strangers to its concerts from the beginning of its existence. Following the example of the procedure for the admission of ladies to its concerts, the society's 1773 rules state that strangers may be admitted "only by Tickets, from a Manager, signed and directed as before specified." When Josiah Quincy visited Charleston in 1773, he recorded that David Deas gave him a concert ticket.[99] Similarly Jonathan Mason's journal states that he attended a concert in 1805 as the guest of Frederick Rutledge. As the society's concert series grew into a well-established Charleston institution, however, the protocol surrounding the admission of gentlemen strangers diverged from the relatively straightforward policy concerning ladies. Shortly after the Revolutionary War, the society took steps to further control—but not preclude—the attendance of nonmembers at its concerts.

While strangers with guests' tickets were permitted to attend individual concerts, the admission policy for the postconcert dancing was more liberal—at least in the society's early years. By February 1785, however, the society's managers reported that "inconveniencies have been found to arise to the Members of the Society, from persons, Non Subscribers, coming into the CONCERT-ROOM, after the CONCERT is over." Rather than requiring a stranger's ticket to control this apparent breach of security, the managers imposed a geographic criterion for such guests by declaring that "no person, except Strangers and Citizens residing upwards of forty five miles from Charleston, will hereafter be admitted after the Concert is over."[100] Perhaps owing to the awkwardness of interrogating potential guests about the distance of their residence from Charleston, these "inconveniencies" continued. In December of 1785, therefore, the society imposed a uniform admission requirement for the entire evening's entertainment. From that time on, the managers announced, "no persons whatever, but members, will be admitted during the evening, except with a Ticket, sign'd by a Manager."[101]

In the years after this change, gentlemen strangers continued to be a standard part of the society's concert audience. An editorial review of the St. Cecilia Society's anniversary concert in 1792, for example, mentioned that in addition to the fashionable ladies present, there were "a number of gentlemen strangers" as well.[102] The society's guest policy faced a new challenge in the summer and fall of 1793, however, when Charleston received a flood of refugees from the French West Indian colony of St. Domingo. Many of the sufferers who sought refuge in this city were wealthy planters and merchants whose fortunes had been swiftly and violently erased in the island's slave revolts. As social peers of Charleston's wealthy elite, some were welcomed as guests at the society's concerts. By the end of October 1793, however, such hospitality exhausted the patience of some members who apparently felt that a double standard applied to the French guests. Seeking to limit the practice, the society then published a reminder that "by one article of its constitution no foreigner can be admitted after three months residence in the city. Several members desire that such a rule will not be forgotten, as no American gentlemen can be admitted by that rule without becoming a member."[103]

Unlike the elaborately engraved season tickets issued to members, the temporary passes issued to visiting gentlemen were improvised objects, made from any sort of paper on hand at the moment the verbal invitation was extended. When Rhode Island native James Brown IV (1761–1834) visited Charleston in early 1794, for example, he received an interesting impromptu ticket to the 23 January St. Cecilia concert from Samuel Gaillard (1770–1795). The precise circumstances in which Brown obtained this entrée is not known, but the fact that his improvised "stranger's ticket" was written on a playing card—the seven of hearts—suggests that he and Gaillard were enjoying a relaxed evening of gentlemen's amusements when the invitation was issued (see figure 4.3).[104]

The society's great prosperity in the 1790s and early nineteenth century undoubtedly attracted large numbers of visitors seeking entrance to its events. In response the society ultimately arrived at a more complex set of regulations to permit approved persons to obtain tickets under specific conditions. In 1807 and 1808 the St. Cecilia Society published several amendments to the standing "rules for the Concert Room" that demonstrate how changing times required the society to refine its definition of a "stranger" and to make allowances for long-term or repeat visitors. The complexity of these provisions may seem pedantic, but they reveal a studied effort to achieve a balance between extending hospitality to worthy guests and maintaining the requisite degree of exclusivity. According to these early-nineteenth-century sources, strangers were entitled to free admission (with the customary ticket from a member), "during the first season next after their arrival in Charleston," so long as they had not been admitted as such "at any preceding season within the term of five years." Strangers excluded by this provision, however, were permitted to apply to a manager for an individual ticket, "for which they shall pay Five Dollars" (roughly $77 in 2005). Inhabitants of South Carolina were not considered strangers "merely on account of any absence from the state, unless such absence be of at least Five years duration, or unless they declare themselves permanently settled in some other state or country." For the slightly reduced price of four dollars, however, "Gentlemen, inhabitants of this state, not members of this society, and who reside upwards of forty miles from Charleston," were eligible to receive tickets to individual concerts. The appeal of the St. Cecilia's concerts was apparently so great, in fact, that the society provided further allowances for strangers to purchase "tickets for the season, for which they shall pay Forty Dollars" (roughly $620 in 2005). These amendments to the society's concert admission policies came with a simple caveat, however: "that no gentleman, stranger, shall enjoy the privilege of a purchased ticket for the night, or a subscription ticket for the season for more than THREE years."[105]

A good example of how these regulations were put into effect is provided by the case of Gabriel Manigault. Manigault, who had been elected a manager of the St. Cecilia Society in February 1796, moved to Philadelphia in 1805 and the following year resigned his membership in the organization. Shortly thereafter, he changed his mind about quitting the society and wrote to his brother Joseph in Charleston, who was then one of the managers, inquiring

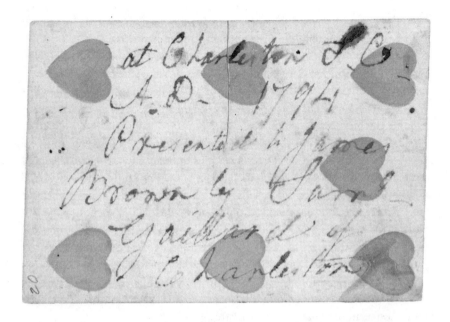

4.3. Two sides of a "stranger's ticket" admitting James Brown, Esquire, to the St. Cecilia Society concert on 23 January 1794. The face of the card contains an inscription from Samuel Gaillard of Charleston, while the back is signed and dated by the society's treasurer, William Robertson. Courtesy of the Rhode Island Historical Society (RHi X3 7900/7901)

about the status of his membership. In early 1807, Joseph replied, "I have yet given you an answer concerning your being a member of the St. Cecilia Society. Mr. Owen [word missing] sent in your resignation, before he received your letter countermanding it, and as it was recorded in the books of the society, you could not be re-admitted, without an application. I think however it is of no consequence, as you certainly may go to the concerts, as a stranger, for some time, unless you should prefer being re-admitted on your return."[106]

The complexity of the regulations concerning the admission of strangers into the St. Cecilia Society's concerts testifies to the cumulative experience of the society's managers in dealing with this matter. The combination of social exclusivity and cosmopolitan musical entertainment at these concerts proved a powerful attraction that required the creation and enforcement of practical solutions in order to maintain the requisite degree of control. Although the admission of strangers was rarely mentioned in the society's advertisements after 1808, it is clear that well-defined rules were in place during its final years as a concert organization. More than a decade after the cessation of its concerts, the set of rules adopted by the society in 1831 was dominated by regulations concerning the admission of "strangers."

AN EXAMINATION OF THE SOCIETY'S ADMINISTRATIVE issues demonstrates that the structure and management of the early St. Cecilia Society had much in common with those of the numerous concert societies in mid-eighteenth-century Britain. The replication of such a well-established model endowed the society with a firm foundation that sustained it for many decades. Circumstances unique to Charleston required extensive modifications, however. These changes—such as the modification of the St. Cecilia Society's rules, the decreasing frequency and duration of its meetings, the migration of its annual election dates, the gradual increase in its use of advertising, the variation of its performance season, the increasingly systematic distribution of tickets, and the earnest fine-tuning of its policies regulating the admission of nonmembers into its audience—reveal much about social and cultural priorities in late colonial and early national Charleston. Like many, but certainly not all, of the subscription concert series in eighteenth-century Britain, the St. Cecilia Society's activities were managed by its members rather than by the hired musicians who performed at its concerts. While this fact may seem unusual to some modern readers, it serves to underscore the role of music in the social life of that era. The men who administered the quotidian affairs of the society were active participants in this cultural endeavor rather than merely passive auditors. For them and their audience, the enjoyment of music was as dependent on the careful cultivation of the proper social environment as on the selection and execution of the music itself.

The Finances

FROM ITS INCEPTION IN 1766, THE ST. CECILIA SOCIETY was neither a struggling commercial venture driven by professional musicians nor a loose confederation of capricious amateurs. Rather, the society was established as a voluntary corporation managed by wealthy planters, transatlantic merchants, lawyers, and bankers who brought a great deal of business experience to bear on their pursuit of concert patronage. Although the basis of its existence was the annual subscription paid by its members, the St. Cecilia Society's financial operations went far beyond the simple collection of dues. During the half century of its concert series, the society's financial dealings ran the gamut from candles for lighting to real-estate mortgages, with a trail of internal litigation along the way. Although none of its bankbooks or account ledgers has survived, there is trace evidence of a wide variety of financial matters during the society's concert era, including the price of its subscription, the scope of its investments, the range of its miscellaneous expenses, its contracts with and salaries for hired musicians, and the collection of arrears. Combined with the known fiscal practices of other contemporary organizations, this evidence of the society's attention to long-term financial management reveals a commitment to musical patronage heretofore unknown in the early United States. The men managing the activities of the St. Cecilia Society may have been amateur musicians, but they were also businessmen who applied their collective experience to the society's financial administration and ensured its survival through fluctuating economic conditions. The society's fortunes were not immune from reversals and frustration, but through planning and perseverance its officers kept the music playing.

Subscriptions

The St. Cecilia Society's first and most general means of generating capital was its annual subscription fee, about which a substantial amount of evidence has survived. The earliest known reference to its subscription is found in an extant account book of Henry Laurens, who recorded a payment of £25 South Carolina currency "to the St. Cæcilian Society" on 17 September 1766, barely a month before the society's inaugural concert.[1] At that time £25 of local currency was worth about £3 11s. British sterling, an amount roughly equivalent to $382 in 2005. When the society's first set of rules were "finally confirmed" seven years later, presumably after having been in effect for several seasons, the sixth rule specified that members were obliged to pay the same £25 annual-subscription fee at the anniversary meeting each November (see appendix 2). In addition to this yearly fee, the seventh rule required each member to make a one-time payment of £35 (£5 sterling or roughly $535 in 2005) for his "entrance," or admission to membership, which included the first year's subscription money. The first suggestion of an increase in subscription cost appeared just over two months after the society's first set of rules was formally adopted, when it announced that at the general meeting of February 1774, "the Question, Whether. or Not, the Annual Subscription of the Members shall be encreased, will then be determined."[2] The outcome of this discussion is not known, but increases definitely took place over the years.

By the autumn of 1785 the annual subscription was £5 and the entrance fee was £10—though both sums were now calculated in an updated South Carolina "sterling" that was nearly on par with British sterling (roughly $428 and $856, respectively, in 2005).[3] At the turn of the nineteenth century, at least by the spring of 1802, the annual subscription was raised slightly, to £5 10s.[4] Rather than indicating an increase in the value of membership in the society, however, this new subscription rate probably represented the society's efforts to keep pace with the rising inflation experienced during the final years of the eighteenth century.[5] The society's new set of rules, adopted in the spring of 1803, finally abandoned the British-influenced monetary system and set the annual subscription fee at $30 (roughly $515 in 2005). The revised rules of 1803 also required (or allowed) members to pay the subscription in three installments: "at every *general* meeting, each member shall pay into the hands of the Treasurer, for the use of the Society, *Ten Dollars*."[6] The power of the dollar fluctuated over the next two decades, but its relative value was consistent enough for the $30 subscription rate to be continued from 1803 through the end of the society's concert activity in 1820.[7] By 1831, a decade after the cessation of its concert series, the society's annual subscription had dropped to $21 (roughly $472 in 2005).[8] The abandonment of the society's concert series may not be the only explanation for this decrease, however. Commodities prices steadily declined after the Panic of 1819, so that at the beginning of the 1830s the buying power of the dollar was greater than it had been in 1803.[9]

Although there are few examples of subscription concert prices in late-eighteenth- and early-nineteenth-century America with which to compare these figures, there are plenty abroad. The average concert series subscription in London during the second half of the eighteenth century, for example, was £5—the same as in contemporary Charleston. In comparison with other concert organizations that included both amateur and professional performers, therefore, the cost of subscription to the St. Cecilia Society's annual concerts was commensurate with that of many gentlemen's music societies in contemporary Britain, but less than that of the most exclusive London series that featured all-professional orchestras.[10]

Investments

Annual subscriptions were not the St. Cecilia Society's only source of income. By the early 1770s the society had enough capital that it began to accumulate stock (such as musical instruments, furniture, and silver) and to issue bonds, or loans, at interest to its members. In an age before the establishment of public banking institutions in British America, voluntary organizations such as societies and clubs served as the major sources of credit for their communities. For members of local organizations such as the South Carolina Society, the Charleston Library Society, and many others, access to this credit was one of the benefits of inclusion.[11] The affluent South Carolina Society, for example, began as a modest social organization in the 1730s and in its early days was known as the "Two Bit Club" because of its subscription charge. By 1776, however, it had accumulated "a sum not less than £68,787.10.3, current money" (roughly $941,500 in 2005).[12] Despite losses sustained during the American Revolution, the stock of this society—which included bonds, promissory notes, and rents received from investment properties—increased to £16,779.8.2 sterling (roughly $1,527,000 in 2005) by 1790.[13] The privileges of membership in the St. Cecilia Society, therefore, went far beyond the enjoyment of sophisticated musical entertainment. With surplus funds available at interest and an exclusive membership including the state's leading merchants, landholders, and politicians, the society represented a powerful financial attraction.

The interest generated from such investment capital could either be reinvested or spent on expanding the organization. Although no details of the St. Cecilia Society's lending capabilities in its early years are known, it is certain that by the time the society approved its first set of rules, it had funds above and beyond those necessary for the operation of a yearly concert series. The 1773 rules, for example, testify to this fact in articulating the responsibilities of the treasurer. On his election to office, he was required to "take Charge of all the Ready Monies, Bonds, Securities, and other Effects, belonging to the

Society," and was not "on any Account, to pay, or lend at Interest, any of the Society's Monies, but by Order of the Society, or the Order of the President, together with the Approbation of the Managers." Four years later, in the early days of the Revolution, the St. Cecilia Society called its members together for the anniversary meeting in November 1777. The tenor of the meeting was practical rather than celebratory, however, as it was necessary "to devise some means of discharging the debts of the society, either by applying part of the Society's stock to that purpose, or enforcing the payment of the long arrears due to the Society."[14] The outcome of this appeal is not known, but it is clear that less than a year later the society did have some surplus cash. On 21 August 1778, the day after its regular quarterly meeting, the St. Cecilia Society purchased a bond for £2,250 South Carolina currency from the newly formed state government.[15] Unfortunately the state's new paper currency, established nearly at par with the old provincial money, was rapidly depreciating in value, and by August 1778 it was worth less than a third of its original value.[16] This investment was relatively small compared to those of some wealthy individuals and several other social organizations in South Carolina, but, to its credit, most of the society's assets were probably still out on loan, or not yet collected, in the form of arrears.

The details of how the society's funds were invested are not known, but considering that Charleston's leading businessmen—many with international connections—were among its members, there can be little doubt that the society's money remained in familiar hands. In fact, when commercial banks were finally opened in Charleston in the 1790s, the managers of the St. Cecilia Society were invariably included among the directors of these institutions. With the financial experience of men such as Thomas Wright Bacot, John Stevens Cogdell, William Crafts, John Splatt Cripps, Henry William deSaussure, James Miller, Edward Penman, Arthur Gordon Rose, Nathaniel Russell, and Arnoldus Vanderhorst, there can be little doubt that the society's funds were aggressively invested for maximum return.[17]

At the St. Cecilia Society's first general meeting following the British evacuation of Charleston, the society's finances were of primary concern. The advertisement for this meeting on 10 April 1783, announced that "all persons indebted to the Society for interest on their bonds, are hereby requested to pay the same immediately."[18] Despite the economic hardships in the wake of eight years of war, the society once again began to prosper. Little more than a year after the British evacuation, the St. Cecilia Society ensured its future financial security by petitioning for incorporation.

On Tuesday, 3 February 1784, the clerk of the South Carolina House of Representatives, meeting at the State House at the corner of Broad and Meeting Streets in Charleston, recorded that "a petition was presented to the House

from the Members of the Saint Cæcilia Society praying to be incorporated."
The speaker of the House, Hugh Rutledge, a manager of the society, ordered
that the petition be referred to a committee, and appointed Thomas Bee, John
Faucheraud Grimké, and Isaac Motte for the purpose. According to the journal of the South Carolina Senate, these committee members were the very
gentlemen who had submitted the petition.[19] On 5 February the committee
reported to the House their opinion that the petition should be granted, and
the House gave them leave to prepare a bill for the same. The text of their bill
to incorporate the "St. Cæcilia Society" was twice read aloud before the House
on Thursday, 19 February, and then sent to the Senate for their consideration.
Over the next two weeks the bill was passed back and forth between the two
houses for the required three readings. After the House performed its final
reading on Saturday the twenty-eighth, the bill received its third reading in
the Senate on Tuesday, 2 March. On the morning of Wednesday, 10 March,
the House declared the bill a legal act and ordered the state seal be affixed to
it. At five o'clock that afternoon, the Senate and House gathered in the Senate
chambers to ratify various acts jointly , including no. 1199, "An Act for Incorporating the St. Cecilia Society."[20]

    The preamble to the society's act of incorporation states:

> WHEREAS, several persons, inhabitants of this State, have associated
> themselves together, and by voluntary contributions raised a consider-
> able fund, which is now placed out at interest on bonds, and collected
> a number of musical instruments, books and other property, with the
> laudable intention of encouraging the liberal science of music, and are
> desirous of having the said society incorporated, thereby to put them
> upon a more solid and lasting foundation than they could be by their
> voluntary subscriptions only.[21]

The principal purpose of incorporating the society, as articulated in this preamble, was to strengthen its financial framework. Although still a social
organization dedicated to advancing "the liberal science of music," the St.
Cecilia Society also became in the eyes of the law "one body corporate and
politic, in deed and in name" that could legally exist in "perpetual succession."
Beyond the collection of its annual subscription money, therefore, the society
was also empowered to make purchases or leases of any kind so long as the
total value thereof did not exceed £500 sterling (roughly $41,000 in 2005)
each year, to receive money and assets by way of donations and subscriptions,
and to sell, exchange, or give away any of its property the members saw fit.[22]

    Since the society's own financial records have not survived, the full extent
of its investments and loans cannot be determined. Evidence of two loans has
survived, however, among Charleston's public records. Both Joseph Farr and

O'Brien Smith, planters with property in St. Paul's and St. Bartholomew's parishes, respectively, mortgaged some of their real estate as security on bonds for £200 (roughly $15,000 in 2005) plus interest. In August 1794 Farr mortgaged to the society 984 acres of swamp and high land in St. Paul's Parish.[23] In March 1795 Smith mortgaged 496 acres "more or less" on a branch of the Ashepoo River in St. Bartholomew's Parish. These mortgages both state that the bonds were executed on the same day as the mortgages. Writing across the recorded copy of Smith's mortgage, the society's treasurer made a note canceling the mortgage: "I Thomas W. Bacot Treasurer of the Saint Cæcilia Society, being duly authorized, do certify that the said Society have rec'd full payment and satisfaction for this mortgage as appears by an Entry in the Bank Book of the Society made by their late Treasurer Edward Darrell, whereby the said Mortgage & the bond therein recited becomes null and void to all intents & purposes whatever—Given under my hand and Seal the 28th June 1804."[24] Had the society's early bankbooks, mentioned in Bacot's note, survived the Civil War, they would have afforded great insight into the financial management of this concert society. Nevertheless, the records of the society's accepting mortgages from Farr and Smith provide important proof of its financial diversity and stability.

Miscellaneous Expenses

The society undoubtedly had a variety of small expenses in the course of its regular concert series, but there are few surviving records of such matters. In Scotland, however, the extant record books of the Edinburgh Musical Society provide an invaluable source from which one might infer the similar expenses of Charleston's St. Cecilia concerts. The treasurer's account of the Scottish society's expenditures for the 1769–70 concert season, for example, includes much more that the performers' salaries (which are listed in decreasing order of importance). The account also notes payments for having the harpsichord tuned, to a clerk "for attendance & receiving the tickets," to two "Centinels attending the Concerts," for the printer's services, to "Cash and Annuity for the Hall," and for more mundane but necessary items such as coal, tallow candles, lamps, music, and tickets.[25]

Although no financial record of this expense has been found, the St. Cecilia Society, like the Edinburgh Musical Society, employed guards at its concerts to receive or inspect the patrons' tickets. During his attendance of a St. Cecilia concert in March 1773, Josiah Quincy recorded that he "was met by *a Constable with his staff*," to whom he offered his ticket. Reading the name inscribed by David Deas on the ticket, the officer addressed Quincy "*by name*" and told him to proceed toward the concert hall. Quincy stated that he was then met by a "white waiter, who directs me to a third to whom I delivered my ticket, and was conducted in."[26] In a city whose population was dominated by enslaved Africans and African Americans, who usually received no payment for their labor, Quincy's note that these attendants were white indicates that the society would have paid them for their services. The society probably also hired a white servant to conduct the flow of carriage traffic to and from its events; for example, in early 1819 the society announced that "a person will be employed to attend to this arrangement."[27] While no record of the society's employment of guards in the nineteenth century has been found, the practice surely continued, given the society's emphasis on regulating the guests at its concerts. During this period, in fact, the employment of guards to restrict entrance to exclusive social events was a common occurrence. In February 1805, for example, Jonathan Mason recorded that he attended a Tuesday evening "picnic" in Charleston, at which "the gentlemen of the town resort to the concert-room, where they dance, play cards, and sup." Mason later recalled that he had "passed a pleasant evening; but the institution has its inconveniences. It is not guarded sufficiently against the admission of improper company." Following the performance of the St. Cecilia Society's concert at the same venue later that week, however, Mason observed that "everything [was] conducted with much propriety," no doubt owing in part to a more rigorous screening of patrons.[28]

Unlike the Edinburgh Musical Society, Charleston's St. Cecilia Society never constructed its own concert venue and thus was obligated to lease space for its events. While the various sites used for its performances are not unknown, only one piece of evidence has been found illustrating the society's expenses in this matter. On 1 December 1813 the society's secretary, John Cripps, wrote a note to "certify that Mr. Sollée has received for several years from the St. Cecilia Society the sum of sixty dollars each night for the use of his Rooms until 12 o'clock." This rental charge may seem inconsequential to the modern reader, but in 2005 this $60 was worth roughly $850—a figure comparable with the rental fee of a modern hall capable of holding several hundred people.[29] If the society's membership was still fixed at 120 members in 1813, and it is known that the annual subscription cost at that time was $30, then this one-night rental fee amounts to less than 2 percent of the society's annual income from subscriptions alone; estimating an average of eight concerts per season during this era, this expense represents less than 14 percent of the annual subscription income. With the addition of interest from investments and loans, the society could thus comfortably afford to hire a hall, contract with professional musicians, maintain a library of music, and equip its performances with all the accouterments necessary for polite and fashionable concerts, including its own collection of musical instruments.

Like the Edinburgh Musical Society and other gentlemen's music clubs in Britain, the St. Cecilia Society is known to have hired, purchased, and maintained a collection of instruments for the use of its members at its concerts. Although no record of the number, variety, or value of these instruments has survived, several references to this collection are found in eighteenth-century sources. In November 1766, one month after the first known St. Cecilia concert, for example, an anonymous newspaper notice stated "a Harpsichord is wanted on hire by the quarter." Interested parties were asked to direct their applications to Robert Wells, the printer of the newspaper and Charleston's largest retailer of music and musical instruments.[30] This brief appeal cannot be securely linked to the St. Cecilia Society, of course, but its timing and context certainly suggest a connection to the newly formed concert organization. When debts forced the dancing and music master Thomas Pike to liquidate his assets in 1773–74, one of the items offered at his final estate sale included "a Spinnet, which could not be sold before, as he was under contract with the St. Coecilia Society for the Use of them."[31] Nearly a decade later, when the society was reactivated in early 1783 after several years of dormancy, its officers publicly requested "those who have in possession any of the instruments or other effects belonging to the Society, to give notice thereof to the Treasurer."[32] A year later, the preamble to the St. Cecilia Society's act of incorporation stated simply that the society had "collected a number of musical instruments, books and other property."[33]

The society may have purchased these instruments from one of several general merchandise importers who retailed musical supplies in colonial Charleston. On at least one occasion, however, the society is known to have made a purchase through a more direct channel. In April 1792, almost immediately following a meeting of the "committee on musical matters," the St. Cecilia Society sent instructions to Thomas Pinckney to purchase a piano and some concert music during his upcoming trip to London. Pinckney, a cellist and long-standing member of the society who had spent the bulk of his youth in England, was on his way to serve as the new American ambassador to the Court of St. James. Before departing on 19 April, Pinckney received a brief letter from the society's treasurer, the English merchant Edward Penman: "Sir,— In pursuance of a resolution of the St. Cecilia Society, I beg leave to enclose you one hundred pounds sterling in bill of exchange on London in your favor, and I am directed to request your excellency to purchace for their use a grand pianoforte, with twenty pounds worth of the best modern music for a concert, and to have the same shipped from London by the first vessel."[34]

Pianos and modern concert music were readily available in Charleston in 1792 at the music store of London native Thomas Bradford, but, as this request demonstrates, the St. Cecilia Society chose to use Pinckney's journey to bypass this retail establishment. The Charleston Library Society, founded in 1748 as a gentlemen's subscription library, exercised a similar practice in the eighteenth century. Rather than purchasing titles from reasonably well-stocked local suppliers, the Library Society relied exclusively on London booksellers to build its collection. This practice not only facilitated the ordering of specific titles, regardless of their distribution in the colonies, but also allowed the library to seek out the best prices and the most accommodating service.[35] The St. Cecilia Society's instructions to Pinckney in 1792 suggest a similar rationale: the society preferred to have its music and instruments selected by one whose refined and discriminating taste was readily acknowledged by his peers. By having its agent select an instrument at the source of production, the society could also avoid the risk of purchasing a "London runner," a second-quality piano exported by unscrupulous agents to the far reaches of the international market.[36] Furthermore, a direct purchase would save the society money by avoiding the customary retail markup and allowing its agent to negotiate the details of packing and shipping. The £100 forwarded to Pinckney was a substantial sum, representing approximately $8,700 in 2005. While modern grand pianos can cost far more than this amount, the portion allocated by the society for a piano in 1792 was ample to purchase a smaller, more delicate grand of that time. Likewise, the £20 (roughly $1,740 in 2005) allocated for the purchase of music would have been sufficient to procure many dozens of the latest orchestral scores, concerti, chamber works, and songs. Less encumbered by the concerns of copyrights and royalties, published music cost far less in Pinckney's day than in ours.

One aspect of the operation of a subscription concert series that the accounts of the Edinburgh Musical Society do not mention is newspaper advertising. Although St. Cecilia Society advertised its activities with varying degrees of regularity over the years, this service was an important means of communication with its members. The survival of a *Charleston Courier* cashbook allows us to examine the society's expenses for placing advertisements in that paper from January 1803 (when the *Courier* commenced operation) through March 1805. During this period the society placed twenty separate advertisements in fifty-one issues of the *Courier*—including notices for meetings, concerts, postponements, and a "Notice to Debtors." The total charge for these months of advertising was $27.52, representing an average of about $12.25 per year (roughly $210.00 in 2005).[37] The *Courier* was not the only paper in which the society published its various notices, however. At that time its advertisements commonly appeared simultaneously in the Charleston *City Gazette* and *Times* as well, a fact that effectively tripled the society's advertising expenses. While this triplicate expenditure may seem excessive, the total cost was probably about 1 percent of the society's annual operating budget. As Charleston's population expanded beyond its modest colonial numbers, surely the society could comfortably afford the luxury of ensuring clear communication with its members.

Contracts and Salaries

As with subscription concert series in eighteenth-century Europe, the orchestra of Charleston's St. Cecilia Society was composed of both amateur and professional musicians. The professionals were usually contracted to perform for an entire season, although visiting soloists (especially singers) might be engaged to appear for shorter periods. Much as today, the salaries paid to such eighteenth-century professionals represented only a portion of their annual income, which they supplemented by teaching music, retailing and repairing instruments and accessories, and performing in other contexts. Very little data concerning the society's contracts with professional musicians or their salaries has survived, but even the limited amount of extant evidence suggests that career musicians in eighteenth-century Charleston received salaries commensurate with those in contemporary Britain.

Although the society also spent money on a variety of other items, salaries paid to professional musicians undoubtedly represented the society's largest expense. During the first few seasons of the St. Cecilia concerts, when the society was just beginning to accumulate capital, it probably relied more on amateur talent than on hired musicians. By 1771, however, the society was actively recruiting professional staff to enlarge its orchestra. The society's 1771 recruitment advertisement mentions its willingness to "agree" or contract with professional musicians for terms of one to three years. For the next half century the employment of professional musicians was a consistent feature of the society's operations, even though extant references to this practice are scarce. One advertisement announcing the commencement of the society's 1786–87 concert season, for example, mentioned the managers "having engaged the performers for the season."[38] Additionally advertisements near the conclusion of several concert seasons reminded members to pay their arrears in order to fulfill the "Salaries of the Performers," who "expect to be paid off as their Contracts expire."[39] Although this practice may have been unprecedented in eighteenth-century British America, it was common among the numerous concert series in the United Kingdom.

The well-preserved financial records of the Edinburgh Musical Society provide an excellent model for imagining the St. Cecilia Society's expenses for professional musicians. In 1771 this organization paid £489 9s. 2d. to sixteen performers, and in 1777 it spent £616 17s. 6d. for twenty-two musicians (though such "reckless recruitment" precipitated serious financial problems).[40] These figures represent an average salary of roughly £29 per annum for each musician, though the orchestral leader and principals were paid between two and five times the salary of the rank and file.[41] Similarly the financial accounts of the summer concert series at the Dublin Lying-in Hospital during the years

1760–84 show that salaries ranged from as little as a few pounds each for infrequently used brass and percussion players to more than £100 for violin and vocal soloists. The average salary for musicians performing at this series was roughly equivalent to that of their colleagues in Edinburgh.[42] If the St. Cecilia Society paid a similar average of £29 to its salaried performers in the 1770s, it could have afforded to hire at least ten professionals per season.[43] The few extant references to the society's contracts with hired musicians confirm that its salaries were indeed similar to these figures.

The earliest reference to the value of St. Cecilia Society musicians' salary is found in Josiah Quincy's journal of his 1773 visit to Charleston. No doubt repeating a figure meant to sound impressive, Quincy reported that the St. Cecilia Society paid a yearly salary of 500 guineas to violinist John Joseph Abercromby. Even without knowing the modern value of this sum, the context of this statement suggests that Abercromby received a very large amount of money. Quincy did not specify the whether he meant 500 guineas in British sterling or in the colonial currency of South Carolina or his native Massachusetts, but sterling would have been the common reference mark for him and his Charleston hosts. In 2005 the approximate value of 500 guineas sterling in 1773 was roughly $53,000—a sum that would have consumed the St. Cecilia Society's entire annual income. Even the Edinburgh Musical Society, whose membership included a larger percentage of the very wealthy and was able to recruit some of the finest musicians in Europe, could not have afforded such an expense. At the end of the 1769–70 season, for example, that society paid its star performer, the castrato Giusto Ferdinando Tenducci, £105 sterling plus £22 1s. in receipts (probably from a benefit concert).[44] If Quincy's report of Abercromby's salary is not simply an exaggeration, it is possible that he may been told that the St. Cecilia Society paid the violinist 500 guineas in South Carolina currency, which would have equaled about £75 sterling (roughly $7,630 in 2005). While this figure represents a respectable salary for an orchestral musician of the early 1770s, it certainly does not elicit the sense of awe suggested in Quincy's journal. It is more likely that Quincy heard that Abercromby earned 500 guineas sterling a year as a violinist in Charleston, and—not knowing that orchestral musicians commonly supplemented their income by teaching, retailing, and performing in other contexts—he assumed that the extravagant salary came solely from the St. Cecilia Society. Even if this qualified salary statement is closer to the truth, however, Abercromby's earnings as a musician in late colonial Charleston are still quite impressive by any standards.

Quincy's 1773 journal also provides another reference to the St. Cecilia Society. While at dinner with the Sons of St. Patrick on 17 March 1773, Quincy heard "two solos on the French horn by one who is said to blow the

finest horn in the world" and added that the St. Cecilia Society paid this performer fifty guineas for one season.[45] While this figure is certainly within the
range of realistic salaries for the period, eighteenth-century brass players did
not usually earn quite this much. Since the orchestration of concert repertoire
during this era placed more emphasis on the string section, brass players were
less essential to the band and thus usually received lower wages. If this particular musician did receive a salary of fifty guineas from the society, he must
truly have been talented.

The most reliable reference to the salary of a professional musician in the
St. Cecilia Society's orchestra is to the compensation of organist and violinist
George Harland Hartley. Hartley's relationship with the society began imme-
diately after his arrival in Charleston in early 1773, but he was obliged to flee
South Carolina four years later because of his allegiance to the British Crown.
After settling in Bristol, England, Hartley was among the many loyalists who
sought compensation for the loss of property and professional income in
America. In 1787 a board of commissioners of the British treasury reviewed
his claim, which included an annual income conservatively estimated at £450
sterling (roughly $41,500 in 2005). Of this professional income, the commis-
sion noted that "from a Musical Society called the St. Cæcilia Society he used
to receive about £80 [sterling] Per Annum for Playing the Harpsicord [sic] at
their Concerts." While this salary (roughly $8,500 in 2005) may be on the
upper end of the scale for orchestral musicians in the 1770s, it is not unusual
for one considered to be an "eminent musician" as Hartley was.[46]

In his *Statistics of South Carolina,* published six years after the cessation
of the St. Cecilia Society's concert series, architect Robert Mills stated that "at
one time it [the society] gave annual salaries of 2 to 300 dollars, to secure first-
rate professors."[47] While nearly two hundred years of inflation make it difficult to grasp the modern equivalent of this dollar amount, the wording of
Mills's statement makes this salary range sound like an impressive sum. In
reality, it represents a very average range. The amounts given by Mills in 1826
dollars are roughly equivalent to a range of $3,926 to $5,889 in 2005. These
modest figures are consistent with the average salaries of British orchestral
musicians, however, and may be taken as a realistic estimate of the St. Cecilia
Society's payments in the early years of the nineteenth century.

Arrears

Within a few years of its founding, the St. Cecilia Society had accumulated a
quantity of capital surpassing its annual expenditures on its concert series. The
annual subscription received from its members, however, remained the society's main source of income, on which it depended to satisfy its many obligations. In an era of limited specie and paper money, it was not uncommon for

merchants, retailers, and social organizations to exercise patience in receiving payment for goods and services. A man's promise of payment was often enough to secure credit, until his behavior demonstrated otherwise. As one might expect, some members of the St. Cecilia Society took advantage of this situation, either by innocent carelessness or by design, and the society was forced to stir them to attention. In the course of the society's five decades of concert activity, however, the issue of arrears escalated from an innocuous nuisance to a painful and debilitating affliction.

The first mention of members in arrears appeared at the end of the St. Cecilia Society's first concert season. On 3 April 1767, the society's treasurer, Isaac Motte (son of the treasurer of the province of South Carolina), published a reminder that "those Gentlemen who have omitted to pay their subscription money are desired to pay it to the treasurer."[48] When the society drafted a formal set of rules in 1773, the continuation of members in arrears prompted the society to include a clause to deal with this delinquency. Rule 6, which specifies the amount of the annual subscription money, also describes the consequences of failure to comply: "Upon Notice from the Treasurer, in Writing, of his Arrears due to the Society, whether those Arrears be for his Annual Subscription, his Dinner-Expenses, or any other Fines incurred by him in the Society, any Person neglecting or refusing to discharge the same, at the next General Meeting of the Society, he shall be no longer deemed a Member."

Six months before the final approval of these rules, however, the society had already published a reminder of rule 6 to its members in arrears. In May 1773 the members were requested to attend the regular general meeting scheduled for that month "in order to dine together, pay up their Arrears, and transact the Business of the Society;—when it is expected, that those Members who are in Arrears, will be punctual in paying the same, as they will be liable to be read out, agreeable to the 6th Rule."[49] Whether or not the society backed down from its threat to enforce the sixth rule is not known, but requests for members to pay their arrears accompanied advertisements for each of the society's quarterly meetings in 1774.[50] In July of that year the society announced that at the August meeting the delinquent members "will certainly have the sixth Rule enforced against them, agreeable to a Resolution of the society at their last Quarterly Meeting."[51] The so-called certainty of this threat was apparently not strong enough motivation, however, so the society passed another resolution relative to arrears at its 1774 anniversary meeting. The advertisement for the society's meeting in February 1775 stated that it is "earnestly requested of the Members to come prepared to pay up their Arrears and Part of their Contribution Money, agreeable to the Resolutions of the 24th [22d] of November last." In the period of tension just before the Revolution, the need to settle the arrears owed to the society became increasingly important. In February 1775, toward the end of what would prove to be its last regular concert season for eight years, the society pleaded for cooperation, "as the Demands on the Society are pressing, and the Performers expect to be paid off as their Contracts expire; the Managers therefore hope they will be enabled to fulfill the Engagements of the Society; every Person who neglects paying his Arrears at the Quarterly Meeting, will, by the 6th Rule be no longer deemed a Member of the Society, and on that Day be excluded, of which those concerned are desired to take Notice accordingly."[52]

Three months later, however, the society repeated the same request, reiterating that "the demands on the Society are preparing, and the performers depend upon being paid off, as their contracts expire."[53] Although the society was fewer than ten years old, the arrears of some members had already extended for long periods. When members were called to celebrate its anniversary in 1777, the society again threatened the sixth rule against "those who have neglected to pay up their arrears for some years past."[54] After two years of dormancy during the early years of the Revolution, the society's debts had reached a critical point. The objective of this meeting was to resolve the situation either by liquidating some of the society's stock "or enforcing the payment of the long arrears due the Society." Although no concerts had been held since the conclusion of the 1774–75 season, the performers had apparently not yet received their salaries for that year. Discharging these debts, therefore, was as much a question of honor as of justice to the musicians. In consideration of the exigencies of the times, the society published a sober reminder of its obligations: "Gentlemen will be pleased to consider that the honour of the Society is concerned in paying those who have administered to their amusement, who have already been too long kept out of their due, and will therefore, it is hoped, make a point of giving their attendance, in order to prevent the continuance of so great a hardship."[55] The society must have found the necessary means to discharge its debts, whether by selling stock or collecting some of the arrears, for by February 1778, the notice for its next general meeting offered to "excuse those who have too long neglected to pay their arrears."[56] Despite this offer of amnesty, in August 1778 the society was again asking "that those in arrears will come prepared to discharge them." By the anniversary meeting three months later, the society expressed hope "that those members who are still in arrears, will recollect the repeated notices they have had to discharge the same" and renewed its threat of enforcing the sixth rule against "all those who neglect to avail themselves of this notice."[57]

When the society revived its concert series in the autumn of 1783, the issue of arrears was not far behind. Nearly all the society's notices for its regular quarterly meetings from 1784 onward state that the members are expected to pay up their arrears. The pleas began calmly enough but soon escalated in urgency. In early 1784 the society hinted, "Such Members as are in arrears, will be pleased to come prepared to discharge the same."[58] By the November of that year, the society "earnestly requested" those members who "remain in arrears" to be prepared to pay the same.[59] In February 1785, those in arrears were "particularly called upon to discharge the same, otherwise the 6th Rule will positively be enforced."[60] The threat of the sixth rule was reiterated throughout the remainder of 1785, and in January 1786 the society gave notice that "all those in arrears are reminded, for the last time, that unless they pay the same on that day, they will assuredly be read out of the Society."[61]

At the end of 1786, the continuation of arrearages prompted the society to issue a new threat: that the treasurer would not issue tickets to any member "until he has paid up his arrears before the last anniversary."[62] In February 1787 the society again advertised that "all those in arrears, are reminded, for the last time, that unless they pay the same on that day, the sixth rule will most assuredly be enforced against them."[63] These repeated promises to enforce the sixth rule sound like empty threats, and without the society's own records we can never know how many members were actually excluded for their failure to pay their arrears. That the society was in fact enforcing the rule, however, is demonstrated in the advertisement for its quarterly meeting in May 1787: "those in arrears are once more reminded, that the Society will continue to enforce the sixth rule against all defaulters."[64]

Rather than passively waiting for members to tender their delinquent funds into its hands, the society took active steps to pursue defaulters. As articulated in the society's sixth rule, before being excluded from the society, members would receive a notice "from the Treasurer, in Writing, of his Arrears due to the Society." In 1787 Francis Kinloch was outraged and embarrassed to have received such a notice from Jacob Read, the society's treasurer. In a letter to Read, dated 3 August 1787, Kinloch made his displeasure clear:

> Sir, On my return from Haddril's [Haddrell's] point some time ago, I
> found a writ left here by your order for the amount due by me to the St.
> Cæcilia Society—I can truly say, that no such paper ever disgraced this
> house before, nor is it a circumstance easily to be forgotten. I have only
> to request, that you would be pleased to inform me what the amount is
> agreeably to the installment act, & that you would send some person for
> the money. I hardly thought that I should ever have recourse to the pro-
> tection of the installment law in any of my private concerns, but the
> whole business will be then of a piece. I remain, Sir, yours Fr. Kinloch.[65]

The act of issuing such writs denoted a certain lack of faith in the debtor, and Kinloch clearly bristled at the idea of being singled out among his peers for this deficiency. Other members who received similar writs no doubt felt likewise, and their caustic rejoinders may have engendered some reluctance in the society's treasurers to pursue those in arrears with appropriate rigor.

Despite the enforcement of its stated rules, the scourge of chronic arrearages continued to affect the finances of the St. Cecilia Society. The problem was not simply members being late with their payments but rather some neglecting to make any payments for years at a time. It was perhaps exacerbated by true defaulters, members who were excluded after having made no payments at all. This practice not only diminished the honor of the society by taking advantage of its good faith in extending credit to gentlemen but also plunged the society into debt. By October of 1788 the matter had reached a crisis point, as expressed in a public notice of an extra meeting of the society's officers:

> St. Cœcilia Society. At a meeting of the president, vice president, and managers of the St. Cœcilia Society, on Monday, the 6th October, the treasurer having reported a state of the funds and debts due by the Society, with the arrears due by the members, it was unanimously *resolved,* that an advertisement be inserted in the public papers, earnestly requesting that every member in arrears, with [will] pay the same to the treasurer, on or before the 1st Monday in November, on the evening of which day there will be a meeting of the managers, and informing them, that unless this reasonable requisition is complied with, it will be impossible to continue the concerts the ensuing season. By order of the president and managers. Arch. Broun, Treasurer.[66]

One month later, the society called its members together for the annual meeting with the usual announcement of an afternoon meeting and an evening concert. Included in this advertisement was a final, calm reminder of the necessity of discharging debts: "The members are earnestly intreated, as they regard the interest of the society, to pay up their arrears, or such part as was due on the last anniversary."[67] Following this anniversary announcement, the topic of arrears is absent from the society's newspaper advertisements for the next three years. This silence does not mean that the matter was resolved successfully, however. As evidence from the early nineteenth century demonstrates, the society's warning that it would be "impossible to continue the concerts" was in earnest. In November 1788 the society's concerts were discontinued and not resumed until November 1790.[68] Although the members continued to meet and dine together at quarterly meetings, the society presented no concerts during the 1788–89 and 1789–90 seasons other than the obligatory concert on St. Cecilia's Day.

In October 1791, less than a year after the resumption of its regular concert schedule, the society resumed publishing reminders for members to discharge their arrears.[69] In November 1792 this request was announced with particular urgency, for the society stated that there was "a necessity for discharging some debts due by the Society."[70] A substantial revision of the society's rules appears to have taken place at its anniversary meeting that year, and at a meeting of the managers in early January 1793 it was "resolved, that the 6th rule of the society be published, and that the same will be strictly enforced in future." Accordingly the full text of the revised sixth rule appeared in the *City Gazette:*

> RULE 6th. On every anniversary, each member shall pay, into the hands of the treasurer, for the use of the Society, the Sum of five pounds sterling, discharge his arrears, and receive an annual ticket for admittance to the concerts, signed by the president and impressed with the Society's seal, without which ticket he shall not be admitted.
>
> Any person upon notice from the treasurer in writing, of his arrears due to the Society, whether those arrears be for his annual subscription, his dinner expenses, or any other fines incurred by him in the Society, neglecting or refusing to discharge the same at the next general meeting of the Society, he shall be no longer deemed a member.[71]

In advance of its quarterly meeting the following month, the society published the mildly worded request "that the few members who are in arrears, will be so obliging as to come prepared to pay."[72] Members in arrears were again requested "to come prepared to pay" at the quarterly meeting on 16 May 1793, "as the salary of the performers will be due on that day."[73] The relative calm of these notices, which seems to suggest a growing compliance with the sixth rule, was quickly dispelled, however. After countless pleas for its members to pay their arrears in a timely manner, the St. Cecilia Society at last resorted to threats of litigation. At that May general meeting, the society "*resolved unanimously,* That all members of this society who are in arrears this day, above the sum of two pounds ten shillings, shall be sued without respect to persons; and that the treasurer do insert this resolution in the *City Gazette,* twice a week for six weeks; and at the expiration of that time place all accounts in the hands of the Society's solicitor."[74]

As an incorporated entity, of course, the society was legally empowered to sue and to be sued.[75] In fact, the ability to take legal action against members in arrears and other defaulters may have motivated the society to seek incorporation in the first place. At the expiration of this six-week period in the summer of 1793, the society's notice for its quarterly meeting on the 15 August announced that "such members who are in arrears above fifty shillings [£2 10s.], on the 20th instant, will please to observe that on that day the books of the Society will be placed in the hands of their solicitor."[76] These stern threats must have produced the desired effect, as there are no records of any suits brought forward by the society during this time.

The persistence of members in arrears was not fully resolved in the autumn of 1793, however, and notices relative to this issue continued to appear with the advertisements of each quarterly meeting through the remainder of the decade. The society's tactics of enforcing payment did take a new direction, though. According to a resolution passed at the quarterly meeting in August 1795, the society established a direct link between the receipt of a season ticket and the payment of arrears: without discharging the latter, a member was not entitled to the former. The enforcement of this resolution seems to have been irregular, for at the anniversary meeting in November 1797 "a resolution was entered into, directing the Treasurer to put in force immediately, the resolve of the 13th of August, 1795." In advance of the meeting in February 1798, the society gave notice that "the members in arrears are requested to take notice of this resolution, and to come prepared."[77] Dissatisfied with the effectiveness of these resolutions, however, the society continued to refine its methods of enforcing the payment of debts. The advertisement for the society's August 1798 meeting requested the presence of its members "to take into consideration some resolutions then to be proposed, and which are of much importance to the Society."[78] Instead of passing a more stringent rule, the result of this meeting was a loosening of the 1795 resolution: "Those in arrears of Five pounds and upwards, who do not pay up, will not be entitled to Tickets."[79] Members indebted to the society for less than £5—or less than one year's subscription—were, of course, still permitted to receive their season tickets. Even with this liberal allowance, the burden of debts to the society continued to grow. By the spring of 1800 the nonpayment of arrears—which included dinner expenses and miscellaneous fines in addition to the normal subscription fee—finally reached a breaking point. The *City Gazette* of 22 April 1800 included a blunt ultimatum to those members indebted to the society: "Last Notice. St. Cecilia Society. The Members who are in arrears five pounds and upwards, are now called upon for the last time to pay up their respective arrears before Friday next the 25th inst. as the solicitor of the Society will on that day positively commence suits against all who disregard this notice, without any discrimination of persons." The first suit, against James Alexander Wright, a former manager of the society, was before the Charleston District Court of Common Pleas by June 1800. William Robertson served as the society's solicitor in the first several cases, but on his being elected president of the society in February 1802 the task was undertaken by the partnership of Joseph Peace and Langdon Cheves.[80] Over the next three decades there were a total of forty suits for arrears concerning thirty-three defendants, with seven being sued twice.[81] The most active year was 1802, when suits against twelve members were tried between February and July. While Peace and Cheves represented the society in a majority of these cases, extant court papers show that the young Cheves, later president of the second Bank of the United States, often appeared alone to prosecute the society's suits. A number of cases in which Peace and Cheves are named as solicitors also include the notation "case proved by Thos. W. Bacot," the society's treasurer between February 1801 and February 1806.[82]

Even after the society commenced suing members in arrears, it continued to grant season tickets "to all members whose arrears are less than five pounds."[83] By October 1801, however, even this liberal allowance was reduced by half, as the society warned its members to "please observe, that by a late resolve of the managers the treasurer is directed not to issue a ticket to any member who shall be in arrears above fifty shillings [£2 10s.]."[84] When the society adopted a new set of rules in the spring of 1803, rule 6 was reincarnated as rule 3, the second section of which specified that

> Any member, upon notice from the Treasurer, *in writing,* of his arrears
> due to the Society, (when such arrears shall amount to one year's contri-
> bution or upwards) refusing or neglecting to discharge the same before,
> or at the next general meeting of the Society, shall be forthwith sued;
> and it shall be the duty of the Treasurer, *upon penalty of incurring the
> arrearage himself,* to place the account of such defaulter in the hands of
> the Solicitor for that purpose; who, without delay shall sue the same. It
> shall also be at the discretion of the Society to read out such member, or
> to continue him as they shall think proper.[85]

Despite the explicitness of these regulations, irregularities in their enforcement persisted. As this revised rule suggests, the society's treasurers in previous years appear to have made personal exceptions in their distribution of season tickets to members in arrears. Alexander Inglis Jr., for example, was never sued by the society, but when he paid his arrears in July 1801 he owed £23 6s. 8d., making him more than four years behind in his subscription.[86] In future seasons the society's treasurer risked his own money as well as his honor in deviating from the letter of the law.

The new rules enacted in the early nineteenth century also brought other irregularities to light. For many years leading up to the turn of the century, members denied their season tickets on account of arrearages had been able to attend concerts by bluffing their way through the door. At the beginning of the 1803–4 concert season, however, the treasurer of the society explicitly reminded members to apply to him for their season passes, "as it is contrary to an express rule of the Society for any gentlemen to be admitted into the concert room without producing his ticket."[87] In spite of all these measures, the blight of arrears continued to linger on the society's finances. The threats of fines, lawsuits, and exclusion had not been sufficiently effective. In February

1805 the society threatened another drastic measure—public exposure of defaulters—at its general meeting: "A list of arrears will be exhibited for the inspection of those Members who will feel a gratification in paying what may be due by them, to enable the Treasurer to maintain the credit of the Society, by settling with the Performers at the end of the season, (which will expire in a few weeks) and to prevent the disagreeable necessity of his enforcing the third rule against all who shall owe a year's contribution and upwards."[88] Apparently too few members took advantage of this warning to assuage the society's financial pressures. One month later the society announced that it was turning over the list of arrears to Daniel Bruckner, an agent of the South Carolina Bank, who would act as its collector:

> The Concert season having expired, and the Salaries of the Performers become due, the Members are respectfully and *earnestly* entreated to pay *Mr. Daniel Bruckner,* who is authorized to collect the same, the arrears due by them, as per list in his hands. Those gentlemen who stand indebted $40 *and upwards,* will, on and after the 10th of April next, please settle with *Langdon Cheves, esq.* Solicitor to the Society, in whose hands a list will on that day be placed, to be sued in the City Court; and such as are indebted from $30 to 40, will please discharge the same on or before the 15th day of August next, when a list will be handed to the Solicitor for legal recovery.[89]

In advance of the August 1805 general meeting, the society tried yet another method of inducing payment from its members. Weeks before that meeting the society reminded its members, "particularly those who have received circular letters from the Treasurer," to come prepared to settle their debts.[90] In spite of public appeals, collectors, and circular letters, a few members allowed their arrears to continue and thus were served with legal writs.

In the autumn of 1807, the third section of the society's rule 5 stipulated that "no member shall have the right of admission to a concert . . . whose arrears shall amount to one year's contribution." To prevent unauthorized exceptions from being granted, the rule further stated that "in case the Treasurer shall infringe this rule, he shall be subject to a fine of *Five Dollars*" (roughly $84 in 2005).[91] At the anniversary meeting in November 1807, however, the society approved revisions to several rules, which it "ordered to be published for general information." Among these was another shift in enforcement strategy:

> RULE III. *Section 3d.* It shall be the duty of the presiding officer of every Anniversary Meeting, immediately after the reading of the Minutes to call over the name or names of such members as may be indebted for

three years arrears, and if no person present, shall forthwith discharge
such arrears, together with all costs and charges which may have accrued
thereon, or become answerable therefor, such member or members
name or names shall be accordingly struck off, and an entry thereof
made on the journals—And in case there shall be no meeting on the
anniversary, the above proceeding shall take place at the next regular
meeting thereafter.[92]

As might now be expected, complications with the satisfaction of arrears persisted. The society called an extra meeting on 8 August 1808 "upon business
of very particular importance" and in advance of the regular general meeting
ten days later pleaded, "It is indispensably necessary that the members should
come prepared to pay their arrears, and it is confidently expected they will
avail themselves of this notice."[93] At that meeting, however, the society again
revised the wording of the third rule, resulting in a retightening of the provisions: the duration of tolerated indebtedness was reduced from three to two
years.[94] In November 1809 the society published an "extract from the 5th
Rule, which has lately been altered." From this point through the remaining
years of its concert series, the society bluntly stated that it would no longer
tolerate arrearages:

> Sect. 3. No member shall have the right of admission to a Concert, with-
> out a *Ticket for the Season,* to be signed by the *President* and countersigned
> by the *Treasurer,* who shall not grant such Ticket of admission to any
> member whatever, *unless the arrears due by him to the Society, at the time
> of his application for a Ticket, be* Fully *discharged;* and in case the Treasurer
> shall infringe this Rule, he shall be subject to a fine of *five* dollars.[95]

No further stern notices were published in the newspapers, but the litigation
against members in arrears continued until 1829. Advertisements for the society's general meetings occasionally reminded members to attend and settle
their arrears in the years after 1809, but the chronic shortfalls in the society's
annual subscription seem to have abated.

There can be little doubt that the society's decision to resort to legal
action against those in arrears caused friction and discomfort among its
membership. As a corporate body, however, the society had to pursue payment of these debts in order to survive. The number of defendants sued represents only a fraction of the society's members, but their arrears nonetheless
formed a considerable amount of money distributed over several years. In
terms of length of arrears, the society's most extreme offender was Charles
Goodwin, who was sued in June 1803 for arrears dating back to his entrance
to the society in September 1785. After Goodwin had enjoyed nearly eighteen

years of membership, during which he had made only a few small payments, his liability for this debt seemed beyond question, but somehow he felt justified in his nonpayment. On being served with a writ notifying him of the suit, Goodwin immediately wrote a hurried note to the society's solicitors, Joseph Peace and Langdon Cheves, informing them "I shall dispute the claim the Society set up ag.ᵗ me & will with pleasure try the question at the June Court."[96] The society's largest suit for arrears was against James Hamilton Sr. In June 1802 Hamilton was successfully sued for $289.52 in arrears dating back to May 1794 (roughly $5,243 in 2005). Following this judgment, Hamilton wrote a promissory note to the society's treasurer, but then refused to honor the note when it matured twelve months later. Accordingly he was sued again in February 1807 and ordered to pay the first judgment, plus interest on his note and additional court costs—a total of more than $300.[97]

The society's suit against Charles Pinckney (1757–1824), a wealthy South Carolina planter and prominent national politician, provides a good example of the society's collection difficulties and the consequences faced by its defendants. In June 1807, during his fourth term as governor of South Carolina, Pinckney was sued for arrears dating from 1802 through 1806. The society's court action was successful, but Pinckney, whose finances were already in a state of deep distress, continued to withhold payment even though his membership continued. In accordance with the society's threats, he was sued again in 1809 for the initial judgment and for arrears accumulated since the first suit. The society won this case as well, but Pinckney's debt to the society was not satisfied for another decade. While the amount of his arrears was smaller than that of some other members who were sued, the difficulty his case presented to the society led to a bitter conclusion. A note penciled on the 1809 judgment against Pinckney succinctly states that the defendant had been "Sued & Read out."[98]

An examination of the list of members sued for arrears to the society reveals that the defendants were among the wealthiest and most influential citizens of South Carolina. Their refusal, or inability, to render payment to the society thus seems uncharacteristic. It is possible, of course, that these well-heeled patrons may have felt their socio-economic or political status constituted a right to admission and thus exempted them from the pedantic requirement of paying for inclusion in this elite circle. This may have been the case in some instances, but another, more specific, reason was probably a work as well. During the years when the problem of arrears was most pronounced—between the conclusion of the American Revolution and the final closure of the African slave trade at the end of 1807—Charleston's (and South Carolina's) economy experienced a great shortage of cash. The planters and merchants who amassed or sustained fortunes during these years dealt largely in long-term credit and had very little in the way of liquid assets. While on paper their wealth may have been impressive, there was in reality very little cash available for the more mundane expenses of life. For men with large sums of money tied up in transatlantic trade, real-estate speculation, and human chattel, therefore, the expenses of the St. Cecilia Society's concerts may have seemed too trivial to even acknowledge.

THE SURVIVING DETAILS OF THE ST. CECILIA SOCIETY's financial activities provide an opportunity to examine the operations of a significant cultural organization in early America. As the proprietor of a series of events, it collected subscription money from its members and contracted with numerous individuals. As a corporate body, the society protected and invested its funds, accrued property, and pursued debtors. The fact that these practices closely echo the fiscal management of similar musical organizations in contemporary Britain testifies to the strength of the connection between the Old and New Worlds in the eighteenth century. In late colonial and early national Charleston, however, the exigencies of the region's plantation economy created difficulties that might have put an end to similar institutions abroad. The St. Cecilia Society counted the wealthiest men in South Carolina among its membership, but their habitual inattention to their debts to the society continually sapped its financial strength. Despite this persistent problem, the society's concert patronage endured for more than a half century, and the organization itself continues to thrive today. Such perseverance was owing in part to the collective financial acumen of its managers, of course, but certainly the members' passion for music played an important role in ensuring the society's long-term survival.

The Venues

DURING ITS YEARS OF CONCERT PATRONAGE, the St. Cecilia Society never constructed its own performance hall, nor did it retain any existing venue for its exclusive use. Rather the society shared performance spaces with a variety of other organizations whose membership usually overlapped with its own. As in contemporary Britain, the society's activities were held in multipurpose rooms that also hosted events such as meetings, dancing assemblies, exhibitions, plays, auctions, lectures, and feasts. So well established was the St. Cecilia Society's presence, however, that a few of the spaces it occupied became known as "the St. Cecilia Society's Concert Room" or simply "the Concert Room." Nevertheless, the society's activities at any one venue were never more than semipermanent and always subject to circumstances beyond its control. Between 1766 and 1820 the St. Cecilia Society's events were held at eight different locations, all situated within a few blocks of Charleston's urban center: the long room at Dillon's Tavern (later called the City Tavern), Pike's Assembly Room, the South Carolina State House, McCrady's Long Room, Charleston's City Hall (in the Exchange Building), the Carolina Coffee House, Sollée's Concert Hall, and the South Carolina Society's Hall (see figure 6.1). While the amount of physical space and the degree of elegance at each of these sites varied considerably, all compared favorably to the venues used for subscription concerts in contemporary Europe. The society's periodic transferal from one venue to another was not simply a progression from small, plain spaces to larger, more elaborate ones. Rather, these movements reflect the society's desire to engage the most commodious venue possible, for its status as a privileged association of the city's elite provided the society with sufficient clout to retain the most fashionable and exclusive sites available in Charleston.

Most concerts in early-eighteenth-century Britain were performed in large rectangular rooms, or "long rooms," situated within taverns and coffeehouses. Such spaces typically formed part of a larger complex of rooms and could be hired out for private social events. As in the ballrooms of modern hotels, the food and beverage needs of the long room's guests were supplied by the house kitchen and its staff. Most of these early concert venues were either enlarged or destroyed in subsequent generations, making it difficult to form generalizations about the size and format of such performance spaces. Nevertheless, it is not unreasonable to estimate that during the first

6.1. Concert venues in Charleston, 1765–1821. The distance between B and E is 0.6 miles.

A. Carolina Coffee House, **B.** Charleston Theatre, **C.** Church Street Theatre (1773–83), **D.** Dillon's Tavern / City Tavern, **E.** Exchange Building / City Hall, **F.** Fayolle's Long Room, **G.** McCrady's Tavern and Long Room, **H.** Orange Garden, **I.** Pike's Assembly Rooms / French Theatre / Church Street Theatre / City Theatre / Concert Hall, **J.** Queen Street Theatre (1736–67), **K.** St. Andrew's Hall, **L.** South Carolina Society Hall, **M.** South Carolina State House / Charleston County Court House, **N.** Vauxhall Garden (1799–1812) half of the eighteenth century such multipurpose rooms ranged in size from roughly 500 to 1,500 square feet of floor space.[1] More specifics have survived about the assembly and concert rooms used in the second half of the century. For example Hickford's Great Room in London, the home of the prestigious Bach-Abel concerts between 1764 and 1774, measured 50 feet by 30 feet (1,500 square feet).[2] The oval-shaped concert room in Edinburgh's St. Cecilia's Hall, opened in 1762, was built within a rectangular space measuring approximately 63 feet by 35 feet (about 2,200 square feet). Hanover Square Rooms, which became the chief concert venue in late-eighteenth-century London after its opening in 1775, measured 79 feet by 32 feet (a little over 2,500 square feet).[3] Continuing this gradual increase in dimensions, it is estimated that the average European concert room of the 1780s and 1790s contained about 2,800 square feet, including the space for both musicians and audience. There were, of course, a few larger and grander concert venues in eighteenth-century Europe. The nearly square Salle des Cent Suisses at the Tuilleries in Paris, home of the Concert Spirituel between 1725 and 1784, for example, contained more than 3,100 square feet of floor space. The rectangular Gewandhaus in Leipzig, which opened in 1781, provided more than 4,200 square feet for the performers and audience.[4]

Comparisons with large venues in major metropolitan cities are not entirely appropriate, however, for the population of Charleston never approached that of London, Edinburgh, Paris, or Leipzig. Concert series in the provincial cities of the United Kingdom and throughout Europe during this time were routinely held in smaller venues, the sizes of which were scaled down in proportion to the local population. The eight concert spaces used in Charleston during the tenure of the St. Cecilia Society's concert series ranged between roughly 1,000 and 3,600 square feet and thus demonstrate a successful effort to match established European standards. The society's concerts began in a commodious tavern long room, not unlike that used by similar organizations abroad, and eventually occupied larger and more specialized assembly rooms. This journey was not without complications and setbacks, however. After years of patronizing alternative venues of varying shapes and sizes, the society's venerable concert series ended in a coffeehouse long room not unlike that in which it began.

From 1766 to 1771 the St. Cecilia concerts were held in Charleston's most prominent public house, or tavern, located at the northeast corner of Broad and Church streets. This venue, in fact, had been the site of almost every concert in the city since 1737.[5] So central was this establishment to Charleston's social and business life that it was colloquially known as "the Corner," and its habitués were called the "Corner Club."[6] Although this establishment prospered for most of the eighteenth century, its name changed periodically with each new proprietor. In the autumn of 1766, when the St. Cecilia Concerts began, the tavern was known as Mr. Dillon's house, or simply Dillon's, after its lease holder, Robert Dillon. Like taverns and coffeehouses in England and in other American cities, there were several side rooms for private meetings in addition to the main reception room. The concerts and the dancing that always followed were held in a private "great room" on the second floor with an adjoining "apartment."[7] A plat dating from 1787, when the building was still in use as a tavern and concert space, shows that this "house" was actually a conglomeration of buildings (see figure 6.2). The main rooms were located in a large brick "Mansion" facing Broad Street, behind which a detached kitchen, stables, and miscellaneous out buildings were located in an enclosed yard. Also behind the mansion, running along the east side of Church Street, was an adjoining building containing a long room approximately 65 feet long and 25 feet wide, with an exterior piazza or porch along the eastern side.[8] In this rectangular space of approximately 1,625 square feet, the musicians probably would have stood (all except the cellists and harpsichordist) at one end of the room in a semicircular array, as was typical for eighteenth-century orchestral musicians.[9] From October 1766 to the end of 1771, five and one half seasons, all the St. Cecilia concerts were performed in this long room.

In the fall of 1771 the dancing master and musician Thomas Pike (ca. 1735–after 1787), one of the founders of the St. Cecilia Society, announced he was constructing a "New Assembly Room" nearly double the size of Dillon's great room.[10] When this new venue finally opened in early 1772, the society's concerts were immediately transferred to it. Pike's Assembly Room (or Rooms) was located on the west side of Church Street between St. Michael's Alley and Tradd Street, about one and a half blocks south of Dillon's Tavern. This facility contained several spaces: two drawing rooms, each 20 by 40 feet, a room 68 feet long for fencing and dancing, and a large assembly room measuring 40 by 80 feet (3,200 square feet), all built above a raised basement used for wine storage.[11] The entire structure was situated more than 50 feet back from Church Street and was accessed by a narrow passageway. Carriages were evidently obliged to deposit their passengers at the foot of the passageway, forcing well-dressed patrons to walk the distance from the street to the door. In November 1772, less than a year after its opening, a concert event to alleviate this inconvenience was advertised at Pike's Assembly Room: "the whole Sum that may be raised on this Occasion, to be laid out for a covered Way and elegant Portico next the Street; thereby to enable Ladies and Gentlemen always to go to the New Suite of Rooms without being incommoded by the Weather."[12]

A little more than a year after its opening, Josiah Quincy attended a St. Cecilia concert at Pike's Assembly Room in March 1773. His record of that event provides some valuable clues as to the size and arrangement of this performance space.[13] Quincy confirmed that the hall was in fact "situated down a yard," but his description of its entrance does not mention the presence of a covered walkway. Arriving at the main building—approximately 120 feet long

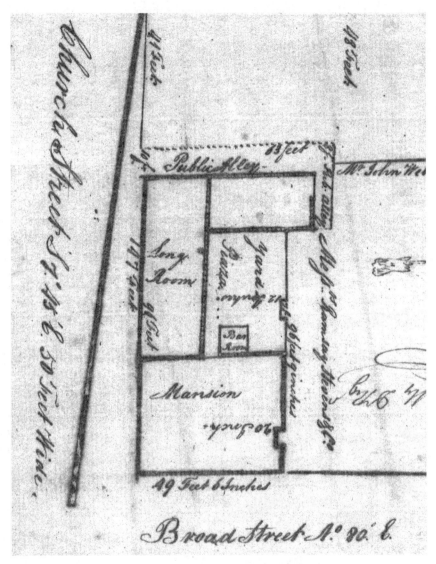

6.2. A 1787 plat of Robert Dillon's Tavern, then known as the City Tavern. Note the location of the "Long Room" north of the "Mansion." The diagonal line in Church Street is part of a compass arrow pointing northward. Courtesy of Charleston County Register of Mesne Conveyance (RMC)

and 40 feet wide—he pronounced it "a large inelegant building" and described the concert room itself as being "preposterously and out of all proportion large." Using the terminology of his day, Quincy noted that this room had "no orchestra for the performers, though a kind of loft for fiddlers at the Assembly." By this he meant the room lacked a raised platform for the musicians to perform upon during a concert, but that one of the walls (probably the west wall, farthest from the street) contained an elevated gallery, or "loft," in which the musicians would stand during the dancing assemblies (see figure 6.3). This feature was common to many eighteenth-century social facilities, as it maximized the floor space available for dancing assemblies. For concerts, however, the musicians were arranged on the floor with the audience, as Quincy indicated, "all at one end of the hall and the company in front and on each side."

Shortly after completion of this elaborate performance space, Thomas Pike was overwhelmed by the debts he had incurred in the course of the project. In the autumn of 1773 he was obliged to forfeit most of his personal and real property, including his Assembly Room, in order to satisfy his creditors.[14] When Pike's extensive lot in Church Street was put up for sale in August 1773, the assignees of his estate, the Reverend Robert Smith and merchant Philip Hawkins, gave notice to prospective buyers that "this Building is subject to an

6.3. Detail from an anonymous eighteenth-century illustration of the dance "Sir Fopling's Airs," showing at left a typical musicians' loft of that era. Courtesy of The Winterthur Library: Joseph Downs Collection of Manuscripts and Printed Ephemera

Incumbrance of a Night, for the Subscribers [Smith and Hawkins] to use it once a Week, for Four Years to come." Since Smith, the rector of St. Philip's Church, was also an officer of the St. Cecilia Society, it seems logical to conclude that the "incumbrance" was placed on behalf of the fortnightly St. Cecilia concerts and Charleston's unadvertised fortnightly dancing assemblies, which took place at the same venue in alternate weeks. The notion that Smith's assistance to Pike was given in the interest of the St. Cecilia Society is further strengthened by the fact that the assignees (Smith and Hawkins) distributed the "first Dividend" to Pike's creditors on St. Cecilia's Day, 22 November 1773.[15]

Although Pike technically retained title to the property, his assignees leased this venue to the Dutch-born merchant Jacob Valk, who used the commodious space to display and auction off the property of other estates, including furniture, plantations, and slaves.[16] When Pike left Charleston for Philadelphia in July 1774, he asked the Reverend Smith to act as his attorney in discharging his Charleston debts. Perhaps aware of Pike's loyalties to the British Crown, Smith transferred the property into his own name, an action that prevented the state from confiscating it as the property of a known loyalist.[17] Johann David Schoepf, visiting Charleston immediately after the Revolution, expressed shock at this arrangement, noting that Smith "not only had no hesitation in a matter of furthering the pleasure of his parishioners, but . . . made no scruple of receiving the rent; whereas in the New England states the bare thought of such a thing would have disgraced any minister."[18] Unfettered by such prudish concerns, the St. Cecilia Society continued to hold its concerts at this venue through 1778, which by the autumn of 1774 had become known as Mr. Valk's Long Room. Besides concerts, dancing assemblies, and auctions, Valk's room was also used for social gatherings, including one on the Fourth of July 1778, when David Ramsay gave an address on the second anniversary of the Declaration of Independence before the president, vice president, and legislature of South Carolina at "the Concert-Room at Mr. Valk's."[19]

Following the surrender of Charleston on 12 May 1780, the British and German occupying forces established their own series of subscription concerts and dancing assemblies. Rather than using the commodious Assembly Room or the venerable tavern at the corner of Broad and Church streets, however, they appropriated the South Carolina State House as their performance venue.[20] Constructed in the mid-1750s at the northwest corner of Broad and Meeting streets, the State House was originally a large two-story brick building; after a fire in 1788, however, a third floor was added and the interior reconfigured (see figure 6.4). In 1765 visiting Philadelphia merchant Pelatiah Webster received a tour of this building and commented on the second-floor meeting rooms of South Carolina's bicameral legislature. Both the Council Chamber (for the royal governor and his council) and the Assembly Room (for the Commons House of Assembly), said Webster, were about 40 feet square. The Assembly Room was decorated much more simply than the Council Chamber, which was elaborately "decorated with many heavy pillars & much carving, rather superb than elegant."[21] Although the original plan of the State House is lost, a recent architectural survey suggests that these rooms could not have been more than 32 feet square, yielding just over 1,000 square feet of floor space each.[22] The Council Chamber, with its "superb" appointments overlooking the corner of Meeting and Broad streets, was undoubtedly used as the concert room, though several adjoining small chambers and the Assembly Room may have also been open to the concerts' promenading patrons. Representing a foreign presence in an occupied city, the British commanders must have chosen the State House as the site of their entertainments because it served as the stronghold of their precarious government, off-limits to rebellious Americans. Even as a concert venue, however, it was not entirely secure, as one musician reported having his violin stolen from "the State-House room since the last Concert."[23]

6.4. South Carolina State House, built in the mid-1750s as a two-story structure. After a fire in 1788, the interior was reconfigured, and a third floor was added in 1790. It is now the Charleston County Historic Courthouse. Photograph by the author

Shortly after the British evacuation of Charleston on 14 December 1782, the citizens of Charleston quickly moved to reestablish their former social life. Unfortunately Pike's Assembly Room was soon destroyed by fire. On Thursday evening, 27 February 1783, a fire broke out during a dancing assembly and quickly consumed the entire structure, including a theater next door that David Douglass had constructed for his American Company of Comedians in the autumn of 1773.[24] The melancholy event was recorded in a letter by Eliza Wilkinson, a young lady eagerly anticipating the return of festive soirées. After an exhilarating carriage ride to the Assembly Room, Miss Wilkinson wrote to a friend, "we got to the Room safe."

> It was finely Illuminated, and the Musick play'd sweetly, so sweetly that I cou'd not keep my feet still; it Inspired me with a Strong inclination for dancing; I promised myself some agreeable, happy hours.—but ah! how precarious and fleeting are all subliminary enjoyments! there was but two minuets danc'd and the third begun; when the Gentlemen came and advis'd us to quit the Room, for the house was on fire, and the Assembly was Immediately broke up, and away we scamper'd; powder'd Beaus & Belles huddl'd away; and left our Spacious, Elegant Room to consuming fire: which soon reduc'd it to dust and ashes. Ah! how fallen!—I stood for hours in the Balcony of a house at some distance, gaz'd, moraliz'd and made a thousand reflections on the blazing spectacle which was so conspicuously exhibited."[25]

One local paper noted that "the spirited Exertions of the Inhabitants, and a Party of Continental Soldiers, sent on purpose, prevented the Flames from spreading any further; and had the Pumps and Engines been in proper order, the Fire might entirely have been extinguished at the beginning." The mercantile firm of Henry Shoolbred and Benjamin Moodie, whose inventory had been stored below the assembly rooms and in the theater, published their thanks to the public and to General Nathanael Greene and his Continental troops for their efforts, and tactfully requested the return of their property that "may have been moved in a Hurry to Places unknown to them." Apparently many of the inhabitants who participated in the firefighting efforts had also helped themselves to the salvaged goods. Governor John Mathews (a founding member of the St. Cecilia Society) and his privy council issued a stern public order commanding the return of the "vast Quantity of Furniture, Goods and Effects" that had been "hastily thrown into the Street." Perhaps indicating that the state itself had some investment in the hall or its contents, the order threatened prosecution for felony theft against those neglecting to return salvaged goods. In addition to depriving the city of its fashionable concert hall and theater, this fire also exacted a substantial monetary toll. One estimate calculated the total value of goods and property lost at between thirty and forty thousand pounds sterling (roughly $2,347,000 to $3,130,000 in 2005).[26]

After a lapse of several years during the Revolution, the St. Cecilia Society's concerts recommenced in the autumn of 1783. Owing to the loss of the assembly room in Church Street, the concerts returned to the tavern at the corner of Broad and Church streets, now called simply the "City Tavern." Its new proprietor, William Thompson, announced to the city's ladies and gentlemen that the tavern's long room would be "elegantly fitted out for their reception, in the view of accommodating dancing-assemblies, societies and clubs, to whom every attention will be given." Actually the St. Cecilia Society had never fully abandoned this venue. While its concerts were transferred to Pike's Assembly Room in early 1772, the society's members continued to gather at this tavern for business meetings, which always included a large repast. Although its name changed as proprietors came and went (Dillon's, Holliday's, Swallow's, Ramadge's), the City Tavern remained the principal meeting place for the nonconcert activities of the society between 1766 and 1788.[27]

The return of the concerts to the City Tavern was intended to be a temporary move, or so Count Francesco Dal Verme was told when he visited Charleston in December of 1783. In a letter to his father, Dal Verme noted that the city of Charleston appeared to be "the best constructed of any I have seen in America," but added that "much of it, however, was burned and destroyed last year by the enemy." To illustrate the losses, Dal Verme cited Pike's assembly hall as an example: "even the hall for dancing suffered the same fate while the inhabitants were using it to celebrate the order received by the English to evacuate the city. What a loss! Another hall has already been substituted for temporary use, in which a ball or a concert is held on alternate Thursdays during this season."[28] Six months after Dal Verme's visit, the Union Kilwinning Lodge of Freemasons announced its plans for a more permanent venue. Although the lot on which Pike's assembly hall had been built, still held by the Reverend Robert Smith, remained unimproved for several more years, the adjacent lot to the south was offered as a substitute. This property, owned by the Union Kilwinning Lodge, had been leased to David Douglass in 1773 for the construction of the playhouse that also burned in the fire of 1783. In May of 1784 the lodge advertised its plan to build not another theater, but a multipurpose hall:

> To the Public. The Members of the Union Kilwinning Lodge, since the
> burning of the playhouse, and the adjacent Dancing Assembly Room,
> having been solicited to build upon their lot, where the play-house once
> stood, a Suite of Public Rooms; Give Notice, that, in consequence of
> such request, they intend erecting, upon the foundation of the Late
> Theatre, such a Suite of Rooms, properly calculated for the reception

and accommodation of the Ladies and Gentlemen, as well as for the use
of any Public Society or Societies, that may think it proper to frequent
them. Any Person inclinable to undertake to build the same, is desired
to give in his proposals (with Estimates) to the Subscriber [John Troup]
at No. 53 Tradd-street; and, where the Ground-plan and elevation of said
intended building may be seen.[29]

Despite the fact that a design for the hall had already been drafted, the
Masonic plan did not come to fruition. Just a few months later, in September
1784, the Union Kilwinning Lodge announced that "finding it impracticable
from the smallness of their fund, to build the intended suit [sic] of rooms on
their lot, whereon the play-house lately stood," they would instead lease the
lot for a term of five years.[30] For nearly two decades to come, therefore, the
concerts of the St. Cecilia Society continued to be held in alternative venues.

Although the City Tavern served as the principal venue for St. Cecilia concerts in the years immediately after the Revolution, a number of private concerts and balls were apparently held at the South Carolina State House in late
1783 and early 1784. Open only to a select group of participants and not publicized in any newspaper, these private soirées garnered little public attention
until 10 March 1784, the day the state legislature gave final approval to the St.
Cecilia Society's act of incorporation. That morning a newspaper reported that
the society had performed a "grand Concert in the State-House" the previous
evening, Tuesday, 9 March, "at which were present a numerous company of
Ladies, and the Honorable the Members of the Senate and the House of Representatives, with a number of other gentlemen."[31] Such exclusive, recreational
use of public property by a private body did not sit well with the nascent
republican element of the city, however. The rhetoric of equality and brother-
hood that had sustained the spirit of Revolution continued after the war and
led to the rise of opposing political factions. Those who had previously commanded respect and authority simply by right of their wealth and social position were now confronted with demands for equal representation from among
the lower classes. One week after the announcement of the St. Cecilia Society's
concert at the State House, the situation came to a dramatic head.

On St. Patrick's Day of 1784, a slave woman named Beck, sent on an
errand to the City Tavern by statesman John Rutledge, asked permission of
the tavern's proprietor to observe a celebratory artillery display in Broad
Street from a second-floor window. The proprietor, republican supporter
William Thompson, was outraged by Beck's "impertinence" in asking for such
liberty in his house and ordered her to leave without completing her errand.
On hearing of Thompson's harsh refusal, Rutledge sent a note to the tavern
curtly demanding an explanation for the callous treatment of his messenger.

Thompson obliged this request by marching two and half blocks up Broad Street to the statesman's home to deliver his reply in person. After unleashing an abrasive condemnation of Rutledge's haughtiness for taking Beck's side, Thompson followed up his verbal attack with a written challenge to a duel. At the State House the next day, Rutledge described the unpleasant encounter to his fellow representatives and reminded them that it was unlawful to invite a gentleman of the legislature to meet on the field of honor. The House of Representatives ordered Thompson's arrest for committing "a gross insult on and undeservedly injurious to an Honorable Member of this House, and a flagrant Violation and breach of the privileges thereof" and immediately confined him to jail.[32] The newly formed Marine Anti-Britannic Society, composed of republican zealots, congratulated Thompson "for his spirited, manly, and patriotic conduct" in standing up to Rutledge, "when *Aristocratical principles* endeavored to subvert and destroy every *genuine idea* of *real republicanism*."[33] In the ensuing hearings Rutledge noted that Thompson's prior insolence to several gentlemen during the concerts and dancing assemblies at the City Tavern had precipitated the removal of those events to alternative venues. This testimony was seconded by the wealthy, European-educated Gabriel Manigault, who claimed to have also witnessed Thompson's ill treatment of his fashionable guests. "Mr. Manigault lies," Thompson railed back at the "Nabob Tribe" of aristocrats, "and if he offers this to my face, by the Eternal God I will kick his A_ _E."[34] Thompson's wife, keeping a cooler head, appealed to the managers and subscribers to the city's dancing assembly (virtually identical with those of the St. Cecilia Society). "Tho' deprived of her Husband," she assured the fashionable set, "they shall be as *elegantly* provided for, during his confinement, as at any other period since the commencement of the Assembly."[35] The managers of the dancing assembly countered by announcing that they would again conduct their entertainments at the State House.[36] A delegation from the Marine Anti-Britannic Society presented an address from "a great number of Respectable Inhabitants" to Governor Benjamin Guerard demanding that he "not sanction any Public Dances, or dissipating Feast, at the State House." They argued that "the growth of luxury, profusion and dissipation is too conspicuous in this land" and that the use of the State House for private events was contrary to the "true Republican spirit" for which the Revolution had been fought. Furthermore, they asserted, such usage recklessly endangered the safety of valuable public records. Governor Guerard, undoubtedly a participant in the music and dancing soirées at the State House, duly advised the Senate to cease such "Evening Entertainments," but then announced that he would defer to the judgment of the president of the Senate, Bristol native John Lloyd, who was empowered to superintend the use of the facilities.[37]

The tension between William Thompson and the aristocratic element of Charleston was quietly resolved by May 1784. So far as is known, no further concerts or dancing assemblies were held at the State House. As if to underscore the resolution, the St. Cecilia Society published an extraordinary advertisement signifying that its concert on 22 April was to be performed "at the usual place." Thompson was released from custody but soon announced that he had been "called" back to his native Pennsylvania and would relinquish his lease of the City Tavern. In October 1784 James Milligan became the proprietor of this establishment, which continued to host the city's dancing assemblies and St. Cecilia concerts for several more years.[38]

Milligan's tenure at the City Tavern was not without its own dramatic incidents, however. During one evening's entertainment at the tavern in early 1785, an argument between the proprietor and five musicians erupted into a brawl. The musicians, whose names are now lost, filed suit against Milligan "to recover damages for injuries received in the course of a beating," and the case was heard in the Court of Common Pleas on 18 August 1785. As noted with levity in the local press, the events of the trial, in which the litigants were represented by two members of the St. Cecilia Society, "relaxed the rigid, inflexible muscles of the gravest."

> The five plaintiffs brought a terrible account of maims and bruises, and one in particular gave a hint of a journey that he had undertaken, in company with his colleagues that will no doubt throw new light on many contested points of sacred and profane history. One of the *Five Plaintiffs* being interrogated as to the language used on the occasion, said *Mr. Milligan bid us all go to hell*—Well, what then?—*We went*—What to Hell?—*Yes.* The jury gave the Five Plaintiffs One Shilling damages, which, considering the length and danger of a journey to Tartarus, and back again, will not pay traveling expenses.
>
> General [Charles Cotesworth] Pinckney was counsel for the defendant, and in a very able defense of his client, he observed that the plaintiffs had themselves been the aggressors, by abusing Mr. Milligan in his own house, which was his *Castle.* When Mr. [William Loughton] Smith came to reply on the other side, he observed that he had the highest respect for the abilities of his learned friend, but believed that he was the first person since the days of Don Quixotte that had ever taken an *Inn* for a *Castle.*[39]

Less than a year later, during the lively Fourth of July celebration in 1786, the proprietor's wife, Mrs. Milligan, was nearly killed by the collapse of one of the tavern's exterior balconies. While the local members of the Society of the Cincinnati were feasting, perhaps in the tavern's venerable long room, they crowded onto a balcony to view the banners and streamers hung from various houses and across the streets in the city's center. Their weight proved too much for the structure, however, and the balcony's frame rained down on the throng below. Fortunately for Mrs. Milligan, who happened to be among those on the street, a rope strung between the balcony rail and a nearby house checked the fall of the main timbers and prevented a fatal injury.[40]

In the spring of 1788 the proprietorship of the City Tavern once again changed hands, and by late August the building was advertised to be let and "immediate possession given." On 22 August, within days of the first notice that the tavern was vacant, the St. Cecilia Society convened an emergency meeting at "Mr. McCrady's tavern" to discuss "business of great importance to the Society."[41] While the topic of discussion at this meeting may have been the society's troubled financial status, it seems also that the members needed to select an alternative venue for society meetings and concerts. For the anniversary meeting that November, the society's managers "resolved they should dine at Mr. McCrady's, on Saturday the 22d." The anniversary concert, however, would be performed as usual "in the evening at the City Tavern." By January 1789 the dancing master Thomas Turner advertised that he had moved his dancing academy "to the house lately the *City-Tavern*, where he resides."[42] Following this change, no further concerts of any kind were advertised to take place at this site. After more than fifty years of hosting musical performances, the City Tavern ceased to function as a concert venue.

The closure of the City Tavern at the end of 1788 was of little immediate consequence to the St. Cecilia Society, however, because the members' numerous debts to the society caused its fortnightly concerts to be suspended during the 1788–89 and 1789–90 seasons.[43] Several public concerts took place at McCrady's Tavern during the years 1789–90, but it is not clear when the first St. Cecilia concert was performed at this new location.[44] Starting in August 1788, however, all the society's meetings were held at McCrady's. It seems likely, therefore, that the society's only advertised concert in 1789, performed on 22 November, was also held at this venue.

The main building of Edward McCrady's Tavern was a three-story brick house overlooking East Bay Street and the busy commercial wharves on the Cooper River. Surrounded by storefronts, warehouses, and maritime concerns, it was certainly not the most fashionable site in Charleston, but the St. Cecilia Society had few alternatives. Like the City Tavern, McCrady's was actually a cluster of multipurpose buildings. The main house, or mansion, opened during the Revolutionary War, was followed in subsequent years by a series of ancillary structures. In 1788 McCrady built behind the main house— and connected by a piazza over an arcade and brick-paved courtyard—a two-story brick building with a kitchen below and a single room above.[45] A survey of the property made in October 1800 shows that this "long spacious room" on the second floor, known as McCrady's Long Room to this day, is approximately 25 feet wide and 55 feet long, with the narrow south end fronting Unity Alley (see figure 6.5). There are two fireplaces along the west wall, and a number of large windows along the south and east walls.[46] The room has undergone some alterations over the years, but it has survived into the twenty-first century with many of its original features intact. The ceiling in the long room is still 16 feet high, for example, and the original "orchestra" is still present. At the north end of the room is a wall pierced by a large central opening flanked by a doorway on each side (see figure 6.6). The central opening functions much like a proscenium arch and leads the eye into a recessed performance area that apparently functioned as an "orchestra" for eighteenth-century performers. This area measures approximately 25 feet wide and 19 feet deep, but to accommodate an anteroom above the orchestra, and perhaps in an effort to direct the sound outwards into the main room, its ceiling is only 8 feet high.[47] When this feature is added to the dimensions of the long room proper, the result is a respectable total of 1,850 square feet of space for entertaining.

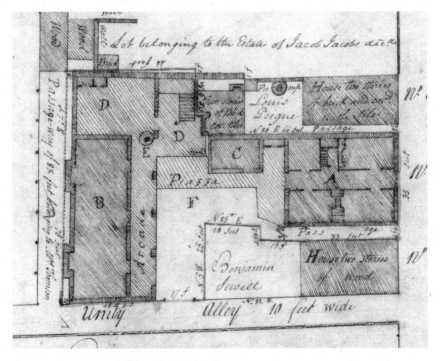

6.5. Plat of Edward McCrady's Tavern (letter A) and Long Room (letter B), surveyed by Joseph Purcell in October 1800. Courtesy of Charleston County RMC

With the closing of the City Tavern in late 1788, McCrady's Long Room became Charleston's principal venue for concerts and other social events over the next several years. Besides the St. Cecilia Society's performances, other organizations such as the St. Andrew's Society, the South Carolina Society, and the city dancing assembly held their meetings and feasts here. Visiting musicians held benefit concerts in the long room, and, for lack of a proper theater at the time, this venue also hosted makeshift dramatic performances.[48] The Society of the Cincinnati entertained George Washington here when he visited Charleston in May 1791, and concluded its elegant dinner for the president with a performance by a "choir of singers." During the summer of 1792 the room was also used to display seven "elegantly superb" pianofortes, recently imported from London on the ship *Britannia*.[49] Even as Charleston's newest and most commodious assembly room, however, McCrady's Long Room apparently did not quite suit the St. Cecilia Society. After the 1790–91 season the society moved its concerts to yet another venue, though this change was not predicated on some trouble with Mr. McCrady. Rather, it was motivated by President Washington's visit to Charleston in May of 1791 and by the society's attempt to secure a more exclusive space for its activities.

6.6. The north end of McCrady's Long Room, showing the recessed "orchestra." Photograph by the author

During Washington's week-long stay in Charleston, the upper floor of the city's waterfront Exchange Building was fitted with amphitheater-style seating for a series of gala events, including a concert sponsored by the St. Cecilia Society. The two-story Exchange, the "noble appearance" of which impressed Josiah Quincy on his arrival in 1773, had been completed in 1771 after nearly four years of construction. It stands on the east side of East Bay Street, at the eastern terminus of Broad Street, and occupies the site of the old Council Chamber that had hosted the earliest advertised concerts in Charleston in the early 1730s. As the principal commercial building for this busy seaport, the central block of the first floor of the Exchange was designed as a public arcade that could be entered from the street to the west or from the harbor to the east through several arched openings (see figure 6.7). The Great Hall or central room of the upper floor is more elegantly appointed and was undoubtedly intended for more exclusive activities. When Charleston was incorporated in 1783, this space was appropriated as the City Hall, and it served as such until 1818. With a floor plan measuring 40 by 46 feet (1,840 square feet), this room is nearly identical in area to McCrady's Long Room, though its nearly square shape stands in contrast to the St. Cecilia Society's previous concert venues.

6.7. The west facade of Charleston's Exchange Building, constructed 1768–71. The Great Hall is in the center of the top floor. Photograph by the author

The acoustical space of this hall is further enhanced by its great height, which is achieved through the use of 14-foot paneled walls and 3-foot crown moldings surmounted by a 6-foot cove ceiling.[50] After much restoration work in the late twentieth century, the Great Hall appears today much as it did in the 1790s. A trio of tall windows in both the east and west walls provide panoramic views of the Cooper River and the city, while large central fireplaces anchor the north and south walls. Twelve columns with capitals of the Ionic order punctuate the perimeter of the room and draw the eye upward to the sky-blue ceiling (see figure 6.8).

President Washington spent a week in Charleston, during which he was feted by a number of local organizations and societies. On the evening of Wednesday, 4 May, the city corporation, comprising the intendant (mayor), city council, and other public officials, held a grand feast and ball for the president in City Hall. The following evening, the St. Cecilia Society, whose membership included the gentlemen of the city corporation, presented a special concert in honor of Washington's visit. Eliza Bowen Ward, a visitor from Rhode Island, attended Wednesday's ball and was invited to the concert. In a letter to Mary Bowen, she described the ball and her reasons for not attending the St. Cecilia's concert:

> I was last night at the *Presidents* ball—and such a ball I never desire to
> be at again—for I was *crowded—jammed*—and *mashed* to *pieces*. . . .
> crammed up in a corner on the fourth seat, elevated it is true but
> there were three seats before us so closely squeezed that not a soul of
> our acquaintance could come within gunshot or rather *tongue-shot* for
> two hours.
>
> I believe you can easily imagine it when I tell you there were
> upwards of four hundred people in the room. After these four seats
> [rows] of ladies quite round the room the whole square was crammed as
> full of gentlemen as it could be to all appearance. . . . to night is the con-
> cert—Mrs. Miller sent to us to go with her . . . the music will be fine and
> the charity boys are to sing. . . . The concert must be half-finished by
> this—but I cannot regret not being there it is so tremendous hot—what
> think [you] of the thermometers being ninety degrees in a passageway—
> they removed it to a dining room and it soon rose to ninety three.[51]

Later reports confirm that the hall was temporarily altered to accommodate the audience, though Miss Ward's allusions to the placement of four-tier amphitheater-style seats around the room provide the best description. A brief newspaper account on Saturday mentioned that the band had "played in the orchestra," suggesting that the musicians were arranged on the floor (or perhaps on a low dais) in the center of the tiered seating. The dimensions and

materials of this seating arrangement are not known, but it must have been
large enough to accommodate a sizeable ensemble. For this concert the St.
Cecilia Society's performing forces were augmented by those of the Amateur
Society (an unknown quantity), thus creating an orchestra of between twenty
and thirty performers, if not more.[52] Added to this band was the choir of St.
Philip's, consisting of about twelve boys from the city's Orphan House.[53]

Notwithstanding Miss Ward's troublesome experience, the St. Cecilia
Society's opinion of its concert at City Hall in May 1791 was not entirely unfa-
vorable, for the following October its managers "resolved, that the concerts
for the ensuing season do commence at the city hall, on *Thursday Evening,* the
13th instant, at seven o'clock."[54] Why the society chose to continue its activities at this municipal facility rather than return to McCrady's commodious,
purpose-built long room is unclear, but this decision may have been motivated by the desire for greater privacy. As with its use of the State House in
1784, the St. Cecilia Society, whose membership included most of the local
elected officials, may have preferred to use its collective political clout to
appropriate a grand public space for its private use rather than share a busy,
multipurpose venue with a host of other individuals and organizations. The
room still served as Charleston's City Hall, however, so the amphitheater-style
seating constructed for Washington's visit must have been made in such a way

6.8. The Great Hall in the Exchange Building. Courtesy of the Old Exchange Building

as to facilitate its temporary removal. The tiered seating was probably disassembled during the meetings of city council, and then raised again for special events such as the concerts of the St. Cecilia Society. The newspaper notices for another very public concert held at City Hall in 1791 confirm this theory. Hoping to draw a large crowd for their 20 October concert to benefit the city's newly founded Orphan House, the musicians forming the Amateur Society advertised that "an amphitheater will be erected for the accommodation of the company."[55]

Despite the prestige and exclusivity afforded by City Hall, this venue also came with practical shortcomings. The square shape of the performance area may have been poorly suited to the dance styles of that period, and the tiered seating undoubtedly complicated the customary transition from concert to ball. The several anterooms flanking the Great Hall may have been too small and too crowded with city records to accommodate the perambulation and conversation of guests during the evenings. Perhaps more important, the building lacked the facilities to meet the food, beverage, and sanitary requirements of large, mixed-sex gatherings. Catered feasts had been presented at the Exchange during the president's visit, of course, but these were very exceptional events. Owing to these deficiencies, the St. Cecilia Society announced in November 1791 that its anniversary meeting, which was to include "much business of the society and of much importance to attend to," would be held at a new location: Williams's Coffee House. Following the disposal its regular business, however, the society reminded its members that "there will be a concert as usual in the evening, at the City Hall." By then end of the 1791–92 concert season, the logistical challenges faced at City Hall forced the St. Cecilia Society to seek yet another venue. At a monthly meeting of the society's managers on 6 February 1792, it was resolved "that on account of the badness of the weather the concert on Thursday the 9th instant should be held at M'Crady's and continued till further notice; and that agreeable to the rules the quarterly meeting of the society should be at the same place on Thursday the 16th inst."[56] Although it is not clear why the weather would have diminished the appeal of the Exchange, it seems likely that the open arcade on the first floor rendered the Great Hall too drafty and cold for the performers and audience to bear during the winter months. Considering the hall's lack of kitchen facilities, the winter weather may have also impeded the delivery of catered refreshments to the venue.

In less than a decade since the renascence of its concerts in 1783, the St. Cecilia Society had held its events in four different venues. In the autumn of 1792 it prepared to commence a new concert season by returning to a space it had deserted the year before. This retrograde move, whether distasteful to the society or not, was again to prove short-lived. In September 1792 Edward

McCrady gave notice of his imminent retirement, and by November John Hartley Harris ("alias William Laycock, formerly of London") assumed proprietorship of the tavern and long room.[57] Although Harris's Tavern continued to be a popular and successful establishment, he catered to a more middle-class, democratically minded clientele, hosting meetings of such groups as the Republican Society, the Ancient York Masons, and the Société Patriotique Française.[58] The St. Cecilia Society's memory of friction with republican elements several years earlier at the City Tavern surely induced its Anglophilic, patrician membership, the majority of whom supported the nascent Federalist Party, to seek a more exclusive venue for its concerts and meetings. John Williams's recently expanded coffeehouse, owned by St. Cecilia member Adam Tunno, provided a suitable alternative.

Williams first opened his Carolina Coffee House at the corner of Tradd and East Bay Streets, overlooking the busy commercial wharves, in December of 1785. By the autumn of 1787, however, he had moved the establishment one block westward on Tradd Street to the northwest corner of Bedon's Alley. Although composed largely of structures used originally for both commercial and residential purposes, the east end of Tradd Street was then becoming more genteel as the city's commercial center crept northward.[59] The Carolina Coffee House—named after the establishment in Birchin Lane that served as the London business office for Carolina merchants from the 1670s well into the nineteenth century—soon became known as the gathering place of upper-class gentlemen and a number of exclusive social organizations. Although this establishment was not the first in Charleston to be styled a "coffeehouse," it was certainly the most enduring.[60]

In the autumn of 1792 John Williams announced to his customers that, "for their better accommodation," he had built two large rooms "fitted up in a stile of particular elegance, and will be ready for the assemblies on Thursday next, great care having been taken to have them well aired, to prevent the danger of ladies taking cold." Shortly thereafter, the managers of the St. Cecilia Society "resolved, that the concerts should commence on the Anniversary, being the 22d instant, at Williams's new room; to begin precisely at seven o'clock in the evening, and to be continued at the same place, every second Thursday during the season. The society are to dine together at Williams's on the anniversary." Tradd Street being rather narrow, and Bedon's Alley even more so, the society's managers attempted to forestall traffic congestion by adding "N.B. It is entreated that carriages will put down with their horses heads towards the bay, and take up with their heads to Church-street."[61]

Despite his assurances, Williams's new room was evidently not sufficiently commodious for the company that patronized his coffeehouse. In August 1793, just before the commencement of the following social season, he announced to the ladies and gentlemen of Charleston "that for their better accommodation than last winter, he has built, and is fitting up additional apartments for their convenience; and assures them that no *expense, taste,* or *attention;* shall be wanting to make the amusements of the approaching season agreeable." Shortly after Williams's announcement, the St. Cecilia Society —just entering its most prosperous era—commenced its 1793–94 concert season at the early date of 5 September. Because of the renovations at Williams's coffeehouse, the society was obliged to give notice that day that "the first concert of the season will be in City Hall This Evening, to begin at seven o'clock." A fortnight later, however, Williams's apartments were finally ready, and the society immediately advertised the continuation of its concert season "at Williams's New Concert Room."[62]

In light of the polite conversation and socialization that accompanied eighteenth-century concerts and dancing assemblies, it is significant that Williams sought to improve his venue by constructing additional "apartments," or adjoining rooms, for use during such entertainments rather than by enlarging or ornamenting the concert room itself. Other than Williams's own description of these spaces. however, no evidence relative to the dimensions of the long room at the Carolina Coffee House has yet been found. Nevertheless, the society's tenure at the Carolina Coffee House for nearly a decade suggests that its size and amenities were sufficient for its exclusive subscription concert series.

Over the next several years, the society's concert season continued along a similar pattern at this venue with little change or incident, though in 1794 the society did feel the need to ask once again "that the gentlemen will direct their servants to draw up their carriages from the Bay towards Church-street, to avoid accident or confusion."[63] The St. Cecilia Society's concerts at Williams's Carolina Coffee House became such an established fixture that other events at this venue occasionally referred to the performance space as "the St. Cecilia Concert room" or "Williams's Concert Room." The most commonly used designation, however, was simply "Williams's Long Room," echoing the generic terminology of previous concert venues in Charleston.[64]

In February of 1799 John Williams gave notice that he was "declining the public business," and by mid-April Catherine Coates had announced that she had taken "those commodious and extensive Buildings, in Tradd-street, known by the name of The Carolina Coffee-House."[65] Accordingly, when the St. Cecilia Society commenced its concert season that October, it gave notice that the performances would take place "at Mrs. Coates's Coffee-House, at the usual hour." Her proprietorship of the Carolina Coffee House continued into early 1802, but the society's tenure at this venue expired shortly before Mrs. Coates's lease on the property.[66] The usual quarterly meeting of the St. Cecilia

Society, scheduled to take place at the coffeehouse on 20 August 1801, was moved with very little advance warning and no explanation to the "hotel" of Francis St. Mary (or François St. Mery) in Queen Street. More important than this sudden change of venue, however, was the concern of the meeting itself: "The members are particularly enjoined to assemble at an early hour, as some business of importance relative to the funds of the society, will be laid before the meeting."[67] Although the topic of this discussion may have been the ongoing litigation against members in arrears, which had commenced in June of 1800, the business at hand could have been the question of removing the society's concerts to a new and perhaps more expensive venue.

In late October 1801 the society announced that "the Concerts for the ensuing season will commence on Thursday next, the 29th inst. at the building late the City Theatre, Church-street." As it had done nearly a decade earlier, when the concerts were first removed to Williams's Coffee House, the managers added instructions for the disposition of carriages: "it is particularly requested that all carriages will set down with their horses heads towards Tradd-street, and take up with their heads towards Broad-street." Two weeks later, when the society's gave notice of its next concert, this new venue was designated "Concert Hall."[68] For the next fifteen seasons, during which the St. Cecilia Society enjoyed a prosperous existence, its concerts were such a regular feature at this new venue that it was occasionally called the "St. Cecilia Society Concert Hall."[69]

Originally built as a theater, Concert Hall had only a brief life as a playhouse, which has been noted by several historians the early American stage. Its long period of use for the performance of music, however, has been all but forgotten, even by local historians.[70] Concert Hall also served as Charleston's largest and most prestigious meeting space during the first two decades of the nineteenth century. The city's elite gathered here for events ranging from orations on morality to civic fetes to performances by East-Indian jugglers.[71] Although it never had exclusive title to this hall, the St. Cecilia Society held more of its concerts here than at any other venue. In fact, the fate of Concert Hall seems to have been closely intertwined with that of the society. For these reasons, and also because of the many extant descriptions of the site, the annals of Concert Hall merit a close examination.

During the twentieth century several scholars published descriptions of the theater that was later converted into Concert Hall. These descriptions exhibit a number of inconsistencies and misunderstandings, however, that have hindered the discovery of its exact location.[72] Despite this confusion, the preponderance of the evidence—of which there is a considerable quantity—clearly demonstrates that Concert Hall (alias French Theater, Church-Street Theater, City Theater) was built on the site of Thomas Pike's Assembly Room.

As with the plan announced by the Union Kilwinning Lodge in 1784 to build a social hall on the foundation of David Douglass's theater, Concert Hall was probably even built on the brick foundation of Pike's earlier venue.[73]

In the years after the February 1783 fire that consumed both Pike's Assembly Room and Douglass's theater, these two lots remained unimproved. Shortly after that fire, a three-story brick double tenement was erected on the lot just south of the ruins of Douglass's theater.[74] In the early twentieth century, this tenement—and the courtyard behind it—was known locally as "Cabbage Row." In DuBose Heyward's novel *Porgy* (1925) and George Gershwin's opera *Porgy & Bess* (1935), however, it was immortalized as "Catfish Row." For those familiar with the geography of Charleston, this landmark may serve as a point of reference for imagining the site of Concert Hall.

In October 1792 Pike's former property was offered for sale and described as being "as valuable a vacant lot as any in the city." Although Pike's Assembly Room had burned in 1783, the lot still contained "an arch way . . . sufficient to receive a carriage" and "the remains of several brick buildings."[75] The property was now in the hands of John Roberts, a tailor who had purchased it from Thomas Pike's assignee, the Reverend Robert Smith. In August 1793 Roberts sold the property to John Sollée (d. 1820), a refugee from the violent slave revolts in St. Domingo who had recently settled in Charleston.[76] Hoping to capitalize on the large influx of other refugees from the West Indies, Sollée embarked on a plan to erect a French-language theater on the vacant lot. During the spring and summer of 1794, the local population knew this new playhouse as the "French Theatre" or "Comedie Francaise."[77] French refugees continued to tread its boards over the next several years, but during the 1794–95 season this venue was called simply the "Theatre, Church-Street," and by November 1795 it was styled the "City Theatre." Well into the nineteenth century, even after its transformation into "Concert Hall," however, each of these titles continued to be used interchangeably to describe the venue built on the ruins of Pike's Assembly Room.

Sollée's theater, by contemporary accounts, was not an especially elegant edifice, nor was it built with a view to timeless permanence. Construction was well underway in early 1794 when, on 23 February, "in consequence of a remarkable high wind, the frame of the new French theater, erected in Church-street, was entirely blown down, and part of the brick work demolished." Despite this major setback, the theater opened on 10 April 1794.[78] The theater was thus built in the brief period of about six weeks, suggesting that the brick remnants of Pike's building may have been substantial enough to hasten its completion.[79] According to Charles Fraser, barely a teenager at the time, the new theater met with the "frantic enthusiasm" of the Charleston public, who were then enamored of all things French. A correspondent calling himself "a Friend to Truth" later explained that the city's inhabitants, "from the laudable motive of encouraging the distressed theatrical performers from St. Domingo, gave so decided a preference to the French Style, as to make it all the rage, and it became the ruin and destruction of the very theater [the Charleston Theatre, in Broad Street] they would have promoted."[80]

After two seasons of competition with the Charleston Theater, the success of Sollée's French Theater caused the other venue to cease operations. In the spring of 1797, a supporter of the dormant Charleston Theater lashed out at Sollée and his company for their competitive practices and called the French Theater a shabby imitation of the Charleston Theater in Broad Street, with "their papered panels, their second hand lusters, their gewgaw trappings, meretriciously displayed in their BARN." To Sollée's defense, "Liberalitas" responded, "and what a scandalous thing it was to say anything against the house, to call it a barn, just because they do not choose to run themselves over head and ears in debt to gild and ornament without being able to pay for it." Applauding the economy of this theater, he added, "a good piece may be as well represented in the Church Street Theatre as to the house, as in Covent Garden or any other of the elegant London Theatres that make such a noise in the world."[81]

Like Pike's earlier venue, Sollée's theater was set back approximately 70 feet westward from Church Street. Similarly the French Theater was accessed from the street by a narrow passageway, about 12 feet wide and 52 feet long, which bisected the lot.[82] In an advertisement promoting her benefit night at the French Theater in the summer of 1794, Mme. Placide assured the public "that the yard leading to the theater is rendered commodious for the reception of carriages."[83] Despite this improvement, the yard was still exposed to the elements. On reaching the western end of the passageway leading from Church Street, patrons were obliged to stop at a gate before proceeding approximately 20 feet further to the theater's lobby entrance. In January 1796, after an evening of inclement weather frustrated those attempting to enter the theater, Sollée gave notice that "for the accommodation of the Ladies, the passage from the gate [to the theater] shall be immediately covered, and tickets will be delivered at the gate, to prevent delay and confusion at the door."[84] The passage from the street to the gate was still exposed, however, and thus a source of annoyance to patrons of the theater. In the midst of complaints about his management of the theater in March 1798, Sollée sought to appease his critics by promising to pave and cover the entire passageway from Church Street to the theater's lobby.[85]

According to newspaper advertisements in the late 1790s, Sollée's theater included a pit, upper and lower boxes, and a gallery—the standard arrangement of many eighteenth-century theaters.[86] There were apparently several chandeliers suspended from the ceiling, for in November 1799 "the Middle

Chandelier, belonging to the Church-street Theater" was advertised as part of a sheriff's sale, "levied on as the Property of John Sollee, at the suit of William Brown."[87] Although it may have been smaller than the Charleston Theater and some theaters in New York and Philadelphia, it was not an unusually small venue. While in Amsterdam in March 1797, Mary Stead Pinckney, second wife of Charles Cotesworth Pinckney, wrote to her niece Mary Izard in South Carolina that she had attended that city's French theater. Comparing this venue to those in Charleston, she remarked "this theater is very neat, but smaller than that of Church Street."[88]

In February 1796, almost two years after opening the theater, Sollée advertised the opening of a "Long Room lately built adjoining the City Theater . . . for the accommodation of the Public . . . as a Coffee-House."[89] On the heels of this advertisement, the partnership of James Claret and John Michel announced their intention "to open a Coffee-Room, in the City Theater, situate in Church-street; where they will have every kind of suitable Liquors," and further noted that "as the intended Coffee-Room has its entrance inside of the City Theater, they give notice, that every day of Performance, none can be admitted in the Coffee Room, without a play ticket, from the hours of two o'clock in the afternoon." Messrs. Claret and Michel dissolved their partnership in June 1796, but the "Coffee Rooms of the City Theater" remained open for many more years under the proprietorship of John Sollée.[90] Receptive to a diverse clientele and notorious for spirited revelry, Sollée's coffeehouse inevitably drew the ire of some of his neighbors. One high-minded citizen implored the City Guard and the elected warden of this quarter to perform their duty "to suppress all vice and immorality in the city," especially that conducted "at the sink of dissipation, the long-room of the City Theater."[91]

In the final years of the eighteenth century, Sollée's theater was further expanded and improved. In March 1798 Sollée announced, "the theater is to be enlarged ten feet, the addition in brick, and covered with slate." In January 1799 he added that the City Theater was "undergoing an extensive alteration, being considerably enlarged and beautified, surrounded by a Brick Wall, and secured by a Terrace on each side of the Roof." Two months later, however, an accident occurred in which "the lobby, leading from the lower boxes to the stair case, gave way in an instant, by which twenty or thirty persons were precipitated upon the croud [sic] of people under them, who were at the same time pressing out of the pit." In order to allay public concerns for the safety of the theater, Sollée published a testimonial from the city's master carpenters that the building had been duly inspected before the commencement of the season, and that the repairs to the lobby would be similarly inspected.[92]

The last dramatic performance at the City Theater took place on 28 March 1800, after which Alexander Placide and his company of comedians transferred back to the Charleston Theater in Broad Street. Sollée later stated that he had agreed with the managers of the Charleston Theater that "the amusements of the friends of Drama, shall not be disturbed hereafter by any opposition between the two Theatres; the principal condition inserted in the written agreement being that the City Theater shall be shut up for any kind of Dramatic performances whatever."[93] In accordance with this agreement, Sollée endeavored to find a new use for his Church Street property. At the end of 1800, he announced: "The City Theater has been converted, at a very great expense, into elegant and roomy accommodations for Public Balls, Concerts, &c. The Anacreontic Concert Room, is by far superior to any of the kind in America, and bids defiance to those of Europe, whether for ornament, site or convenience. The said room shall be lighted up This Evening, from six o'clock to nine, to shew to the curious that what is said is not exaggerated. N.B. On New-Year's Day, there will be a Masquerade Ball, in the evening, to last till midnight." A second masquerade ball was announced for mid-January 1801, for which "proper improvements and accommodation have been made since the late Ball for the greatest conveniency of those who are fond of the above amusement." Sollée reported a week later that owing to "the great encouragement given to the Masquerade entertainments," these balls would be continued at the "Concert Room." Confirming that the hall was still arranged as a theater, however, Sollée added that, "according to some friendly advice, proper regulations shall be established. No admittance on the stage but for the Masks. The visitors are requested to stay in the boxes, which are appropriated for themselves only, and may hold five hundred people."[94]

The success of his masquerade balls provoked Sollée to propose an even more extensive plan. On 19 January 1801 he announced that he had "converted the whole of his theater in such a manner as to afford to the city a new kind of entertainments, not only for large societies, but also for public amusements, such as balls, concerts, &c." The new entertainments that Sollée proposed bore a strong resemblance to the long-established private activities of the St. Cecilia Society, however. At the refurbished theater, he announced plans for "the Anacreontic Concert," an annual series of twelve performances "consisting chiefly of vocal music with accompaniments of instruments," which "will always be over before nine o'clock, so as to let the subscribers to the said concert have a ball which will last till twelve o'clock." Like the St. Cecilia concerts, Sollée stated, "the music for the concert and ball shall be executed by the same band and well selected among the professors of music." This proposal may have been designed to attract citizens excluded from the St. Cecilia Society, but not unlike that elite organization, Sollée's Anacreontic Concert was to be limited to one hundred subscribers who would each "have the right to bring two ladies with him."[95]

Sollée continued to improve his venue, advertising in late January that "many alterations have also been made since the last ball, and there is a private passage for the spectators to go to the Refreshment Rooms, without crossing the stage as before, which precaution will avoid much confusion. None but those with masks shall be admitted on the stage." By the middle of March 1801 the *City Gazette* was reporting that "a floor was erected over the pit," but that the "lower boxes, of an amphitheatrical shape" were still in place. Later that month Sollée repeated that "the hall is to be converted in to the form of a Concert Hall," which he zealously promoted as "the most convenient place in the city for any public festival for the citizens of Charleston."[96] The plans for the Anacreontic Concert must have evaporated, however, as no mention of that new series appears after the commencement of the St. Cecilia Society's 1801–2 concert season at this venue.

In addition to transferring its concert performances to the new Concert Hall, the St. Cecilia Society announced in November 1801 that its anniversary meeting would take place "at the Long Room in Church-street, adjoining Concert-Hall."[97] That space (or perhaps its staff) must not have been quite ready for the accommodation of such an event, for on the day of the meeting the location was suddenly changed to the house of Margaret Daniel, a free woman of color who sold pastries in Church Street.[98] Not until August 1803 did the St. Cecilia Society commence its business meetings at "Sollee's Long Room in Church-street, adjoining the Concert Room."[99] After one year of meetings there, however, the business meetings were transferred back to the Carolina Coffee House, where they remained for two years, through August 1806.[100] For the next decade after August 1806, all the St. Cecilia Society's business meetings—with only four exceptions—took place at the long room adjoining Concert Hall.[101]

Although the St. Cecilia Society regularly held its concerts at Concert Hall in the early years of the nineteenth century, it did not hold an exclusive lease on the property. Following the society's first concert there in October 1801, the former theater was also the site of almost all other concerts that took place in Charleston over the next two decades. Just as with Pike's (or, more precisely, Valk's) rooms in the mid-1770s, Concert Hall and the rooms adjoining it were often used for large auctions—principally of furniture—in the early decades of the nineteenth century.[102] The Reverend Abiel Abbot, visiting Charleston in the autumn of 1818, recorded his impressions of a visit to Concert Hall: "It is an extensive room, and was hung all round with prints to be exposed at auction; among them is a considerable number executed by eminent artists."[103] Most of these public sales took place within the hall itself, but several were advertised as taking place "under the Piazza of the Church-street Theatre."[104]

As these advertisements suggest, the physical transformation from theater to concert hall was a gradual process. The theater's box seats, for example, were still present in the former French Theatre during the spring of 1801. Such seating in eighteenth-century theaters typically required interior pillars for support—an architectural feature that partially obstructed the view of some audience members. By December 1802, however, advertisements for a performance of ventriloquism and "miscellaneous experiments" at this venue stated "that new arrangements are made at the Theatre Church-street, so that all the spectators will have an opportunity of seeing without interruption."[105] A year later, in November 1803, Sollée announced further alterations to this property, which he now called the "State Coffee-House and Restaurateur Hotel." With his typical flair for hyperbole, Sollée boasted "that since the existence of this city, no plan of the kind could be better recommended for its advantage towards the public utility, and adapted to the conveniences of the best part of the company." Sollée's description of this venue provides many more details as to its internal arrangement:

> Among the citizens of this place, (and even strangers) there are but few unacquainted with the extensive lot, and the many different kinds of conveniences adjoining the City Theatre. It is to avail himself of these conveniences, and turn them to the use of the Public, that the subscriber has lately made a considerable alteration in the distribution of the Concert Hall, Assembly Room and Card Room, which stand on the same floor, give a beautiful prospect of upwards of two hundred feet. There is no such public accommodation in the Northern States. The Concert Hall is 66 feet, by 40; the Assembly room is nearly 80 feet by 30; and the Card Room is 40 feet by 24. Consequently, the three Rooms together, are calculated to contain an assembly of nearly 300, who may dance and play cards, at ease; and what has never been seen in America, all the company may sit at supper in the same room. As it appears from the disposition of many members, that the Assemblies are to be, this season, at the place above mentioned, the subscriber is very happy to announce, not only to the members who compose the St. Cœcilia Society, the Assemblies, Clubs, &c. but also to the Public in general, that he has contracted with two white Cooks, of distinguished abilities, who will attend, not only Dinners and Entertainments bespoken, but also the Restaurateur business, in its various branches, and in a style hitherto unknown in Charleston. All the buildings adjoining the City Theatre, will be appropriated for the use of Assemblies, Societies, Clubs, Select Parties, &c. Coffee-House, under the denomination of the State Coffee-House, and Restaurateur Hotel.[106]

Sollée continued to promote his redesignated venue into 1804, apparently with some success. In January of that year he assured the Charleston public of an orderly house by emulating the practices of the St. Cecilia Society: "To avoid all kind of confusion, no more than one hundred tickets will be sold to gentlemen, with the right of admittance for one or two ladies, for each ticket. Refreshments will be provided, and the St. Cecilia Society's rules and decorum strictly observed."[107] As with many his other ventures, however, Sollée's plan appears to have stalled. Although the new physical arrangement of his property found ample patronage, the designation "State Coffee-House and Restaurateur Hotel" appeared in but a single advertisement.

In September 1809 the St. Cecilia Society called an extra general meeting and an extra meeting of its managers at "Mr. Sollee's Long Room."[108] The minutes of these meetings are not extant, but the meetings were probably held to discuss the further alteration of Concert Hall to better suit the society's needs. Some sort of construction began in the early autumn, and in early November the continuing renovations delayed the start of the society's concert season. "The Concerts will commence," the society then announced, "as soon as Mr. Sollee's new Concert Hall is finished, which will probably be in the course of 10 or 15 days." The society's anniversary meeting was held, as usual, at "Mr. Sollee's Rooms" on 22 November, and the first concert was finally performed on 30 November.[109] No further advertisement or description of this "new Concert Hall" appeared, suggesting that it was merely an improvement of the existing concert room.

The fortnightly concerts of the St. Cecilia Society continued for several more years at Concert Hall, which in the spring of 1813 was still considered "the handsomest room of the city."[110] During 1814, however, the hardships of war with Britain affected both the society and its concert venue. The society advertised only one concert during the 1814–15 season and that not until well after the restoration of peace, in March 1815. John Sollée's Concert Hall suffered a similar setback in 1814, when years of financial confusion culminated in the property being wrested from his control.

From the beginning Sollée's financial management of his Church Street property had been the subject of much criticism. When he purchased the property in 1793, he inherited from its previous owner a mortgage that haunted him for years to come. During the hall's tenure as a theater, he and the managers of the Charleston Theatre, led by Alexander Placide, had very public disagreements about the payments of the annual lease and the existing mortgage. Placide and his partners claimed that often they had been forced to make both payments because of Sollée's tangled finances. Indeed, the records of the Charleston County courts from the turn of the nineteenth century show that filing suit against John Sollée was a popular activity. To the chagrin of many parties, Sollée transferred title of the property into his wife's name, thus using her comfortable inheritance as protection against his own shortcomings. Nevertheless, Concert Hall (or at least a seven-year lease thereupon) was many times scheduled for public auction for nonpayment of annual taxes. These sales appear to have been averted, but by 1814 the friction over Sollée's financial management of the property had come to a head when the Court of Equity judged that the lot Sollée originally purchased in August 1793 should be auctioned off to the highest bidder.

In advance of the sale, which took place on 12 July 1814, a small plat was drawn to illustrate the "Plan of a lot on which Mr. Sollee's Theater is built" (see figure 6.9). It shows a "passage" approximately 11 feet wide leading 52 feet and 6 inches westward from Church Street to the main body of the lot, which is 50 feet wide. At the end of the passage is a small (probably fenced) yard approximately 20 feet deep, leading to a "Lobby" between 25 and 30 feet wide and approximately 75 to 80 feet deep. Adjoining the western end of the lobby is a "Long Room" approximately 40 feet wide and nearly 100 feet long. Both structures lie along the northern line of the lot and are apparently bounded by the brick wall Sollée added in January 1799. There is no barrier on the southern edge of the lot, indicating free access to the adjoining property, on which Sollée had constructed other buildings.[111] This plat, which provides only the outline of the lot and its buildings, depicts the property as it appeared after two decades of construction and renovation. Its lack of detail leaves many questions unanswered, especially that of the internal arrangement of the various rooms within these two buildings. By comparing the plat

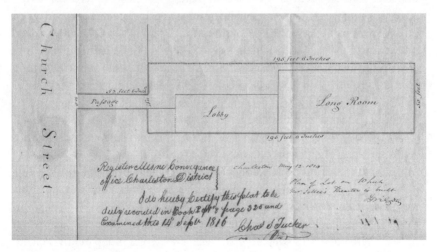

6.9. Plat of John Sollée's Concert Hall, May 1814. From the collections of the South Carolina Historical Society

to John Sollée's earlier descriptions of the venue, however, this sparse representation becomes more meaningful.

Sollée's November 1803 description of the former theater's internal arrangement specifies the existence of three rooms all standing "on the same floor": a concert room ("66 feet by 40"), an assembly room ("nearly 80 feet by 30"), and a card room ("40 feet by 24"). Although depicted without exact dimensions, the two structures in this 1814 plat conform to Sollée's earlier description. The estimated proportions of the 1814 lobby match closely those of Sollée's 1803 assembly room, and the combined dimensions of the concert and card rooms, each 40 feet wide, fit neatly into the long room depicted in the plat. As described in 1803, therefore, Sollée's Concert Hall encompassed 2,640 square feet of floor space. If the separation between that space and the adjoining card room was later removed, or was composed of moveable dividers such as pocket doors, then the combined floor space of Sollée's Long Room (approximately 90 by 40 feet) would create an impressive 3,600 square feet of performance space. This figure exceeds that of Pike's Assembly Room (80 by 40 feet), the foundations of which were ostensibly used for the construction of Sollée's theater in 1794. By remembering that the depth of Sollée's theater was "enlarged ten feet" in the spring of 1798, however, the 1814 survey can be accepted as accurately reflecting the various alterations described in the Charleston newspapers over the previous two decades.

The highest bidder at the July 1814 auction of Concert Hall was William Grogan, a Charleston attorney representing the English family of Sollée's wife, Harriet Neyle Sollée. Grogan later sold the property back to Sollée's wife but placed it in care of several trustees and out of her husband's reach.[112] Mrs. Sollée was represented in this second transaction by her son, Frederick W. Sollée, as well as by Henry H. Bacot, then treasurer of the St. Cecilia Society, and Samuel Prioleau, then a manager of the society. Whether these men acted as agents of the St. Cecilia Society is not known, but the society's long relationship with Concert Hall and John Sollée suggests that it felt some interest in the property.

Grogan's transfer of the Concert Hall property to Harriet Sollée, which was finalized in June 1816, authorized her to "occupy such part of the said premises as shall be deemed necessary for the residence of herself and her family," as they had apparently done since 1793. The conveyance also permitted Mrs. Sollée to rent or lease any of the other several buildings on the property for any length of time she thought proper, though not exceeding two years.[113] During his tenure as proprietor, John Sollée had executed such rental and lease agreements, in which the St. Cecilia Society was apparently a client. It appears that Mrs. Sollée leased Concert Hall to the French dancing master Pierre Tastet, for his weekly dancing assemblies soon became the principal attraction at the hall and he its principal spokesman in the ensuing several years. Tastet first held his annual pupils' ball at Concert Hall in April 1813, and by the autumn of the following year moved his weekly "long rooms" to this venue.[114] Then in the autumn of 1816, just a few months after the formal transfer of this Church Street property into Harriett Sollée's ownership, the St. Cecilia Society's concerts were once again removed to the Carolina Coffee House in Tradd Street. Although the society published no explanation for this move, the sale of Concert Hall and Tastet's strong presence there may have been a contributing factor. Tastet's own advertisements suggest another motivation, however: that the hall was falling into disrepair and was no longer elegant enough for the society's entertainments.

In the autumn of 1815 a room was added above Concert Hall, perhaps lowering the ceiling height of the concert room.[115] This alteration was serious enough that the managers of a benefit concert that October "deemed it prudent to ascertain the security of Concert Hall" and to publish a "certificate for the satisfaction of the public" from a committee of house carpenters. Having been called on "to survey the alterations made, and to ascertain the strength of the Building," the carpenters reported that they were "unanimously of opinion, that it is substantial, and can accommodate, with safety, any Company the Concert Hall may contain, be it ever so numerous."[116]

In October 1816 Tastet announced that on account of the "elegant alterations that are going on at Concert Hall, and the damp weather which prevented its being finished at time," his weekly dancing assemblies there would be temporarily postponed. Tastet was forced to delay his "long rooms" until early November, however, "on account of the freshness of the Painting at Concert Hall."[117] In May 1817 an advertisement for Mr. Blanchard's exhibitions of "lofty tumbling" and rope dancing at Concert Hall included a testimonial from four master carpenters, who "having been called upon to give our opinion, and to survey the work done to a wall adjoining, but not immediately connected with the Concert-Hall, declare, that the props now put up to the said wall, will make it secure, and free from danger, as long as they remain there."[118] The following November, Tastet once again advertised the commencement of his dancing season at "the Concert Hall, Church-street, which has undergone a complete repair, and is decorated in a good style."[119] Signifying that the public's patronage of Concert Hall had waned, Tastet soon announced that "Gentlemen belonging to the St. Cecilia Society, Charleston Assemblies, Cotillion Parties, and Social Assemblies, who choose to witness the improvements made at Concert Hall, for the best accommodation of societies, are welcome to their free entrance, and will confer a favor by doing so to either Mr. Tastet or the Proprietor." Even in the autumn of 1819, the former patrons of Concert Hall were being solicited to return to this venue. Tastet, "having taken the lease, jointly with [the musician] Mr. Andral," again announced "they are repairing it in such a manner as to make it convenient and agreeable for the use of Societies and select Parties."[120] Their pleas went unanswered, however, as neither the St. Cecilia Society nor any other of Charleston's elite social clubs were again regular patrons of Concert Hall. As late as 1823 the hall was promoted as having been "lately repaired in carefully examined by faithful workmen," but the last advertised musical performance there took place in April 1825.[121] Two months later, the "large Wooden Building, generally known as Concert Hall," including a "large handsome Chandelier, and a number of Wooden Benches," was sold at auction and removed from Mrs. Sollée's lot.[122]

In November 1816, four months after the formal transfer of Concert Hall to Mrs. Sollée's trustees, the St. Cecilia Society's concerts and business meetings returned to the Carolina Coffee House.[123] In the fifteen years since the St. Cecilia Society had last held its concerts in this coffeehouse, the property had changed hands several times. In October 1816, James Whitehurst announced that he had leased the property and that "the Ball and Supper Rooms are handsomely painted and fitted up for parties." A year later Whitehurst repeated that "the *Ball Room* is commodiously and well fitted up for the convenience of Balls and Cotillion Parties."[124] When President James Monroe visited Charleston in the spring of 1819, however, the St. Cecilia Society sought a different, even more exclusive venue for its "Concert and Ball, in honor of the President of the United States."[125] This event, held on a Saturday evening some two months after the conclusion of the society's regular season, took place at the hall of the South Carolina Society, situated in Meeting Street one block south of Broad Street and just a few yards west of Concert Hall (see figure 6.10). This large two-story brick building on a raised basement, completed in 1804 and still in use, contains a commodious ballroom on the second floor measuring 73 feet deep and 29 feet wide (2,117 square feet). Crowned by a cove ceiling 18 feet high, this room also includes a small semicircular music gallery at the eastern end, mounted above columns and entablature of the Composite order (see figure 6.11).[126] On the evening of 1 May 1819, about 150 gentlemen dined with President Monroe at St. Andrew's Hall in Broad Street. Afterward "the company retired at an early hour, to attend the splendid Concert and Ball given by the *St. Cecilia Society,* at the South Carolina Hall; which was attended by a very large assemblage of Ladies, to whom the President had the pleasure of paying his respects.[127]

Unlike its concert for President Washington nearly thirty years before, this grand event did not induce the St. Cecilia Society to continue its regular entertainments at the hall of the South Carolina Society. In the autumn of 1819 the society's concerts and balls were resumed at the Carolina Coffee

House, now operated by R. Heriot.[128] At just over fifty years old, the society's subscription concert series was now older than any of the available performing spaces in Charleston. Like those structures, the series and the society's commitment to concert patronage were showing signs of age and fatigue. Fashionable balls replaced concerts with increasing frequency during the

6.10. South Carolina Society Hall, west facade. This structure was completed in 1804; the portico was added in 1825. Photograph by the author

1819–20 season, and at last, in the spring of 1820, the society performed its final regular concert in the old ball room of the Carolina Coffee House.

More than five decades after its founding, the St. Cecilia Society's concert series had migrated across Charleston's urban landscape, inhabiting eight different venues, all within a narrow geographic area. Without its own proprietary concert space, the society was obliged to adapt to a variety of changing circumstances in order to secure the degree of privacy and comfort required for its fashionable entertainments. Despite this inconvenience, the performing spaces available in eighteenth- and early-nineteenth-century Charleston were not inconsistent with those used by subscription concert societies in contemporary Europe. In the era before the advent of the large, Romantic symphony orchestra, concert organizations rarely built halls for their own exclusive use. Multipurpose rooms situated within structures catering to a variety of other activities were in fact the norm rather than the exception for concerts during the Classical period. Ranging in size from just over 1,000 square feet in the Council Chamber of the South Carolina State House to 3,600 potential square feet in John Sollée's Concert Hall, the venues patronized by the St. Cecilia Society were neither unusually small nor extravagantly

6.11. The east end of the ballroom of South Carolina Society Hall. Photograph by the author

grand in comparison with those on the other side of the Atlantic. Performing space was not the only requirement for the society's events, of course. A genteel setting, auxiliary spaces for conversation and refreshments, and some measure of security from intrusion were also important elements contributing to the success or failure of these concerts. All eight of the halls patronized by the St. Cecilia Society during the tenure of its concert series fulfilled these requirements, though with varying degrees of satisfaction. Some of the society's venue choices were clearly precipitated by circumstances beyond its control, while others were motivated by the appearance of fresh opportunities. In either case, however, these migrations reflect the society's perpetual desire to capitalize on its collective social status in order to engage the most fashionable and commodious rooms available in the city.

7

The Performers, 1766–1792

THE STORIED WEALTH AND CULTURAL REFINEMENT that characterized Charleston during the late eighteenth and early nineteenth centuries endowed the city's elite families with both the means and the desire to cultivate a musical atmosphere emulating that found in the urban centers of contemporary Britain. As a testament to the success of their efforts, Charleston developed a reputation on both sides of the Atlantic for providing alluring opportunities to professional musicians. Foremost among the reasons for the city's attractiveness to performers was, of course, the subscription concert series of the St. Cecilia Society. Arising from an association of amateur performers in the 1760s, the society actively sought to enlarge and improve its retinue of musicians, creating a respectably sized ensemble within the first decade of its existence. Throughout the remaining years of its concert activity, the society "was long celebrated for its liberal encouragement of musical talent," as former concert manager Charles Fraser remembered, "for no performer of any reputation ever came to Charleston without receiving its patronage."[1] While the society's own records of its relationships with professional musicians are lost, the surviving fragmentary and circumstantial evidence clearly supports the spirit of Fraser's assertion. By encouraging amateur as well as professional musicians over a span of five decades, the patronage of the St. Cecilia Society played a significant role in both increasing and sustaining Charleston's musical population.

When viewed as a whole, the fragmentary evidence of the society's patronage of musical talent forms a rewarding chronological narrative. This chapter will examine the evidence from the first half of the society's concert-giving era, from 1766 through 1792. During this quarter century of activity, the society began as an association of amateur performers and continued to rely on nonprofessional talent throughout its decades of concert patronage. In its early years the society also established relationships with resident professional musicians who had emigrated from Europe. By the early 1770s the concert series was successful enough that its managers began the active recruiting of high-caliber performers to Charleston. The Revolutionary War scattered most of the musicians forming the St. Cecilia Society's orchestra, leaving it with a much-depleted roster at the war's conclusion in 1783. In the first decade of recovery after the war, however, the society reestablished a band of musicians by patronizing resident performers as well as those drawn to Charleston by the city's reputation for musical taste.

Gentlemen Amateurs

According to the memoir of Charles Fraser, whose Scottish-born father, Alexander, had been a founding member of the St. Cecilia Society in 1766, this musical organization was "originally an association of gentlemen amateurs, who met together to indulge a common taste and to pass an agreeable hour."[2] This statement is consistent with musical practices in mid-eighteenth-century Europe, especially in the United Kingdom, where subscription concert series during the second half of the eighteenth century regularly included amateur performers. In an age before the emergence of professional orchestras independent of court and church, amateurs and professionals were familiar companions.

Among the numerous subscription concert societies that appeared in eighteenth-century Britain, the participation of gentlemen amateurs was a ubiquitous phenomenon. In fact the rise of such concert organizations was inextricably linked to the presence of amateur performers. Since Britain's population of professional musicians was concentrated in London, concerts there inevitably enjoyed a higher percentage of hired performers. Outside London, however, concert societies were largely composed of amateurs, and one could just as easily take an instrument and perform as sit in the audience and listen.[3] From the founding of the Edinburgh Musical Society in 1728, the members' participation in the weekly concerts was mandatory. Despite a relaxation of this rule as the society expanded, a "reasonable degree" of musical competence continued to be the first requirement for membership.[4] In his 1777 London essay, "Some Thoughts on the Performance of Concert Music," Robert Bremner directed his practical advice to the amateurs who participate in concert orchestras, or, in his words, "those gentlemen who laudably meet together to improve, and feast on their own musical performances."[5] Viewed in context of these British societies, the participation of gentlemen—and even lady—amateurs in the concerts of Charleston's St. Cecilia Society should be understood as the continuation of a well-established tradition.

The love of music was "an early characteristic of the people of Charleston," Fraser wrote, "and very generally cultivated by them as an accomplishment."

Fraser himself played keyboard instruments, and his mentor and much older brother, Alexander Jr. (1750–1798), may have fostered his early musical studies.[6] In the 1790s the two shared a sketchbook that contains a rather juvenile pencil portrait of a violinist who might be Alexander, a St. Cecilia manager through most of that decade (see figure 7.1). Evidence taken from the city's colonial-era newspapers also supports Fraser's remark about early amateurs. In 1753 the German immigrant musician Frederick Grunzweig advertised to teach a variety of instruments and to instruct his students "so as to enable them to play the most difficult pieces of music in concert."[7] For his benefit concert in the autumn of 1760, Edward Wallace received the assistance of "the Gentlemen who are the best Performers, both in Town and Country."[8] In Charleston in the early 1760s, remembered George Milligen-Johnston, there were "often Concerts of vocal and instrumental Music, generally performed by Gentlemen."[9] For his "Concert of Vocal and Instrumental Musick" in the autumn of 1765, Thomas Pike was assisted "by the Gentlemen of the place."[10] Reflecting on the cultural development of the state, David Ramsay noted in his *History of South-Carolina* (1809) that music occupied the attention of many amateurs, though with less success than dancing. Excellence in music, observed Ramsay,

7.1. Pencil sketch of an unknown violinist, probably by Charles Fraser, ca. 1793. From a sketchbook titled "Sketches from Nature," on deposit at the South Carolina Historical Society from the Estate of Maud Winthrop Gibbon

"requires not only a natural talent, but sedulous attention and long practice. There are many in Carolina, who, possessing all these advantages, arrive at a distinguished eminence, but more, who after spending considerable sums of money, scarcely exceed mediocrity, and soon forget the smattering they had previously acquired."[11] The praise of one's peers, especially that of young ladies, was indeed a powerful incentive for young gentlemen of that era to labor at music. When "Lucinda" complained publicly about the discordant sounds of a gentleman practicing the flute near her home in 1805, for example, "Old South" defended his noble efforts by observing that "young men, fond of pleasing amiable females, are often persuaded to attempt difficulties, of any *nature*, which might render themselves agreeable to the *softer* sex."[12]

Musical instruments are listed in the estate inventories of a number of the approximately two hundred men identified as members of the St. Cecilia Society up to 1820. Keyboard instruments are especially common, but German (transverse) flutes and violins are also frequently found.[13] Many of the men identified as members of the St. Cecilia Society, and many probable members from that same social sphere, are known to have been practicing amateur musicians. A few examples will prove sufficient to illustrate this point. The Pinckney brothers, Charles Cotesworth and Thomas, are best remembered for their active role in local, national, and international politics, but during quiet periods of the American Revolution they both passed the hours playing cello. They most likely acquired this skill during their long youthful years in London, as did the Drayton brothers, William Henry and Charles, who had violin tutors while studying abroad in the early 1760s. Arthur Middleton is known to have performed on the German flute, an accomplishment no doubt acquired similarly during his studies in London. William Loughton Smith spent much of his time in London during the Revolution playing violin with a group of other gentlemen amateurs. The cosmopolitan merchant Joseph Dulles was remembered as an accomplished performer on the piano, violin, and flute. John Stevens Cogdell, grandson of the English organist John Stevens, was said to be proficient on the French horn as well as keyboard instruments.[14] The English-born Reverend Henry Purcell, rector of St. Michael's after the Revolution, was probably not related to the renowned seventeenth-century composer of the same name, but, quoting a seventeenth-century musical rebus written in honor of the celebrated musician, the man of God was similarly described as one "who in Musick's compleat."[15]

The participation of amateur performers was a consistent feature of the St. Cecilia Society's concerts from its inception in 1766 until their cessation in 1820. Gentlemen amateurs were to be found primarily among the orchestra, but occasionally stepped forward to present songs, perform chamber music, and perhaps act as concerto soloists. Such participation was not confined to this exclusive society, however, as there is copious evidence that amateurs regularly performed at the more public benefit and charity concerts in Charleston during the same period.[16] A November 1772 concert given to raise money for improvements to Pike's Assembly Room, the St. Cecilia Society's concert venue, advertised that the "vocal part" would be performed by "a Gentleman, who does it merely to oblige on this Occasion." In September 1788 the St. Cecilia Society was preparing to have some of its sheet music bound and asked that any "gentlemen of the society" with the society's music in their possession return it to the managers. For her benefit concert in April 1806, Antoinette La Roque was "assisted by all the gentlemen of the Orchestra, with the addition of some Amateurs in the instrumental part." The makeup of this orchestra was more clearly identified in the advertisements for her benefit concert in April 1807, at which Miss La Roque was accompanied by "the Gentlemen of the Orchestra of the St. Cecilia Society, and other Amateurs." For his benefit concert in March 1817, Mr. Norton announced that "the Orchestra will be full—some of the Amateurs have consented to give their assistance." Although the St. Cecilia Society's concerts ended in the spring of 1820, amateur participation in Charleston's concert life continued for many years. For example the advertisements for Mr. Nicolas's benefit in May 1821 stated "the Orchestra will be numerous, as most of the Professors, and several of the Amateurs have volunteered their services." The orchestra for Mr. Aimé's concert in July 1823 was similarly "composed of Gentlemen Professors and Amateurs of this City."[17]

Gentlemen were not the only nonprofessionals to appear before concert audiences in Charleston. Lady amateurs also appeared in concerts as both instrumentalists and vocalists, but, as in European concerts of the day, they were not found among the body of the orchestra. Their instrumental appearances were restricted to the role of concerto soloists or perhaps in an ensemble, such as in a song or duet performance.[18] Speaking of the ladies of Charleston in the early 1760s, for example, George Milligen-Johnston noted "many sing well, and play upon the Harpsichord and Guitar with great skill." Peter Valton's benefit concert in February 1773 included "among other Select Pieces . . . A Concerto on the Harpsichord, By a Lady, a Pupil of Mr. Valton's." During the British occupation of Charleston during the American Revolution, the benefit concerts of both Gaetano Franceschini and John Abercromby included "a Harpsichord Concerto by a Lady" and "a Concerto Solo upon the Harpsichord, by a Lady." Miss La Roque's benefit concert in April 1807, accompanied by "the Gentlemen of the Orchestra of the St. Cecilia Society, and other Amateurs," included "a lady of considerable merit as a performer on the Harp." At P. H. Taylor's benefit concert in March 1816, managed by three gentlemen of the St. Cecilia Society, a "Lady amateur" performed a song "in the style of the celebrated Signora Catalani" and a duet with German guitarist Charles Thieneman.[19]

Despite the large number of references to the participation of amateurs in concerts in Charleston between 1766 and 1820, no evidence has yet been found to positively identify any of the amateur performers who participated in the concerts of the St. Cecilia Society. Amateurs, according to the social mores of the day, performed for their own enjoyment and eschewed any public recognition of their efforts or merits. For this reason their names were never mentioned in connection with these performances. The ability to perform in concert was itself a sign of one's cultural refinement and one's financial status (having ample leisure time to practice), but to have allowed one's name to appear in print would have been viewed as either a dishonorable lack of modesty or a sign of financial distress.

Since it is not possible to reconstruct the number of amateur performers at the society's concerts, it is also impossible to know the proportion of amateurs to professionals, or how this ratio changed as the society evolved over its first five decades. While it is known that the participation of gentlemen amateur performers in concerts continued in Charleston beyond the end of the St. Cecilia Society's concert activity, it may be likely that the number and proficiency of these performers declined in the early decades of the nineteenth century. Owing to the increasing technical demands of concert music in the early nineteenth century, as well as changing cultural values in the early Romantic period, the decrease of amateur participation in concerts during the first half of the nineteenth century is widely acknowledged—in Charleston, throughout the United States, and abroad.[20] Despite the lack of concrete evidence, therefore, it is probably safe to hypothesize that the contingent of amateurs performing in the society's orchestra was smaller near the end of the St. Cecilia Society's concert-giving era than in previous decades.

Early "Masters"

Having begun as "an association of gentlemen amateurs," the St. Cecilia Society was, according to Fraser, "afterwards increased in numbers and resources."[21] No orchestra rosters have survived to document this increase, but circumstantial evidence suggests the size of the society's band probably doubled in the years between its founding in 1766 and the outbreak of the American Revolution. While part of this increase can be attributed to the growth of the society's membership, the expanding engagement of professional musicians, or, in the terminology of the day, "masters" of music, also played an important role.

Among the thirty-seven founding members of the society, as named in Wilmot Gibbes deSaussure's post–Civil War notes, were four professional musicians: Benjamin Yarnold, Anthony L'Abbé, Thomas Pike, and Peter Valton. In addition the core group of members undoubtedly included a healthy number of capable amateur musicians who augmented the band as the first concert season commenced. A ratio as low as 20 percent of the initial membership—low even compared to the subscription concerts in provincial England—would have yielded an orchestra of about a dozen players, including the four professionals. This number is, of course, a conjectural estimate, but—based on the personal background of the known early members—it is also a very conservative figure, and the number may well have been higher.

The instrumentation of the society's early orchestra is equally unclear. The four professional players may have been skilled on several instruments, as was typical of career musicians in the eighteenth century.[22] Yarnold and Valton were both employed as church organists but probably played orchestral instruments as well. Little is known of Yarnold's musical training, but it is almost certain that Valton was trained on a variety of instruments during his youth at the Chapel Royal. Thomas Pike is known to have performed as a soloist on French horn and bassoon, and, as a dancing master, he probably played the violin as well.[23] Although he was active as a musician in Charleston for more than thirty years, no evidence has been found to determine what instruments Anthony L'Abbé may have played in the society's concerts.[24]

Beyond these four professional musicians, there is no known evidence of other hired performers participating in the first several seasons of the St. Cecilia Society's concerts. A survey of the Charleston newspapers for the 1760s and early 1770s demonstrates, however, that there definitely were other professional musicians in Charleston during this time.[25] During the first decade of the society's existence, there was only one other perennial opportunity for professional musicians in Charleston: the exclusive annual series of subscription dancing assemblies held during the customary autumn-to-spring social season. Considering that, until about 1807, when subscription dancing assemblies began to proliferate in Charleston, the membership and management of the "city assemblies" was nearly identical with that of the St. Cecilia Society, the same can probably be said of the musicians who performed at each of these events.[26] Despite the intriguing similarities between these two organizations, even less is known of the band heard at the assemblies. The five musicians who acted as plaintiffs in the 1785 lawsuit against James Milligan may well have constituted the entire performing ensemble at the city assemblies. If this small number is accurate, then there can be little doubt that the opportunity of performing at the St. Cecilia Society's concerts was the primary attraction for the many musicians who settled in or visited Charleston in the decade after 1766.

There were several dancing masters besides Thomas Pike active in Charleston during the 1760s and early 1770s. Teachers of this polite accomplishment usually performed on the violin in the course of their instruction, and thus they may have been skilled enough to perform in an orchestral context.[27] The paucity of evidence about the activities and movements of all of these musicians, however, renders their participation in the society's concerts a matter of speculation. The most prudent conclusion is simply that during its first several seasons the society's orchestra included only a small number of professional musicians. In fact, the society may have desired to limit expenses until its accumulated assets (which could be lent out at interest), substantially exceeded the expenses of hired musicians and other miscellaneous costs associated with an annual series of concerts.

Expansion and Recruitment

By the end of the 1770–71 concert season, the society had gained enough momentum to expand its activities. Clear evidence of this change appeared in mid-April 1771, five years after the society's founding, when it published an advertisement that was repeated in the Charleston newspapers for three months and also appeared in papers in Philadelphia, New York, and Boston (see figure 7.2).[28]

The positions mentioned are essential to the structure of an orchestra of that era, and thus it cannot be assumed that by publishing this advertisement

Charlestown, South Carolina, April 11th, 1771.

THE St. CŒCILIA SOCIETY Give Notice, that they will engage with, and give suitable Encouragement t , MUSICIANS properly qualified to perform at their CONCERT, provided they apply on or before the first Day of October next. — The Performers they are in Want of are, a *First* and *Second Violin, Two Hautboys* and a *Bassoon,* whom they are willi g to agree with for *One, Two* or *Three* Years.
JOHN GORDON, President.
THOMAS L*n*. SMITH, Vice-President.

7.2. The first St. Cecilia Society recruitment advertisement, from *South-Carolina and American General Gazette,* 10–17 April 1771. The text is dated 11 April, a Thursday and the date on which the society's managers probably met to draft the notice. Courtesy of the Charleston Library Society the society simply meant to fill vacancies in its orchestra. Rather, it seems more likely that the society was using its accumulated financial strength to hire highly skilled professionals to take over positions formerly filled by amateurs or mediocre professionals and thus to increase the caliber of the orchestra. The knowledge of who filled these openings, and when and from whence they arrived, is now lost, but it is clear that in the months following this advertisement the number of professional musicians in Charleston increased significantly. To understand the success of this recruiting effort we must remember that in the eighteenth century the circulation of newspapers extended far beyond their home cities. Ship traffic routinely carried American newspapers to taverns and coffeehouses in Britain and the West Indies, just as many foreign and domestic papers could be read in similar establishments in Charleston. By repeating its advertisement in the local papers for several months, therefore, the St. Cecilia Society could rest assured that word of its musical needs would reach British musicians through such news outlets as the Carolina Coffee House in Birchin Lane, London. A number of musicians, certainly more than the five specified in this advertisement, arrived in Charleston during the months after its first publication, and if the size of the society's orchestra in the spring of 1771 is conservatively estimated at between ten and fifteen instrumentalists, then by the autumn of that year it grew to at least fifteen to twenty players. The city's flourishing taste for music, as suggested by this advertisement, may have been incentive enough to attract musicians who did not gain the advertised positions.[29] The society may also have been simultaneously recruiting musicians through a more conventional method: private correspondence.

The extant records of other subscription concert organizations, such as the Edinburgh Musical Society, demonstrate that orchestral vacancies were usually filled through private correspondence rather than through public advertisement. Relying on friends and business contacts, the officers of these concert societies sent letters far and wide asking for suggestions and recommendations.[30] During its first several decades of operation, Charleston's St. Cecilia Society, too, may have enjoyed the services of agents in Britain to help it locate musicians, but no direct evidence of this activity has been found. The society did profit indirectly, however, from its connections to Charleston's business community and through the influence of the Church of England. Merchants in eighteenth-century Charleston communicated with European agents as a routine part of their business. By using their experience to fulfill noncommercial needs, these merchants also played an important role in advancing the cultural life of early Charleston. The examination of a few examples of this activity will provide a model for imagining how the St. Cecilia Society may have recruited musicians from abroad.

During the colonial period the Church of England served an important role in Charleston's cultural life. As the established church of the colony, it received support from the public treasury and administered civic matters. The two principal urban parishes in Charleston, St. Philip's and St. Michael's, were governed by a group of vestrymen and churchwardens composed of the city's elite Anglican citizens: prosperous merchants and planters with strong connections to Britain. When these churches needed supplies, be it ministers, bells, clocks, or organs, they turned to their familiar commercial contacts in England for assistance.[31] When they required organists, the churches likewise relied on friends and agents to help them procure the best talent available. The Church of England was, therefore, responsible for setting the high-water mark for musicianship in the city and for the whole province of South Carolina. The importance of these recruits went beyond the walls of the church, and church officials were undoubtedly aware of this influence. By recruiting the best possible candidates from England, the parishes received not only the best in church music, but also the best music teachers for the community and the best instrumental performers for their concerts.[32]

Charleston merchants and planters used their business experience for noncommercial secular purposes as well. Forming the nucleus of the Charleston Library Society, for example, they engaged booksellers and manufacturers of scientific instruments in London to satisfy their intellectual pursuits. During the late 1750s the Library Society patronized London bookseller James Rivington as its official supplier of books, pamphlets, and periodicals.[33] Rivington's connections to Charleston's cultural life went beyond literary matters, however, as is demonstrated by an incident involving Benjamin Yarnold in the spring of 1758. When Yarnold, then organist at St. Philip's Church, declared his intention of returning to England in early March, the church's vestry immediately wrote to Rivington for assistance in finding a replacement organist. While the vestry's choice of agent may seem odd, it was based on several prior experiences with the bookseller. Some months before, Rivington had been instrumental in recruiting the Reverend Robert Smith, later a president of the St. Cecilia Society, to St. Philip's. Five years earlier Rivington had also acted as a liaison between some Charleston gentlemen in London and Richard Langdon, organist at Exeter Cathedral, who had expressed a willingness to immigrate to South Carolina.[34] In need of a high-caliber musician, the gentlemen of St. Philip's vestry turned to an agent familiar to them from a variety of contexts, and sought to capitalize on his connections to London's musical life. In late colonial Charleston, therefore, the need to conduct transatlantic business as efficiently as possible caused the commercial, spiritual, intellectual, and musical aspects of life to become intertwined.

The use of private correspondence to fill specific cultural needs was a standard practice in eighteenth-century Charleston, but it was also frustratingly slow. The case of George Harland Hartley (ca. 1740–1792), who performed in the St. Cecilia Society's orchestra from early 1773 through the spring of 1775, provides a clear example of this phenomenon. Hartley's immigration to Charleston illustrates both the difficulties involved in recruiting professional musicians through private communication and the benefits of the society's relationship with Charleston's commercial community and the Church of England.

In late May 1768, after more than a decade of threatening to return to England, Benjamin Yarnold notified the vestry of St. Michael's Church (his post since late 1764) that he was definitely taking a twelve-month sabbatical.[35] By June of 1769, John Stevens, another English immigrant musician, had been serving as Yarnold's substitute for at least six months. The details of why Yarnold did not return are unknown, but by 1770 it is clear that the church was trying to recruit a permanent replacement in England. In December of that year Thomas Loughton Smith, a former vestryman of St. Michael's, founding member of the St. Cecilia Society, and "eminent Merchant" of Charleston, wrote from London to say that he "had been disappointed by the Person he had engag'd for Organist of this Parish."[36] The problem was the church's method of securing the organist's salary: it promised a yearly income of at least £50 sterling that was collected from a voluntary subscription among the parishioners. The lack of secure salary apparently discouraged organists from venturing overseas, for one year later John Nutt, a London commercial agent with substantial interest in South Carolina trade, complained to the vestry of "the difficulty he found in sending out an Organist of Merit, without being assur'd of a settl'd handsome Salary."[37]

Eighteen months after Yarnold's departure, in December 1770, a "Carolina Gentlemen" lately returned from Boston—probably Pierce Butler, an Irish officer in the British Army who had just settled in Charleston—recommended to the vestry of St. Michael's "one Mr. Hartley at Boston . . . as a proper Person for that Office." Despite the recommendation, the vestry decided "not to ap[p]ly to any Person till Mr. Nutt found he could not procure one" and wrote asking him "to make a Speedy proper & thorough enquirey for such a Person & give the earliest intelligence wheth[e]r he cou'd positively succeed or not."[38] Twelve months later, Pierce Butler told the vestry that George Harland Hartley, now in Barbados, had written him and expressed his continued interest in the organist position. Butler "gave such flattering Accounts of his great Abilities as an Organist" that in December 1771 the vestry decided to make a formal invitation to Hartley and to inform Nutt "to decline any further Look out for an Organist, as they were in expectation of receiving one from the West Indies."

Their offer of compensation to Hartley mentioned only the "certainty of £50 Sterling" from St. Michael's, but added that "a Performer of your Merit & Abilities in execution equal to the pleasing Acc[oun]ts laid before the Vestry in Your favour, can scarce fail of meeting with a suitable encouragement."[39]

When John Stevens died suddenly in June 1772, Hartley had still not yet arrived and the vestry of St. Michael's was forced to appoint another temporary organist. Almost immediately thereafter the vestry learned, through another letter sent to Pierce Butler, that Hartley had not received the invitation of December last. A new invitation was sent, but this time St. Michael's offer contained an enticing supplement: "It is with Pleasure we inform You that the Plan of Our St. Cæcilia Society has been lately extended. From the President of that Society [probably Thomas Loughton Smith] You have a letter enclosed whose Offer, together with the Church & the prospect of teaching, which from the present Taste for Musick here, is very favorable, we hope will be sufficient Inducements for You to come & reside here."[40] George Harland Hartley finally arrived in Charleston from Antigua in January 1773—some four and a half years after Benjamin Yarnold had vacated the organist's bench at St. Michael's. By early February, Hartley was featured as first violinist in Peter Valton's benefit concert.[41]

The difficulties inherent in recruiting professional musicians from abroad during this time, combined with the society's limited initial budget, undoubtedly played a part in constraining the size and caliber of the St. Cecilia Society's early orchestra. Without a well-established, transatlantic reputation, the society during its early years could not wait passively for musicians to apply for positions in its band. It relied on communication and inquiries sent through private channels, such as local merchants, British agents, and Carolina gentlemen sojourning abroad. The society no doubt experienced some frustration with the delays inherent in transatlantic communication during the eighteenth century and thus sought a more direct method. Its 1771 recruiting advertisement, broadcast throughout the American colonies and in Britain through public newspapers, probably represents the society's desire to satisfy its musical requirements in the most expeditious manner then possible.

Whether the extension of the St. Cecilia Society's plan mentioned in the letter to Hartley in the summer of 1772 was a belated reference to the society's 1771 recruiting advertisement or represented a further expansion of its orchestra is not known. The society's activities were clearly increasing, however, as musicians continued to arrive in Charleston. In March 1773 the society announced the beginning of a more regular, fortnightly concert schedule.

In the last several seasons before the Revolution interrupted the society's regular concert schedule, several other performers of note appeared in

Charleston under the patronage of the St. Cecilia Society. Just when or by what means the violinist John Joseph Abercromby (ca. 1745–after 1808) arrived in South Carolina is not clear, but after attending a St. Cecilia concert in early March 1773 Josiah Quincy described him as "a Frenchman just arrived" who "can't speak a word of English." Although the scion of a old Scottish family, Abercromby had been raised by his mother in her native town of Arras and then educated at the Jesuit College at Douai, French Flanders (now in northern France). Thus Quincy's impression of this violinist can be ascribed to his Continental education, and Abercromby's family connections in the county of Edinburgh may have facilitated his immigration to Charleston.[42] Quincy noted that he "played a first fiddle and solo incomparably, better than any I ever had heard." Comparing Abercromby to violinists active in contemporary Boston, Quincy clarified his judgment by adding that he had several times heard solos played by John Turner and William Sampson Morgan, the latter claiming to have been a pupil of the famed Italian violinist Felice Giardini.[43]

Details of the arrival of the Italian violinist and composer Gaetano Franceschini are also lacking, but his relationship with the St. Cecilia Society is made clear by his benefit concert at the end of the 1773–74 season, which was performed with "the permission of the Honourable the President, the Vice President, and Members of the St. Coecilia Society, and the Assistance of the Gentlemen Performers."[44] In 1769 Franceschini had published in Amsterdam two sets of six trio sonatas, which were republished in London by Robert Wornum about 1773. Friends or agents of the St. Cecilia Society then in London, therefore, probably arranged Franceschini's immigration to Charleston.[45]

When David Douglass's American Company of Comedians performed in Charleston during the 1773–74 season, the St. Cecilia Society probably engaged some of its theatrical musicians and singers. While it is not known how many instrumental performers may have been included in this troupe, there were several singers among the company who were definitely heard at concerts in Charleston in the spring of 1774. On Peter Valton's benefit concert in February of that year, an event sponsored by the St. Cecilia Society, Valton was joined by several vocalists from Douglass's company, including the Misses Hallam, (Maria) Storer, and Wainwright, as well as Mr. Wools. Although the advertisements for Franceschini's April 1774 "Grand Concert of Vocal and Instrumental Music," which was also sponsored by the society, fail to name the vocalists for that performance, the same theatrical singers were most likely included.[46] In later years, when a theater company became a permanent fixture in Charleston, the St. Cecilia concerts regularly featured professional singers. Thus it seems logical to surmise that members of Douglass's company appeared at the St. Cecilia concerts during the 1773–74 season.[47]

In the autumn of 1774, the apex of the St. Cecilia Society's pre-Revolutionary activity, Peter Van Hagen (ca. 1750–1803) and his companion, the vocalist known only as Signora Castella, arrived in Charleston and immediately began to advertise their musical skills. Introducing himself as "Organist and Director of the City's Concert in Rotterdam, lately arrived from London," Van Hagen demonstrated that he was well acquainted with the practices of subscription concert series.[48] It seems likely that the St. Cecilia Society played a role in recruiting these two musicians to Charleston, for immediately after their arrival they presented a joint benefit concert "with the approbation" and "by Permission" of the managers of the St. Cecilia Society.[49]

Thus by the mid-1770s the St. Cecilia Society had assembled an impressive group of musicians, including Peter Valton, Anthony L'Abbé, Thomas Pike, Gaetano Franceschini, John Joseph Abercromby, George Harland Hartley, Peter Van Hagen, Signora Castella, and undoubtedly several other professional musicians then residing in Charleston. When Josiah Quincy recorded his observations of the St. Cecilia concert he attended on 2 March 1773, he described only selected parts of the orchestra he heard: pairs of "bass-viols" (violoncellos) and French horns, a first violin, and harpsichord. Judging from these clues, however, we can estimate that the society's orchestra at that time numbered about twenty musicians and was probably composed of equal numbers of amateurs and professionals.[50] Although Quincy did not attend the society's next concert, on 16 March, he did have another opportunity to hear some of the society's musicians. On the evening of 17 March, St. Patrick's Day, Quincy "feasted with the Sons of St. Patrick" and during dinner heard "six violins, two hautboys and bassoon, with a hand-taber [perhaps an Irish bodhrán] beat excellently well." After dinner the company was entertained by "six French horns in concert—most surpassing musick! Two solos on the French horn by one who is said to blow the finest horn in the world: he has fifty guineas for the season from the St. Cecilia Society."[51] At such a social event, it seems unlikely that amateurs would have participated in the music making during their celebratory feast. Thus the ten musicians who performed during dinner were probably all professional musicians, although none are identified. Furthermore the six French horns that played after dinner were probably drawn from among the ten violinists who played earlier, as it was not uncommon at that time for professional musicians to double on both string and wind instruments. Quincy's observation that one of the horn players was a paid professional in the employ of the St. Cecilia Society suggests that all these musicians, whether professional or amateur, may have also participated in the society's concerts. This possibility is strengthened by the fact that the membership of the Sons of St. Patrick was not exclusively Irish and, like most of Charleston's elite social clubs, overlapped a great deal with the sphere of gentlemen composing the St. Cecilia Society.[52]

Although fragmentary, these clues about the size of the society's orchestra are sufficient to draw comparisons with contemporary practices elsewhere. Orchestras in Britain during the second half of the eighteenth-century usually ranged between ten and twenty-five performers.[53] At the fashionable resort city of Bath, England, for example, the band at the Pump Room formed "the backbone of all professional activity in the city" for most of the eighteenth century. Following a slight increase in 1751, however, this orchestra consisted of only eight musicians. The orchestra of the Oxford Musical Society, almost an exact contemporary of Charleston's St. Cecilia Society, maintained an average of about twenty performers, including both professionals and amateurs, during the late eighteenth and early nineteenth centuries. The professional contingent of the Edinburgh Musical Society steadily increased from its founding in 1728 throughout the next several decades: six performers received payments in 1749–50, twelve in 1759, and sixteen in 1771. The professional contingent of its orchestra grew to twenty-two musicians by 1777, but financial shortfalls soon proved this extravagant increase to have been an instance of "reckless recruitment." Compared to this sampling, therefore, the orchestra of Charleston's St. Cecilia Society, as it existed by the mid-1770s, could easily be described as an average-sized band.[54]

Revolution and Recovery

By the late spring of 1775, the political climate in Charleston had grown so tense that the city's social life seems to have ground to a halt. Facing slim prospects for a continuation of musical patronage, or perhaps unsympathetic to the American cause, many musicians chose to leave Charleston. Gaetano Franceschini, for example, gave notice of his imminent departure from Charleston in April 1775, just as the concert season of the St. Cecilia Society was winding down.[55] Louis Vidal—who arrived in Charleston from Philadelphia in July 1774 claiming to have been "for a considerable Time, First Player on the French Horn in the Court of Portugal"—performed during that autumn and then announced his intention to leave Charleston for the French West Indies in December.[56] In August 1776 Anthony L'Abbé sailed from Charleston for "a French Port," bearing letters from statesman-merchant Henry Laurens to contacts in London.[57] Similarly James Juhan left Charleston to wait out the Revolution in French St. Domingo.[58] Peter Albrecht Van Hagen and Signora Castella probably fled Charleston in late 1775 as well, but no evidence of their movements has been found.[59] Because of his refusal to recognize the independence of South Carolina from the British Crown, George Harland Hartley was dismissed from his post as organist of St. Michael's in July 1776.[60] John Joseph Abercromby traveled to Edinburgh in early 1777 on family business.[61] Thus, in the early stages of the

American Revolution, Charleston's population of professional musicians was seriously depleted.

Following the occupation of Charleston by British forces in May 1780, an active concert life soon reappeared. This fact was owing in part to resources among the occupying army and in part to musicians who either remained in the city or returned in the wake of the army. Just weeks after the city's fall, violinist John Joseph Abercromby was among the citizens who signed a letter welcoming the British forces.[62] Anthony L'Abbé and Joseph Lafar, who had both volunteered in the local militia in 1778 and may have participated in the unsuccessful defense of Savannah, laid down their arms.[63] So did dancing and music master Andrew Rutledge, who had served as the local deputy wagon master general.[64] Peter Valton volunteered his services at St. Michael's Church when it was reopened under British control. Some musicians who had previously fled, such as Franceschini, now returned. The loyalist musician John Mills, who previously had been denied the position of clerk at St. Michael's Church and was exiled from the state in 1778, assumed the organist's bench at the British-controlled St. Philip's.[65] Thomas Pike returned to Charleston as a captain in the British army with a reputation as an accomplished swordsman.[66]

Concerts and dancing assemblies, cosponsored by the occupying British and German regiments and loyalist citizens, commenced in late autumn 1780 and continued into May 1781. "The Last Garrison Subscription Ball for this Season," the *Royal South-Carolina Gazette* announced in May, "will be held as usual, at the State-House, on Saturday the 12th instant, to commemorate the *reduction* of Charles-Town." The musical forces for both the city's concerts and dancing assemblies, it seems, were augmented by members of the occupying army, for on 23 May 1781 "the Band of Musick of the Hessian regiment of Dittfourth [Dittfurth]" gave a concert "immediately after candle-light" at the State House, for "the Ladies and Gentlemen that used to frequent the Assemblies, the Gentlemen of the Army, Navy, and most respectable part of the Inhabitants."[67] A second season of concerts commenced in October 1781 and concluded in May 1782.[68] A German witness to this series later reported hearing an orchestra of twenty instrumentalists: "In Charleston there were concerts twice a month, by four first and three second violins, two violas, two violoncellos, two bassoons, one harpsichord, two clarinets or oboes, two flutes and two horns. The price of the ticket was half a guinea. We met there the following musical artists: *Franciskini* [Franceschini] an Italian and good violinist, *Ebercromby* [Abercromby] a Scotchman, also a violinist, *Walton*, a harpsichordist, born in Charleston [Peter Valton of London]," and "an oboist of the third regiment, by name of *Smith*, was a particularly powerful performer."[69]

When the British army evacuated Charleston in December 1782, many of the musicians who had performed during the occupation—especially the regimental musicians—took their leave as well.[70] Thus it is not clear how many professional musicians were in Charleston when the St. Cecilia Society recommenced its fortnightly concert series in the autumn of 1783. During his brief stay in Charleston in the early months of 1784, the German physician Johann David Schoepf observed "there are publick concerts, at this time mainly under the direction of German and English musicians left behind by the army, for as yet few of the natives care greatly for music or understand it." Schoepf's statement is a bit of a mystery, however, as no concerts of any kind were advertised during his residence in the city.[71] What musicians were left behind by, or defected from, the British army is not known, nor at what concerts they may have performed.

Charleston's economy and social life slowly recovered after the return of peace, but the growth of its cultural life was stymied by a remnant of the conservative war-era mentality: a legal ban on theatrical entertainments. After the Revolution, Charleston, like most American cities, enacted prohibitions against theatrical performances that were to linger for several years.[72] Despite restrictive legislation passed in September 1783 and in March 1787, numerous "recitations" of dramatic scenes and English operas were given between March 1785 and January 1790. Since Charleston's only theater had burned in February 1783, these performances were staged by itinerant players at a variety of locations: the city's Exchange, McCrady's Long Room, the "Great Room" at the foot of Tradd Street (formerly John Williams's first Carolina Coffee House), and Harmony Hall (later called "the Lecture Room") just outside the city limits.[73] These were but passing entertainments, however, and the concert series of the St. Cecilia Society remained the principal attraction for professional musicians who considered a trip to Charleston. In the decade following the conclusion of the American Revolution, it is possible to identify only a few musicians who were definitely associated with the concerts of the St. Cecilia Society. Regardless, the city enjoyed the talents of several familiar performers, as well as those of a number of new arrivals.

Peter Valton remained in Charleston throughout the war, but died in February 1784.[74] Jervis Henry Stevens replaced Valton at St. Philip's and served as the church's organist for the next thirty years.[75] Anthony L'Abbé continued his musical career in Charleston until his death in 1798, when the members of the St. Cecilia Society were summoned to attend his funeral.[76] John Joseph Abercromby lingered in Charleston for several more years before credit problems drove him northward.[77] Benjamin Yarnold, who had left for England in the summer of 1768, wrote to St. Cecilia Society member John Faucheraud Grimké in late 1783 to enquire about opportunities in Charleston. The vestry of St. Michael's instructed Grimké to advise Yarnold that they would give him "every Encouragement in their Power," and in late December 1784 he returned to his former post as organist of St. Michael's.[78] After his death in June 1787, Yarnold's duties at St. Michael's were continued by his son William for almost two years while the vestry sought to import a new candidate "from Europe." The younger Yarnold resided in Charleston for at least another decade and thus may have participated in the city's concert life.[79]

The English flautist William Brown, who immigrated to British-occupied New York in 1783, made an appearance in Charleston in the spring of 1784. For his concert in late April of that year, Brown described himself as having "lately arrived from Philadelphia."[80] The length of his residence in Charleston is not known, but by early 1785 he was again performing in Philadelphia.[81]

The dancing master Joseph Lafar, having arrived in 1777, advertised the opening of Charleston's first "Music Shop" in late 1785, but the venture apparently did not last.[82] In late 1786 he attempted to start his own subscription series of fortnightly concerts and assemblies but met with little success.[83] After presenting a benefit concert in February 1786, Lafar apparently left Charleston sometime in 1788.[84] His return in early 1791 was coincident with a charity concert "for the benefit of a numerous family in distress" sponsored by the St. Cecilia Society at McCrady's Long Room on 18 March 1791. Although neither the name of this family nor those of the performers were given, Lafar was likely the recipient of the society's benevolence.[85] In the advertisements for a similar concert on 16 June 1791, Lafar described himself as "lately returned to this city" and stated that, after having suffered "a series of misfortunes," he had been "advised by some of his friends, to attempt this method to alleviate the distress of his family."[86] The misfortunes of Lafar's family continued after his death in 1795, for on 9 March 1797 another charity concert was held "for the Benefit of Mrs. Lafar, the Widow, and Children, of the late Mr. Joseph Lafar, Musician." Although it is not stated explicitly, the St. Cecilia Society seems to have been a tacit sponsor of this event.[87]

More successful in the music retail business was Thomas Bradford, who in February 1788 opened "Bradford & Co. Musical Instrument Makers in General, from their Manufactory, Fountain Court, Cheapside, London." Apparently representing a branch of an English musical-instrument-making family, Bradford ran Charleston's sole music store for the next twenty years. After his death in 1803 his wife, Christiana, managed it for several more years. A versatile music teacher and instrument technician, Thomas Bradford never advertised instruments of his own construction nor presented a concert for his own benefit. He was, however, frequently mentioned as a distributor of tickets for others' concerts, and he may have performed as well.[88]

There were several other musicians in postwar Charleston about whom little or nothing is known. One Mr. Simcolin applied for the organist position at St. Michael's in May 1783, but was rejected because the vestry was of the opinion that he "does not perform Church Music, so perfectly as to authorize us to appoint him to the office of an Organist."[89] In the spring of 1785 one Mr. Brandon advertised to copy music and to teach violin at his "Music School."[90] A flautist named Mr. Franks, probably William Franco, appeared as a concerto soloist in the autumn of 1787, and possibly again in 1788.[91] Caspar Cumin is listed as a "violin player" in the Charleston city directory of 1790.[92] While nothing is known about the connections of these musicians with the St. Cecilia Society, there is clear evidence that the society did employ musicians who were simply passing through. The return of Maria Storer to Charleston in 1785 not only provides such evidence but also the earliest proof that the St. Cecilia Society hired professional singers for its concerts.

Storer arrived in Charleston from Jamaica, where she had lingered during the Revolution, in late March 1785. Although on her way to England, she was persuaded by unknown parties to remain in Charleston for some time.[93] The opportunity to perform at the concerts of the St. Cecilia Society undoubtedly played some part in her decision to stay in Charleston, for by early May, if not earlier, she was singing at the society's fortnightly concerts.[94] Storer announced a benefit concert for 17 May, but later postponed it "by the advice of her friends" to 20 June.[95] This concert, billed as "the last Night of her Performance," was postponed indefinitely when Storer abandoned her plans to leave Charleston.[96] In the meantime Miss Storer performed three of the "most select Anthems" from Handel's *Messiah* at St. Michael's Church on Sunday, 26 June, for which she received six guineas (roughly $550 in 2005) from the vestry "as a Compliment for her services."[97] New England educator Noah Webster, who had just arrived in Charleston to peddle his new spelling book, attended this musical event. An advocate of American psalmody and the dissemination of sacred vocal music, Webster was not impressed with Storer's performance: "An odd affair this, for a woman to sing for her own benefit; but I put a quarter of a dollar in the plate. She sang well in the modern taste, but I cannot admire it."[98] The performance was advertised as being for a charitable cause, but some members of the audience, including Webster, apparently believed that Storer performed solely for her own remuneration. Storer, "impatient to remove from her character the odium thrown on it by a report now in circulation," published a public rebuttal to these rumors. Even if her circumstances had been so desperate as to induce her to seek charity, she stated, "her *own feelings* would effectually prevent her appealing to *theirs,* through so *public,* so *indelicate* a channel."[99]

In light of Storer's decision to extend her stay in Charleston, the St. Cecilia concerts were continued through the summer of 1785, during which time she performed on several occasions.[100] Considering the general respect and admiration expressed for Maria Storer's vocal talents and the temporary nature of her stopover in Charleston, it is likely that the society extended its concert season to such unusual lengths to take full advantage of the limited opportunity to enjoy hearing her voice. Storer finally had her benefit concert on 12 October, but further information on her participation in the St. Cecilia concerts is lacking. When she departed for New York in late January 1786, however, the *Charleston Evening Gazette* alluded to her performances with the society by remarking that during her stopover in Charleston she had "afforded so much amusement, by her vocal abilities, to the polite circles of this city."[101]

During Maria Storer's extended season in Charleston, Henri Capron, a French cellist and singer, arrived in Charleston from Philadelphia in late June 1785. Like Storer, Capron found encouragement from the St. Cecilia Society soon after his arrival. At the performance of Thursday, 11 August, the *Evening Gazette* reported that "the St. Cecilia Concert was better attended last night than it has been for some time. Two of the senses, at least, were completely gratified; to please the eye there was present the most shining beauties in Charleston; to gratify the ear—Miss Storer and Mr. Capron." He probably continued performing for the society through the 1785–86 season, but evidence to confirm this is lacking.[102] Capron, "lately from Europe," soon advertised himself as a teacher of singing and the violoncello. He had a benefit concert on 10 January 1786, for which he described himself as "a stranger in this country, ignorant of its language, and known but to few of its inhabitants." In February 1786 he added English guitar to his teaching repertoire, but his tenure in Charleston did not last much longer.[103] Capron returned to Philadelphia by September 1786, by which time he was preparing subscription concerts in that city.[104]

While financial difficulties caused a suspension of the St. Cecilia Society's concerts between November 1788 and November 1790, Charleston's reputation for the liberal encouragement of music continued to attract musicians of the highest caliber. Despite what some scholars have said about the poverty endured by most professional musicians in eighteenth-century America, musical life in Charleston was advanced enough to enable some musicians not only to flourish but to improve their social standing.[105] The activities of several musicians in the late 1780s illustrate this point.

In the early autumn of 1787, roughly a decade after his family had fled Charleston during the American Revolution, the young violinist Alexander Juhan (ca. 1765–1845) returned to South Carolina.[106] Juhan's skills on the violin were not unfamiliar to those in Charleston, as one of the local newspapers carried a report in the summer of 1786 of an elaborate charity concert recently held in Philadelphia. It mentioned the performance of a violin concerto by "Mr. Juhan, who not only displayed the most promising talents, but a taste and execution which proved arduous practice, and gave universal satisfaction."[107] Juhan's presence in Charleston from the autumn of 1787 through at least 1798 was relatively low profile.[108] Although no evidence has been found to confirm a link between Juhan and the St. Cecilia Society, his professional and personal prosperity in South Carolina suggests that he received ample encouragement. Having married the daughter of prosperous and influential Charleston merchant Daniel Bourdeaux in 1792, Juhan was able to retire from the musical profession by 1804 and live comfortably on his plantation near the Lower Three Runs of the Savannah River (near modern Allendale, South Carolina).[109]

The patronage of the St. Cecilia Society may have also played a significant role in the professional success of Jacob Eckhard (1757–1833), who arrived in Charleston in the autumn of 1786. So widespread and varied was Eckhard's musical activity in Charleston that his 1833 obituary observed that he was "regarded in our city as the father of music." A native of Hesse Cassel, Eckhard arrived in America in 1776 as part of the German forces recruited by Britain to serve in the American Revolution. At the conclusion of the war he settled in Richmond, Virginia, but he was then invited to serve as organist of St. John's Lutheran Church in Charleston. Soon after his arrival, a posthumous tribute informs us, Eckhard received an important career boost: "His extraordinary acquirements in this profession, soon attracted the notice of the community, and an equanimity, cheerfulness and affability of demeanor, rendered him particularly fitted for the station to which he had assumed; accordingly a requisition was made upon his services, which whilst it advanced his pecuniary interests, introduced him in the best and most respectable circles of Society. His station gave him more popularity than is derived from many of the other professions."[110]

Although the author of this anecdote was careful not to name the parties who had made this "requisition" of Eckhard's services, his later prominence in Charleston musical life suggests that it was the St. Cecilia Society that had advanced Eckhard's "pecuniary interests" and social connections.[111] In addition to performing as organist at St. John's and later at St. Michael's, Eckhard also performed as pianist in solo sonatas, concerti, and chamber works at a multitude of concerts in Charleston over a span of four decades. A truly versatile musician, he was also a composer, conductor, vocalist, violist, and piano retailer.

Circumstantial evidence strongly suggests that Samuel Rodgers, who arrived in Charleston in May 1789, was connected with the St. Cecilia Society.[112] Rodgers had been a pupil of Benjamin Cooke, a celebrated English composer, organist at Westminster Abbey, and conductor of the Academy of Ancient Music for more than thirty-five years. Acting on information then circulating in London about St. Michael's search for a new organist, Rodgers wrote in December 1788 to John Faucheraud Grimké, the same man to whom Benjamin Yarnold wrote when he sought to return to Charleston. Grimké passed Rodgers's letter on to the vestry of St. Michael's, whose rector, Henry Purcell, replied "I am happy in being the Instrument of assuring you that they were not a little rejoic'd at the Prospect of having the Organist's Place filled by a Gent. that Dr. Cooke has ever taken by the Hand & patronized. We are under infinite Obligations to that Gentlemen, & shall cheerfully embrace every opportunity of testifying it." Purcell assured Rodgers that the church vestry "will ever think it their Duty to promote your Interest, & second your Views." In regard to the city of Charleston in general, Purcell added "and upon the whole—from the Temper & Habits of the People—the healthiness of the City, & the Emoluments that You will enjoy, I'll be bold to say, You will quickly applaud yourself for the Change You are about to make."[113] Unlike the 1772 offer made to George Harland Hartley, the offer to Rodgers from the representatives of St. Michael's did not mention the possibility of performing at the St. Cecilia Society's concerts. This omission was probably because the society's concerts had been suspended in November 1788 and were not resumed until November 1790, more than a year after Rodgers's arrival. In addition to his duties at St. Michael's, Rodgers taught harpsichord (later piano) and German flute and also imported pianos for sale.[114] Although he never presented a concert for his own benefit, Rodgers was active in Charleston's musical life until his death in 1810.

If it was not directly involved, then the St. Cecilia Society's liberal encouragement of music in Charleston was at least indirectly responsible for advancing the career of the violinist Michael Benoit Poitiaux (ca. 1771–1854). A native of Brussels, Belgium, Poitiaux came to Charleston in 1787 in the employ of an English merchant.[115] His skills on the violin soon attracted attention in the community, however, and he was encouraged to pursue a new line of work. By September 1792 Poitiaux announced that he "now determined to devote all his time to the study and practice of his music," having "removed the cause which prevented him from teaching the art of playing on the violin." He considered "this public notice the more requisite, as he has had several applications from gentlemen who wished to be instructed by him, at a time when a different line of occupation obliged him to decline receiving any scholars."[116] Poitiaux resided in Charleston for several more years, and his 1796 benefit concert was the largest, most elaborate concert in the city's early history.

Following the steady increase of the St. Cecilia Society's fortunes and orchestra in the 1770s, the decade after the American Revolution was clearly a period of recovery and rebuilding. There were many obstacles that hindered this process: a number of the society's members had either been killed during

the war or sided with the British and departed; many of the society's principal musicians had either fled or died; the loss of Pike's Assembly Room forced
the society's performances to migrate among four smaller venues; and difficulties with the collection of arrears caused a temporary suspension of its concerts. Despite these impediments, the St. Cecilia Society persevered in its
mission to "encourage the liberal science of music." Performers who had
endured the war years in Charleston were rewarded with continued patronage, and some of those who immigrated to Charleston found sufficient
encouragement to settle permanently. The society's resources were not as
robust as they had been before the Revolution, but events on the horizon were
about to change this condition radically.

The Performers, 1793–1820

AFTER HAVING ASSEMBLED A BAND OF MUSICIANS from at least six European nations by the early 1770s and having luxuriated in cosmopolitan musical entertainments on the eve of the American Revolution, the members of the St. Cecilia Society must have been frustrated to face the task of rebuilding its retinue of musicians during the postwar depression of the 1780s. Money was scarce, old social and business networks had been disrupted, and musicians were not so easily drawn to Charleston as they had been in earlier days. The society's difficulties did not last indefinitely, however, for the opening of the Charleston Theatre in early 1793 and the nearly simultaneous arrival of refugees from St. Domingo brought an unprecedented number of musicians to Charleston. In the wake of these developments, dramatic and musico-dramatic entertainment became a permanent fixture of Charleston's cultural life, and a sizable number of professional musicians—instrumentalists and singers—were present in Charleston on a nearly continuous basis. By sharing performers with the local theatrical establishment and actively encouraging the settlement of many refugees, the St. Cecilia Society's concerts enjoyed a profusion of talent over the ensuing two decades. These convenient and mutually beneficial arrangements allowed the society to reach a new plateau of activity around the turn of the nineteenth century, but its increasingly passive reliance on these sources of labor ultimately contributed to the cessation of the society's long-standing concert series.

The Establishment of a Permanent Theater

Were it not for the interruption of the American Revolution, Charleston would probably have maintained an active theatrical life throughout the 1770s and 1780s. The war brought theatrical exhibitions to an abrupt end, however, and soured much of the population against such extravagant public entertainment.

It was not until December 1791 that the state legislature finally passed an act to permit the exhibition of theatrical entertainments (upon payment of a £100 license fee) and the construction of a new theater.[1] By late spring of 1792 Thomas Wade West and John Bignall, managers of the Virginia Company of Comedians, announced their plans for a new theater in Charleston, complete with a frontispiece and stage doors "after the manner of the new opera house in London."[2] The site chosen was a vacant green space that had been used as a parade ground for military exercises, toward the southwestern end of Broad Street.[3] Funds were raised through the sale of shares, and in subsequent years the managers of the theater were answerable to its shareholders, who held title to the property. Following months of construction delays and the sale of additional shares, the Charleston Theatre in Broad Street opened in February 1793.[4]

The opening of the Charleston Theatre was a significant moment in the city's cultural life, but in this area it was overshadowed by the contemporary developments in Boston, New York, and Philadelphia. Far more populous than Charleston and relatively close together, these northeastern cities formed the hub of post-Revolutionary American theatrical activity and were also the destination of most actors arriving from Britain. The managers of the Charleston Theatre, therefore, recruited most of its players from among the northern theaters and brought them to perform in Charleston from autumn through spring. In this manner, theater audiences in Charleston saw and heard much of the same repertoire and many of the same performers as those in Boston, New York, Philadelphia, and other cities along the eastern seaboard.

Like other theaters in late-eighteenth-century Britain and America, the Charleston Theatre presented English-language drama, which, in the custom of the day, frequently included the interpolation of music and dancing. English "operas," or dramatic works with spoken dialogue and numerous songs, were also a standard part of the theater's offerings. In a narrow pit immediately in front of the stage sat the theater's orchestra or band, which was separated from the audience by a low wall or barrier. In addition to accompanying the vocal numbers, the orchestra also performed instrumental music before the curtain rose and in the intervals between acts.[5] According to one of its musicians, the orchestra of the Charleston Theatre in the spring of 1794 comprised thirteen performers, including string, wind, and brass instruments.[6] At the end of the theatrical season much of the Charleston company dispersed to pursue opportunities in cooler, busier northern cities, while others remained on a more continual basis and created new postseason diversions for local audiences. Vauxhall Garden, opened in 1799 by theater manager Alexander Placide, was the most prominent of these summer attractions. Until Placide's death in the summer of 1812, this venue

provided regular summer concerts and encouraged many singers and orchestral musicians to reside in Charleston year round.[7]

The St. Cecilia Society and the theater were the principal employers of
musicians in Charleston between 1793 and 1820 but the relationship between
these two institutions was not adversarial. On the contrary, there is copious
evidence that the society enjoyed a symbiotic relationship with the musicians
attached to the local theaters.[8] Professional musicians affiliated with the society routinely appeared at the theater and in other performing contexts in
Charleston, as they would have done in other American and European cities.
Charleston and its surrounding countryside had a rather small free white
population that could sustain only so many professional musicians. There
were not, as one might find in a larger city, separate orchestras for the theater,
the St. Cecilia Society, and the other musical organizations that formed and
dissolved over the years.[9] During this period, there was essentially one pool of
instrumental performers who supplied the various musical performances of
the city.

The unity of orchestral forces in Charleston is succinctly demonstrated by
several concerts given by "the gentlemen of the orchestra" in the early years
of the nineteenth century. Advertisements for a benefit concert for "the gentlemen of the Orchestra" in January 1802 named only a few soloists, all associated with the Charleston Theatre. Confirmation that this was the same band
heard at the St. Cecilia Society's concerts is provided by a programming note:
the concert featured a "Grand Overture" by resident musician Robert Leaumont, which had been "performed for the first time at the Anniversary Concert of the St. Cecilia Society."[10] The benefit concert for "The Gentlemen of
the Orchestra" at Vauxhall Garden in September 1805 included all the theater
musicians summering in Charleston, who were "on this occasion . . . assisted
by a number of Amateurs."[11] A Passion Week "oratorio," intended "to follow
the plan of the Spiritual Concert in Paris," was given in March 1807 "for the
Benefit of the Gentlemen who compose the Orchestra of the St. Cecilia Society." It included not only musicians from the theater, gentlemen amateurs, and
refugees from St. Domingo, but also a chorus of children from the Charleston
Orphan House.[12] These examples demonstrate that the collective orchestral
musicians in Charleston, appearing in different roles depending on the day of
the week and the month of the year, constituted a single ensemble—one that
in September 1808 was in fact described as the "Orchestra of Charleston."[13]

Further evidence of the overlap in the musical forces of the theater and
the society's concerts is suggested by the performance calendars of these two
organizations. While the seasons of the theater and the St. Cecilia Society
were roughly identical, their respective managers were careful to avoid scheduling events on the same evening. Thursday evenings were reserved for the

society's concerts (and the fortnightly subscription dancing assemblies), while theatrical performances generally took place on Monday, Wednesday, and Friday evenings. There were occasional performances at the theater on Thursday evenings, however, but these anomalies occurred during the periods when the St. Cecilia concerts were suspended, such as during the Christmas and New Year's holiday season or before and after the concert season.[14] The motivation for avoiding schedule conflicts between the society and the local theater undoubtedly arose from their overlapping personnel rather than similar audiences, for while the society's concerts were private events, the theater was a more "republican" entertainment and thus open to a more diverse audience than St. Cecilia's. Some members of the St. Cecilia Society no doubt attended the theater, but others may have avoided its less-exclusive atmosphere.

It is significant that the managers of the Charleston Theatre between 1793 and 1820—Thomas Wade West and John Bignall, Alexander Placide (and his assistants), Charlotte Wrighten Placide, Joseph Holman, and Charles Gilfert —are all known to have cooperated with the St. Cecilia Society on a number of special events.[15] Such collaboration may have been more obligatory than coincidental, however. Most of the known theater shareholders were also officers of the society, and thus the managers of the theater may have been compelled by this relationship to curry their favor and accommodate their requests.[16] Considering both the extent and the nature of the relationship between these two institutions, the managers of the Charleston Theatre may have acted as proxy agents for the society, playing a role not unlike that of the St. Michael's vestry in its negotiations with George Harland Hartley in the early 1770s. During their recruiting trips to Boston, New York, and Philadelphia, Charleston theater managers may have been empowered to inform prospective theater musicians that qualified performers could find employment both at the city's theater and at the St. Cecilia concerts. Such an arrangement would have been mutually beneficial: the presence of the theater in Charleston ensured a steady supply of potential performers for the St. Cecilia Society's concerts, while the reputation of the society may have helped attract high-quality musicians to the city.[17] Relying on the professional connections and efforts of the theater managers, therefore, the St. Cecilia Society found that its need to recruit musicians to Charleston after 1793 either diminished significantly or evaporated completely.[18]

Despite the potentially lucrative combination of performing at the city's new theater and at the St. Cecilia concerts, Charleston's theatrical managers found many musicians in the nation's larger northeastern cities reluctant to venture southward because of Charleston's unhealthy reputation. In addition to the torrid heat of the summer season, the months of July, August, and September were known to constitute a dangerous season to be in the city. Various illnesses, principally yellow fever, were an omnipresent danger during these months, especially to new arrivals to Charleston. The combination of extreme heat, low-lying marshes, and poor sanitation standards created an atmosphere ripe for the spread of disease. So common was the demise of new arrivals during the late summer and early autumn that their death was customarily attributed to "stranger's fever."

By the end of the eighteenth century there were many performers among the theatrical companies of Boston, New York, and Philadelphia who had summered in Charleston at one time or another and were familiar with Charleston's unhealthy reputation. In his description of travels in America at the turn of the nineteenth century, Englishman Charles William Janson went so far as to describe Charleston as "the Grave of American Performers."[19] Displaying a familiarity with the rigors of the performer's life, Janson lamented, "Charleston has proved a grave to the theatrical corps in America. The high salaries given there, from the great plenty of money, and riches of the principal inhabitants, who are great amateurs, drew thither numbers of performers on the expiration of their engagements with the northern managers." As a result of the mortality in Charleston, Janson remarked, "the American stage is at present somewhat depreciated, and it is not to be expected that England can spare a supply of such performers . . . with the celerity with which a Carolina climate may carry them off."[20]

Gottlieb Graupner, later an eminent oboist in Boston, performed only briefly in Charleston in the mid-1790s, probably because he was present when four members of his Boston theatrical company—two singers and two instrumentalists—succumbed to stranger's fever in the summer of 1796.[21] In 1805 retired violinist Alexander Juhan advertised to sell part of his extensive plantation, recommending it to "any gentleman who wishes to remove from an unhealthy situation on the seaboard, to a more healthy one in a higher part of the state." In August 1807 the managers of the "Theatre Picturesque and Mechanique" in Charleston announced the final week of their presentations, after which "the Artists who are strangers to our climate, will be obliged to leave the city, during the sickly season."[22] One can imagine that musicians who traveled to Charleston probably received the same advice from their peers as that given to British consul William Ogilby in 1830. Before embarking for Charleston, Ogilby was warned that this southern city may become his final resting place. "I have not much fear of this tho'," he recorded in his diary, "and yet my brother Consul at New York told me to take my coffin with me."[23]

Despite these dangers, the Charleston Theatre, and consequently the orchestra of the St. Cecilia Society, was usually staffed with a robust complement of performers. The earliest evidence of the society's employment of theater musicians does not concern the members of the orchestra, however.

Instead, the first clue to the relationship between these two organizations appears just two months after the opening of the theater, in the St. Cecilia Society's announcement that Mrs. Decker and Mr. Chambers, members of West and Bignall's theatrical troupe, "will each favor the company with a song" at its concert on 4 April 1793.[24] Over the ensuing years many other theatrical singers were heard at benefit concerts in Charleston, including those sponsored by the St. Cecilia Society. Perhaps the most intriguing example occurred in March of 1811, at the benefit of violinist Jean-Claude LeFolle. His concert, which was performed "*under the particular patronage of the St. Cecilia Society,*" included the vocal talents of the young actress Eliza Poe, mother of the celebrated writer Edgar Allan Poe (1809–1849).[25] Only a few singers were named in the advertisements for the society's regular concert series, however. Shortly after her arrival from New York with the theatrical company in the autumn of 1801, for example, the St. Cecilia Society announced that the young English singer Dorothea Broadhurst would perform a song "in each act" of its first concert of the season on 12 November.[26] Advertisements for the society's anniversary meeting two weeks later contained the usual reminder that "there will be a Concert in the Evening," then added "in each act songs by Miss Broadhurst and Messrs. Darleys, sen. and jun. of the Charleston Theatre." The society's anniversary concert in 1803 was similarly advertised, noting the performance of three different theatrical stars: "The vocal parts by Mrs. Placide, and Messrs. Hodgkinson and Marshall."[27]

Two of these last-mentioned singers deserve further mention because they seem to have enjoyed special relationships with the St. Cecilia Society. Even before her marriage to French acrobat and theatrical manager Alexander Placide in the summer of 1796, Charlotte Wrighten Placide was a fixture of both the theater and the concert stage in Charleston.[28] For nearly twenty years she appeared as a vocal soloist and in vocal ensembles in nearly every benefit concert held in the city—including many sponsored by the St. Cecilia Society. Mrs. Placide may have been a regular performer at the St. Cecilia concerts in the years after her marriage, although little evidence to support this assertion survives. Following the death of her husband in the summer of 1812, Mrs. Placide attempted to continue the family's management of the Charleston Theatre for the 1812–13 season. The exigencies of the new war with Britain curtailed Charleston's social life, however, and forced her to close the theater in January 1813. During what would be her last spring in Charleston, Mrs. Placide presented a "Concert and Ball" in February 1813, which was advertised as being given "under the immediate Patronage of the St. Cecilia Society."[29]

Undoubtedly the most striking event sponsored by the St. Cecilia Society (and the most informative for modern readers) was the concert it sponsored for the benefit of the orphan children of the celebrated theatrical singer John

Hodgkinson (1767–1805) in October 1805. Although he died in New York, Hodgkinson had only recently left Charleston after serving as acting comanager of the city's theater for three seasons. In early October 1805 the *Charleston Courier* announced that "we are happy to be able to report that the Managers of the St. Cecilia Society have determined to give a Concert in a short time for the benefit of the Orphan Children of the deceased Mr. Hodgkinson." To induce citizens to attend this special event, the initial notice stated that "the benevolent inhabitants of Charleston need not be reminded of the amusement and edification which they have frequently received from the Theatrical Talents of Mr. Hodgkinson. It may not be improper, however, to mention, that during his residence in this town, he gratuitously performed at every concert and play that was given for charitable purposes."[30] Further explanation of the motivations behind this charity event was published the following week: "The deep impression made upon the minds of the citizens of Charleston, by the sudden and melancholy death of the late Mr. Hodgkinson, and the strong sense of his merits, in public as well as private life, during his residence among them, have induced the *Managers of the St. Cecilia Society* to propose to a liberal and humane public, a *Concert for the benefit of his two Orphan Children,* to be performed on Thursday Evening, the 17th instant, at the *St. Cecilia Concert Room, Church-street,* to begin precisely at seven o'clock."[31]

For reasons not known, probably on account of rehearsals, this charity concert was postponed several times and finally set for 29 October. The delays may have been related to the anticipated arrival of the favorite theatrical singer Mrs. Oldmixon (née Georgina Sidus, 1763?–1836), whose well-publicized arrival in the schooner *Sally* from Philadelphia the day before the concert added to the air of anticipation.[32] "Immediately upon her landing," reported the Charleston *City Gazette,* Mrs. Oldmixon was "waited upon by some of the gentlemen who manage the concert this evening, to sing for the benefit of Mr. Hodgkinson's orphans. She displayed the most anxious desire to contribute every thing in her power to serve the children; but at the same time expressed her doubts whether, exhausted as she was with fasting, sickness and fatigue, during a tempestuous passage of many days, she would have strength enough to meet the Charleston audience, for the first time, without manifest disadvantage." To aid the children and "to oblige the managers and the public," however, Mrs. Oldmixon soon consented to sing, "saying that she would rely upon the liberality of the company to make allowance for her situation."[33]

The managers of the St. Cecilia Society were not alone in their zeal to support Hodgkinson's children, for "in every capital city, from Maine to this of Charleston, the good people are almost tumultuously rushing forward to contribute their share to this great and virtuous works of providing for the

Orphans." Stressing the importance of this cause and the anticipated wonders of the performance, the local press stated that "the circle of Charleston will not fail duty to appreciate the merit of the Professors and Amateurs of Music, who have voluntarily stepped forward to exert themselves, and display their powers at the Concert, for the Children's benefit This Evening. We will not wrong the people of Charleston, so far, as to suppose it possible, that on such an occasion, any one who can possibly attend, will be absent."[34]

In an unprecedented gesture, the *Charleston Courier* published a lengthy postconcert "Communication" that provides a detailed and colorful description of the proceedings at the charity performance:

> Seldom has the St. Cecilia Concert-Room witnessed a more crowded or brilliant audience than graced it on Tuesday evening last; never an occasion which reflected more honour on the benevolent affections of those who attended. As the object of the Concert was noble and kind, so we are persuaded the success of it must have been considerable. The amiable motives which carried so many needed no other return, than the feelings of their hearts; but they received all that additional gratification which fine melody and rich harmony can impart. The music which Mrs. Placide selected, and the charming strain in which she executed it, was in perfect consonance with that amiable lovely character which her soft and engaging manners have impressed upon the people of Charleston.
>
> Mrs. SULLY [wife of actor Matthew Sully Jr.] performed a concerto on the piano, with an execution and taste which attracted the admiration of all who had heard her.
>
> With that enchanting voice which has so often delighted the ears of those who can feel and appreciate its effect and power, Miss LAROQUE [Antoinette La Roque] sang an ariette from the celebrated Opera of Nina. When the time approached for the appearance of Mrs. OLDMIXON, expectation was on tiptoe—the hum of conversation was hushed into silence, and all were anxiously solicitous to hear if report of her great vocal talent had outstripped her merits; and tho' aware of the fatigue she had undergone in a long and stormy voyage from the North, and the little strength which one day's rest could be supposed to give; yet their anticipations were great, and were only to be exceeded by the powers she exhibited.—She was several times interrupted by bursts of plaudits, which could not be restrained; and when she had concluded, such a continuation of applause followed as testified an admiration and astonishment never before witnessed in that concert-room. The taste with which she sung, and the expression she threw into the tender passages of the beautiful music of GIARDINI, the command she possessed over a voice

of uncommon compass, and modulated with nicest accuracy, and the height to which she ascended, making a double octave from G. can only be credited by those who have had the delight of listening to the necromancy of her notes. The public must be highly gratified at an accession so valuable to the Theatre; and Mr. PLACIDE deserves their thanks and patronage for his taste and exertions in bringing forward talents so rare and admirable as Mrs. O's.[35]

No lists of the repertoire and the performers were published in advance of this concert, but several postconcert notices provide further insight into the society's operation. A few days after the concert, in early November 1805, the society published its thanks to five professional singers and seventeen instrumentalists. An "extract from the Minutes" of the monthly meeting of the society's board of managers shows that it was "unanimously *Resolved,* That the thanks of this Board be presented to Mrs. *Placide,* Mrs. *Oldmixon,* Mrs. *Sully* and Miss *Laroque;* and Messrs. *Sully & Story;* also to Messrs. *Leaumont, Eckhard, Carrere, Miniere, De Villers, Tomlins, Peyre, Noel, Remoussin, A. Remoussin, Labatut, Muck, Stone, Eckhard, jun.* and *Heulean* [Heulan] for their polite and generous assistance to the Concert of the late Mr. Hodgkinson's Orphan Children." A postscript in the next day's paper stated that "the name of Mr. Brunet was inadvertently omitted among those of the gentlemen to whom the thanks of the Board of Managers of the St. Cecilia Society were presented."[36]

At the end of November, the *Charleston Courier* published a letter from theater manager Alexander Placide to Stephen C. Carpenter, coeditor of that paper, regarding the receipts from the charity concert. Placide stated that the performance produced $537.50 (roughly $8,905 in 2005), minus the expenses, which amounted to $59 (roughly $977 in 2005).[37] Although Placide may have calculated the receipts for this concert, the funds were handed over to the St. Cecilia Society, who had sponsored the event. The society, whose membership overlapped with the trustees of the Charleston Orphan House, then extended its role of musical patron to that of benefactor for Hodgkinson's orphans. In a rare glimpse into its financial capacities, the society published a full description of its plans for this money six weeks after the concert:

St. Cecilia Society. The President having called the attention of the Managers to the sum of money collected at the Concert given by the *St. Cecilia Society,* for the benefit of the Orphan Children of the late Mr. Hodgkinson, the Treasurer was called upon for a report, whereupon he exhibited a statement whereby it appeared that the nett balance of 414 dollars and 25 cents, had been deposited in the Bank by the President and Treasurer.

The Board then took into consideration the disposition thereof, and, after having received some information relative to the Children of the late Mr. Hodgkinson, entered into the following resolutions.

1st. That the nett amount remaining from the collection made at the Benefit Concert given by the St. Cecilia Society, as well as such other sums of money as may be paid into their hands for the like purpose, be invested in Bank or Funded Stock, for the benefit of said Children, which shall be paid or assigned to them in equal proportions, on their respectively attaining the age of twenty-one years, or day of marriage, which shall first happen.

2d. That the interest or dividends of such Stock or Bank Shares, be paid annually as received, to such persons as may be entrusted with the custody of the persons of the children, to assist in their education and maintenance, if the same should be necessary.

But as the managers have been informed, and believe, that several respectable persons in this state are desirous and have generously offered to take upon themselves the care and expense of the maintenance and education of the unfortunate Orphan Children of the late Mr. Hodgkinson, till married, or otherwise satisfactorily settled, free from all charge, which plan is calculated to fit them for moving with comfort and respectability, in whatever walk of life it may be the will of God to guide them, and will assure them a small accumulated capital on their entrance into life—It is further resolved, that, in the event of the said Children being thus eligibly placed, the annual dividends or interest arising from such Bank or Funded Stock, shall be invested in the purchase of other Stock for their benefit.

That the President and Treasurer be requested and directed to carry into effect those resolutions; and that the President and Treasurer of this Society, for the time being, shall be Trustees for the purposes aforesaid. John S. Cogdell, *Secretary.*[38]

The planning and forethought that went into the education fund of Hodgkinson's orphans is a valuable demonstration of the nature of the St. Cecilia Society's relationship with the world of professional players. These proceedings reveal that the society did not regard its hired performers as mere anonymous employees; rather, it extended friendship and protection—true patronage—to its favorite musicians. The assistance rendered to the orphans of John Hodgkinson was not the first demonstration of the St. Cecilia Society's benevolence toward musicians, however. In fact, the society had earlier provided extensive, repeated support to a specific group of musicians: refugees from St. Domingo. Arriving shortly after the opening of the Charleston Theatre, these refugees provided a significant boost to the musical vitality of Charleston in general and the St. Cecilia Society's concerts in particular. The list of musicians who participated in the concert for John Hodgkinson's orphans demonstrates that by the turn of the nineteenth century these French-speaking refugees formed the majority of the society's orchestra.

The opening of the Charleston Theatre in the spring of 1793 was contemporary with a wave of pro-French sentiment that swept through Charleston. During the theater's first season there were a number of public and private celebrations that, in the words of Charles Fraser, "exhibited the most extravagant and enthusiastic sympathy in behalf of the French revolution."[39] When an army of mulattos and former slaves set fire to Le Cap François, a major city of St. Domingo in June 1793, this sympathy paved the way for the arrival of thousands of French refugees who began streaming into Charleston and other eastern seaports in the summer and autumn of 1793.[40] Among these refugees were professional musicians, veterans of French theaters and subscription concerts, as well as gentlemen planters who had acquired considerable musical skills as part of their privileged education. Bereft of their former livelihoods, both these groups made significant contributions to Charleston's musical life.

Before their return to Charleston in the autumn of 1793, managers West and Bignall of the Charleston Theatre wrote from Norfolk, Virginia, to state that their company had recently been enlarged by players from England and Philadelphia. In addition, a letter printed in the Charleston *City Gazette* in September 1793 announced that "their orchestra is augmented by several good performers on wind instruments, &c. from the Cape [Cap François], in consequence of which, Charleston, the ensuing season, may with truth boast of having the best performers and most regular conducted theatre on the continent."[41] Soon after their arrival in Charleston, Messrs. Remy Victor Petit, Le Roy, Pierre Joseph Foucard, Philip Villars, and Duport—French musicians "instructed by the most eminent professors in their line in Europe"—joined forces with performers from the Charleston Theatre, including Michael Benoit Poitiaux and James West, to present concerts for their own benefit.[42]

Meanwhile, in the summer of 1793, a number of gentlemen representing the leading merchants and planters of Charleston formed a new organization known as the Benevolent Society. Their stated mission was to circulate a subscription "for the purpose of raising a fund to be applied to the relief of the necessitous of every country, who may come amongst us." Despite this vague description, the real purpose of their subscription was to assist the refugees pouring out of St. Domingo.[43] Many of the officers of this new society were, of course, also members and officers of the St. Cecilia Society.[44] This overlap was more than just a coincidence, however, for just a month after the formation of this relief organization the St. Cecilia Society announced that it would hold a special meeting "to take into consideration the propriety of bestowing the funds of the society to the encrease of the Benevolent Society."[45] While the outcome of this meeting was not publicized, the society's continued interest in the welfare of the French refugees was made manifest six months later, when on 6 March 1794 the St. Cecilia Society presented a "Grand Concert, for the benefit of the distressed inhabitants of St. Domingo, now in this city," at the Charleston Theatre. Rather than naming the entire band, the printed program for this concert named only the soloists: theatrical singers Mr. and Mrs. Chambers, Mr. Clifford, and Mr. West, as well as the pianist Mrs. Sully and violinist Mr. Petit. As an event sponsored by the St. Cecilia Society, the presence of its managers ensured that a certain degree of decorum and order was observed during the performance. No doubt this was the message conveyed in the final line of the program: "None but the managers admitted on the stage."[46]

Capitalizing on the recent immigration of large numbers of refugees to Charleston, St. Domingan native John Sollée opened his French Theatre in April 1794 with a separate dramatic company and band. To staff the orchestra of this second theater, Sollée engaged a number of his fellow countrymen who had fled the recent slave uprisings and, like the managers of the Charleston Theatre, recruited professional musicians from northern theaters.[47] At that same time three refugee musicians who had joined the Charleston Theatre, Francis Lecat, Joseph Brunet, and J. B. Daugetty, published an open letter to its manager, Thomas Wade West, demanding permission to play at Sollée's French Theatre as well. Despite their impoverished condition since fleeing St. Domingo, West was reluctant to encourage the existence of a rival theater and thus forbade such sharing of personnel.[48] In a city the size of Charleston, this lack of cooperation might have proved fatal to Sollée's venture, but his theater did not perish. Its success was not so much a reflection of the city's increasing ability to attract and sustain a larger pool of professional musicians, however, as it was the result of an unusual circumstance: the recent mass exodus from St. Domingo. The sudden influx of French refugees into Charleston gave such a boost to the city's musical life that during 1795–96 one Citizen Cornet was able to sustain a Vauxhall "after the Parisian fashion," complete with "an excellent Orchestra of French Music."[49]

In the long term, however, the two rival theaters could not sustain competition in such a small city. The Charleston Theatre closed in the spring of 1796, and its players merged with those of the French Theatre, now called the Church-Street or City Theatre. Following this union, a portion of the musicians in the now-combined theater orchestra migrated back to the northern states while some of the recent French immigrants settled permanently (or died) in Charleston. The city's musical population was far from devastated, though. A "Grand Musical Festival" held at the Charleston Theatre on 6 July 1796, given as the benefit of violinist M. B. Poitiaux, performed Haydn's *Stabat mater* and other instrumental works with an ensemble that included vocal soloists, chorus, and a "full orchestra of upwards of thirty performers." The makeup of this band, which included "the most eminent professors and amateurs in town," included "one organ, twelve violins, three basses [cellos], 5 tenors [violas], six oboes flutes and clarinets, two horns, one bassoon, one pair kettle drums, in all 30 [31]." Thus with the cooperation of professional instrumentalists, St. Domingan refugees, and gentlemen amateurs, a large ensemble, even by contemporary European standards, was possible in Charleston.[50]

In the spring of 1800 the city's theatrical managers and stockholders worked out an agreement to reopen the Charleston Theatre in Broad Street and to use the Church Street venue for nondramatic entertainments.[51] After six years of rapid growth since the opening of these playhouses and the influx of refugees, Charleston's theatrical and musical life soon settled into a more regular pattern of activity. The relative calm that accompanied the turn of the nineteenth century was short-lived, however, as the pulse of the city's musical life was again quickened by the sudden arrival of new talent. In late 1803, after a decade of fighting with insurgents, France announced its decision to cede control of St. Domingo to the armies of former slaves. Echoing the events of exactly a decade earlier, a stream of French-speaking refugees, including many professional musicians and talented amateurs, began pouring into Charleston.

In late December 1803 and January 1804 a pair of subscription concerts "for the benefit of an unfortunate family, lately arrived in Charleston, from the island of St. Domingo" were presented at Concert Hall by a mixed ensemble of "professors and many amateurs." Although the St. Cecilia Society may not have been solely responsible for these events, the advertisements tactfully noted that "the rules and decorum observed at the St. Cecilia Society, will be strictly adhered to."[52] On 28 February 1804, two months after the formal proclamation of the sovereign nation of Haiti, the St. Cecilia Society presented another "Concert and Ball, for the benefit of a number of Distressed Inhabitants from St. Domingo, Who have lately arrived in Charleston." This event was given at "the St. Cecilia Society's Concert Room, in Church-street (the use of which Mr. Sollee, the proprietor, has kindly offered, free of expence)," and included the talents of Charlotte Wrighten Placide, John Hodgkinson, Mr. Marshall, "several Amateurs," and "the gentlemen composing the Orchestra of the St. Cecilia Society" (see figure 8.1). Soon afterward, the managers of this charity performance (that is, the managers of the St. Cecilia Society) announced their intention to deliberate on the mode of distributing the concert receipts, which "equaled their most sanguine expectations," and solicited applications for aid. Interested parties were directed to submit their requests,

CONCERT and BALL,

FOR THE BENEFIT OF A NUMBER OF
Distressed Inhabitants from St. Domingo,

Who have lately arrived in Charleston,

Will take place THIS EVENING, at the St. Cecilia Society's Concert Room, in Church-street, (the use of which Mr. Sollee, the proprietor, has kindly offered, free of expence) and will commence precisely at 7 o'clock.

The following is the arrangement of the MUSIC.

ACT I.

Grand Symphonie,	Haydn.
Song, " While successful proves the Gale," by Mr. Marshall,	Reeve.
Quartetto, on the Clarinet, by an Amateur,	Furche.
Song, " Lovers who Listen," by Mrs. Placide,	Storace.
Rondo,	Haydn.

ACT II.

Overture, from the Opera of Lodoiska,	Kreutzer
Song, " Dieu ! ce n'est pas pour moi," from the Opera Oedipe, by an Amateur,	Saccine
Concerto, on the Piano Forte, by an Amateur,	Dusseck
Song, " Leave not the Man of Worth without a Friend," by Mr. Hodgkinson,	Saccine
Finale,	Pleyel

Madame Placide, Messrs. Hodgkinson and Marshall and several Amateurs, together with the gentlemen composing the Orchestra of the St. Cecilia Society, have generously volunteered their services on this occasion.

Tickets, each admitting one gentleman, (who can introduce as many ladies as he may please) at 3 dollars each, may be had on application to either of the subscribers, who are appointed managers.

> James Lynah,
> John Mitchell,
> Joseph Manigault,
> O'Brien Smith,
> Wm. S. Hasell, } Managers.
> Thomas W. Bacot,
> Peter Freneau,
> George Jouve,
> Simon M'Intosh.

February 28.

8.1. Program for the St. Cecilia Society's charity concert for refugees from St. Domingo, from the *City Gazette and Daily Advertiser*, 28 February 1804. Courtesy of the Charleston Library Society "stating the number and situation of each family, and their place of residence," to Thomas W. Bacot, then treasurer of the St. Cecilia Society. In order to maximize the benefit of the collected funds, representatives of the St. Cecilia Society joined with a committee of Charleston City Council and a "Committee of Benevolence" representing the city's French community, to oversee the distribution of aid.[53]

As the Charleston Theatre began its 1804–5 season, the *Charleston Courier* remarked that "the Orchestra had been considerably enlarged," thanks in part to the participation of newly arrived refugees.[54] West Indians continued to arrive in late 1804 and into the new year, precipitating the need for additional funds to relieve their suffering. Plans for yet another concert to aid the Haitian exiles were announced at the beginning of 1805, to be held again at "the St. Cecilia Society's Concert Room."[55] The managers for the event were drawn from the experienced gentlemen of the society, as usual, but on this occasion they received assistance from several noteworthy gentlemen: John Francis Soult, J. E. A. Steinmetz, and Don Diego Morphy—the local consuls representing France, Prussia, and Spain, respectively.[56] The concert proved to be a high-water mark in Charleston's musical life, for, as the *City Gazette* reported, it was "more numerously attended . . . than any other that has heretofore been given; the rooms were literally crowded, and prepared to view a display of elegance and beauty that is not often witnessed." Attended by as many as a thousand guests, the concert reportedly brought in "upwards of sixteen hundred dollars" (roughly $26,500 in 2005), after expenses, to aid the destitute refugees.[57]

By the turn of the nineteenth century Charleston's St. Cecilia Society was at the peak of its musical activity. Its concerts were frequent, well attended, and graced by an abundance of talented performers. Thanks to the immigration of many St. Domingan refugees, the society's orchestra was predominantly composed of French musicians. Of these many musicians, a few, such as Messrs. Le Roy and Duport, left Charleston during the theatrical confusion of the late 1790s. Most of these refugees settled permanently in this city, however. Violinist Remy Victor Petit, for example, may have become the leader of the orchestra at the Charleston Theatre, for he directed the "Grand Musical Festival" there in July 1796. On his death three years later, Petit was remembered as "master of music in the Concert of St. Cecilia."[58] Philip Villars likewise survived in Charleston for nearly a decade after his arrival in 1793.[59] Clarinetist and composer Pierre Joseph Foucard (ca. 1756–1818), a native of Valenciennes in northeastern France, appeared in countless concerts in Charleston over a period of nearly twenty-five years.[60] Despite being denied permission to perform at the French Theatre in April 1794, violinists Francis Lecat (ca. 1758–1839) and J. B. Daugetty (d. 1807) spent the rest of their lives as professional musicians in Charleston.[61] Louis DeVillers (ca. 1766–1831), a native of France, also arrived in Charleston in the mid-1790s. In addition to performing at a myriad of concerts in Charleston, he operated a retail music store for more than twenty-five years.[62] William Noel, a native of St. Domingo, was active in Charleston as a violinist between at least 1802 and his death in 1808.[63]

Many of the refugee musicians from St. Domingo were *grand blancs,* or wealthy planters and merchants, who, in an effort to repair their broken lives, turned their musical accomplishments into a new vocation in Charleston. This transformation is best articulated in a promotion for the 1805 benefit concert of multi-instrumentalist Robert Leaumont. A former planter in St. Domingo, decorated veteran of the American Revolution, and published composer, Marie-Robert de Castile, Chevalier de Léaumont (1762–1814) arrived in Charleston via Boston in 1799 and soon became leader of the Charleston Theatre's orchestra. In April 1805 the *Charleston Courier* described him as "a gentleman who once luxuriated in honourable rank and affluence, but by the sad reverses of an unpropitious fate, has been driven to the mortifying, but we maintain honourable expedient, of making provision for a numerous family, by practicing as a profession that which was originally acquired as an elegant accomplishment, and exercised only as an amusement."[64] Other refugee musicians in Charleston were of a similar mold. The brothers Remoussin—Daniel (ca. 1781–1814), Arnold (1783–1820), and Augustus (1784–1829)—were sons of the Chevalier Marie-Paul Daniel Remoussin (1740–after 1820), and were once "numbered among the wealthiest planters" in St. Domingo.[65] The most active of these brothers, Arnold, was identified in March 1809 as the "Leader of the Band" at the Charleston Theatre.[66] Henri Dovivier Peire (or Peyre, born ca. 1777), a stepson of the Chevalier Remoussin, played music and taught dance in Charleston.[67] Similarly Joseph Brunet (ca. 1748–1808), a native of Paris, was remembered on his death as having been "twice reduced by the storm of the French revolution, from the exalted station of a judge and a commissary under the administration of St. Domingo too [*sic*] great extremities."[68] Arriving in Charleston in 1793, Charles Carrere (1762–1829) left behind "a handsome property" in his native St. Domingo and spent the next thirty years as a performer and teacher of music.[69] Jean-Jacques Heulan (ca. 1771–1832) attracted music students by advertising himself as "formerly a Planter of the West-Indies, having been educated in the best Colleges in Europe."[70] Jean-Jacques Miniere (born ca. 1768), a planter who fled Cap François in 1803, was also active in Charleston's musical life for several years.[71]

As gentlemen planters stripped of their property, many of these refugee musicians found not only employers but friends among the circle of the St. Cecilia Society. The career of (Pierre) Isadore Labatut (ca. 1768–1856), a multitalented gentleman who arrived in Charleston in the mid-1790s, provides an excellent example of this phenomenon. The "son of the commander of the island of Tortuga" (just north of St. Domingo), whose family arrived penniless in Charleston, Labatut provided for himself and his young wife, the former Mlle. Remoussin, by capitalizing on the artistic accomplishments acquired through his privileged education.[72] In December 1799 Margaret Izard Manigault, the wife of St. Cecilia Society manager Gabriel Manigault, wrote to Josephine du Pont in New York about their mutual friends Monsieur and Madame Labatut. Regarding Labatut's efforts to sustain his family, Mrs. Manigault wrote "He is extremely industrious, & a very good husband. Takes lodgers, boarders, scholars. Teaches drawing, & music, & French. Plays at the Theatre, at the Concert, with the Military Band [at Vauxhall Garden]. Does every thing, & is esteemed."[73] The concert at which Labatut performed was undoubtedly the concert series of the St. Cecilia Society, of which the Manigault gentlemen were long-time members. From these varied activities the Labatuts managed a fairly comfortable existence, though certainly not as luxurious as their situation in prerevolutionary St. Domingo. The following year Mrs. Manigault informed Mrs. du Pont that Mons. Labatut "continues to work like a horse & with all his exertions makes about 1200 dollars a year [roughly $18,940 in 2005]. That is very well, & he provides for [his wife's] every comfort."[74]

Not all the formerly wealthy refugees who benefited from the patronage of the St. Cecilia Society were men, however. Several women amateurs, not trained to pursue careers as professional musicians, presented their musical talents before the circle of the society in order to support their distressed families. Among these was a young lady whose vocal prowess brought her to the attention of the St. Cecilia Society. The amateur singer Antoinette La Roque probably arrived in Charleston as a child sometime in the 1790s and performed anonymously before her name became known to the public in 1804.[75] On 5 April 1804 Miss La Roque received a benefit concert and ball, the managers and ticket agents of which were also managers of the St. Cecilia Society. A note accompanying the initial advertisement stated the motivation for this concert, perhaps for the benefit of those who had not yet had the luxury of hearing her more private performances: "Madame La Roque arrived here from St. Domingo, with her daughter Miss La Roque, and several younger children, stripped of all means of subsistence. Miss La Roque has given the aid of her voice on various occasions in this city, for the benefit of others, at Concerts and Oratorios; and she now is encouraged to hope that she may obtain, from the kindness of the citizens, some relief for her distressed mother and her family."[76]

A year later, on 18 April 1805, Miss La Roque presented another concert for her benefit, for which she "humbly" solicited "a portion of that liberal patronage and support, which so eminently characterizes the respectable inhabitants of this city." Tickets were to be had from a long list of sixteen gentlemen, identified as "*Officers and Managers of the St. Cecilia Society.*"[77] A pre-concert puff described La Roque as having been "born in affluence and reared in the lap of ease and luxurious elegance" and offered a musical preview of the concert: "Those whose souls can harmonize with the 'Concord of Sweet Sounds' will be much gratified by attending this Concert. Hodgkinson and Story will exert their vocal powers to please. To which will be added, the unrivalled sweetness of Miss Laroque's voice. The celebrated Overtures from Nina [by Nicolas-Marie Dalayrac], Lodoiska [by Rodolphe Kreutzer] and the young Henry [Etienne-Nicolas Méhul's *Jeune Henri*], will be performed; and a Concerto on the Piano will exhibit the talents of the youngest Remoussin [Arnold] upon that instrument."[78] Another puff recommended the instrumental selections as "uncommonly fine," and assured the audience that "the Ariettes selected by Miss La Roque, for her voice, are singularly beautiful; and will, no doubt, be sung in the finest style of taste and melody." "Exclusive of the above inducements," the anonymous correspondent added, "all who are disposed to be liberal to merit, or benevolent to distress, will gratify the noblest feelings of the heart, by taking tickets, and swelling the receipts of the Concert."[79]

Cognizant of the value of the patronage she received in Charleston, Miss La Roque published a public thanks after the concert "to tender her best respects and unfeigned thanks to those Ladies and Gentlemen who honored her Concert with their attendance on Thursday last." Directing her gratitude more specifically to the gentlemen of the St. Cecilia Society, she also requested "that the Gentlemen who were so kind as the assist her in the disposal of tickets and undertake the management of the Concert, as well as those Gentlemen who volunteered their services in the performances thereof, will accept her very grateful acknowledgements."[80]

Antoinette La Roque appeared in a number of public concerts in Charleston between 1804 and 1807 and received two more concerts for her own benefit in April 1806 and April 1807. As with her previous benefits, these events were advertised as being given "under the patronage of the Managers of the St. Cecilia Society" and performed with assistance from "Gentlemen of the Orchestra of the St. Cecilia Society."[81] Considering that each of Miss La Roque's benefit concerts took place in April during the years 1804 through 1807, it is possible that she was a regular performer at the St. Cecilia Society's concerts for at least four seasons and at the end of each received permission to present a concert for her own profit. This venture into the musical profession was but a brief chapter in Miss La Roque's life, however. Shortly after her benefit concert in April 1807, the local press announced that Miss La Roque had recently married a French merchant in Charleston named Peter Robin.

Mrs. Robin's name does not again appear in published concert programs in Charleston until February 1813, at a benefit for Mrs. Placide sponsored by the society, after which her name appears not at all. It is not clear whether she continued singing at the St. Cecilia concerts, but it is certain that she withdrew from public performances.[82]

In contrast to Miss La Roque, pianist Jane Labat appears to have embraced the opportunity to capitalize on her musical talents; in fact, she turned it into a family business. The wife of French merchant André Labat (born ca. 1771), Madame Jane Labat arrived in Charleston in early 1807 and quickly attracted the attention of the city's musical amateurs.[83] By exhibiting her talents at the private musicales held in the drawing rooms of the city's elite families, Madame Labat appears to have secured immediately the support of the gentlemen of the St. Cecilia Society. In early March 1807 the *Charleston Courier* carried the announcement that "a Grand Concert and Ball, Will be given on Thursday, 12th instant, at the Concert Room, in Church-street under the patronage of the Managers of the St. Cecilia Society, for the benefit of Madam Labat, whose wonderful powers on the Piano Forte have never been equaled in this country, and perhaps unrivaled in Europe, and have excited the astonishment and admiration of all those who have had the pleasure of hearing her exquisite performances." The gentlemen of the orchestra assisted Madame Labat for this performance, as did vocal soloists Filippo Trajetta and Antoinette La Roque, and nine-year-old pianist Mademoiselle Ursule Labat. The day before the performance, however, a brief postponement notice was published, the wording of which underscores the interdependence of the city's musical resources: "Madam Labat's Concert and Ball, are postponed until Friday Evening, in consequence of Mrs. Placide's Benefit taking place [at the theatre] on Thursday. There will be but one Concert of the St. Cecilia Society [remaining] this season."[84] After another postponement, Labat's concert was finally performed on 17 March. An anonymous communication to the *City Gazette* of that day provides an unusually specific testimony of Madame Labat's talents: "Nothing in the United States has ever approached the performances of Madam Labat; who was considered, even in Europe, to have rivaled, if not surpassed, all the *first-rate* performers—Nothing, indeed, can equal the brilliancy of her touch—the distinctness and rapidity of her execution, unless it be the delicate and exquisite taste and feeling, with which she gives the most enchanting expression to the composer's ideas."[85]

Although the date of Labat's arrival is unclear, she may have been performing regularly with the St. Cecilia Society during the spring of 1807, for just two days after the society's final concert of the season she was advertising the sale of a new shipment of Erard pianos from Paris, as well as "the handsome Piano, with four pedals, on which she played at the St. Cecilia Concert,

should any person be desirous of purchasing the same."[86] In the months following her March 1807 concert, Madame Labat displayed her "elegant," "well-
known talents" and "uncommon powers" on the piano at a number of benefit
concerts for other musicians.[87] Noting "the kind reception she has met with
in this city," she extended her thanks "to the public in general, and in particular to the Managers of the St. Cecilia Society, for the favors already conferred
on her; the continuation of which, she now solicits, as a Teacher of both Vocal
Music and Forte-Piano; having been prevailed upon by the solicitations of her
friends, to fix her residence here."[88] Despite her announcement of settling in
Charleston, Madame Labat left the city at some point and then announced her
return, "lately from London," in June 1812.[89] In subsequent years, through at
least 1817, Madame Labat performed in several benefit concerts (as did her
young daughters, the pianist Ursule and the singer Constance) and continued
to sell imported pianos.[90]

For these lady and gentleman refugees, the act of turning one's "elegant
accomplishments" into a professional vocation could easily have been seen as
a step downward on the social ladder and thus represented a serious risk to
the family's reputation. Yet their distress was real and, being strangers to the
city and the language, allowed little choice but to find a ready means of support. The intervention of the St. Cecilia Society, with its well-established reputation for decorous behavior, sophisticated musical taste, and exclusive
social sphere, allowed these unfortunate refugees to capitalize on their talents
with a minimum of embarrassment or injury to their reputations.

In consequence of the profusion of musicians in Charleston in the early
years of the nineteenth century, including many others not named here, the
St. Cecilia Society enjoyed a bountiful concert life. The musical atmosphere
was so vibrant, in fact, that the professional musicians in Charleston formed
and incorporated their own subscription concert series: the Philharmonic
Society. Between March 1809 and May 1812 this organization provided a parallel, but not necessarily competitive, musical outlet that gave these musicians
another opportunity to capitalize on their talents. Although little is known
about its audience, the names listed in the act to incorporate the Philharmonic Society in 1810 clearly indicate that it was composed of the same theater musicians and St. Domingan refugees who performed at other concerts
in Charleston—including those of the St. Cecilia Society.[91] This new society
was a purely commercial venture, with the musicians themselves acting as its
officers and managers.[92] By presenting its fortnightly subscription concerts at
an alternative venue (the long room of dancing master and violinist Peter Fayolle) on a different night of the week (Tuesday rather than Thursday), the
Philharmonic Society represented an alternative to the St. Cecilia Society
rather than its rival.[93] Thus with record numbers of musicians inhabiting the

city and its audiences rapidly enlarging, Charleston enjoyed an unprecedented level of musical activity in the early years of the nineteenth century.

Declining Numbers of Musicians

In the years after 1793, the prosperity of the St. Cecilia Society's concerts was owed in large part to the numbers of musicians brought to Charleston by the theater and by the revolts in St. Domingo. The society's interdependent relationship with the theater and the refugee community ensured it a ready supply of talented performers and perhaps lulled it into a more passive form of musical patronage. This reliance on external sources to staff its concerts left the society vulnerable to changes beyond its control in Charleston. Such was the case in the years after the War of 1812: the society experienced great difficulty in sustaining its orchestra when the duration of the theater company's annual residence in Charleston began to diminish. The musical contingent of the Charleston Theatre was still numerous and talented, but it began to spend less time in the city. Compounding this problem was the graying of the resident population of St. Domingan refugee musicians, who, by the 1810s, were quietly fading away. While other pressures, social and economic, also contributed to the St. Cecilia Society's difficulties in its final years as a musical organization, its inability to form an orchestra independently of the theater company was a major factor in its withdrawal from concert activity. This fact is clearly demonstrated by the succession of dramatic changes to Charleston's musical scene between 1812 and 1820.

The summer of 1812 was marked by a pair of events that had significant consequences for concert activity in Charleston. The declaration of war against Great Britain in June was the culmination of several years of political and economic unease and presaged a suspension of high spirits. Almost simultaneously, the death of Alexander Placide, the long-time manager of the Charleston Theatre, in July 1812 caused a serious interruption in the city's theatrical routine.[94] His widow, Charlotte Wrighten Placide, attempted to start the theatrical season in early January 1813, but the "dormant liberality of the Charleston public"—no doubt caused by the war with Britain—forced her to abandon the season after a few nights.[95] For the remainder of the War of 1812, a further two seasons, the Charleston Theatre lay empty. During this time the city's population of professional musicians did decline slightly, but not as dramatically as during the Revolutionary War. Drawing on the St. Domingan refugees and theater musicians who had settled permanently in Charleston, and with the continued assistance of amateurs, there were still sufficient numbers of performers in the city to assemble an orchestra for the concerts of the St. Cecilia Society. Nevertheless, the general contraction of the city's musical life during the War of 1812 is demonstrated by the demise of the Philharmonic Society.

Following the conclusion of its concert season in May 1812 the Philharmonic Society advertised only anniversary concerts in the spring of 1813 and 1814. No further advertisements of this organization appear after the death of its president, Robert Leaumont, in August 1814.[96]

The renascence of the Charleston Theatre in the autumn of 1815 renewed the supply of seasonal musicians to the city, creating the opportunity for Charleston's concert life to be reinvigorated. Changes were soon underway, however, that reduced the seasonal tenure of the theatrical corps in Charleston and, by extension, eroded the orchestra of the St. Cecilia Society. The agent most responsible for this upheaval, the manager of the city's theater, was not a faceless, remote adversary of the society. On the contrary, that person, German-born musician and composer Charles Gilfert (1786–1829), was an intimate acquaintance of the society who had personally benefited from its patronage.

Gilfert was somewhat of a celebrity in early-nineteenth-century Charleston. In his reminiscences of theatrical life during that era, Dr. John Beaufain Irving (1800–1881) posed a rhetorical question: "who in our community, at that time, did not know Gilfert by sight, and [had not] been struck by some of his remarkable ways?"[97] Gilfert had a long history with the society and was friendly with many of its members. Before taking up residence in the manager's apartments in the Charleston Theatre, he kept an "open house" at the western end of Price's Alley, "which he dignified by the title of 'Brandenburg Castle.'" Here Gilfert daily entertained his friends, patrons, and, in his words, the "lads of the village." This entourage included not only musicians and actors, but also Charleston artists, writers, and many gentlemen of the St. Cecilia Society.[98]

Charles Gilfert's career in Charleston was underway by at least January 1807, when he presented a concert and ball for his own benefit.[99] He had arrived as one of the seasonal musicians of the Charleston Theatre, and accordingly was prone to migrations between this city and theaters to the north. In December 1809 he became the organist at St. John's, then Charleston's only Lutheran church.[100] The following December, Gilfert announced that he had "made Charleston his place of residence" and opened the Gilfert & Co. retail music store in Broad Street.[101] In May 1811, however, Gilfert's participation in a duel obliged him to flee Charleston for some time.[102] By the end of the following spring he was back at the theater in Charleston, where he became a citizen of the United States immediately after the declaration of war with Britain in June 1812.[103] Sometime after the closing of the Charleston Theatre in early 1813, Gilfert left Charleston and became leader of the orchestra first at the Theatrical Commonwealth and then at the Park Theatre in New York.[104] After his father-in-law, English actor Joseph Holman, reopened the

Charleston Theatre in the autumn of 1815, Gilfert and his new bride made their way to Charleston as well.[105] Gilfert's talents as a performer and composer were much admired in Charleston, and his return to the city did not go unnoticed. His benefit concert in March 1816, managed by several gentlemen of the circle of the St. Cecilia Society, was attended by a "crowded and fashionable audience" who judged that the music, "particularly Mr. G.'s performance on the Piano, gave the most complete satisfaction."[106] Days later, Gilfert was scheduled to appear at the benefit concert of the theatrical singer P. H. Taylor. In a letter to Margaret Izard Manigault in Philadelphia, Martha Coffin Derby, a New England resident wintering in Charleston, recorded the anticipation for this performance felt among the city's music lovers: "We have heard Madame La Batte [Labat] and Mme. Bridone [Virginia Bridon] this evening will present a trial of skill between the former and Guilford [Gilfert]—they both play at Taylor's Concert and as the Musicians (Taylor being a great favorite with them) intend to do their *best,* great expectations are raised. Opinions differ with respect to Mde. la Batte and Guilford—the former's friends here will not allow of a comparison. Mr. D[erby] I think leans to Guilford as having more soul—more genius."[107]

When the Charleston Theatre began its season in November 1816, its advertisements boldly announced "the ORCHESTRE is placed under the direction of Mr. Gilfert."[108] In its second season following the conclusion of the War of 1812, the Charleston Theatre was not only revived, but its musical forces were expanded. "In addition to several of our veterans," the *Southern Patriot* observed in November 1816, "Mr. Holman has brought from England and the Northward an accession of numbers and of talents." Directing his attention to the theater's orchestra, the newspaper's correspondent was equally sanguine: "In the Music, also, those who have long regretted the want of an excellent band, will perceive, in this respect, a striking and desirable improvement. . . . As to the *morale* of the musical corps, it is almost sufficient to say, that the leader of the band is Mr. Gilfert—whose talents, both in composition and execution, are too well known, and indeed too well felt by *amateurs,* to need any commendation from us. The whole band, in our humble estimation, taken together, forms a body of better talent and experience, than we have been gratified with, for several years."[109]

Although Charleston audiences may not have known it at the time, when Holman assumed the management of the Charleston Theatre in the autumn of 1815, he did so with the intention of making the city the hub of a circuit of southeastern theaters. This idea was not entirely new. Under the management of Alexander Placide, the corps of the Charleston Theatre had occasionally played short engagements in cities such as Augusta, Savannah, and Richmond. On two occasions at the beginning of the nineteenth century, in

December 1801 and January 1803, the concert schedule of the St. Cecilia Society had been interrupted "on account of the absence of some of the Performers, with the Theatrical Corps at Savannah."[110] In contrast to these brief forays, however, Holman envisioned a network of southern theaters operated by a large, divisible company. During the next two seasons in Charleston, Holman's less-than-scrupulous management alienated much of the local community and thwarted progress toward this goal.[111] Following Holman's sudden death in August 1817, Gilfert inherited not only the management of the Charleston Theatre but also the plan for a southeastern theatrical circuit. Dr. Irving, who witnessed this transition firsthand, later recalled that "a new era of theatricals may be said, then, to have commenced."[112]

After assuming Holman's management duties, Gilfert brought his theatrical company from New York (where they had summered) to Norfolk, Virginia, where they performed from 14 October until 1 December 1817.[113] Their delay in returning to Charleston was motivated in part by the epidemic of yellow fever that was then raging in the city.[114] The *Southern Patriot* looked forward to the arrival of an early frost, which would allow the social calendar to commence: "With the return of the season, which always brings gaiety, business, fashion and enjoyment in its train, our city will again put on the smiling face it always presents during the winter months." The first frost did not occur until 18 November, after which the *Charleston Courier* announced that citizens "may now venture to our city with the utmost security."[115] Receiving this news in Norfolk, Gilfert wrapped up his performances in that city and journeyed back to Charleston, opening the Charleston Theatre on 12 December 1817.

During the Charleston Company's engagement in Norfolk that autumn, the St. Cecilia Society advertised no concerts. In addition to the absence of the majority of the city's orchestral musicians, the society's members were no doubt as wary as the theatrical players of gathering in Charleston during this severe sickly season. After the epidemic subsided, however, the society moved to commence its concert season. With Gilfert and company still out of town, the society called an extra meeting in early December to discuss "business of importance"—surely concerning its arrangement with the musicians of the Charleston Theatre's orchestra.[116] The society's first concert did not take place until 29 January 1818, by which time Gilfert had divided the Charleston Company and sent half to perform in Augusta, Georgia, from 14 January to 4 April 1818.[117] Continuing its nearly half century tradition of fortnightly Thursday concerts, the next St. Cecilia concert was scheduled for 12 February. By 6 February 1818, however, the society announced that "it being found impracticable to procure an Orchestra for the society for the present season, a Ball will take place on Thursday Evening, 12th inst."[118]

In addition to the complications caused by the society's arrangements with the theater musicians, an air of melancholy hung over Charleston in the early months of 1818. In February the *Courier* noted that the annual Jockey Club races "have been uncommonly meagre and uninteresting—offering little to excite or reward attention." Searching for an explanation for this fact, the correspondent observed, "We are growing more serious—perhaps more intellectual." The shock of the many deaths caused by the recent autumnal fevers still hung over the Charleston community. "The atmosphere of grief has dampened our feelings—and our harp is hung upon the willows. . . . 'How can we sing,' asked the Israelites, 'in a strange land.' How can this city forget its recent sufferings, and plunge into the clamorous festivities of the season."[119] In spite of the lingering melancholy and the complications in assembling its orchestra, the St. Cecilia Society upheld its fortnightly schedule of performances through the end of March 1818. Of these remaining three performances, the society presented another ball followed by two concerts. For the first time in its long history, the society had substituted balls for concerts, yet its total of five events that spring still represented a reasonably average post–New Year's schedule. In the ensuing years, however, the logistical complications caused by the new touring circuit of the Charleston Theatre got worse. The 1817–18 season—so problematic for the St. Cecilia Society's musical endeavors—proved to be the longest Gilfert ever kept his company in Charleston again.[120]

In the autumn of 1818, Gilfert once again commenced his theatrical performances in Norfolk before playing a brief but intense period in Charleston between 28 October and 27 November. During the company's short residence, the St. Cecilia Society advertised a concert for 12 November. Two days before the performance, however, the society abruptly announced that "in consequence of the arrangements made at the *Charleston Theatre* for the present week, which deprive the society of the use of its Orchestra, there will be a BALL at the *Carolina Coffee-House,* on Thursday Evening next, in lieu of the Concert." Although the theater company was in town, it was performing on an unprecedented daily schedule—including the evening of 12 November. The musicians of the theater's orchestra, who formerly had Thursday evenings free, were thus not at liberty to prepare for the St. Cecilia Society's scheduled concert. At the end of November, Gilfert took his company to Savannah for a two-month engagement. During this absence, the society held one concert before Christmas (probably staffed by a reduced orchestra of resident professionals), followed by two balls in January. The Charleston Theatre was reopened at the beginning of February 1819, after which the St. Cecilia Society performed a single concert. Its season was abruptly terminated, however, when Gilfert and company suddenly returned to Savannah for the entire month of March. The return of the theatrical corps in early April enabled the society to present a "splendid Concert and Ball" for President James Monroe on 1 May 1819.[121]

In the autumn of 1819 Gilfert announced a bold scheme to present two concurrent companies in the theaters of his southeastern circuit. His divided company played in both Norfolk and Richmond during the early months of the season (thus avoiding yet another epidemic of deadly fevers in Charleston).[122] Gilfert and part of his company then performed in Charleston from 12 December 1819 to 18 May 1820, during which the St. Cecilia Society presented three balls and two more events designated "concert and ball." This nomenclature was common enough in early-nineteenth-century Charleston, but before its performance for President Monroe, the St. Cecilia Society had never employed it. Since its inception the society had concluded each concert evening with dancing, but this new designation suggests a change in emphasis. Perhaps representing a dilution of the spirit of the previous concerts, these two "concert and ball" events were the last regular musical performances of the St. Cecilia Society's lengthy concert tradition.

Problems with Gilfert and the Charleston Theatre continued for several years after the St. Cecilia Society presented its last concert. By the spring of 1820 Gilfert's responsibilities as the director of a dual theatrical company had separated him not only from his ostensible home base of Charleston but from almost all musical activity in general. At some point, probably in 1818, Gilfert turned over the direction of the theater's orchestra to the violinist Mr. Nicola, who continued in this capacity through the 1820s. During the brief 1820–21 theatrical season, Gilfert did not appear in Charleston until mid-March 1821, entrusting the managerial duties of the Charleston Theatre to an assistant. In the spring of 1822, a number of lawsuits over unpaid debts caused Gilfert, known to be a compulsive gambler, to lose his lease on the Charleston Theatre as well as his stock shares in the property, and by late May of that year, he was jailed for the debts he had incurred during his efforts to establish a widespread network of theaters. This was not the end of his career as manager of the Charleston Theatre, however; Gilfert remained in Charleston until early 1825, during which time he functioned as the "quasi manager" of the theater before moving to New York.[123]

As Gilfert and his contemporaries no doubt realized, the erratic residency of the Charleston Theatre company in the years 1817 through 1820 represented a serious blow to the St. Cecilia Society's long-standing annual concert series. In retrospect we can imagine that the complications and frustrations arising from these circumstances, including the cancellation or postponement of many concerts over several seasons, contributed greatly to the society's decision to withdraw from concert patronage. Since the opening of the

Charleston Theatre in 1793, the society had relied on that institution to ensure the nearly continuous presence of professional musicians in the city in order to staff its concerts. This logical and efficient arrangement allowed the society to relax any concerns about finding qualified musicians to fill vacancies in its orchestra and to focus instead on a more passive enjoyment of music and socialization. As a result of this well-established passivity, however, the society was not prepared to cope with the disturbances caused by Gilfert's theatrical migrations. During its last several concert seasons, the society tried to make the most of the situation by presenting a reduced number of performances. By the spring of 1820 the St. Cecilia Society's difficulties in "procuring" an orchestra reached a breaking point. Founded as a musical society more than fifty years earlier, the society found that the sudden lack of performers threatened its very purpose. Rather than mounting an aggressive attempt to remedy the situation and to preserve its long-standing tradition, the society opted to forgo concerts in favor of a limited number of balls each season.

The Form and Musical Content of the Concerts

THE CULTIVATION OF MUSIC FORMED THE PRINCIPAL MISSION of the St. Cecilia Society's early activities; yet few details about the specific music it nurtured have survived. While the society did frequently publish preperformance notices of its concerts during the five decades of its musical activity, it never publicly advertised the content of any of its regular concerts. Knowledge of this musical content evidently remained with the society—in its own library of musical scores, in its secretary's records, and in the private papers of its audience. A few pieces of direct evidence are known to have survived, but the destruction of the society's records and the papers of many of its members in 1865 obliterated the primary sources relating to this matter. Despite this limitation, sufficient circumstantial evidence exists from other musical activity in Charleston during this time to produce a reconstruction of the form and musical content of the society's concerts.

From its emergence in 1766 to its withdrawal from concert patronage in 1820, the musical activity of the St. Cecilia Society was concurrent with the life cycle of an aesthetic era musicologists describe as the Classical period. During this time the society's concerts echoed the practices of those in contemporary Britain by cultivating a cosmopolitan musical aesthetic based on the works of contemporary European composers. The repertoire heard at British concerts formed a primary influence for those in Charleston, but the French music introduced by St. Domingan refugees after 1793 also had a noticeable impact. The society's concerts featured a mix of orchestral music, concerti, chamber music, and vocal music written by composers who, while they may have once enjoyed some celebrity, have been largely forgotten by modern concert audiences.

The Influence of British Models

The emergence of Charleston's St. Cecilia Society in 1766 was contemporaneous with a significant transformation of musical taste then taking place in
England. Specifically the society's concert series began in the wake of a major
shift in musical repertoire that took place in that country around the year
1760. Prior to that time the repertoire, styles, and genres associated with the
musical era now known as the Baroque period held sway. With the arrival of
music and musicians representing the latest Continental style in the 1750s and
early 1760s, a new aesthetic era was underway. In his multivolume *General
History of Music,* published between 1776 and 1789, Charles Burney described
the revolutionary nature of this transition: "Content with our former posses-
sions and habits, we went on in the tranquil enjoyment of the productions of
Corelli, Geminiani, and Handel, at our national theatres, concerts, and public
gardens, till the arrival of Giardini, Bach, and Abel; who soon created schisms,
and at length, with the assistance of Fischer, brought about a total revolution
in our music taste."[1] London audiences were captivated by the suave, cantabile
melodic style introduced by the Italian violinist Felice Giardini (1716–1796)
on his arrival in London in 1751 and by the Italian opera singers recruited to
perform on England's stages. The arrival of orchestral music by German composer Johann Stamitz (1717–1757) and his Scottish pupil Thomas Erskine,
Earl of Kelly (1732–1781), in the late 1750s introduced London concert audiences to the elaborations on the simple and elegant Italian *galant* style made
famous by the court orchestra of the elector of Mannheim. The permanence
of this new musical aesthetic was cemented in the early 1760s by the arrival of
Carl Friedrich Abel (1723–1787) and Johann Christian Bach (1735–1782),
who collaborated to present their own subscription concert series.[2] With the
assistance of German oboe virtuoso Johann Christian Fischer (1733–1800),
the Bach-Abel concerts were the most celebrated and fashionable subscription
concert series in London between 1765 and 1782.

By combining the melodic simplicity that characterized Italian music of
this period with Germanic harmonic sensibility and colorful orchestration,
composers from across Europe collectively contributed to the creation of the
remarkably uniform musical aesthetic that musicologists describe as the Classical style. Emerging in southern Europe during the 1750s and spreading
northward, this new cosmopolitan style—which, like contemporary architecture, embraced the virtues of linear clarity and formal symmetry—became
the lingua franca of European composers during the second half of the eighteenth century.[3] Despite some opposition from traditionalists, the adoption of
this musical language in Britain during the 1760s and 1770s relegated "native"
music to the cultural sidelines.[4]

The fact that the emergence and initial flowering of this musical aesthetic in London was contemporary with the peak period of colonial South Carolina's economic and cultural connection with Britain is an important clue for understanding the musical character of the nascent St. Cecilia Society. During the 1760s and early 1770s, the commercial and cultural traffic between these two locations provided ample opportunities for Charlestonians to learn about or to experience firsthand the latest British and European musical fashions. Charleston native Peter Manigault (1731–1773), for example, near the end of his extensive schooling in London in February 1754, wrote home to his ailing mother with a remedy for her sufferings. Were she in London, Manigault declared, "I would have waited on you to see the new Italian Singers & Dancers who are just arrived from Naples: There you would have felt such Power of Music, & seen such just Action in the Singers, & such easy & proper Motion in the Dancers, as for the time w[oul]d have suspended all sense of Pain.—These People have so tickled my Ears with their Italian Airs, that tis high time I should leave England, or I shall spend all my Money upon them."[5] Manigault, whose two English-educated sons later served as officers of the St. Cecilia Society, was clearly entranced by the Italian performers who invigorated London's musical scene with the latest in *galant* musical fashions. Charleston native Ralph Izard (1741–1804), a musical amateur and connoisseur of all the arts, had a parallel experience some years later while traveling in Europe.[6] After purchasing a house in London in 1771, Izard and his family embarked on an extended tour of the Continent. In a January 1775 letter written from Naples to a Charleston friend, Izard drew on his experiences in London to opine about the present state of music in Italy: "The music in this country, has not answered my expectation. The performers in the opera, at London, are superior to those at Florence and Naples. There was no opera at Turin, when I was there, and the inhabitants of Rome are too devout to suffer any in the holy city. With regard to instrumental music, I am persuaded that, all Italy united, could not produce such a concert as Bach's and Ables [Abel's]."[7]

The numerous advertisements of music retailers in Charleston during the late eighteenth and early nineteenth centuries testify to the steady flow of musical fashions from London and regularly emphasize the newness of these imported works. Starting in 1756, Robert Wells, who published the St. Cecilia Society's first newspaper notices and its first set of rules, repeatedly advertised the availability of the "newest music" and instruments at his "Great Stationary and Book Store." His contemporary, Nicholas Langford, also imported music and instruments in partnership with Jervis Henry Stevens, later librarian of the St. Cecilia Society. Shortly after the Revolution, Charles Morgan and then William P. Young imported large quantities of new music from London, including a variety of composers "too tedious to enumerate."[8] Thomas Bradford, among the most active of these merchants, announced in early 1788 that he carried "all the new Operas, now performing in London, and the latest music for all instruments, composed by the most eminent masters in Europe." In 1789 Bradford sold music "for all instruments, judiciously selected from the works of the most exquisite masters, whose compositions will continue to be imported as soon as published in Europe." In the summer of 1792 he boasted that he had just imported from London "the greatest variety of new music by Pleyel, Hayden [Haydn], &c. and other exquisite masters, too extensive to enumerate, but far superior in quantity and quality to any music hitherto imported into this country."[9] Well after Bradford's death, other Charleston music retailers such as Jacob Eckhard and Louis DeVillers continued to stress the recent vintage of their merchandise, including, for example, "the latest musical publications, consisting of Concertos, Quartettos, Trios, Sonatas, with the newest English Songs, &c."[10]

In contrast to the copious evidence of imported musical fashions in Charleston, a number of reports, advertisements, and concert programs published in the local newspapers demonstrate that a few musicians residing in Charleston during the late eighteenth and early nineteenth centuries did compose some concert music. Very little of this music has survived, or at least has yet surfaced.[11] Consistent with the dearth of direct information about the musical content of the St. Cecilia Society's concerts, there is not sufficient evidence to determine conclusively the society's attitude toward the performance or cultivation of such works. As with other aspects of its endeavors, however, a viable hypothesis can easily be drawn from a comparison with contemporary subscription concert series in Britain. Throughout the second half of the eighteenth century and into the early nineteenth century, British concerts were dominated by the performance of musical fashions imported from the Continent, while music written by native British composers was generally relegated to an inferior status. The large amount of music composed in Britain by Continental musicians—such as J. C. Bach, Muzio Clementi, and Ignaz Pleyel, to name only a few—was exempted from this prejudice, however. Such musical bias was part of the cachet of the subscription concert series and was akin to their policy of social exclusivity.[12] Inclusion in such a society provided access to an esoteric cultural milieu that reinforced the distinction between the fashionable and the mundane. By comparison the purpose of the St. Cecilia Society (according to its own act of incorporation) was to promote an appreciation of the science of music—not in the community at large but among its exclusive social sphere. The achievement of this goal required the performance of music sanctioned by authorized and accepted standards of taste. In eighteenth- and early-nineteenth-century Charleston, this standard was established by the concert societies of London and their preference for the latest Continental imports. If locally composed music was in fact performed at the St. Cecilia Society's concerts, it is likely that the society's attitude toward this repertoire was influenced by a variation on the British bias: music composed locally by British or European musicians would receive preference over the productions of native composers. In the absence of more robust evidence, however, this hypothesis cannot be proven with certainty.

Regardless of such questions, it can be stated with confidence that the society did not seek to foster the creation of a regional or national style. Although Charleston was for many generations considered the cultural capital of the American South, the musical repertoire cultivated by the St. Cecilia Society bore no relation whatever to what is colloquially known as "Southern Music." The predominantly rural mixing of Anglo- and/or African American influences, which gave rise to such phenomena as American country music, spiritual songs (both Anglo- and African American), minstrel music, and the blues developed on entirely separate paths from the imported, cosmopolitan music heard at the St. Cecilia concerts. In this respect Charleston's musical culture was not necessarily unique, for much of the same music—and often the same musicians—were also heard in contemporary American cities such as Boston, New York, Philadelphia, and Baltimore. What was unique to Charleston, however, was the social context in which this music was fostered. Given that the St. Cecilia Society was cultural byproduct of the region's plantation economy and its dependence on chattel slavery, that its "aristocratic" gentlemen occasionally fought duels and imbibed liberally of fine imported wines, and that its members were preoccupied with manners and appearances, the society itself may certainly be described as a kind of "southern" phenomenon. The musical legacy of this society, however, is too urbane and cosmopolitan to be limited by such a label.

The Formal Structure of Concerts during the Classical Period

There are but three pieces of direct evidence to illustrate the form and musical content of the St. Cecilia Society's regular concerts: a newspaper notice from December 1773 requesting the return of several bound volumes of the society's music, a handbill for the society's 1778 anniversary concert among the papers of Charles Drayton (1743–1820), and Charles Fraser's brief reference to a handbill from November 1815 in his *Reminiscences*. In contrast to this dearth of evidence, the programs of most charity and commercial concerts (those organized by professional musicians and open to the public) advertised in Charleston between 1765 and 1820 were published in the local newspapers. Without a fixed audience, the musicians who presented these performances, usually for their own benefit, were compelled to offer a preview of their content in order to attract patrons.

The amount of detail provided in their programs ranges from a simple list of genres or composers to a comprehensive list of titles, composers, and performers. As a whole they offer considerable evidence of the concert repertoire of this era. Most, if not all, of the musicians performing at public concerts in Charleston between 1766 and 1820 were affiliated with the orchestra of the St. Cecilia Society. While their benefit concerts were open to the public, much of their audience (and their managers, when identified) also overlapped with this private organization. Since these commercial concerts were a sort of offspring of the society's concerts, the published programs for the public events of may be accepted as evidence of the musical content of the St. Cecilia Society's concerts, for studies of similar concert organizations in contemporary Britain have demonstrated that beyond slight differences in program emphasis, benefit concerts at this time were nearly indistinguishable from those of the parent organization. In fact, musicians presenting their own benefit concerts abroad are known to have borrowed musical scores from their host organization for such events.[13]

The musical content of eighteenth-century British concerts was frequently made known to audiences through the distribution of printed handbills. This practice was not mandatory, however, and it often depended on the nature of the event. The advance publicity surrounding commercial concerts such as benefits, for example, usually announced the musical fare in an effort to attract an audience, while concerts that were part of a series and were performed at regular intervals, especially those including amateur performers whose attendance was not always reliable, were not necessarily advertised with printed handbills. In fact, owing to the paucity of rehearsals, the absence of performers, and the vagaries of music copying, the content of many eighteenth- and early-nineteenth-century polite concerts was not fixed until the last minute.[14] For many polite concert series, therefore, the advance printing of a paper program was often a luxury that may have been realized only for special occasions such as anniversaries.

No information has yet been found to indicate how often the St. Cecilia Society printed concert handbills. If the society distributed bills to its members at each of its regularly scheduled concerts, the number printed over a period of five decades may have exceeded forty thousand.[15] The fact that only one extant program has yet surfaced, however, suggests that the musical content of the society's regular concerts was not determined until a very late hour, and, as a consequence, printed bills were not regularly distributed at society events. Conversely the repertoire for anniversary concerts and other special events was probably selected far enough in advance to facilitate the distribution of printed handbills, such as the extant November 1778 bill and that mentioned by Charles Fraser for November 1815. Even in this limited scenario, the potential number of printed bills would exceed five thousand. Whether the society printed bills for its regular concerts or only for anniversaries, it seems very likely that there are extant St. Cecilia handbills still in private hands or languishing in distant archives.

The survival of many printed handbills and broadsides from various British concerts—of both commercial and polite varieties—enables us to draw generalizations about the format and musical content of these events. By the middle of the eighteenth century the programs of concerts in Britain had developed a rather standardized format, the construction of which was intertwined with the genres of music contained therein. In general they featured a broader range of musical genres than modern concerts, and typically included orchestral music, chamber ensembles, and concerti, as well as vocal music. Rather than separating these genres into discrete sections, British concerts were usually constructed according to a plan that included either two or three "acts," or sections, each of which contained a mix of genres.[16] Each act of a concert usually opened with an orchestral piece, labeled either an overture or symphony, and similarly concluded with a piece involving the full band.[17] Between these orchestral bookends, songs, chamber music, and concerti would be performed in alternation. While this range of musical fare may seem overly miscellaneous to the modern concert patron, we must remember that the audience in the Age of Enlightenment derived satisfaction from such variety of musical genres and textures.[18] In an era characterized by a more homogeneous musical style than has been witnessed in recent generations, this alternating pattern provided diversity while also maintaining a sense of formal coherence. The basic structure of these concerts—their division into acts and the succession of contrasting genres—remained securely in place well into the early nineteenth century.[19] Auditors of this era were familiar with these conventions and knew what to expect when they subscribed or purchased a ticket. The practice was so standardized, for example, that when Gaetano Franceschini advertised his April 1774 "Grand Concert of Vocal and Instrumental Music," an event sponsored by the St. Cecilia Society, he needed only to suggest the content in an abbreviated manner: "A Solo and a Concerto on the Violin by Mr. Franceschini, Concerto on the Viol d'Amour &c. &c. &c."[20]

The first concert in Charleston for which the program was printed in the local newspaper was Thomas Pike's subscription concert of October 1765. Prior to this event, the phrase "Concert of Vocal and Instrumental Musick" was regularly used to advertise performances without providing any clues to their musical content. Of the eighteen known concert programs published in Charleston between 1765 and 1800, only four are arranged in three acts, and each of these events was associated with the St. Cecilia Society. Three of these particular programs date from between 1774 and 1782, an era of predominantly *galant* repertoire the relative brevity of which allowed for a greater number of works to be heard in a single concert than in later decades. The fourth three-act program, dating from 1794, represents an anomaly when compared to other concerts in post-Revolutionary Charleston and abroad.[21] Between 1800 and the termination of the St. Cecilia Society's concert activity in 1820, the concert programs published in Charleston are consistently arranged in two acts or parts.[22] While this small amount of evidence does not constitute sufficient proof to reach a definitive conclusion about the internal divisions of the St. Cecilia Society's concert programs, it does suggest a likely scenario. Considering the emphasis on polite sociability at its musical events, it is not difficult to imagine that the society would have favored the three-act model; it provided an additional interval in which to socialize, and its shorter blocks of music were less taxing on those who may have preferred to move about freely. Whether or not the society's programs were similarly consolidated into two acts after 1800 is a question that may never be settled unless additional concert programs come to light.

Just as with the format of concert programs, the "slight differences" between the musical content of "polite" concerts (organized by amateurs) and "commercial" concerts (organized by professionals) in Britain were echoed in Charleston as well. The principal difference between these two varieties of concerts was one of emphasis rather than of substance and was influenced by the agent(s) responsible for organizing the event. The selection of music performed at the St. Cecilia Society concerts probably fell to its managers, and was probably relegated to the society's "committee on musical matters" rather than to its more highly skilled hired professionals. Such a practice would have been consistent with what is known about other "polite" concert series in contemporary Britain: the content of eighteenth- and early-nineteenth-century concerts was generally determined by the organizers rather than by the principal performers.[23] The repertoire heard at polite concerts, such as those of the St. Cecilia Society, therefore, reflected the musical ideologies or tastes of the management and (presumably) the organization's select membership. Generally speaking, polite concerts featured a wider range of musical genres and composers than public concerts. In terms of instrumental repertoire, polite concerts usually featured more full-ensemble orchestral music—a choice that may have been influenced by the performing skills of the amateur contingent of the ensemble. In contrast the repertoire heard at commercial concerts reflected the choices of more highly skilled performers who sought to showcase their talents in an effort to attract a broader audience and to maximize profits. Thus while they also contained vocal and orchestral music, commercial concerts generally included a higher proportion of music with opportunities for soloistic display, such as songs, chamber music, and concerti. A good example of this trend may be seen in the program for pianist Charles Gilfert's 1810 benefit concert (see figure 9.1), which includes four songs and two sets of variations for solo piano. To some degree, of course, the professionals' choices were influenced by the musical tastes of the community at large, for novelties had the potential of deterring patrons with fixed tastes or expectations.[24]

Mr. GILFERT's
Concert,
This Evening, July 19,
At Mr. FAYOLLE's LONG-ROOM,

The Orcheftr under the Direction of Mr. LEAUMONT.

ACT I.

Grand Sinfonia, - - - - - - -	Krommer.
Song, 'No indeed not I,' (by Mifs S. Sully)	Hook
Air, with variations on the Piano-Forte, (by Mr. Gilfert)	Gilfert.
Song, 'La Clef des Coeurs' (by Mr. Guilbert)	Guilbert.
Overture to Lodoifka, (by Particular Defire)	Kreutzer.

ACT II.

Overture to Nina, - - - -	Daleyrac.
Song, 'Conftant Kate' (by Mr. Sully)	Hook.
Variations on the Piano-Forte, (by Mr. Arnold Remouffin)	Remouffin.
Song, 'Seclufion's Sacred Bower,' (by Mifs Sully)	Atwood.
Concerto on the Piano-Forte, (by Mr. Gilfert)	Steibelt.
To conclude, by Particular Defire, with the Serenading Waltz,	Gilfert.

☞ The Concert to begin precifely at 8 o'Clock.

9.1. Broadside for Charles Gilfert's benefit concert in Charleston, 19 July 1810. From the collections of the South Caroliniana Library

The Content of Charleston Concerts

The dozens of concert programs published in the various Charleston newspapers during the half century of the St. Cecilia Society's musical era contain references to hundreds of individual musical works. Some of these pieces are only vaguely described (for example, "a French song"), while a few are identified quite precisely ("Fourth Concerto on the Clarionet, Michel"). The majority of these works are only partially identified, however, usually citing the musical genre and the composer's surname ("Quartetto, Pleyel").[25] Nevertheless, these extant programs, taken as a whole, represent an invaluable resource for the study of Charleston's musical life. This material not only establishes a catalog of the musical fare heard at concerts during this era, but it also provides an index, as it were, of the city's musical taste. While it must be acknowledged that these programs do not represent the musical content of the St. Cecilia Society's regular concerts in as direct a manner as would be preferred, this material cannot be said to misrepresent the organization that formed the backbone of Charleston's concert life between 1766 and 1820. To some indeterminate degree, therefore, the musical tastes represented in these programs reflect the musical preferences of the St. Cecilia Society. Despite this caveat, the insight provided by this large body of evidence forms an important and necessary part of the present examination of the society's musical activity.

A detailed analysis of the evolving musical tastes represented in the dozens of extant Charleston concert programs is beyond the scope of the present project, and may not be entirely feasible considering the limitations of the extant evidence. The following pages offer an overview of this data, which has been collected largely from extant Charleston newspapers. It is included here to illustrate the substance of concerts in Charleston during the latter part of the eighteenth century and the first two decades of the nineteenth, and thus to provide a model for imagining the musical content of the contemporaneous concerts of the St. Cecilia Society. For the convenience of presentation, this evidence is arranged according to the four genres that filled the concert programs of this era: orchestral music, concerti, chamber music, and vocal music.

Orchestral Music

Concerts featuring solely orchestral repertoire were rare in eighteenth-century Britain and so were concerts devoid of orchestral music. Considering the infrequency of these extremes, they can hardly be expected to have occurred in contemporary Charleston.[26] As with their European counterparts, orchestral music served as the major structural element of concerts in late-eighteenth- and early-nineteenth-century Charleston. In nearly every known concert program, orchestral music opened and closed each act. Because of the centrality of this genre, orchestral music may be seen as a kind of barometer of musical taste in Charleston and its core musical organization, the St. Cecilia Society.

Since orchestral music generally formed the major landmarks of concert programs, it is tempting to hypothesize that multimovement works such as symphonies may have been divided up and their individual movements performed over the course of a concert. Owing to the paucity of information given on these programs, it is difficult to form a strong conclusion about this matter. While this practice of dividing a symphony into individual movements may have taken place at some Continental concerts, evidence suggests that those in Charleston, at least during the eighteenth century, followed the British custom of performing symphonies without interruptions.[27] Extant programs from Charleston concerts of the first two decades of the nineteenth century, however, include references to what may have been individual movements from larger orchestral works. During these years independent works labeled *minuet, andante, rondo,* and *finale,* by composers such as Haydn or Pleyel, occasionally appear within concert programs on which "grand overtures" or symphonies by these same composers are also listed.[28]

The term *orchestral music* encompasses a wide range of subgenres such as symphonies, overtures from operas, oratorios, or plays, and other works that employ a full band with minimal use of soloists. In fact, a proper appreciation for the orchestral content of Charleston concerts during the period in question is contingent on an understanding of the contemporary fluidity of this terminology. In Britain during the second half of the eighteenth century, the term *overture* was used interchangeably with the term *symphony* and its nominal variations (such as *sinfonia, simfonia,* and *symphonie*). Although the term *overture* had a variety of musical connotations in mid-eighteenth-century Europe, it referred most significantly to the three-movement Italian opera overture, which had evolved into an independent concert genre by the 1750s and served as the prototype for the mature Classical symphony. The overture in the Italian manner was popularized in England by George Frideric Handel (1685–1759), among other immigrant composers, and was imitated by native-born musicians such as Thomas Arne (1710–1778), William Boyce (1711–1779), and Maurice Greene (1696–1755). Two-movement overtures also existed in mid-eighteenth-century England, usually as introductory music at the beginning of odes and other multimovement vocal works. Each of Benjamin Yarnold's *Six Overtures for the Harpsichord of Piano Forte,* for example, consists of two contrasting movements, generally arranged in a fast-slow pairing. These uncomplicated, *galant* works—which were published in London around 1780 but composed some years earlier—probably represent the reduction of orchestral scores for keyboard performance.[29] More significant, the London-based music publisher Robert Bremner (1713–1789) published sixty

Continental symphonies between 1763 and 1783 in a widely distributed series titled *Periodical Overtures*. This use of the term *overture* endured well after Bremner's series, however, for even when Haydn's mature symphonies were performed in London in the late 1790s they were styled "grand overtures."[30] It is reasonable to conclude, therefore, that unless designated as being from a specific opera, oratorio, or play, the term *overture* or *grand overture* was likewise used in Charleston concert programs of the late eighteenth century to describe a multimovement orchestral work that we would now label a *symphony*. For the sake of clarity the following discussion will consider the symphony and the true operatic overture separately.

Symphonies

What orchestral music may have been performed in the first years of the St. Cecilia Society's concert series is not known. The advertised program for Thomas Pike's 1765 concert does not include any independent orchestral works, nor do any other extant source until the handbill for the St. Cecilia Society's 1778 anniversary concert. A clue to the kind of orchestral music heard in Charleston in the late 1760s may be found, however, in a 1767 letter from Harriott Pinckney of Charleston. Just before her older brother Charles Cotesworth Pinckney, a founding member of the St. Cecilia Society, returned home after many years of schooling in London, she sent him a request for a supply of the latest musical fashions, explaining "I am at a great loss for Musick as they don't import any choice [works] here for sale and we never get any but what we particularly send for." Harriott begged her brother to send home "Bach's Sonata's [*sic*], Bach's Symphonies, ye royal shepherd [a 1764 English opera with music by George Rush, including a three-movement overture], The cunning Man [Jean-Jacques Rousseau's *Le Devin du village* (1752), adapted by Charles Burney as *The Cunning Man* (1766)] which we have had a great Character of here, I believe it was originally wrote in French by Rousseau[,] and Abel's Overtures."[31]

In terms of orchestral music the most significant of Miss Pinckney's requests were the symphonies of J. C. Bach and the overtures of Carl Friedrich Abel—German composers whose works were still considered novelties to London audiences in 1767. In fact, the introduction of the early Classical style to England in the 1760s is largely attributable to these gentlemen, who took up residence in London early in the decade. The publication and performance of their orchestral works brought to England the latest musical fashions from Germany—then the orchestral nursery of Europe—and marked the beginning of a new era in British musical history. The primary appeal of the exclusive Bach-Abel concert series, established in 1764 and so highly regarded by Charlestonian Ralph Izard, was the performance of orchestral works by contemporary German instrumental music—specifically that emanating from the court of the elector of Mannheim, whose orchestra was then the envy of all Europe.[32] The success of this new orchestral style was greatly enhanced by Robert Bremner's serial publication of *Periodical Overtures* (1763–1783) in the new Germanic style. These overtures (really symphonies) are all scored in an eight-part instrumentation that became the standard for the early Classical symphony: two oboes (clarinets or flutes occasionally substituting), two horns, first violins, second violins, violas, and basses.[33] Consistent with the musical practices of the period, the bass part was to be performed by a cello, double bass, and (ideally) bassoon, with a keyboard instrument realizing the composer's harmonic figures ("figured bass").[34]

Considering the strength of Charleston's desire to emulate fashionable British culture, it is likely that this new Germanic symphonic idiom was heard at the St. Cecilia Society's concerts from its earliest days. Confirmation of this hypothesis does not appear until the 1770s, however, by which time the society's acceptance of the Mannheim-influenced repertoire was well established. In December 1773, providing valuable evidence of its musical preferences, the society published an appeal for the return of several orchestral parts: "Whereas the Tenor and thorough Bass Parts of the Overtures of Handel, Martini, Abel, op. 1. and 4, Lord Kelly and Richter's Symphonies, op. 2, bound up together, and mark'd No. 1. belonging to the St. COECILIA Society have been for some Time missing, supposed to have been borrowed, any Person possessed of the same, is desired to return them to the Treasurer of the said Society."[35] Similarly the orchestral music heard at the society's anniversary concert in November 1778, according to the extant handbill shown in figure 9.2, included five independent overtures or symphonies: the fourth and second symphonies of Johann Anton Filtz (1733–1760), the "2d Symphony . . . 2d Sett" by Friedrich Schwindl (1737–1786), the "1st Overture . . . Opera 2d" by Franz Xavier Richter (1709–1789), and the "4th Overture" by Lord Kelly. Not only did each of these composers represent the so-called Mannheim School of orchestral composition, but works by each of these men were also included among the symphonies published serially by Robert Bremner in London. The next extant concert program to specify genres and composers' names, that for Gaetano Franceschini's May 1782 benefit concert, demonstrates the continued prevalence of this symphonic repertoire in Charleston. As with the 1778 concert, Franceschini's concert included six orchestral pieces (labeled either "overture" or "sinfonia") written by the same Germanic composers heard at concerts in contemporary London: Abel, Schwindl, and Josef Myslivecek (1737–1781).[36]

From the 1760s through the early 1780s the symphonic music heard at concerts in Britain and in Charleston was dominated by works influenced by the Mannheim idiom, which was itself a refinement of the Italian operatic

Sт. COECILIA.

ANNIVERSARY CONCERT,

MONDAY, November 23, 1778.

ACT I.

Overture in the MESSIAH

A SONG

A FLUTE CONCERTO

4th Symphony of FILTZ

ACT II.

2d Symphony by FILTZ

Harpsichord SONAT

A SONG

2d Symphony by SCHWINDL, 2d Sett.

ACT III.

1st Overture by RICHTER, Opera 2d.

A SONG

A Solo on the VIOLIN

4th Overture by Lord KELLY,

FINIS.

9.2. Handbill for the 1778 St. Cecilia anniversary concert (approximately 5.5" by 7"). Courtesy of Drayton Hall, a historic site of the National Trust for Historic Preservation in the United States overture of the late Baroque era. By the mid-1780s, however, a new orchestral style was in ascendancy in Europe and in Britain: the four-movement "Viennese" symphony, made famous by the most celebrated composer of the late eighteenth century, Franz Joseph Haydn (1732–1809).[37] Evidence of the Viennese element in Charleston can be dated to the subscription concerts held in the city during the British occupation of 1780–82. According to a letter from a German officer garrisoned in Charleston during that time, local audiences heard compositions by Haydn as well as those of J. C. Bach, C. F. Abel, Carl Joseph Toeschi (1731–1788), Johann Stamitz, Antonin Kammel (1730–1784), Lord Kelly, J. C. Fischer, Joseph Schmitt (1734–1791), Johann Christoph Möller (1755–1803), and Vaclav Pichl (1741–1805).[38] The earliest known specific reference to the performance of a Haydn symphony in Charleston dates from October 1787, at the benefit concert of violinist Alexander Juhan.[39] From that time onward, well into the 1820s, more symphonies (or "grand overtures") by Haydn appeared on Charleston concerts than symphonies by any other composer. In terms of frequency of performances, the symphonic composers heard in Charleston after Haydn were younger adherents to the same musical idiom: Ignaz Pleyel (1757–1831), Wolfgang Amadeus Mozart (1756–1791), Adalbert Gyrowetz (1763–1850), and Franz Krommer (1759–1831), in descending order of frequency.[40] This evidence is corroborated by a simple but informative remark in Charles Fraser's 1854 *Reminiscences:* "I have a bill of the performances at one [St. Cecilia concert] given in November, 1815, on which I find the names of Pleyel, Haydn, Mozart, and Kromer [Krommer], all, then, as they are now, very favorite composers."[41] In addition to these, a few "grand overtures," or symphonies, by composers less familiar to modern audiences were also heard at local concerts between 1793 and 1820: Domenico Cimarosa (1749–1801), François-Joseph Gossec (1734–1829), Marie-Alexandre Guénin (1744–1819), local composer Robert Leaumont, Louis Massonneau (1766–1848), Tommaso or Filippo Trajetta, Johann Baptist Vanhal (1739–1813), Peter von Winter (1754–1825), and even the obscure Joseph Aloys Schmittbaur (1718–1809).[42]

The earliest known Charleston performance of a symphony, or "grand overture," by Ludwig van Beethoven (1770–1827) took place on 10 April 1805, at a Passion Week oratorio concert under the direction of German-born musician Jacob Eckhard. The fact that a symphonic work by Beethoven appeared on only one other known program before 1820, another oratorio directed by Eckhard on 2 April 1806, can be explained by at least two hypotheses.[43] First, while Beethoven's symphonies have long since been recognized as the most significant orchestral works of the early nineteenth century, if not in the entire history of the genre, Charleston audiences during this time may have preferred the lighter, more conventional works of the above-named

composers. Second, Charleston's cumulative musical resources were probably
not sufficient to meet the orchestral forces and technical skill necessary to
perform a Beethoven symphony, at least those from his Third Symphony (the
Sinfonia eroica of 1803) onward.

Overtures

A perusal of the extant Charleston concert programs from the half century
under consideration reveals that the number of symphonies included on the
programs of the 1790s and early nineteenth century is generally lower than on
programs of the 1770s and early 1780s. After 1800, in fact, the inclusion of but
a single symphony per concert was not a rare occurrence. This alteration does
not necessarily suggest a diminishing affinity for the symphony, however;
rather, it was probably the result of the increasing duration of symphonic
music in the 1780s and subsequent decades. Since the concert portion of the
St. Cecilia Society's performances probably lasted about two hours, the
reduced number of symphonies during the last thirty-odd years of its concert
series suggests a desire to confine the musical portion of the evening within
the bounds of a well-established time frame. Despite this change, orchestral
music continued to be an important part of the concert experience in Charleston. For while the number of symphonies listed on extant programs from the
last three decades of the St. Cecilia Society's concert activity declined, the
inclusion of English and French operatic overtures became an increasingly
common occurrence. Generally cast in a single movement, operatic overtures
occupied less than half the performance time of a mature Classical symphony,
as exemplified by the works of Haydn, Pleyel, and others, and yet these works
satisfied the need for full-band music on the program.

 The performance of orchestral overtures lifted from larger works was not
new to Charleston in the 1790s. The earliest known example of this practice
dates from Thomas Pike's 1765 concert, when the overture to Handel's oratorio *Scipio* was performed.[44] The St. Cecilia Society's 1773 advertisement for
missing orchestral parts mentions the "overtures of Handel."[45] The next extant
complete program in Charleston, from the St. Cecilia Society's 1778 anniversary concert, includes the overture to Handel's most famous oratorio, *Messiah*.
Over the next several decades, there were several more known performances
of overtures from Handel's oratorios, including those from *Sampson, Esther*,
and the *Occasional Oratorio*.[46] The fact that most of these performances took
place within the context of semisacred oratorio concerts, however, suggests
that the inclusion of Handel's oratorio overtures at secular concerts fell out of
fashion in Charleston by the 1780s.

 From the 1790s onward, operatic overtures became regular components
of the local concert repertoire. It is perhaps no coincidence that this increase

was contemporaneous with dual events that had a dramatic influence on the vitality of Charleston's concert life: the opening of the Charleston Theatre and the arrival of French refugees from St. Domingo. Besides performing tragic, comic, and sentimental plays imported from London, the theater also presented English operas and musical farces, as well as English adaptations of French *opéras comiques*.[47] Not all the operas from which concert overtures were excerpted were performed at the local theater, however, and it is significant that the majority of these works represent a Parisian rather than a strictly London repertoire. Thus the opera overtures performed at concerts in Charleston at the turn of the nineteenth century were not selected because they came from favorite works of the local stage; instead it appears that the preference for French opera overtures reflected the tastes and experiences of the French musicians who formed a majority of the city's musical professionals at that time. The influence of the distressed émigrés who augmented Charleston's musical life was not limited to a single genre, of course. South Carolinian William Elliott (1778–1863) succinctly acknowledged the scale of their contribution in 1816 while summering in New England. Comparing the expanding cultural scene in urban Massachusetts to that of Charleston, an amused Elliott remarked to his fiancée, Ann Smith, "the Bostonians are as much indebted to us, for their taste in music, as we are to the Emigrants from France!"[48]

The three opera overtures most frequently performed in Charleston were first performed in Paris but not associated exclusively with France, for they were heard in Britain as well as in other American cities. The multipart, "grandly regal" overture to *Henry IV; ou, Le Bataille d'Ivry* (1774), written for the ascension of Louis XVI by Jean-Paul-Gilles Martini (1741–1816), was the most frequently performed overture in Charleston; it is included on more than a dozen extant programs from the late 1780s through 1817.[49] Rodolphe Kreutzer's celebrated overture to *Lodoiska* (1791) was heard at least as many times, but in a narrower span of time—between 1804 and 1817.[50] The overture to Christoph Willibald Gluck's *Iphigenie en Tauride*, in two parts labeled "The Calm" and "The Storm," was included on a number of programs between 1796 and 1811 and represents the third most performed overture in Charleston during this era.[51] Although taken from a 1779 French work that was not performed in its entirety in Charleston, this overture by Gluck (1714–1787) became popular among English-speaking audiences by virtue of the fact that it was published in London in 1783 as the last installment of Bremner's *Periodical Overtures*.

In contrast to these three widely performed orchestral works, a number of the overtures performed at concerts in Charleston reflect the influence of the city's population of French musicians. The performance of orchestral selections from the Parisian *opéras comiques* (and occasionally *grands opéras*) of the 1780s through the early 1800s cannot be connected to contemporary British musical fashions, for London critics often rejected this music as too light and frivolous for their concerts. Because French-trained musicians formed a majority of South Carolina's music professionals between 1793 and about 1820, however, this repertoire was presented more liberally in Charleston than in London.[52] For example, overtures to the grand opera *Panurge dans l'île des lanternes* (1785) and the comic operas *La Caravane du Caire* (1783) and *L'épreuve villageoise* (1784)—all by André-Ernest-Modeste Grétry (1741–1813)—were performed in Charleston several times between 1793 and 1816.[53] The overtures to no fewer than five comic operas by Nicolas-Marie Dalayrac (1753–1809) were heard in Charleston between 1805 and 1817: *Nina, ou, La folle par amour* (1786), *La Soirée orageuse* (1790), *Renaud d'Ast* (1787), *Camille; ou, Le Souterrain* (1791), and *Les Deux Petits Savoyards* (1789).[54] The overture to *Jeune Henri* (1797) by Etienne-Nicolas Méhul (1763–1817) also received repeated performances in the early years of the nineteenth century.[55] Overtures to *Le calife de Bagdad* (1800) and *Jean de Paris* (1812) by François-Adrien Boieldieu (1775–1834) were both played in 1816.[56]

A number of other noteworthy operatic overtures were heard in Charleston, but with an infrequency that precludes the formation of any conclusion about their presence on concert programs. The performance of many, but not all, of these works is probably linked to contemporary performances of their main dramatic works at the local theaters. Such overtures include those from Nicolas Dezède's *Blaise et Babet* (1783), Michael Kelly's *Blue Beard* (1798), Cimarosa's *Il matrimonio segreto* (1792), Pierre Gaveaux's *Le Petit matelot* (1796), Pierre-Alexandre Monsigny's *Le Déserteur* (1769), Robert Leaumont's own overture to Michael Kelly's pastiche *The Forty Thieves* (1806), Samuel Arnold's pastiche *Love and Money* (1795), James Hook's *The Fortress* (1807), and Mozart's *Die Zauberflöte* (1791).[57]

Symphonies Concertantes

Concerts in late-eighteenth- and early-nineteenth-century Charleston would not have been au courant without the inclusion of another species of symphony then in fashion: the *symphonie concertante*. Originating in Paris in the 1770s, this hybrid of the symphony and the concerto was soon embraced at London concerts, and works of this sort were composed by all the major orchestral composers working in that city in the late eighteenth century (including Haydn, Pleyel, and Gyrowetz, among others). Its combination of colorful instrumental variety with the formal structure of the symphony was attractive to audiences, for its tempered the seriousness of the latter with the vivacity of the former.[58] Charlestonians heard the performance of several *symphonies concertantes* between 1793 and 1813—the peak years during which the refugees from St. Domingo held sway over the city's musical scene. Most of these works are not fully identified, but those that are represent the composers most closely associated with this genre: Pleyel and Jean-Baptiste Davaux (1742–1822). Davaux, in fact, is best remembered for his *symphonies concertantes*, most of which are cast in just two movements.[59]

Concerti

The concerto for instrumental soloist(s) and orchestra was the dominant form of orchestral music in Europe during the first half of the eighteenth century, but the emergence of the multimovement concert overture, or symphony, in the second half of the century soon consigned this genre to a secondary position. British concert audiences had witnessed such a transition by the early 1760s, when the symphonies of the Mannheim school were first being heard in London. In addition to the fact that the St. Cecilia Society did not coalesce until 1766, there is little evidence of any of the concert repertoire heard in Charleston during this decade to illustrate the decline of the Baroque concerto in favor of the Classical symphony. It is significant, however, that Thomas Pike's October 1765 concert—an event that perhaps marked the twilight of the Baroque aesthetic in Charleston's musical history—included no symphonies but no fewer than seven concerti: two for French horn, two for bassoon, one for harpsichord, and the second and fifth of John Stanley's concerti grossi, op. 2.[60] The Baroque concerto grosso, featuring a group of soloists accompanied by a string orchestra, was a prominent musical genre during the first half of the eighteenth century, popularized in Britain through the performance of works by such composers as Arcangelo Corelli (1653–1713), Francesco Geminiani (1687–1762), Handel, and William Boyce. Corelli's concerti grossi were especially popular among gentlemen's concerts in England because their limited technical demands facilitated amateur participation. The popularity of Corelli's concerti endured for more than a century after his death, though performances in the late eighteenth and early nineteenth centuries were largely restricted to less prestigious, provincial concert series.[61] Whether or not such works were part of Charleston's rather cosmopolitan concert scene is difficult to determine without more evidence of the St. Cecilia Society's repertoire, but the German correspondent who commented on the state of music in Charleston during his stay in the early 1780s reported that "Haendel and even Corelli are still loved there."[62] Thus while numerous performances of these works may have taken place in eighteenth-century Charleston, as this firsthand account suggests, only a single advertised performance of a concerto grosso by Corelli has been found—dating from a public concert in February 1793 to benefit the city's new Orphan House.[63]

In evidence from the years immediately after Pike's concerto-laden performance, a clearer picture of the quantity and character of the concerts heard in Charleston begins to emerge. Over the next half century, dozens of works for instrumental soloists and orchestra were performed and advertised in the local newspapers with varying degrees of specificity. In the last years of the St. Cecilia Society's concerts, from about 1817 to 1820, the presence of concerti in Charleston concert advertisements shrank dramatically. This change is probably attributable largely to the sudden decline in the city's population of professional musicians caused by the migrations of the Charleston Theatre troupe during these years. Despite this disruption, the extant evidence for this half century of concert music illustrates the entire breadth of the Classical style—from the mid-eighteenth-century *galant* idiom through the proto-Romantic work of Beethoven's early-nineteenth-century contemporaries. Although a number of different solo instruments were featured, these concerti can be grouped into three categories: works for strings, keyboard, and winds.[64]

Concerti for String Instruments

Of the string concerti advertised in Charleston between 1766 and 1820, works for solo violin emerge as the unrivaled favorite. Only a handful of advertised performances of cello concerti have been found, and none for solo viola.[65] The vast majority of concerti presented in Charleston during this period were for one soloist and orchestra, but there were a few advertised performances of concerti for two stringed instruments.[66]

The violin was a favorite instrument for solo concerti when the St. Cecilia Society established its concert series in 1766, and thus many of the earliest references to the performance of concerti in Charleston involve this instrument. As with all other genres of music heard at concerts in this city during the eighteenth century, few specifics are known about the violin repertoire played in the years before the American Revolution. The earliest known violin soloists at the St. Cecilia Society's concerts, John Joseph Abercromby and Gaetano Franceschini, both presented violin concerti in Charleston in the 1770s and early 1780s.[67] In the few extant programs from this period, the composer of only one work is identified: the Italian-born Felice Giardini. After settling in London in 1751, Giardini promoted the new Italian *galant* musical style through the performance of concerti, orchestral works, and songs, revitalizing the city's concert scene and marking a turning point in British musical tastes. Giardini concerti may have been the works for solo violin and orchestra heard in the early days of the St. Cecilia Society's concerts, but by 1780 the works of two other violinists then popular in London—Wilhelm Cramer (1747–1799) and Francis Hippolyte Barthelemon (1741–1808)—might also have been part of the Charleston repertoire.[68]

As an interesting adjunct to works for solo violin and orchestra, John Joseph Abercromby, the violinist so admiringly described by Josiah Quincy in 1773, appears to have also performed on the viol d'amore during his tenure in Charleston.[69] Although the use of this instrument, with its *scordatura* tuning and sympathetic strings, was fairly widespread in seventeenth-century Europe, by the second half of the eighteenth century the viol d'amore was considered an "ostentatiously elitist instrument" in Britain and on the Continent. This cousin of the violin had a very limited repertoire during the early Classical period, and thus its presence on concert programs in Charleston represented a rare treat, one usually available only at the most cosmopolitan series abroad.[70]

As concert advertisements in Charleston became more detailed in the years after the American Revolution, a better picture of the violin concerti performed in this city emerges. Of the roughly thirty works for violin soloist and orchestra advertised between 1787 and 1818, nearly all include the composers' names.[71] Some of the composers whose concerti were performed in the late 1780s and early 1790s represent a French influence, such as Davaux and Franz Lamotte (ca. 1751–1780).[72] Between 1793 and 1817, however, works by the Italian violinist Giovanni Mane Giornovichi (also known as Ivan Mane Jarnović, 1745–1804) dominated the violin concerti heard at Charleston concerts.[73] The long reign of Giornovichi's concerti was probably because of his participation in prestigious concerts in London during the last decade of the eighteenth century. Similarly British admiration for the Italian violinist Giovanni Battista Viotti (1755–1824) was established by his presence at many high-profile London concerts of the 1790s. It should come as no surprise, therefore, that a number of Viotti concerti were performed in Charleston between 1793 and 1816.[74] In numbers not far behind the works of this Italian virtuoso, violin concerti by Viotti's Parisian student Pierre Rode (1774–1830) enjoyed several performances in Charleston in the short space of time between 1812 and 1818.[75] The concerti of Rodolphe Kreutzer (1766–1811), a prominent French violinist of the early nineteenth century whose name has long been associated with that of a sonata by Beethoven, were not unknown in Charleston, but they did not receive many repetitions.[76]

Concerti for Keyboard Instruments

The number and distribution of keyboard concerti performed in Charleston during the period reflect the transition from the harpsichord to the piano that occurred in the years immediately after the American Revolution. Owing to its limited volume and fixed dynamic range, the harpsichord was not well suited to the *galant* musical style that emerged from Italy and Germany around the middle of the eighteenth century—or to the solo concerto format in general.

By the end of the century, however, the harpsichord was eclipsed by the piano, which proved to be an ideal medium for the mature Classical concerto.

Harpsichords and smaller spinets were regularly advertised in Charleston during the 1760s through the 1780s, both as newly imported and as second-hand instruments; both varieties appear in many estate inventories of this period. The concerto for solo keyboard and orchestra was not a significant part of British concerts during this time, however, and evidence suggests a similar situation in Charleston. Each of the earliest known references to keyboard concerti in Charleston involves a lady amateur. At Peter Valton's concerts in February 1773 and February 1774, lady amateurs, pupils of Mr. Valton, performed concerti on the harpsichord.[77] Similarly a pair of concerts performed in 1781, during the British occupation of Charleston, included harpsichord concerti presented by lady amateurs.[78] Which composers were represented in these performances is not known, but one can hypothesize that the works in the new *galant* idiom imported from the Continent were then in fashion. This category would include the op. 1 concerti of J. C. Bach, published in London in 1763, and those published by his colleague Carl Abel in 1774. Works in this genre by English composers such as Thomas Arne, James Hook (1746–1827), and others may be considered candidates as well.

Much more is known about the music for piano and orchestra that began to be mentioned in advertisements for Charleston concerts during the late 1780s. Small, square pianos were certainly available in England as early as the 1760s, and larger grand pianos were obtainable there by the 1770s. But it was only in the 1790s, after the London piano firm of John Broadwood improved the mechanical action and resonance of the instrument, that the piano emerged as a leading concerto instrument.[79] Thus while harpsichords were occasionally advertised for sale in the Charleston newspapers of the 1790s, their use in concert music was certainly overshadowed by the piano. The frequency with which newly imported pianos were advertised during the 1790s and following decades suggests that a very wide range of instruments, both in terms of size and quality, were to be had in Charleston.

Although its concert career began later than that of the violin, the piano quickly became the preferred instrument for solo concerti in Charleston. Roughly fifty piano concerti were advertised between 1788 and 1819; the number would surely be much higher if we knew more about the content of the St. Cecilia Society's fortnightly concerts. The composers of most of the piano concerti performed in Charleston from the 1790s onward are identified, but a few are not.[80] The earliest known references to piano concerti in Charleston, those from the late 1780s and 1790s, are to works of now-obscure composers. Among these are the east European composers Franz Anton Hoffmeister (1754–1812), Leopold Kozeluch (1747–1818), and Johann Krumpholtz

(1742–1790), whose works were known to local audiences through the importation of British music publications.[81] The bulk of the known piano concerti performed in Charleston during this period, however, were advertised in the early years of the nineteenth century. An examination of these references reveals a preference for the works of three composers associated with the "London piano-forte school": Johann Baptist Cramer (1771–1858), Jan Ladislav Dussek (1760–1812), and Daniel Steibelt (1765–1823).[82] The son of violin virtuoso Wilhelm Cramer, Cramer spent his entire career in London, where his piano works were widely performed.[83] His older colleague Dussek was active during the 1790s in London, where he established himself as a powerful force in piano composition and construction.[84] Dividing his career in the 1790s between Paris and London, Steibelt achieved enormous success in England with his third piano concerto, premiered in 1798 with the subtitle *L'Orage* (The Storm). Some, and perhaps all, of the Steibelt piano and orchestral performances in Charleston were of this celebrated concerto.[85]

While concerti from the "London piano-forte school" dominated this genre in Charleston, their reign was not exclusive. Piano concerti by violin virtuoso G. B. Viotti received at least three performances in Charleston.[86] Works by Giornovichi, Boieldieu, Carolus Antonius Fodor (1768–1846), and Joseph Wölfl (1773–1812) enjoyed slightly fewer advertised repetitions.[87] Only a single reference to the performance of a Mozart piano concerto has been found, relegating Mozart to a group of obscure composers whose works received but a single advertised performance during this period.[88]

Concerti for Wind Instruments

As with the piano, the composition of concerti for solo wind instruments during the second half of the eighteenth century was influenced by mechanical modifications to the instruments themselves—that is, the addition of keys. The most dramatic result of these alterations was the rise of the clarinet as a solo instrument. Still considered a new addition to the concert orchestra by midcentury, the clarinet was by the end of the century an integral part of the Classical tonal palette.

The first known reference to the performance of a clarinet concerto in Charleston dates from late 1793, when Pierre Foucard played an unattributed work for clarinet and orchestra.[89] Over the next quarter century, the clarinet proved to be a very popular solo instrument at local concerts, and Foucard was its leading exponent in Charleston. The number of such works performed rivals, and perhaps even exceeds, the number of violin concerti heard in Charleston during the entire span of the St. Cecilia Society's musical activity.

Works by Michel Yost (1754–1829), better known as Michel, dominated this genre in both Charleston and abroad. The first clarinetist of international reputation, Michel achieved renown through his performances at the Concert Spirituel in Paris in the late 1770s and 1780s.[90] Clarinet concerti by other composers of Michel's generation were also heard, including works by Amand Vanderhagen (1753–1822), François Devienne (1759–1803), Frédéric Nicolas Duvernoy (1765–1838), Xavier Lefevre (1763–1829), Vicente Martín y Soler (1754–1806), and Johann Christoph Vogel (1756–1788).[91] In addition, two European musicians appear to have performed clarinet concerti of their own composition in Charleston: one Dubois, who made several concert appearances around the turn of the nineteenth century, and Auguste Gautier, who migrated along the East Coast with the seasonal theatrical orchestra.[92]

Works for other wind instruments and orchestra may be found among extant Charleston concert programs of this era. The flute was a favorite instrument among gentlemen amateurs during the late eighteenth and the early nineteenth centuries, and a wide variety of music was published for this instrument in Europe. Advertised performances of flute concerti in Charleston are not very numerous in this era, owing principally to the ascendancy of the clarinet late in the century, but the extant references are distributed over the entire period. Works by Johann Christian Fischer and Devienne dominate this repertoire, though an amateur did perform a single flute concerto by Pleyel in 1813.[93] It should come as no surprise that the few oboe concerti advertised during this period were by J. C. Fischer, who completely dominated the oboe scene in London during the second half of the eighteenth century.[94] Although not representative of any musical trend or fashion, it is worth mentioning that but a single reference to a bassoon concerto has been found during the half century in question.[95]

Chamber Music

Since the second quarter of the nineteenth century the concert performance of chamber music has been relegated to events of a homogeneous nature, such as concerts composed exclusively of quartets, or exclusively of solo works. In contrast to this practice, the chamber music included in the mixed-genre concerts of the late eighteenth and early nineteenth centuries included a wider range of instrument combinations within a single program. Furthermore some chamber works of this era were specifically intended for the cooperative performance of amateurs and professionals.

Some varieties of chamber music in vogue during the Classical period had definite amateur connotations, such as the keyboard sonata with obbligato violin or cello accompaniment and works for pairs of violins or flutes. The performance of such works was rare at most British concert series, which relegated avowedly amateur genres to more private contexts.[96] There is not sufficient evidence, however, to determine whether or not this trend was observed in Charleston. It is known that such music was available from local retailers, and Peter Valton's "Opera prima," advertised in Charleston in 1768, was a set of six sonatas for keyboard with violin accompaniment.[97] This choice of genre for his first major set of works probably represents Valton's desire to gratify his students and patrons rather than to produce concert repertoire.

While little is known about the participation of gentlemen amateurs in the chamber music presented at concerts in Charleston, the evidence is more revealing about the role of women. Anonymous lady amateurs certainly did perform chamber music at concerts in Charleston, especially on the harpsichord and, from the 1790s onward, the piano. In addition, the harp, which came into vogue in the 1790s with the arrival of Parisian fashions via England and with the refugees from St. Domingo, was frequently played by young ladies on concert programs of early-nineteenth-century Charleston.[98]

In general, however, it may be safe to conclude that the bulk of the chamber music included on concerts in late-eighteenth- and early-nineteenth-century Charleston was performed by professional musicians. The items marked as "solos" were undoubtedly technically challenging works that showcased the performer's talents. Similarly the trio sonatas that were still part of the repertoire in the 1760s and 1770s and the string quartets that emerged in subsequent decades were usually the domain of professional players.[99]

The varieties of chamber music heard in Charleston during the period in question can be divided into two distinct categories: music for small ensembles (including solos, duos, trios, and quartets), and solo keyboard music, an emerging concert genre of the late eighteenth century.[100]

Ensemble Chamber Music

Pieces identified as "solos" were usually technically challenging works performed by skilled professionals—such as the violin solo by John Joseph Abercromby that Josiah Quincy praised so highly in March 1773. In the parlance of the 1770s, a "solo" did not denote a performance by a singular musician. Rather, it was understood to be a work, usually labeled a *sonata,* for one melody instrument, such as a violin, flute, or cello, accompanied by one or more continuo instruments.[101] Thus Quincy's description of Abercromby's violin solo, as well as other similar references in the early years of the society's existence, allude to what was in fact an ensemble performance.[102] In the decades after the Revolution instrumental solos continued to appear on Charleston concert programs, but without the same regularity as in the late colonial era. Nevertheless, soloists on the violin, flute, clarinet, and cello exhibited their talents by performing works by Kreutzer, Pleyel, and Rode, as well as their own compositions.[103]

Duets for two melody instruments appear infrequently among extant concert advertisements, though this kind of music constituted a substantial part of the printed music available through local retailers.[104] Usually directed at amateur performers, or for instrumentalists accompanying a dance, compositions of this nature were probably considered too slight to merit inclusion on a concert program.

Instrumental trios do not appear to have been a common feature of concerts performed in Charleston, as they are rarely mentioned in extant concert advertisements. This fact does not rule out the possibility that trios were simply restricted to more intimate musical events, for the trio sonata was a major chamber music idiom at the middle of the eighteenth century. As with the solo sonata, however, this kind of composition required more performers than its name implies: the typical realization of a trio sonata included two melody instruments (usually violins), a cello, and a keyboard instrument (either harpsichord or a small organ).[105] Trios of this nature were not unknown in Charleston during the early days of the St. Cecilia Society's concert series. Thomas Pike's October 1765 concert included an unspecified trio.[106] In June 1771 Shad Windsor, husband of harpsichord teacher and organist Ann Windsor, advertised the sale of "Several volumes of Musick, for two Violins and a Bass, by Abel, Boyce, Corelli, Campioni, &c."[107] The society's violinist Gaetano Franceschini published twelve of his own trio sonatas in Amsterdam in 1769.[108] Whether or not these trios for two violins and continuo, evincing the *galant* musical idiom that marked the transition between the Baroque and Classical eras, were performed at the St. Cecilia concerts is not known, but it is difficult to imagine that they were not performed in some Charleston forum during Franceschini's long residency. After the revival of Charleston's musical life in the years after the Revolution, instrumental trios continued to make rare appearances on concert programs.[109] While this fact may represent a continuation of earlier musical preferences, it may also be attributable to the ascendancy of the string quartet in the second half of the eighteenth century and beyond.

The earliest known Charleston reference to the concert performance of a quartet—for strings or other combinations of instruments—appeared in May 1788, when Alexander Juhan presented an unidentified quartet at his benefit. As with other genres of concert music in Charleston, references to quartets in extant concert advertising from this era do not always provide the names of the composers. In some cases, the name of the leader or principal player only is inserted.[110] Of the remaining quartets whose composers are identified, however, the name of Ignaz Pleyel clearly dominates.[111] Other names represented among the quartets performed in Charleston include Rode, Giovanni Punto (1746–1803), Davaux, and Georg-Friedrich Fuchs (1752–1821).[112] The name of the most illustrious quartet composer of the era, Franz Joseph Haydn, does not appear among these extant advertisements, though his quartets were almost certainly available at Charleston music stores during this time. Haydn was clearly revered in Charleston, as his orchestral works were a concert staple in the city. The reason for this omission was not owing to ignorance of these celebrated works, therefore, but rather a matter of taste. Many of the quartets mentioned in extant concert advertisements include a wind instrument, either clarinet or flute, along with the usual violin, viola, and cello. This kind of chamber music—by no means a rarity during the Classical period—was usually written for a skilled wind soloist accompanied by less advanced string players, a fact suggesting that the selection of chamber music at these concerts was influenced by the participation of amateur performers. Furthermore quartets written for a soloist (either a string or wind instrument) and accompanying trio represent a more *galant* French fashion of the Classical period, as opposed to the more complex Germanic idiom made famous by Haydn, in which four advanced players participate more equally.

Solo Keyboard Music

Solo keyboard music was almost certainly heard at concerts in colonial Charleston, though few details of such performances have survived. It is clear that solo sonatas for the harpsichord were heard at concerts by the early 1770s, but none of the composers was identified.[113] These works were probably by such musicians as Arne, J. C. Bach, Pietro Domenico Paradies (1707–1791), Baldassare Galuppi (1706–1785), and others whose works were published in London around the middle of the eighteenth century.

The earliest known keyboard compositions to be identified on a concert program appeared on the one for Alexander Juhan's benefit in October 1787, when he performed a "Sonata Piano Forte" by Haydn, as well as a similarly titled work by himself or his father, James Juhan.[114] It was nearly a decade later, however, before concert advertisements began to name regularly the composers of piano music included on Charleston concerts.[115] Evidence from this period indicates that the solo piano compositions heard at Charleston concerts during the late 1790s and early 1800s were dominated by members of the "London piano-forte school"—Dussek, Steibelt, Cramer, and Muzio Clementi (1752–1832).[116] To this list of illustrious pianist-composers can be added such names as Pleyel, Wölfl, Boieldieu, and even Beethoven.[117]

Performances of a few other miscellaneous keyboard works in Charleston deserve mention. Frantisek Koczwara's phenomenally successful programmatic sonata *The Battle of Prague* (first published in 1788) was included on a few advertised concerts in Charleston in the early nineteenth century. Originally scored for piano accompanied by violin, cello, and percussion, this piece was widely admired in Britain, on the Continent, and in the United States—though in a variety of arrangements. It was especially admired in a solo piano arrangement in Boston, for example, but the few known performances of this work in Charleston specified an arrangement for "full orchestra."[118] A similar piano work, *The Battle of Trenton,* published by English-born composer James Hewitt (1770–1827) in New York and Philadelphia in 1797, was heard on at least one Charleston concert in 1799.[119] Closer to home, Charles Gilfert's own keyboard compositions began to appear with some regularity on Charleston concert programs in the years after the War of 1812—especially his variations on a theme from Dalayrac's opera *Nina.*[120]

Vocal Music

Vocal music was an integral part of all concert programs in Charleston during the Classical period.[121] While duets and even vocal trios were sung on occasion, the majority of these vocal performances were solos.[122] As with concerts in contemporary Britain and in other American cities, most of these solos were excerpted from English operas of the period, but independent "popular" songs of the day were also heard.[123] English-language songs were not the only vocal fare heard at Charleston concerts, however. Thanks in large part to the number of French-speaking refugees who settled in or passed through the city, excerpts from Italian and French operas, performed both in their original languages and in translation, are occasionally found on extant concert programs.

Most extant concert programs of this period do not specify titles or composers of songs. The name of the performer is frequently given, but even this small piece of information is not consistently present. In the years following the establishment of the Charleston Theatre in 1793, however, the listings of vocal selections in concert advertisements became more specific, allowing more precise identification of songs and performers. This change was no mere coincidence, for oftentimes the songs heard at concerts were taken from the English operas, comedies, and farces then performing at the local theater.[124] An examination of the dramatic characters portrayed by theatrical singers suggests that in Charleston, as in Britain, these concert songs were performed mostly by sopranos and tenors—the principal vocal types called for in the solo repertoire of that era.[125]

Singers did not perform songs without instrumental assistance, of course. In elaborate vocal pieces, such as opera excerpts (self-contained, detachable "numbers," according to the style of the era), singers were supported by the orchestra, while simpler songs called for plainer accompaniment. During the early decades of the St. Cecilia concerts, the latter sort of accompaniment would have meant basso continuo (harpsichord and a bass instrument), while from the 1790s onward the piano, harp, and "Spanish" guitar were also employed for support.

English Songs

From the mid-1760s through the early years of the nineteenth century, Charleston concert audiences heard essentially the same English-language songs as their counterparts in Britain. These included works by such composers as Thomas Arne, Samuel Arnold, Henry Bishop, John Braham, Domenico Corri, John Davy, Charles Dibdin, James Hook, William Jackson of Exeter, Michael Kelly, Thomas Linley, Thomas Moore, John Percy, Thomas Pinto, William Reeve, William Shield, John Stevenson, Stephen Storace, and Elizabeth Weichsell. Of these song composers, the most frequently represented were Arne, Hook, Shield, and Storace.

Of the few concert programs published in the Charleston newspapers during the first decade of the St. Cecilia Society's existence, none specifically identifies the songs included. Thomas Pike's concert in October 1765, for example, included an unspecified song in each of its two acts. The following month Peter Valton's benefit concert included "two Songs sung by Miss Wainwright, and two by Miss Hallam," young English theatrical singers making their debuts in Charleston.[126] Despite these vague announcements, the advertisements for the city's largest bookstore provide a hint of what kind of secular vocal music may have been heard at these concerts. In June 1766 Robert Wells, Charleston's principal colonial retailer of imported books and music, advertised that he had for sale the music to Thomas Arne's operas *Artaxerxes* (1762), *Love in a Village* (1762), and *Thomas and Sally* (1760), as well as that of the classic *The Beggar's Opera* (1728; perhaps Arne's updated version of 1759), and "Upwards of 500 single songs, among which are most of the new ones sung at the theatres and gardens in London." In November 1767 Wells offered "a variety of single Songs, Cantatas &c., set to music; the Music in *Artaxerxes, The Summers Tale, Daphne and Amintor,* &c." In May 1774, a year before his return to London, Wells boasted that his bookstore carried "Several thousands of the Best Songs set to Musick."[127] The same English vocal repertoire was continued through the early 1780s, when an anonymous German correspondent recorded his impression of the concerts performed during the British occupation of Charleston: "The arias, which several aristocratic ladies sang at public concerts as *dilettanti* were written in the English language and were composed by Arnold, Dibdin, Pinto, Weichsell and others."[128]

As the advance printing of concert programs became more common in Charleston after the Revolution, the vocal repertoire heard at local concerts can be determined with a greater degree of certainty. A few examples will give a sense of the English songs in vogue at the time. At his benefit concert in

October 1787 Alexander Juhan sang a "Hunting Song" by Percy and an unspecified song by Arne.[129] At a semitheatrical concert in May 1789, Miss Wall sang the anonymous song "The Lark's Shrill Notes," first heard at London's Ranelagh Gardens in the late 1750s.[130] The St. Cecilia Society's concert to assist the Salter family in March 1800 included young Miss Salter singing "Within a mile of Edinburgh" (from Hook's 1793 ballad opera *Harlequin Faustus*) and "The Pretty Waxen Doll" (from Shield's 1791 opera *The Woodman*), while thespian Mr. Chambers sang "The Galley Slave" (from William Reeve's one-act opera *The Purse; or, Benevolent Tar*).[131] At the second benefit concert for the "gentlemen of the Orchestra" in January 1802, Mr. Story, "from the Theatres London and Boston," sang Shield's song "The Wolf" (from Arnold's 1782 opera *The Castle of Andalusia*) and Storace's "There the Silver'd Waters Roam" (from the 1792 opera *The Pirates*).[132] The benefit concert for the mother of the late Dorothea Broadhurst in February 1803 included Mr. Marshall singing Shield's "The Seaman's Home" (from the 1793 pastiche *The Midnight Wanderers*), Mrs. Melmoth singing Arne's "Disdainful you fly me" (from *Artaxerxes*) and Mrs. Placide performing Storace's "Lovers who listen" (from *The Pirates*).[133] John Hodgkinson sang Storace's "The Rose and Lilly" (from the 1791 opera *The Siege of Belgrade*) and "The Son's Invocation to the Spirit of his Father" at Antoinette La Roque's benefit in April 1804, while Mrs. Placide sang Kelly's "No, My Love, No!" (from the 1800 farce *Of Age Tomorrow*). Also that evening they sang Stevenson's duet "Sweet little Margaret."[134] "The Song of 'Sweet Echo'" from Arne's 1738 masque *Comus* was performed by Mrs. Marshall, with flute obbligato played by John Hodgkinson, at Mrs. Whitlock's benefit in April 1805.[135] Charles Gilfert's benefit in March 1807 included Mrs. Claude singing Braham's "The Beautiful Maid" (from the 1802 comic opera *The Cabinet*) and Shield's "The Nightingale."[136] The "Miss Sullys" sang the trio "The Three Sisters" (from Thomas Linley's 1776 comic opera *Selima and Azor*) at Miss Sully's benefit in March 1811.[137] Mr. LeFolle's benefit in March 1811, a performance sponsored and managed by the St. Cecilia Society, included three singers: Miss Thomas sang Kelly's "Turn minutes to seconds," Eliza Poe sang Shield's "Whilst with Village Maids I Stray" (from the 1782 comic opera *Rosina*) and Hook's "Ruddy Aurora," while Cornelia Thomas sang Storace's "Joyous Day" (from *The Siege of Belgrade*).[138] At her benefit concert in February 1813, also sponsored by the St. Cecilia Society, Mrs. Placide sang Hook's "When you tell me your heart is another's" and Davy's "Lovely Ball," while Cornelia Thomas (now Mrs. Burke) sang Kelly's "With My Tambourin" and Shield's "Tuneful Lark."[139] At Mr. LeFolle's benefit in March 1813, Mrs. Placide was featured in two songs by Domenico Corri: "Deep in the Fountain of this Beating Heart" and "In Christian Land" ("Never Kiss & Tell," with harp & flute obbligato, from the 1806 opera *The Travellers*, *or Music's Fascination*). On that same program, Mrs. Placide and Cornelia Thomas Burke sang Storace's duet "Haste Zephyr o'er the glade" (from *The Siege of Belgrade*).[140] Mr. Nichols sang two songs by Braham at the benefit of Mr. Gilles in December 1816: "To Share a Heart that Never Lov'd" and "Said a Smile to a Tear."[141] At Mr. Norton's benefit in March 1817, Mr. Nichols sang Henry Bishop's "The Soldier's Gratitude" (from the 1813 melodramatic opera *For England, Ho!*). Mr. Nichols and Mrs. Waring together sang Moore's "Oh Nanny, wilt thou gang with me."[142] Bishop's "Celebrated Echo Song" (from the 1815 opera *Brother and Sister*) was presented by Mrs. French at her benefit in February 1819.[143]

Italian Songs

English-language songs were not the only kind of vocal music heard at concerts in late-eighteenth- and early-nineteenth-century Charleston. Shortly after the conclusion of the American Revolution, Charleston bookseller Charles Morgan announced that he had just imported from London "Italian Operas and Songs, Periodical ditto [individual songs published as part of a series]" as well as "Vocal English Operas."[144] Italian songs were heard at many sophisticated British concerts, but their performance in late-eighteenth-century America may not have been a likely occurrence. Taking its lead from the example set by London musical tastes, however, the St. Cecilia Society welcomed this Continental repertoire at its concerts—a fact demonstrated by the Charleston performances of Maria Storer in 1785.

English theatrical singer Maria Storer returned to Charleston in early 1785, having earlier performed at the Church Street Theatre during the elaborate 1773–74 season, and was soon engaged to sing at the St. Cecilia Society's concerts. Although the Revolution had compelled her to retreat to Jamaica for the duration of the war, Storer was still respected for her cosmopolitan taste as well as her vocal talents. Shortly after her arrival and her engagement with the St. Cecilia Society, however, a frustrated auditor appealed to Miss Storer through the *Columbian Herald* to revert to a more familiar vocal fare: "A correspondent advises Miss Maria Storer not to introduce any more Italian songs, at the St. Cecilia concert; Italian songs are at best an exotic entertainment, and require a knowledge of the language to give pathos and sensibility. To subdue the heart by affecting and pathetic expression—to inspire kindred emotions—to soothe and to soften the asperities of our nature, ought ever to be the moral pursuit of a fine singer, and she may assure herself that this accomplishment is superior to the wonder of executing difficulties which can only be interesting to the amateurs of science."[145] Exactly what Italian songs Storer was performing is not known, but another notice of her performances with the St. Cecilia Society, published on 1 July

1785, demonstrates that her vocal selections were similar to those heard at the most fashionable and prestigious concert series in contemporary London, the Pantheon concerts and those at the Hanover Square Rooms under Carl Friedrich Abel: "The celebrated cantabile air 'The lamentation of Mary Queen of Scots,' written by Lord Kaims, and set to music by Signor Tenducci, was sung last night by Miss Maria Storer at the St. Cecilia concert, with the highest approbation, and is a proof of the superiority which simple natural melody will always possess over the modern refinements of art."[146] Although its music was composed in a comparatively simple style, obviously more pleasing to a certain portion of the St. Cecilia Society's audience than Miss Storer's Italian fare, this English "Lamentation" was actually the work of two celebrated Italian musicians residing in London: the castrato Giusto Ferdinando Tenducci composed the vocal melody, while Tommaso Giordani was responsible for the instrumental setting. Scored for voice and string orchestra, it was published in 1782 with the notation that it had been "Sung by Sigr: Tenducci at the Pantheon & Mr. Abel's concert &c."[147]

Considering the small size and relative remoteness of late-eighteenth-century Charleston, it is no surprise that Italian vocal works appear infrequently on extant concert programs of this era. Nevertheless, even the small number of such references suggests that Charleston concert audiences were treated to a diet of Italian vocal fashions in similar doses as their counterparts in other American cities and in Britain. At the St. Cecilia Society's concert for the orphan children of John Hodgkinson in October 1805, for example, Mrs. Oldmixon delighted the audience with "the necromancy of her notes" by performing "tender passages of the beautiful music of Giardini," a musical selection that required a compass of a "double octave from G."[148] Although she selected an Italian vocal piece for her Charleston debut, Mrs. Oldmixon was a British singer who had just arrived via the Philadelphia stage.[149]

Operatic excerpts by the Italian composer Giovanni Paisiello (1740–1816) were presented in early-nineteenth-century Charleston on a number of occasions. His celebrated aria "Nel cor più non mi sento" from the opera La Molinara was known in England and in Charleston, though it was perhaps heard more often as "Hope Told a Flattering Tale" in revivals of Arne's Artaxerxes.[150] Similarly selections from Wolfgang Amadeus Mozart's Italian operas occasionally appear on extant Charleston programs, though more often than not in translations.[151] Filippo Trajetta (1777–1854), "Master of Music and Composer, from Naples," performed his own Italian vocal works and those by his father, the celebrated opera composer Tommaso Traetta (1727–1779), during his residency in Charleston between late 1801 and 1808.[152] Arias by several other Italian composers, including Niccolò Piccinni (1728–1800), Giovanni Battista Pergolesi (1710–1736), Domenico Cimarosa (1749–1801), Niccolò

Jommelli (1714–1774), Giuseppi Nicolini (1762–1842), and Giacomo Tritto (1733–1824) were occasionally heard in early-nineteenth-century Charleston, with the choice of language apparently determined by the performers.[153]

French Songs

While the performance of Italian-language songs in Charleston may be explained as an extension of London musical fashions of the late eighteenth and early nineteenth centuries, the appearance of French vocal selections on concert programs during this period is largely the result of the influence of the French-speaking refugees who came to Charleston in the 1790s and early 1800s. Unfortunately only a few of the French vocal pieces included on advertised concerts during the 1790s are identified.[154] The nature of these songs may be deduced, however, from the several French *opéras comiques* that were played at Charleston's French Theatre (also known as the Church Street Theatre or City Theatre) between its opening in April 1794 and its closing at the turn of the century. For example several of Grétry's *opéras comiques* were performed during the late 1790s, and a number of advertised concerts included vocal excerpts from his works.[155] In addition to their overtures, vocal selections from Dalayrac's *Nina* and Boieldieu's *Le Calife de Bagdad* were heard several times in Charleston.[156]

Not all of the French vocal works performed in Charleston can be traced to local stage productions of French operas, however. Many appear to have been the favorites of particular performers, or French songs obtained through London publishers. Several excerpts from François Devienne's *Les Visitandines* appear on early-nineteenth-century concert programs, for example, though that opera is not known to have been staged in Charleston.[157] Several French songs by "Trajetta" were performed in Charleston—after Filippo Trajetta's departure from the city in 1808. While these may have been the work of the young Italian singer-composer, they may also have been excerpts from the French versions of his father's Italian operas produced in Paris during the 1770s.[158] Other French songs by such composers as Giuseppe Milico (1737–1802), Méhul, Jean-Baptiste LeMoyne (1751–1796), Kreutzer, and Henri Berton (1767–1844) each appear on at least one Charleston program during the period under study.[159]

It may surprise modern readers that the majority of the French vocal selections heard at concerts in Charleston during the years of the St. Cecilia Society's concert activity were written by the Italian composer Antonio Sacchini (1730–1786). Although Sacchini resided briefly in London during the late 1770s, the presence of his vocal music in Charleston is more likely attributable to the French immigrants who arrived around the turn of the nineteenth century. The titles performed in this city were taken from the Italian operas that Sacchini reworked for presentations in France in the 1780s, including *Renaud, Oedipe à Colonne,* and *Chimène; ou, Le Cid.*[160]

LIKE MANY OTHER ASPECTS of the city's cultural life during the late eighteenth and early nineteenth centuries, the concert music performed in Charleston during this era demonstrates a strong desire to replicate contemporary British models. From the genres, titles, and composers discussed in this chapter, it is clear that the "polite" and "commercial" concerts in Britain, especially those in London, formed the aesthetic paradigm for similar concerts in Charleston during the city's golden age of music.[161] Charleston was not the only city in the United States to hear such au courant music, of course, as many of the same British publications and even many of the same musicians found their way to New York, Philadelphia, and other cities along the Atlantic coastline. Conditions unique to each community created musical differences and disparities, however, which determined the extent to which this aesthetic model could take root. Anomalies such as the unexpected influx of French musicians and repertoire in the 1790s also spawned variations in this musical melting pot that served to highlight distinctive local flavors. The institutional strength of the St. Cecilia Society and the long-term vitality of its concert series made Charleston a fertile field for a host of European musical transplants. As with the more tangible elements of the city's past—such as its buildings, furnishings, and artwork—the cosmopolitan musical repertoire cultivated in late-eighteenth- and early-nineteenth-century Charleston was an enduring legacy of its colonial British roots. Unlike the mute, decaying artifacts of the past, however, knowledge of the music that once echoed through this city's halls provides a dynamic link to the world of early Charleston. By locating and performing examples of this long-forgotten repertoire in our own time, we can reanimate a vibrant element of the city's past. Our listening habits may be prejudiced by twenty-first century conditions, but the experience would still provide a rewarding opportunity to appreciate the sounds that once captured the imaginations of local concert audiences.

The End of an Era

THE CONCERT SERIES OF CHARLESTON'S ST. CECILIA SOCIETY was sired by the intersection of the colonial passion for emulating the sophisticated culture of London with the new opportunities afforded by a secure and prosperous economy in the wake of the peace of 1763. For the sake of historical simplicity, it would be convenient to ascribe the demise of the society's concert patronage in 1820 to a similarly intersecting pair of events: the gradual "desertion" of the musicians associated with the Charleston Theatre after 1817 and the crippling economic depression caused by the Panic of 1819. Such a conclusion would create a satisfying pair of historical bookends with which to frame the St. Cecilia Society's era as the most prominent musical organization in North America, and it would not be inaccurate. This tidy summing up of the rise and fall of the society's concert series carries with it a tacit implication, however, that does not do proper justice to the musical legacy of this organization. Because the St. Cecilia concerts did not survive this cultural and economic challenge in 1820—after having weathered the hardships of the American Revolution, the postwar depression in the late 1780s, the national embargo initiated in 1808, and the War of 1812—it would be easy to assume that the collective musical ardor of the society's members was in serious decline and that its commitment to furthering its musical traditions was not strong enough to survive the final crises. The continued participation of gentlemen and lady amateurs in polite music making in Charleston after 1820 seems to challenge this neat conclusion, however, and begs for a more nuanced interpretation of the termination of the St. Cecilia concerts. Behind the conspicuous effects of the economic depression and the difficulties in assembling an orchestra, other forces, far less obvious or sudden, were also conspiring to weaken the society's musical traditions in the early decades of the nineteenth century.

Charles Fraser's brief explanation for the demise of the St. Cecilia concerts, published in 1854 and repeated by writers for more than a century and a half, draws attention to the society's difficulty in "procuring" an orchestra as a major factor contributing to the demise of the concerts. In addition to this well-documented crisis, Fraser also makes vague reference to a series of other issues, seemingly less important, that have yet to receive any serious scrutiny. We should not be deterred by the ambiguity of Fraser's text, however, for when viewed from a broader historical context, these ostensibly minor factors undoubtedly contributed to the St. Cecilia Society's transformation around the year 1820 and deserve to be properly acknowledged.

After five decades of concert patronage, Fraser wrote, "the purposes of the society seemed to have been accomplished, and its destinies fulfilled. Change, which is always at work, was silently preying upon its prosperity. As the old members fell off, their places were supplied by younger ones. A rival Society had sprung up. Musical entertainment could be enjoyed elsewhere— new tastes were formed—new habits came into fashion. The love of dancing increased."[1] From this brief abstract of the termination of its concert series, we learn first that the purposes of the St. Cecilia Society were gradually transformed by the inevitable succession of newer, younger members. Such evolutionary turnover is not uncommon among social organizations, of course, and on its own presents no inherent danger to their survival. In the case of this musical society, however, this usually mundane transition proved a serious and effective challenge to the society's original purposes. The continuation of Fraser's explanation succinctly identifies a trio of factors that transformed the ordinary passing of the torch from one generation to another into such a serious threat: the rise of a "rival" musical organization, changing habits and tastes, and the increasing popularity of dancing.

A "Rival" Musical Organization

In a footnote to his explanation Fraser identified "the old Philharmonic Society, incorporated in 1810," as the "rival society" whose presence contributed to the cessation of the St. Cecilia concerts. This organization, which was formed by 1809 and incorporated in 1810, may have diluted slightly the St. Cecilia Society's near monopoly on concert music in early-nineteenth-century Charleston, but its virtual collapse in 1814 rendered it a relatively small threat to the activities of the St. Cecilia Society. At the distance of forty years after the cessation of the Philharmonic Society's concerts, Fraser's memory of its supposed rivalry with the St. Cecilia concerts was probably exaggerated and a bit confused. If the concerts of the Philharmonic Society had succeeded in drawing audience members away from St. Cecilia performances, one might expect the St. Cecilia Society to have faded out of existence rather than the

Phlharmonic Society. Furthermore the band of the Philharmonic Society was composed of virtually the same musicians heard at the St. Cecilia Society's fortnightly series, and their concert schedule was carefully constructed to avoid conflicts with St. Cecilia performances. Although we may never be able to reconstruct the full story of the Philharmonic Society's brief existence, the surviving evidence does not seem to support Fraser's assertion of a rivalry with the St. Cecilia Society. In short, the two musical organizations were too similar to foster a healthy competition, especially in a city with such a small potential audience, and the younger, less exclusive society was short lived.

There was another musical society in early nineteenth-century Charleston, however, whose mission, membership, and audience was indeed sufficiently distinctive to form a sort of rivalry with the St. Cecilia Society: the Union Harmonic Society. Beginning in the autumn of 1817 and continuing well into the 1820s, the various traveling engagements of the Charleston Theatre company and its orchestra caused a significant disruption in Charleston's concert life and contributed to the decline of the St. Cecilia Society's long-standing concert series. The theater company's peregrinations had a more generalized effect on the city's musical life as well. With fewer professional musicians in town, there were fewer benefit concerts and fewer performances of large-ensemble instrumental music. Contemporary with these changes, however, the Union Harmonic Society was able to present large-scale compositions in Charleston with an apparently numerous ensemble. Founded in early 1816 "for the purpose of rehearsing and improving Sacred Music," the Union Harmonic Society made a specialty of performing sacred choral music for the benefit of charitable causes.[2] In contrast to the "fashionable" repertoire heard at the "polite" concerts of the St. Cecilia Society and the Philharmonic Society, the music cultivated by the Union Harmonic Society represented a new ideological direction in the city's musical life.

For an exclusive social group in a small American city, the encouragement of Classical musical repertoire was a part of a desire, born of colonial pretensions, to construct a sense of cultural identity and legitimacy by replicating elements of sophisticated English culture. The performance of a cosmopolitan musical aesthetic, borrowed chiefly from the cultural capital, London, provided auditory proof of the society's urbanity and maturity. As the currency of this Enlightenment cultural model waned in the early decades of the nineteenth century, however, so too did prevailing attitudes toward concert repertoire. The eighteenth-century emphasis on au courant music that offered sensual enjoyment eventually gave way to a new aesthetic. Beginning in late-eighteenth-century England and continuing well into the nineteenth century, concerts underwent a process that has been called "sacralization," whereby a certain repertoire of music was elevated to the status of "classics" and was attributed with an inherent morality and "scientific" perfection that merited an unprecedented degree of reverence and intellectual engagement from the audience. This process eventually spread to concert repertoire in general, and by the middle of the nineteenth century emerged as the dominant musical ideology of the Romantic era. The eighteenth-century "sociable aesthetic," with its emphasis on manners and polite conversation, was gradually discredited and pushed out of the concert world.[3]

While there is no evidence of a causal relationship between the rise of the Union Harmonic Society and the decline of the St. Cecilia concerts, the opposing trajectories of "polite" and sacred music around the year 1820 seem to mark a historic transition in the appreciation of music in Charleston. Although its performances were not as numerous or as regular as those of the St. Cecilia Society or the Philharmonic Society, the Union Harmonic concerts were open to a broader audience and even a broader range of performers than either of the earlier musical organizations. Its performances were nonsubscription events open to the public at large, and its membership apparently included women as well as men.[4] While the majority of the St. Cecilia Society members were affiliated with the Anglican/Episcopal Church, most of the known members of the Union Harmonic Society were members of other Protestant denominations, including Independent Congregationalists, Unitarians, Presbyterians, and Baptists. In these respects, this young concert society represented a new, increasingly democratic ethos of concert music that was then emerging in America and abroad. The general cultivation of sacred music, according to a supporter of the Union Harmonic Society, "affords an image of the harmony which prevails in heaven, and may one day exist on earth. If, for instance, all mankind could at the same moment be employed in singing the same hymn, the whole earth would exhibit one harmonious impulse of pure devotion and brotherly love."[5]

The Union Harmonic Society's emphasis on sacred concert music, especially works composed by Handel, Haydn, and Mozart that were increasingly regarded as classics, linked it to similar musical organizations in northern cities as well as abroad. Like the Handel and Haydn Society founded in Boston in 1815, the Union Harmonic Society eschewed fashionable music in favor of the sacred repertoire as a means of effecting a general moral improvement among the community.[6] The society's "scientific display of vocal and instrumental harmony" at the Circular Congregational Church in Meeting Street in April 1819, for example, attracted about twelve hundred auditors, causing a correspondent to the *Charleston Courier* to remark that "our sister cities of the North, have witnessed and duly appreciated similar exertions 'to rouse the feelings and to mend the heart,' and we are persuaded that the good taste and discernment of this community will not be wanting to foster and encourage this sublime auxiliary of true devotion."[7] Henry Tudor Farmer, an English-born physician-poet, emphasized the moral value of such music in his 1821 address to the members of the Union Harmonic Society, stating "the cultivation and improvement of sacred music is not only essential to the interests of religious exercise, but to the general taste and refinement of a nation. Indeed, it may be added to national rectitude and morality, since those offerings which are dedicated to the Deity, should be of the purest and highest order."[8] The drive to improve morals and society in general through the cultivation of a specific musical repertoire was not a uniquely American phenomenon, of course. It represented the extension of a movement in contemporary Europe, especially in England, which was bolstered in large part by the broadening of public access to musical performances. Charleston's Union Harmonic Society was, therefore, the local manifestation of a broader trend in musical aesthetics.

In its early years the St. Cecilia Society's concerts represented the successful transplantation of a British musical model, one that was well suited to the socio-economic conditions of early Charleston. Similarly the rise of the Union Harmonic Society and the new musical aesthetic it embodied represented a new English export that found ready audiences in this port city—at least at first. While the activities of Charleston's Union Harmonic Society around the year 1820 represent the local version of a powerful international movement toward a more serious ideology of concert music than that left over from the eighteenth century, it was a change that did not take root. After several years of successful activity, even the Union Harmonic Society was struggling for survival by the autumn of 1823. A correspondent calling himself "Carolinian" lamented that the "fundamental cause" of this situation was "want of public spirit," adding that "the Union Harmonic Society has no encouragement from the public, which can readily be seen by a reference to their last Anniversary Concert, when the amounts paid and received, differed about *Twenty-five Cents!*"[9] Although it survived until at least 1828, the rise and fall of the Union Harmonic Society within a relatively short time frame suggests that the majority of the concert-going public in Charleston was not prepared to fully embrace this new, morally charged aesthetic.

Despite the failure of the Union Harmonic Society to establish itself as the new central figure in Charleston's musical life, the implications of its brief existence still provide powerful evidence for determining the reasons behind the collapse of the St. Cecilia Society's venerable concert series. The rise of the Union Harmonic Society at the very moment when the St. Cecilia Society was struggling highlights a significant transformation that was taking place in Charleston's musical climate around the year 1820, one that went beyond the difficulties attributable to a poor economic climate and dwindling numbers of resident professional musicians. For much of its existence as a concert organization, the St. Cecilia Society established and maintained the standards of Charleston's concert life by embracing the performance of a variety of musical genres composed by the most celebrated European masters of the day. Its musical identity was, in fact, intertwined with the life cycle of the musical aesthetic known as the Classical style. In other words the St. Cecilia Society emerged in the early stages of this stylistic period, when British audiences were just beginning to appreciate the cosmopolitan musical language then brewing in Europe; St. Cecilia concerts were at their apex when musical Classicism reached its maturity in the last decade of the eighteenth century; and the society went into decline as the cultural forces that gave rise to and sustained this Enlightenment musical ideology began to fade. The emergence of a new musical aesthetic incompatible to the St. Cecilia Society's well-established traditions—coincident with economic difficulties and a diminished supply of professional musicians—was an effective challenge to its domination of Charleston's musical scene. The society's withdrawal from concert patronage during the ascendancy of the Union Harmonic Society is therefore significant, for it may have been a sign of its unwillingness to embrace the new musical aesthetic and its concomitant social practices. Rather than adapt its half-century-old concert series to the realities of a new musical era, the St. Cecilia Society chose instead to withdraw into a narrower sphere of activities in which its cherished traditions could be sustained.

New Habits and Tastes

The calculated hospitality demonstrated by the regulations for the admission of nonmembers reveals the importance of polite sociability at the St. Cecilia Society's concerts. In eighteenth-century European and early American culture, the cultivation of musical taste was, after all, as much a social ritual for the elite beau monde as an artistic endeavor. The inherently social nature of concert performances was an intrinsic part of the musical aesthetic of this era, and thus transformed such events into a significant forum for mixed-sex interaction within the bounds of a protected social sphere. Conversation was the primary medium for the creation and development of social networks, and, as the complex web of family trees and business partnerships within the St. Cecilia Society's membership demonstrate, a great deal of chatting, negotiating, and flirting took place at their concerts in Charleston.

Sociable conversation was surely an important feature of the St. Cecilia Society's concerts from the start, but in the early years there may have been less talking *during* the music. Josiah Quincy, for example, observed that the ladies' "taciturnity during the performances" at a St. Cecilia concert in 1773 greatly surpassed that of the ladies in Boston, though he did note that the "noise and flirtations after the music" were "pretty much on par."[10] An anonymous German correspondent who witnessed the subscription concerts in Charleston during the British occupation of 1780–82 was not quite as impressed. While he approved of the musical repertoire and the performance of the band, he complained, "silence and attention during the music, however, one does not find in America as it really should be."[11] A review of a St. Cecilia concert in October 1805 noted "expectation was on tiptoe" for the first appearance of the celebrated vocalist Mrs. Oldmixon—so much so that the usual "hum of conversation was hushed into silence."[12]

By the second decade of the nineteenth century, however, the "hum of conversation" at the St. Cecilia concerts was clearly intruding on the music. The society's concerts were now dominated by a younger generation of auditors, the children and grandchildren of the early members, who were apparently less reluctant than their elders to socialize during the performances. The causes for this change, which foreshadowed the end of the society's concert patronage, are the subject of an illuminating series of letters that appeared in the Charleston *Times* in February 1811. Writing under the name "Argus," an anonymous correspondent described a recent conversation he had with "a set of fashionable young sparks," who lamented that "the loquacity of the female sex was daily gaining ground." Ostensibly trying to defend womanhood in general, Argus asked the young gentlemen if they had taken into account the modest behavior of ladies in social situations were silence was appropriate and expected. The unanimous response given by the young sparks shocked Argus. "They all, with one accord, instantly said—'Have you lately visited a St. Cecilia Society Concert?'" Argus answered "No—but surely that's not a place for unceasing conversation." "That is exactly what we say," the sparks rejoined, "but whoever has frequented that chaste and respectable Society's Concerts in former times and now, cannot but draw the lamentable conclusion, that female loquacity is in a most dreadful state of augmentation. Formerly, our venerable grand-mothers would, with most becoming deference to the company they were in, refrain from conversation, at these places, during the performance of the music, and indulged their propensity only during the intervals between pieces." Former generations of ladies had exercised this self-restraint out of respect for others, the young men continued, because they knew that some members of the audience were "amateurs of music" who had come to enjoy the elegant sounds. "Therefore, to make such a noise as to prevent them from hearing, and to affront the performers, who would naturally supposed their music is despised, would not only be indecorous, but also tend to lessen the respectability of the society in the eyes of genteel foreigners, who are courteously invited to partake of its amusements." Out of consideration for those listening intently, the ladies of former years never "overstept the modesty" of their sex. "But times are changed," they complained to Argus, "hence the necessity of a singular request at the top of every Concert Bill—'Silence is requested during the performance of the music!!!'"[13]

Argus's report of this conversation elicited several defensive letters, of course. On behalf of "the rest of the sisterhood," a correspondent calling herself "Celia" pleaded guilty to conversing during the music at the concerts, but explained that the ladies were not fully to blame. Their talking was merely an attempt to instruct and improve the "beaux of the present day," whose breadth of knowledge and conversational topics were unfortunately "confined to the stable and the turf." "With respect to our loquacity at Concerts," Celia concluded, "I think the gentleman has greatly exaggerated, for, although a constant attendant myself, I have never been disturbed by their talking."[14] A more acerbic reply came from "Vindex," who argued that the ladies were "neither exclusively, nor generally, very talkative at musical entertainments." She sarcastically blamed this growing impropriety on the self-important "fashionable young sparks" themselves, who "carry their *utility* so far as even to *support* the *pillars* of the Ball-Room." Far from being the source of the problem, said Vindex, the ladies "have been MADE to talk . . . by the flippant beaux who flutter about them; who, full of self and of pleasing condescension, cannot find it in their hearts to deny the softer sex the pleasure of their fascinating tongues." Convinced that their flirtatious voices were more satisfying to the ladies than the suave music filling the concert room, the young men saturated the air with a hum of prosaic conversation. "No—not even were the divine St. Cecilia herself to descend, and touch the harp's melodious chords," Vindex continued, "would these gentry think her music half so delightful to a lady's ear, as 'Miss, have I the exstatic felicity of beholding you in perfect health?'—'The evening's most warm, I do protest'—is far better calculated to give her entertainment, than [the] sweetest symphonies, or most harmonious strains. And if a 'pray Miss, how's your good mamma, and your kind sisters, and all the rest of the dear family?' be uttered with judicious pathos, and a feeling cadence, 'tis then that, in comparison with this tender phrase, music is mere raven's croak, or screech of owls; and naught is truly musical, but the soft melting tones of the speakers voice." In the final analysis Vindex was unambiguous about the cause of the increasing loquacity at the St. Cecilia concerts: "it is the male sex who talk most, worst, and loudest; and who provoke the female to converse out of season."[15]

Along with the ascendance of Charleston's Union Harmonic Society, the points raised by Vindex, Celia, and Argus about the pervasiveness of light conversation at the St. Cecilia concerts are consistent with a broader international trend in the early decades of the nineteenth century. In the second half of the eighteenth century, much of the beau monde's social life in Britain and British America took place in public forums such as exclusive concerts and balls rather than at small-scale private dinners and salons. With the expansion of communities and the of fragmentation of traditional social stratification in the early nineteenth century, the beau monde faced increasing competition and crowding from the rising middle class, and opportunities for old-style socially exclusive interaction within that sphere diminished.[16] To be sure the growing numbers of genteel private balls, salons, and formal dinners in early-nine-teenth-century Charleston provided new outlets for refined conversation, but their rise also meant the growth of a number of increasingly narrowly defined social cliques.[17] In this new world the St. Cecilia Society's concerts represented a rare opportunity for elite mingling on a large scale, and the social value of conversation, networking, and flirting at such events increased dramatically. For many young gentlemen and ladies of that era, the opportunity for a few minutes of polite conversation within this rarified environment was simply too valuable to allow their desires to be deterred by the performance of music.

A certain amount of talking was to be expected at concerts built on the eighteenth-century Enlightenment model of polite sociability; they were, after all, social events confined to a limited sphere of friends, associates, and family. The toleration of such distracting behavior arose from social necessity inherent in the contemporary ideology of music, and did not necessarily indicate a half-hearted commitment to music as a serious pursuit.[18] Similarly the acknowledged increase in talking during the St. Cecilia concerts does not prove that the society's collective interest in music was in decline in the early nineteenth century, for the appreciation of music remained an important and widely recognized criterion of social status for many years beyond this point. Rather, the increasing tension between conversation and musical perform-ance at the St. Cecilia concerts in the second decade of the nineteenth century resulted from the collapse of two formerly separate social activities into a sin-gle arena. Each had recognized value and was appreciated, but in close quar-ters they were incompatible. At a time when the act of listening to music in Europe and in the United States was evolving into an increasingly serious and morally charged endeavor, this incompatibility could not be tolerated for long. The fact that the St. Cecilia Society withdrew from concert patronage in 1820 probably had less to do with a waning interest in music than it is a demonstration of their acceptance or acknowledgment of the fact that music and social conversation did not belong together anymore, that the mid-eigh-teenth-century ideology of listening to concert music was too narrowly defined to satisfy the tastes and desires of the new age. By abandoning its con-cert series, therefore, the society alleviated a problem that was annoying to its auditors, injurious to its reputation, and impossible to uproot. To paraphrase Charles Fraser, by 1820 the times and habits had changed, and music could be truly enjoyed, in the new sense, elsewhere in Charleston.

The Love of Dancing

The large number of early St. Cecilia Society members who were related by marriage testifies to the society's success in promoting courtship among eligible members of "families of quality" within its exclusive social sphere. With its members representing the primary landowners and most successful merchants of the state, there was ample motivation to establish alliances that would protect and augment family fortunes. Even with the lack of rigid proscriptions against conversing during the musical performance, however, the rather static atmosphere of the concert was not sufficiently conducive to match making. The real socializing at St. Cecilia events took place after the conclusion of the music, in the hours of dancing that followed each concert. No matter how formal or rigid it may have been at the time, dancing afforded far greater opportunities for building and maintaining social relationships.

The Classical style of music in currency in the late eighteenth century may not have imposed strenuous demands on the listener's intellect, but the concert etiquette of that era did require audiences to observe a certain degree of attention and quiet. By definition, therefore, the role of an auditor at a concert is rather passive and static. Dancing affords participants a greater opportunity for active involvement, however, without requiring an increase in intellectual engagement. For many in the St. Cecilia Society's audiences, especially the young bachelors, the postconcert ball carried a far greater appeal than the quiet, passive digestion of sophisticated music. Surrounded by a pageant of the lowcountry's "shining beauties," these young men were understandably eager for the opportunity to hold hands with the ladies of their choice and to engage in socially sanctioned flirting. This fact is clearly demonstrated in a letter written by a frustrated young Thomas Pinckney Jr. (1780–1842) to his cousin Harriott Pinckney following a disappointing visit to a St. Cecilia event. "Things go on in the old style," the young Pinckney reported in early February 1802. "We all went to the last concert [on 28 January], about 9 o'clock. It was quite a sudden thought of my Uncle's [Charles Cotesworth Pinckney's] at whose house we were playing cards; after the company were gone, some one proposed in a joke to go, and my Uncle immediately ordered the carriage, so in we went." Skipping the concert portion of the evening, Pinckney and his family arrived at Concert Hall in time for the postconcert ball. To his great distress, on entering the room he saw his intended belle in the arms of a rival suitor. "I asked Mary [Izard] to dance with me, [but] I saw, with a degree of mortification, I cannot express, Ben [Benjamin Burgh] Smith take *her* out. I could have eaten my fingers off. I should not have cared so much had she danced with a *Gentleman,* but to see that paltry knave, holding both her hands, I could not bear."[19] Such scenes of romance and rivalry were no doubt a standard feature of the St. Cecilia concerts during its decades of concert activity. In fact the opportunity to circulate in such company may have been the primary attraction for some society members. Restricted to an exclusive sphere of wealthy men and infused with an abundance of fashionable and vivacious ladies, the concerts of the St. Cecilia Society—and especially the dancing that followed—served as the most elite social stage in the southern United States.

While the combination of concerts and balls may have been a natural and important feature of the St. Cecilia Society's performances from its founding in 1766, the bond between this pair began to erode in the second decade of the nineteenth century. Charles Fraser's remark that "the love of dancing increased" in the early nineteenth century is certainly borne out by evidence in the newspapers, for in the years between 1808 and the end of the society's concert series in 1820, Charleston witnessed a proliferation of subscription dancing assemblies. Dancing masters such as Peter Fayolle and Jean-Marie Légé, for example, frequently held assemblies to exercise their students' skills, and in 1808 they began advertising tickets to regular "cotillion parties." By 1813 this generic title had been adopted by a formal organization with elected officers and a subscription list that expanded and evolved into the "Charleston Cotillion Parties" by 1819.[20] Similarly the Amicable Assemblies appeared in 1809, and in 1810 changed its name to (or merged with) the Charleston Assemblies. The frequency and organization of its events quickly grew and soon rivaled that of the St. Cecilia concerts. The last year of the War of 1812 brought an abrupt end to its activities, but the Charleston Assemblies was reorganized in early 1816 and continued for years afterward.[21] An advertisement in November 1817 names the three current subscription dancing assemblies as Charleston Assemblies, Cotillion Parties, and Social Assemblies, to which Peter Fayolle added a fourth, the Chorean Assembly, in early 1818.[22]

The rapid rise of these new subscription dancing assemblies in the early years of the nineteenth century did not necessarily form a direct threat to the vitality of the St. Cecilia concerts. Rather, their growing presence indirectly sapped energy away from the society's concert series by promoting the fashion for dance and by enabling a broader segment of Charleston's population to mimic that part of the society's exclusive activities. But the general increase in the love of dancing did succeed in drawing at least some auditors away from the St. Cecilia Society's sphere of influence. As early as 1809, for example, a correspondent to the Charleston *Times* lamented the decline in the city's public support of the musical arts. "Has music (once Northern[ers] named the Carolinians' thermometer) lost its charms?" he asked his neighbors. "Ah no; for the honor of our ancestry let it not be said."[23] Similarly, when French violinist Jean-Claude LeFolle gave a benefit concert "under the particular patronage of the St. Cecilia Society" in March 1811, he found many of the society's members absent. As Margaret Izard Manigault, widow of a long-time member of the society, explained this odd circumstance to her mother in Philadelphia, the fashionable set of Charleston was pre-engaged to attend a private ball on the same evening. LeFolle was "much admired" by the local amateurs, however, so they all purchased tickets for his concert without intending to be present. Offering an oblique apology for this awkward situation, Mrs. Manigault confided to her mother, "our St. Cecilia Society concerts are sadly fallen off."[24]

From these examples, it is clear that during the second decade of the nineteenth century subscription dancing assemblies, not to mention private domestic balls, became the focus of a great deal of social energy in Charleston. The popularity of such activities can be traced back to the colonial period, of course, but, like the emergence of the Union Harmonic Society, the rapid ascendance of fashionable dancing around the time of the St. Cecilia Society's withdrawal from concert patronage points to the beginning of a new aesthetic era. Concerts and dancing, once seen as harmonious companions in the eighteenth century, were increasingly seen as separate events embodying disparate cultural ideologies. As the changing aesthetics of music pulled concert life into a more serious and increasingly passive direction, the rapidly proliferating dancing assemblies provided opportunities for a wider range of participants to actively engage in an elegant alternative form of entertainment. In Charleston and many other cities during the early decades of the nineteenth century, dancing assumed the social importance and allure that subscription concerts had held in the 1760s. Responding to the changing habits and tastes of its members, Charles Fraser remembered, "the concerts were given up, and the society substituted dancing assemblies, which have been regularly continued, every season, with great elegance."[25]

SOMETIME DURING THE YEAR 1827, the young Charleston planter Thomas Middleton (1791–1863) took pen and paper in hand to record an afternoon of congenial musical recreation with eleven of his peers (see figure 10.1). The instruments assembled on this occasion—violin, clarinets, flutes, and guitar—certainly do not represent a conventional musical ensemble of that era, but a number of visual cues shed light on the purpose of the gathering. The conspicuous presence of spirits on the table, the absence of printed music, the gentlemen placing a finger in his ear, and another bowing Middleton's guitar case with a fireplace shovel all convey an informal, jocular mood. According to an inscription on the back of the drawing, it was meant preserve the memory of such gatherings for the descendants of the subjects, and "to convey a pleasing idea of the custom of these times, and the habits of their forefathers."

The sketch represents, in Middleton's words, "a number of gentlemen friends and amateurs in musick, [who] frequently met at each others['] houses to beguile away the time in listening to the soothing strains of their own music." The artist's list of the men present on this occasion includes many familiar names that together suggest a further explanation of the purpose of this event, however.[26] Since most if not all of the "friends and amateurs" depicted here were active in the St. Cecilia Society during the 1820s, it is possible that this sketch represents a moment from a rehearsal for the society's isolated concert at St. Andrew's Hall on 26 June 1827, about which no other information has been found.[27]

Middleton's visual record of this informal rehearsal, assembled in the well-appointed dining room of his brother, Arthur, illustrates the continuation of a practice passed down through generations of wealthy Charleston men. Endowed with the privileges of rank, fortune, and education, they had ample opportunities to gratify their musical desires in the same manner as their grandfathers, whose musical aspirations brought the St. Cecilia Society into existence. The persistence of such music making among Charleston's gentry—both male and female—in the years after the termination of the society's regular concert series provides an important demonstration of their continued passion for music. In the larger public sphere of Charleston and

10.1. *Friends and Amateurs in Musick,* 1827, by Thomas Middleton (1791–1863). Ink wash on paper. Gibbes Museum of Art / Carolina Art Association, 1940.10.01

beyond, the acts of making and listening to music in 1827 were increasingly burdened with a tone of gravity that did not harmonize with the well-established customs of Charleston's gentry. Gathering instead in smaller, more intimate contexts, they chose to preserve their musical traditions in a less ostentatious manner, and to "beguile away the time in listening to the soothing strains of their own music," out of the public eye. This change in the city's cultural life was apparent to contemporary observers as well as later historians. Speaking of Charleston's artistic climate in his *Statistics of South Carolina* (1826), Robert Mills noted "music has always been highly admired and patronized in this city, and still is, though more in a private way."[28]

As it stated in its early years, the St. Cecilia Society's original purpose was to "encourage the science of music." The gentlemen who undertook this cause did so not merely for their recreation and sensual gratification, however, but also because they saw it as their civic responsibility, as the leading citizens of the community, to promote an activity that gave such conspicuous proof of the maturity of their colonial society. Their encouragement of this science, therefore, was less concerned with the general dissemination of music appreciation than with fashioning a musical representation of their exclusive cultural legitimacy. In the deferential world into which the St. Cecilia Society was born, the stratification of social classes was generally acknowledged and observed. The exclusive nature of the society's concerts and its membership was not unusual for that time, and in fact the society may have viewed its private musical patronage as beneficial to the health and prosperity of the community in general. In the decades after the American Revolution, however, the rise of democratic representation in politics caused a ripple that slowly disrupted the traditions of social stratification. As politics and business opened to persons from the lower ranks of society, so too did cultural life. In reaction to this process during the early decades of the nineteenth century, the distinction between established traditions and new practices took on great significance in Charleston.

By the second decade of the nineteenth century, the St. Cecilia Society represented a conspicuous vestige of the more deferential world of the previous century. Although it was neither the oldest nor the biggest social organization in Charleston, the society's concerts represented the largest and most elite mixed-sex events in the region. As social and economic forces gradually reshaped the community, however, the cultural motivations that had inspired the formation of the society's concert series also weakened. The society's role as the local authority on musical taste was challenged by the emergence of a new aesthetic ideology, manifest in the Union Harmonic Society, and its exclusivity was at odds with the new civic spirit embodied in that ideology. Changes in the cultural community surrounding the society rendered its original purpose increasingly obsolete, to the point that its events became more of a ritual of habit than a vital practice. The continuation of the society's existence, if not its concert patronage, after the crisis years leading up to 1820 testifies to the fact that the organization had acquired an importance to its members far beyond its musical patronage. Just as in other cities from New York to London, the changing patterns of society and politics in the early decades of the nineteenth century induced the beau monde of Charleston to withdraw into a more private insular world disconnected from the community's changing tides.[29] Even as a ritual, a mere shadow of its former vitality, the St. Cecilia Society symbolized a treasured link to the past, too valuable to abandon completely. Music, dance, and socialization could now be enjoyed elsewhere in Charleston, but no new phenomenon could challenge the prestige of the St. Cecilia Society.

Conclusion

THE POLYGLOT WORLD OF COLONIAL CHARLESTON, South Carolina, echoed
with the mingling sounds and musical traditions of emigrants from Europe,
Africa, and the Caribbean, as well as those of Native Americans. Like the flags
of many nations flying above the vessels in the city's harbor and along its
crowded wharves, the various languages, musical instruments, and voices
heard in the streets and in private rooms formed a colorful and dynamic part
of the city's character. Such variety piqued the interest of many visitors, but
the broad spectrum of these overlapping sounds, ranging from the "savage"
and mundane to the "scientific" and esoteric, also created a sort of aural chaos
that displeased at least a portion of the inhabitants. In the well-stratified hierarchy of eighteenth-century society, such lack of distinction within the aural
landscape seemed unnatural and dangerous.[1] As one response to this condition, local authorities enacted prohibitions against recreational drumming,
dancing, and "whooping or hallooing" among slaves, who formed the majority of the population, to discourage the ferment of challenges to their power.[2]
Within the free Anglo-European population, however, such restrictive measures could not be used to control or rank the multiplicity of musical traditions
that filled the air, and the rigid social stratification of the era discouraged the
promotion of a homogenized appreciation of music among the various class,
ethnic, and religious groups that comprised the community. An alternative
was to create a private sphere of musical life that, with encouragement from
the highest ranks of society, could set a standard by which other practices
could be compared and judged.

During the brief period of peace and economic prosperity that marked
South Carolina's final decade as a British colony, a select group of wealthy and
ambitious men joined ranks to form a new organization, the St. Cecilia Society, that would demonstrate the maturity of their community and assert their
own cultural authority by sponsoring the performance of an urbane, cosmopolitan repertoire of imported music. In launching such a venture, the founding members demonstrated not only their familiarity with mainstream

musical practices in contemporary Britain, but also their desire to align their cultural lives with acknowledged principles of taste then in currency. The gentlemen of this society actively participated in constructing and nurturing the musical life of their community, for such endeavors reinforced their attempts to demonstrate their economic, social, and political clout. Likewise, the society's choice of St. Cecilia as its eponym was an important element of its self-fashioning. Occupying a strategic middle ground between the rhetoric of secular Classicism and Christian (specifically Anglican) morality in eighteenth-century Britain, this patron saint of music embodied the qualities of virtue, reason, and sensuality with which the society wished to characterize its musical activities and mixed-sex social gatherings.

The society's practices and activities over a half century of musical patronage demonstrate its connection to the prevailing contemporary models in Britain and Europe during what music historians call the Classical period. The administrative structure of the society combined elements of the protodemocratic voluntary organization and the eighteenth-century commercial corporation. Membership was extended only to men of the region's socioeconomic elite, but the audience for the society's performances also included nonmembers of both sexes who were admitted only through a closely monitored approval process. Elected officers managed the society's various activities and formed committees to address specific issues. Its financial operations and policies were shaped by men familiar with the management of large sums of money and with the mechanics of concert patronage abroad. Similarly the practical aspects of the society's existence mirrored those of late-eighteenth-century British concert organizations: the nature and physical dimensions of its performance venues, the participation of amateur performers (both gentlemen and ladies) at its concerts, and its recruitment of and relationship with professional musicians. The extant evidence of the musical language and the musical genres cultivated in Charleston during the late eighteenth and early nineteenth centuries further demonstrates that the society, the local arbiter of musical taste, replicated the form and the musical content of similar organizations abroad—especially those in the nearest capital of musical taste, London. In short, the society was truly the backbone of Charleston's musical life during its five decades of concert activity.

The termination of the society's concert series in 1820 was not simply the result of a waning affection for music but rather was caused by the intersection of several social and economic factors. For years leading up to this transitional moment, the rising volume of polite conversation at its concerts and the growing interest in dancing among its members formed internal signs that the society's original spirit was evolving. As sons and grandsons gradually filled the places of the ambitious colonial gentlemen who had formed the

organization, the habits and tastes of the younger generations gradually sup-
planted the initial purposes of the St. Cecilia Society. These seemingly benign,
internal changes took on greater significance, however, when the decentral-
ization of Charleston's theatrical company, which began in late 1817, kept
most of Charleston's professional musicians on the road for years to come.
After a quarter century of interdependence with the local theater orchestra,
the society's inability to form an orchestra independently of this body exposed
the degree to which the society had withdrawn from the process of actively
recruiting performers. The Panic of 1819, caused by the collapse of a postwar
economic bubble, crippled the local economy and forced many South Carolinians to circumscribe their cultural activities. As a result, the economic climate of Charleston in 1820 was far less conducive to the advancement of
cosmopolitan concert music than was the colonial boom that first nurtured
the St. Cecilia Society in the late 1760s. The simultaneous emergence of a new
musical ideology, based on the reverential appreciation of a limited canon of
timeless "classics" rather than au courant repertoire, further highlighted the
antiquated character of the St. Cecilia concerts. Recognizing that its Enlight-
enment-era customs were of a vintage less cherished by the rising age and
forced to react to external crises, the society chose to focus its energies on sustaining a portion of its exclusive traditions while leaving others to preside over
the city's concert life.

Beyond providing insight into the mechanics of the St. Cecilia Society's
concert series and the specifics of its rise and fall, the material presented in
this study forms a lens with which we may better focus our understanding of
the history of musical culture in colonial British American and the early
United States. At the local level, the emergence, flowering, and decline of this
musical phenomenon mirrors the arching trajectory of Charleston cultural
history between the late colonial era and the beginning of the antebellum era.
The disparate scraps of evidence pieced together here facilitate a better understanding of people, places, and activities that once contributed to the life of
this community: colorful personalities long forgotten, physical spaces transformed by later development, and cultural routines once treasured but now
misremembered. The examination of the local conditions contemporary with
the decline of the St. Cecilia Society's concert series around the year 1820 also
improves our view of a significant point of transition in the history of the
American South. Those same years, according to historians of this region,
mark the advent of the so-called antebellum era, when the waning influence
of eighteenth-century patterns gave way to an increasingly isolationist, self-
consciously southern cultural and political identity. The conditions precipitating the withdrawal of the St. Cecilia Society at this crossroads underscore the
seriousness of this transformation for Charleston and for the entire region.

On the national level the St. Cecilia Society's fifty-four seasons of concert activity demonstrate that—well before the emergence of significant early Romantic musical organizations such as the Boston Academy of Music (founded in 1833) and the New York Philharmonic Society (founded in 1842)— serious and sustained concert activity commensurate with that of contemporary British urban centers was not unknown in the United States. In studies of the rise of European orchestral music in mid-nineteenth-century America, however, scholars of this topic have heretofore argued too forcefully that a tradition of religious psalmody ("unscientific," provincial vocal music) dominated American musical life until forces specific to Boston and, later, New York embraced a morally constructed ideology of orchestral music in the second quarter of the nineteenth century. From that crucible of religious sentiment and Romantic transcendentalism, Americans gradually overcame their misgivings about European secular concert music and proceeded to elevate that art form to the apex of cultural pursuits. While much of this argument is accurate, the decision to overlook the significance of secular concert activity in Boston, New York, or any other American city before the second quarter of the nineteenth century creates the impression of a vacuum that did not exist. Furthermore it perpetuates the too-prevalent conflation of all of eighteenth-century British America under the heading of "New England" writ large.

When compared with what is known about the cultural life of other communities in colonial and postcolonial British America, the active musical patronage of Charleston's St. Cecilia Society appears to be an isolated phenomenon. This study does not attempt to claim that the musical content of the St. Cecilia Society's concerts was more aesthetically advanced than that of concerts in contemporary Boston, New York, or Philadelphia, however, for other studies have demonstrated that much of the same repertoire was being performed in each of these cities in the late eighteenth and early nineteenth centuries. These same studies have also demonstrated the existence of subscription concerts in other American cities during the eighteenth century, though none was apparently as well organized and tenacious as in Charleston.[3] The significance, and perhaps uniqueness, of the St. Cecilia Society, therefore, derives not simply from its concert fare, but also from the early date of its founding, its adherence to established secular models, and its long-term commitment to musical patronage. Only by taking these additional factors into consideration, then, might it be possible to assert that Charleston was more musically advanced than any other American city during this period.

Boston may have led the way in the American adoption of a canon of European orchestral music in the early Romantic era, but it is misleading and inaccurate to characterize this period as a starting point. While the St. Cecilia Society's approach to orchestral music and concert music in general was not as morally serious as that demonstrated by the likes of Boston's Handel and Haydn Society and other mid-nineteenth-century musical organizations in that city, it was perfectly in tune with the European aesthetic ideologies of the era in which that Charleston society flourished. Concert life in Charleston between 1766 and 1820 and that in Boston between 1820 and 1850 cannot and should not be placed in direct comparison, for they represent separate aesthetic eras transpiring in sharply contrasting communities.[4]

Claims of precedent or superiority are not the object of this book. Rather, it is hoped that this study will inspire historians to revisit the early musical development of other American cities, to search anew for documentary evidence and to strive to eradicate the artificial intellectual barriers between musicology and other humanistic disciplines that have impeded our understanding of this era for too long. Only when we have amassed similar studies of early American cities such as Baltimore, Boston, New York, and Philadelphia will we be able to understand fully the musical significance of Charleston's St. Cecilia Society.

Although the material presented here amounts to a microhistory of a narrowly defined time, place, population, and activity, to view it in isolation would be both myopic and anachronistic. The duration of the St. Cecilia Society's concert patronage in Charleston was inexorably linked to the cultural, social, and economic conditions of the broader Atlantic world in the late eighteenth and early nineteenth centuries. The Atlantic triangular trade—slave labor from Africa producing goods in South Carolina for export to Europe—yielded large profits for local planters, merchants, and ancillary professionals. In turn, these Carolina men used their wealth to import material goods, ideas, and talent to satisfy their individual and communal desires for cultural maturity. As this reconstruction of the society's activities demonstrates, concert music was a tool with which an elite sphere of Charlestonians signaled their attachment to and participation in the contemporary cultural ideologies of a distant continent. Changes in the dynamic of this transatlantic phenomenon, caused by such forces as international war, the legal status of the foreign slave trade, and the price of Carolina rice on the international market, had overt consequences for the vitality of the St. Cecilia Society's concert series. Despite these setbacks and inconveniences, the society held fast to the spirit of its original purpose for more than half a century—a fact that testifies to the enduring validity of this transatlantic cultural model. That meaning did evolve over the years, as the British colony of South Carolina transformed into one of the United States, but the society and its musical activities continued to bear the stamp of a foreign pedigree well into the nineteenth century. As a consequence, the various facets of the St. Cecilia Society's character—its management, admission policies, relationships with musicians, and choice of musical repertoire—appear to have more in common with contemporary British musical practices than with the traditionally accepted profile of American musical life during this same period. Perhaps in the future, when we have compiled similar microhistories of concert life in other American cities of the late colonial and early national eras, the musical patronage of this venerable Carolina institution may no longer seem unique. That possibility can never detract from its significance, however, for the gentlemen Votaries of Apollo who founded Charleston's St. Cecilia Society nearly two hundred and fifty years ago represented a blend of transatlantic influences as inimitable as the economic and social conditions that characterized their age. Regardless of whether or not we are ever invited to dance at one of the society's exclusive balls, we can all share in celebrating its heritage. Its activities have touched the lives of men and women from several nations over the past many generations, and we can all benefit from knowing its roots.

Appendix 1

Calendar of St. Cecilia Concerts, 1766–1820

THIS APPENDIX PROVIDES a season-by-season calendar of the St. Cecilia Society's concerts performed between 1766 and 1820. It represents a distillation of data accumulated from extant primary sources, especially the Charleston newspapers of this period. This material should not be taken as a definitive account of the number and frequency of the society's concerts, however, for the discovery of further primary sources in the future may augment and verify these findings. Nevertheless, the present calendar provides a valuable adjunct to the overview of the society's activity presented in chapter 3 and the discussions of its management and the timing of its seasons presented in chapter 4. On its own this data is not sufficient to form an accurate measurement of the society's commitment to concert patronage, of course, but its synoptic presentation can still be useful in the process of reconstructing the society's early history.

Evidence of the frequency of the society's earliest performances, those in its first six concert seasons, is very limited. From March 1773, when it announced the commencement of a fortnightly timetable, the society's concerts took place on a regular schedule during the social season. Most of its concerts between 1773 and 1791 were not advertised, but the adherence to the fortnightly schedule is demonstrated by the fact that occasional deviations from this routine were announced in the newspapers. In addition, occasional postperformance press notices provide evidence of some unadvertised concerts. Starting in the autumn of 1791 the society's concerts were advertised with increasing regularity, and from 1803 through 1820 each concert was individually publicized.

The scheduling of the society's anniversary concert merits special attention. According to the fifth of the society regulations adopted in November 1773, the managers were responsible for scheduling the concerts, "the Anniversary only excepted, on the Evening of which, a Concert shall always be performed." Presumably this fixed anniversary concert was instituted soon after the inception of the society, although none was advertised before the formal adoption of the rules. On the feast day of St. Cecilia, 22 November, the members of the society also held a general meeting and enjoyed a meal together. For many years it was their principal gathering, at which the annual election of officers took place. The practice of performing an evening concert after this meeting was so well established that several advertisements for the society's anniversary celebrations noted simply "there will be a concert as usual in the evening."[1] As the feast day of its patron saint moved to different days of the week, so did the society's anniversary events (though Sunday feast days were consistently observed on Mondays). The predictability of this pattern was upset, however, by the society's advertisement for its thirty-ninth anniversary. In November 1805 it announced that the anniversary meeting would be held on Friday the twenty-second, as customary, but that "a Concert" would be performed "on Thursday Evening preceding" rather than on the evening of the actual anniversary. This small adjustment might seem like a slight disruption of a long-standing tradition, but it proved a more serious omen. For nearly a decade after this 1805 alteration, the anniversary meetings continued to take place on the moveable feast day of St. Cecilia, but the advertisements for these events demonstrate that the anniversary concert was a separate event. During this time, the regularly scheduled concert on the Thursday preceding or following 22 November was appointed the "Anniversary Concert." The last concert designated as such was performed in 1813 on Tuesday, 23 November, after which there is no further mention of an anniversary concert. This separation of the anniversary concert from the anniversary meeting may have been initiated for the convenience of the society's members, whose lives were growing increasingly busy with other commercial and social activities, but it may also have been a sign of something more serious: a decline in the society's general commitment to concert patronage. It is worth noting, however, that the set of rules adopted by the society in 1831 continue to speak of an obligatory concert performed on the anniversary, "unless any intervening circumstances should, in the opinion of the Managers, render it proper or necessary to postpone the same."

The following calendar of concerts draws on five sources: announcements of specific concerts, announcements of schedule changes, postperformance press notices, references in contemporary manuscripts, and concerts implied by the society's fortnightly schedule. This material is divided into fifty-four individual concert seasons, which usually commenced in early autumn and concluded in early spring. Note, however, that the summer performances of 1785, 1794, and 1795 are here divided into artificial seasons commencing in July and ending in June. Each season includes the dates of both known concerts and conjectural performances. Dates given in brackets represent concerts implied by the society's customary fortnightly schedule. The decision to include these conjectural dates is strengthened by the fact that in every case where there is a gap of some weeks or even months between advertised concerts, the interval between the known concerts is evenly divisible into fortnights. The evidence used to reconstruct the performance schedule of each season is provided in an accompanying note. Unless otherwise noted below, the St. Cecilia Society's concerts from 1766 through 1775 were performed on Tuesday evenings. Similarly the society's concerts from 1783 through 1820 were performed on Thursday evenings unless otherwise indicated.

1766–67 Season: Concerts on 14 October; [28 October]; [11 November]; 25 November; [9 December]; 20 January; Thursday, 9 April.[2]

1767–68 Season: Concerts on 20 October; [24 November]; 10 May.[3]

1768–69 Season: No advertised St. Cecilia Society concerts.

1769–70 Season: No advertised St. Cecilia Society concerts.

1770–71 Season: No advertised St. Cecilia Society concerts.

1771–72 Season: No advertised St. Cecilia Society concerts.

1772–73 Season: Concerts on [Monday, 23 November]; 2 March; 16 March, "To be continued every other Tuesday"; [30 March]; [13 April]; [27 April].[4]

1773–74 Season: Concert on Monday, 22 November, and concerts continued fortnightly to an unknown date in the spring of 1774.[5]

1774–75 Season: Concerts on 16 August; [30 August]; [13 September]; [27 September]; [11 October]; [25 October]; [8 November]; [22 November]. Concerts continued fortnightly to an unknown date in the spring of 1775.[6]

1775–76 Season: No advertised St. Cecilia Society concerts.

1776–77 Season: No advertised St. Cecilia Society concerts.

1777–78 Season: No advertised St. Cecilia Society concerts.

1778–79 Season: Anniversary concert on Monday, 23 November 1778.

1779–80 Season: No advertised St. Cecilia Society concerts.

1780–81 Season: No advertised St. Cecilia Society concerts.

1781–82 Season: No advertised St. Cecilia Society concerts.

1782–83 Season: No advertised St. Cecilia Society concerts.

1783–84 Season: Concerts on Saturday, 22 November; 11 December; Tuesday, 9 March 1784; [18 March]; 1 April; 22 April.[7]

1784–85 Season: Concerts on [Monday, 22 November]; 16 December; [27 January]; 10 February; [24 February]; [10 March]; [24 March]; [7 April]; [21 April]; 5 May; [19 May]; [2 June]; [16 June]; 30 June.[8]

1785–86 Season: Concerts on [13 July]; [27 July]; 11 August; [25 August]; [8 September]; [22 September]; [6 October]; [20 October]; [3 November]; [Tuesday, 22 November]; [8 December]; fortnightly concerts continued to an unknown date in the spring of 1786.[9]

1786–87 Season: Concerts on [Wednesday, 22 November]; 7 December; 21 December; fortnightly concerts continued to an unknown date in the spring of 1787.[10]

1787–88 Season: Concerts on 18 October; [1 November]; [15 November]; 22 November; 13 December; 10 January; fortnightly concerts continued to an unknown date in spring of 1788.[11]

1788–89 Season: Regular concerts suspended; concert on Saturday, 22 November.[12]

1789–90 Season: Regular concerts suspended; concert on Monday, 23 November.[13]

1790–91 Season: Concerts on [Monday, 23 November]; [2 December]; [16 December]; [13 January]; [27 January]; [10 February]; [24 February]; [10 March]; [24 March]; [7 April]; [21 April]; 5 May.[14]

1791–92 Season: Concerts on 13 October; [27 October]; [10 November]; Tuesday, 22 November; fortnightly concerts continue "as usual" on 1 December; [15

December]; [12 January]; [26 January]; 9 February; [23 February]; [8 March];
[22 March]; concerts possibly continued through the summer months.[15]

1792–93 Season: Concerts "commence" on 22 November and continue "every second Thursday during the season"; [5 December]; [19 December]; [10 Janu-
ary]; [24 January]; [7 February]; [21 February]; [7 March]; [21 March];
4 April; [18 April]; [2 May]; "last concert" on 16 May.[16]

1793–94 Season: "First concert" on 5 September; fortnightly concerts continue on
19 September, and "will be continued every second Thursday during the season"; [3 October]; [17 October]; [31 October]; 14 November; Friday,
22 November; 28 November; 12 December; concerts "recommence for the
remainder of the season" on 9 January; 23 January; [6 February]; [20 Febru-
ary]; "Grand Concert" for the benefit of French refugees on 6 March;
20 March, "and to continue every other Thursday for one year certain";
[3 April]; [17 April]; [2 May]; [15 May]; [29 May]; [12 June]; [26 June].[17]

1794–95 Season: Concerts on [10 July]; [24 July]; [7 August]; [21 August]; [4 Sep-
tember]; [18 September]; [2 October]; [16 October]; [30 October]; [13 Novem-
ber]; Saturday, 22 November; 27 November; 8 January; 22 January; [5 February];
concert scheduled for 19 February preponed to Tuesday, 17 February; 5 March;
[19 March]; [2 April]; concerts possibly continued through the summer months:
[16 April]; [30 April]; [14 May]; [28 May]; [11 June]; [25 June].[18]

1795–96 Season: Concerts on [9 July]; [23 July]; [6 August]; [20 August];
[3 September]; [17 September]; [1 October]; [15 October]; [29 October];
[12 November]; Monday, 23 November, then suspended; concerts "recommence" on 7 January, "after which the Concerts will be continued every other
Thursday, during the remainder of the Season"; [21 January]; [4 February];
concert scheduled for 18 February postponed to 25 February (probably
because of Race Week); [10 March]; [24 March]; [7 April]; [21 April].[19]

1796–97 Season: Concerts "commence" on 15 September and are "continued every
other Thursday during the Season"; [29 September]; [13 October]; [27 Octo-
ber]; [10 November]; Tuesday, 22 November;"suspended until the second
Thursday in January next"; 12 January 1797, and "continued every other
Thursday during the remainder of the Season"; [26 January]; concert scheduled for 9 February postponed to 16 February for Race Week; [2 March];
16 March; [30 March]; [13 April]; [27 April].[20]

1797–98 Season: Concerts "commence" on 21 September "and will be continued
every other Thursday during the Season"; [5 October]; [19 October];
[2 November]; concert scheduled for 16 November postponed to Wednesday,
22 November; 7 December; 11 January; [25 January]; [8 February]; concert
scheduled for 22 February postponed to 1 March because of Race Week;
[15 March]; [29 March]; [12 April]; 26 April.[21]

1798–99 Season: Concerts "commence" on 4 October; [18 October]; [1 Novem-
ber]; [15 November]; 22 November; and then "suspended until the Second
Thursday in January next"; 10 January; 24 January; [7 February]; 21 February;
14 March; 28 March; 11 April; [26 April].[22]

1799–1800 Season: Concerts "commence" on 31 October; 14 November; [Friday, 22 November]; concerts "recommence" 16 January; 30 January; concert scheduled for 13 February postponed until 20 February because of Race Week; 6 March; 20 March; [3 April]; [17 April]; 1 May; 15 May.[23]

1800–1801 Season: Concerts "commence" on 30 October "and will be continued every Thursday until St. Cecilia's Day"; [6 November]; [13 November]; [20 November]; Saturday, 22 November; concerts; "recommence" on 8 January and are "continued every fortnight during the season"; [22 January]; [5 February]; [19 February]; [5 March]; [19 March]; concert scheduled for 2 April postponed to 9 April because of Passion Week; [23 April].[24]

1801–2 Season: Concerts "commence" on 29 October; 12 November; Tuesday, 24 November; concerts "recommence" on 14 January; "continued every fortnight, thro' the remainder of the season"; 28 January; concert scheduled for 11 February postponed to 18 February because of Race Week; 4 March; 18 March, "which will be the last this season."[25]

1802–3 Season: Concert "commence" on 28 October; [11 November]; Monday, 22 November; 9 December; concerts "recommence" on 13 January and are "continued through the remainder of the Season once a fortnight, except in race week, during which there will not be a Concert"; concert scheduled for 27 January postponed to 3 February "on account of the absence of some of the Performers, with the Theatrical Corps at Savannah," and again to 17 February because of Race Week; 3 March; 17 March; "last Concert, for this season" on Wednesday, 30 March.[26]

1803–4 Season: Concerts "commence" on 27 October; [10 November]; Tuesday, 22 November; concert scheduled for 8 December postponed to 15 December; concerts scheduled to "re-commence" on 12 January, but postponed to 26 January (probably owing to the arrival of refugee musicians) "and thence to be continued during the remainder of the season, once a fortnight"; 9 February; 23 February; 8 March; "Last Concert, during this season" on 22 March.[27]

1804–5 Season: Concerts "commence" on 25 October; 8 November; 22 November; 6 December; concerts "recommence" on 17 January and are "continued once a fortnight through the remainder of the season"; 31 January; 14 February; 28 February; 16 March, "which will be the last this season."[28]

1805–6 Season: Concerts "commence" on 24 October; 7 November; 21 November; 5 December; 16 January; 30 January; 13 February; 27 February; 13 March.[29]

1806–7 Season: Concerts "commence" on 23 October; 6 November; 27 November; 4 December; 15 January; 29 January; 12 February; [5 March]; 19 March, "which will be the last for this season."[30]

1807–8 Season: Concerts scheduled to "commence" on 29 October, but postponed "owing to the indisposition of some of the performers" to 12 November; 26 November; 10 December; 14 January; 28 January; 11 February; 25 February; 10 March; "Last Concert for this season" on 24 March.[31]

1808–9 Season: Concerts "commence" on 27 October; 10 November; 24 November; 8 December; concerts "recommence" on 26 January; 9 February; 23 February; 9 March; Wednesday, 15 March; "last Concert for this season" on 23 March.[32]

1809–10 Season: Commencement of season delayed until 30 November; 7 December; 21 December; 11 January; 25 January; 8 February; 22 February; 8 March; "Last Concert for this season" scheduled for 22 March but postponed to 29 March.[33]

1810–11 Season: Concert scheduled for Wednesday, 21 November postponed to 22 November; 6 December; 10 January; 17 January; 31 January; 14 February; 7 March; 28 March; concert scheduled for 11 April postponed to 18 April.[34]

1811–12 Season: Concerts on 7 November; 21 November; Friday, 6 December; 16 January; 30 January; 13 February; 5 March; 19 March; concert scheduled for 2 April postponed to Tuesday, 7 April, "being the last this season."[35]

1812–13 Season: Concerts on 26 November; 7 January; 21 January; 4 February; Monday, 22 February; 11 March; 25 March, "being the last this season."[36]

1813–14 Season: Concerts on 4 November; Tuesday, 23 November; 10 December; 20 January; "last Concert this Season" on Tuesday, 22 February.[37]

1814–15 Season: Concert on 9 March 1815.[38]

1815–16 Season: Concerts on 16 November; 7 December; 18 January; 8 February.[39]

1816–17 Season: Concerts on 14 November; 28 November; 12 December; 16 January; 30 January; 13 February; 6 March; 20 March.[40]

1817–18 Season: Concert on 29 January; ball on 12 February; ball on 26 February; concert on 12 March; concert on 26 March.[41]

1818–19 Season: Ball on 12 November; concert on 26 November; ball on 14 January; ball on 28 January; concert on 25 February; concert on 1 May.[42]

1819–20 Season: Concert and ball on 16 December; concert and ball on 20 January; ball scheduled for Wednesday, 16 February, postponed to 17 February; ball on 24 February; ball Friday, 10 March.[43]

Appendix 2

Rules of the St. Cecilia Society, 1773

Rules of the St. Coecilia Society Agreed upon and Finally Confirmed, November 22d, 1773 (Charleston, S.C.: Robert Wells, 1774)

I. The Society shall be called the St. CŒCILIA SOCIETY, and consist of One Hundred and twenty Members.

II. There shall be annually four General Meetings of the Society, namely, on St. Coecilia's Day, which shall be the anniversary of the Society, and on the Third Thursdays in February, May, and August; on which General Meetings, the Members of the Society shall dine together.

On the Anniversary, the Society shall break up at Five, and on the other General Meetings at Six o'Clock, in the Afternoon; at which Hours, the Steward shall call for and settle the Bill. Every Member shall be charged Twenty Shillings currency towards defraying the Expence of the Dinner; and in Case of any Deficiency, the same shall be paid by the Members present at the said Meetings.

III. The Society, on their Anniversary, shall elect, by Ballot, a President, Vice-President, Treasurer, and Steward, and Eleven other Members, Residents in Charlestown, who, with the fore-named Officers, shall be constituted Managers for the current Year. And in Case any Member, a Resident in Charlestown, shall, upon his Election, refuse to Serve as Officer or Manager of the Society, such Persons so refusing, if an Officer, shall pay a Fine of Ten Pounds currency; if a Manager, a Fine of Five Pounds currency; and the Society shall proceed to another Election in his or their Room.

IV. On the First Thursday in every Month, there shall be a Meeting of the Managers, at Six o'Clock in the Evening, from the first of October to the first of April; and at Seven o'Clock, from the first of April to the first of October.

In Case of the Death, Resignation, or Removal from Charlestown, of any of the Managers, the remaining Managers are empowered to supply the Vacancy.

But in the Case of the Death, Resignation, or Removal from Charlestown, of any of the Officers, the Managers shall call an Extraordinary Meeting of the Society, giving a Fortnight's Notice thereof in all the Weekly Gazettes: And, on every other Emergency, the same Power is vested in them.

V. The Managers are impowered to fix the Number and Times of the Concerts; the Anniversary only excepted, on the Evening of which, a Concert shall always be performed; also, to regulate every other Matter relating thereto, as well as every other Business of the Society, during the Recess of the Society.

VI. On every Anniversary, each member shall pay, into the Hands of the Treasurer, for the Use of the Society, the Sum of Twenty-five Pounds currency.

Upon Notice from the Treasurer, in Writing, of his Arrears due to the Society, whether those Arrears be for his Annual Subscription, his Dinner Expences, or any other Fines incurred by him in the Society, and Persons neglecting or refusing to discharge the same, at the next General Meeting of the Society, he shall be no longer deemed a Member.

VII. Any Person desirous of becoming a Member of the St. Coecilia Society, shall signify the same by a Letter, directed to the President of the Society; and whenever a Vacancy happens in the Society, the Members present, at their Next General Meeting, have Power to elect, or reject, the Candidate so offering himself; which Election, or Rejection, shall be by Ballot only; and the Assent of Two-thirds of the Members present shall be necessary for the Admission of such Candidate. And every person, on his Election, shall subscribe to the Rules of the Society, and pay to the Treasurer, for the use of the Society, Thirty-five Pounds currency.

VIII. Every member is allowed to introduce to the Concert as many Ladies has he thinks proper, who are to be admitted by Tickets, signed by a Member, and expressing the Name of the Lady to whom each Ticket is presented.

No other Person is to be admitted, except Strangers, and then only by Tickets, from a Manager, signed and directed as before specified.

No Boys are to be, on any Account, admitted.

IX. The Treasurer shall immediately, upon his Election into Office, take Charge of all the Ready Monies, Bonds, Securities, and other Effects, belonging to the Society; and give Bond to the President and Vice-President to be accountable to them, or to the Order of the President and Managers, for the same, Fire and other inevitable Accidents excepted.

He is not, on any Account, to pay, or lend at Interest, any of the Society's Monies, but by Order of the Society, or the Order of the President, together with the Approbation of the Managers.

X. At all Meetings of the Society, not less than Twenty-one Members, and at all Meetings of the Managers, not less than Five Members, shall be a Quorum to transact Business.

All Matters, canvassed at any of those Meetings, shall be determined by a Majority of Votes, the Election of Members only excepted, which, according to Rule VII. is to be determined by, at least, Two-thirds of the Society present at their General Meetings.

The President, or in his Absence, the Vice-President, or, in case of the Absence of both of them, a Person chose as Chairman by the Members present, shall keep due Order and Decorum in the Society.

Every Member, speaking of Business, shall address himself immediately to the Chair.

XI. At every General Meeting, the Society shall proceed to Business at Eleven o'Clock in the Forenoon; and in Case the President, Vice-President, or Treasurer, do not attend at the said Hour, they shall each pay a Fine, to the Society, of Thirty-two Shillings and Six-pence currency; and every other Member, residing in Charlestown, who does not attend at the said Hour, shall pay a Fine of Ten Shillings currency; unless the Society, to whose Judgment all Fines are to be referred, shall, at their next General Meeting, see sufficient Cause to remit the same.

XII. None of the foregoing Rules shall be altered, or any new ones enacted, until they have been proposed and agreed upon at Two General Meetings of the Society.

Appendix 3

Rules of the St. Cecilia Society, 1831

Rules of the St. Cecilia Society Adopted 17th February, 1831 (Charleston, S.C.: A. E. Miller, 1831)

Rule I. *Meetings.*

Section 1st. There shall be annually three general meetings of the Society—namely, on the 22d of November, being St. Cecilia's day, which shall be the anniversary, and on which the members shall dine together—and on the third Thursdays in August and February, at 12 o'clock, M. When St. Cecilia's day shall happen on Sunday, the Society shall meet and dine together on the day following.

Sec. 2d. On the first Monday in every Month there shall be a meeting of the Managers.

Sec. 3d. At all meetings of the Society not less than fifteen members, and at all meetings of the Managers, not less than five, shall form a quorum to transact business; and all matters moved at any of those meetings, shall be decided by a majority of votes—the admission of members excepted.

Provided, nevertheless, that on the abrogation, alteration of, or addition to any of these Rules, there shall not be less than twenty-five members present, two-thirds of whom shall concur in such abrogation, alteration, or addition: and provided also, that any proposition for that purpose shall have been agreed to by a like majority at some one previous general meeting.

Rule II. *Officers and Managers.*

Sec. 1st. The Society shall annually, at the anniversary meeting, elect by ballot, a President, Vice-President, and Treasurer, who shall also act as Secretary, and twelve other members, who, with the fore-mentioned Officers, shall be constituted Managers for the ensuing year, all of whom shall be residents of Charleston.

Sec. 2d. In case of the death, resignation, or removal of residence from Charleston of any of the Managers, the remaining Managers are empowered to supply the vacancy: but in case of the death, resignation, or removal of residence from Charleston of any of the Officers, the Managers shall call an extraordinary meeting of the Society, giving notice thereof in two of the gazettes; and on every other emergency the same power is given to them.

Sec. 3d. The *President,* or in his absence, the Vice-President, or in the absence of both of them, a person chosen as Chairman by the members present, shall preserve order and decorum in the Society; and every member speaking on business shall address himself to the Chair.

Sec.4th. The *Treasurer* shall, immediately upon his election into office, take charge of all the ready moneys, bonds, securities, and other effects belonging to the Society, and give bond to the President and Vice-President, to be accountable to them, or to the order of the President and Managers, for the same. He shall not pay, or lend at interest, any of the Society's money, but by order of the President, together with the approbation of the Managers. He shall, at every general meeting, lay before the Society a list of arrears due from each member; and at each anniversary meeting, a statement of the debts and funds of the Society; also, shall give notice, in writing, to the members when their arrears shall amount to one year's contribution, and proceed as mentioned in the Third Rule.

Sec. 5th. It shall be the duty of the Secretary, under the direction of the Managers, to engage and contract for the dinner, and at the dinner to put an end to the expenses of the Society at 9 o'clock; also, to write the minutes of the proceedings of the Society, and of the Managers at monthly and extra meetings, and to notify the Society of all meetings to be held.

Sec. 6th. The Managers are empowered to fix the number and the times of the Concerts, (there being always one on the anniversary, unless any intervening circumstances should, in the opinion of the Managers, render it proper or necessary to postpone the same); also to prescribe and enforce rules for the Concerts, and for the preserving order and decorum in the room: and to contract for, and regulate every other matter relating thereto, as well as every other business of the Society, during the recess of the Society.

Rule III. *Funds.*

Sec. 1st. At every general meeting, each member shall pay the Treasurer seven dollars for the use of the Society.

Sec. 2d. Any member, upon notice from the Treasurer, in writing, that his arrears amount to one year's contribution, refusing or neglecting to discharge the same before, or at the next general meeting of the Society, shall be forthwith sued; and it shall be the duty of the Treasurer, upon penalty of incurring the arrearages himself, to place the account of such defaulters in the hands of the Solicitor for suit.

Sec. 3d. In case any member shall depart from the State, his contribution shall cease from one twelve-month after his departure, and recommence on his return.

Sec. 4th. It shall be the duty of the presiding officer, at every anniversary meeting, immediately after the reading of the minutes, to call over the names of such members as may be indebted for two year's contribution, and if no person present shall discharge such arrears, or become answerable therefore, it shall be at the discretion of the Society to read out or continue such member.

Rule IV. *Admission of Members.*

Sec. 1st. Any person desirous of becoming a member of this Society, shall signify the same by letter, addressed to the President, at a general meeting; when he shall be balloted for, and on obtaining the votes of two-thirds of the members present, shall be admitted a member. Upon such admission, he shall pay to the Treasurer seven dollars in advance, and subscribe to the Rules, whereon he may receive a ticket for admission to the Concerts, signed by the President, and countersigned by the Treasurer. Each member, on his admission, shall be liable to one year's contribution.

Rule V. *Rights of Members.*

Sec. 1st. No member shall have the right of admission to a Concert or Ball without a ticket for the season, to be signed by the President, and countersigned by the Treasurer; who shall not grant such ticket to any member whatever, unless the arrears due by him to the Society, at the time of his application for a ticket, be fully discharged. And in case the Treasurer shall infringe this Rule, he shall be subject to a fine of five dollars.

Sec. 2d. Any member, on paying his arrears and giving notice, in writing, to the President, may resign from this Society; but, until he has complied with these requisitions, he shall be considered a member, and charged accordingly with his contributions.

Rule VI. *Strangers.*

Sec. 1st. Gentlemen strangers are admissible to the Concerts during the first season, next after their arrival in Charleston, on the application of a member, by tickets expressing their name, dated and signed by one of the acting Managers; said member paying for each ticket, two dollars.

Sec. 2d. The Manager who signs a ticket of admission to a Concert for a stranger, shall require the member who applies therefore to endorse his name thereon, in ink, and if the stranger is not entitled to an invitation, the member endorsing the ticket, shall pay to the Society the sum of five dollars; and if the Manager shall neglect to require the endorsement aforesaid, he, and not the member applying for the ticket, shall be considered as giving the invitation; and it shall be the Treasurer's duty to charge the member or Manager, as the case may be, with the said sum.

Sec. 3d. The day succeeding each Concert, the door-keeper shall deliver to the Secretary the tickets of admission for strangers which he received the preceding evening, who shall hand them to the Chairman of the Managers at their next meeting, when the names of the persons invited shall be read aloud, and if it shall appear to the Board of Managers that any person not entitled to a ticket has been invited, the Secretary shall, the ensuing day, deliver to the Treasurer a list of the names of those improperly invited, by whom and when invited, that the Treasurer may charge such member or Manager as directed in the 2d Section.

Sec. 4th. Inhabitants of this State are not considered strangers, merely on account of any absence from the State, unless the absence be of at least four years duration, or unless they declare themselves permanently settled in some other State or country, in which case they shall be entitled to the benefit of the foregoing Sections.

All residents beyond eighty miles of Charleston shall be also entitled to the privilege of strangers.

Sec. 5th. Gentlemen of this State, not members, who reside beyond twenty-five miles, and within eighty miles of Charleston, and who do not reside in the city any portion of the year, are only admissible on the application of a Member, by tickets from the Treasurer, for which they shall pay five dollars.

Sec. 6th. Officers of the Army and Navy of the United States shall always be entitled to admission to the Concerts or Balls.

Gentlemen who have been members of the Society for five years, after having resigned, [may] be admitted to the Concerts or Balls on the payment of five dollars.

Sec. 7th. No gentlemen, not a member of the Society, can dine with the Society unless by special invitation of the President and Managers.

Sec. 8th. The Managers shall have the privilege of inviting strangers to each Concert without payment; but this privilege is only to be exercised in cases in which the ordinary rules of the Society afford no remedy.

General Resolutions.

Resolved, That any gentlemen smoking tobacco in any of the rooms occupied by the Society during the nights of the Concerts or Balls, before the ladies have retired, shall be fined in the sum of five dollars; and it shall be the duty of the acting Managers for the night, to report those who violate this Resolution to the Treasurer, who shall charge that sum to their accounts.

Resolved, That when the Secretary advertises a Concert or Ball, he shall name in the advertisement, the Manager appointed to sign the tickets of invitation, who shall be one of the acting Managers for such Concert or Ball, which tickets shall be given to each member who makes an application therefor.

Resolved, That upon the return by the Sheriff of a "Nulla Bona" to an Execution issued at the suit of the Society, the Treasurer's duty shall be, to report the same to the Board of Managers at their next meeting, when the Board may order a "Ca. Sa." or otherwise act as the circumstances of the case may require.

Appendix 4

Known Members of the St. Cecilia Society, 1766–1820

THE FOLLOWING LIST includes the names of more than two hundred men known to have been members of the St. Cecilia Society between 1766 and 1820. These names represent only a fraction of the society's total membership during these years, of course, but the loss of the society's own membership records in 1865 precludes the creation of a more complete roster. The names presented here are drawn from a variety of primary source materials. The majority appear in items published by the society in the local newspaper during the years of its musical activities, such as annual election returns (which appeared on thirty-one occasions between 1767 and 1825), notices for meetings and concerts, and notices for topics such as arrears and changes to the society's rules.[1] Records of the society's forty lawsuits against members in arrears provide nearly three dozen further names.[2] Finally some extant personal papers of men active in Charleston during the society's concert era include records of subscription payments. Because of the complexities of the evidence used to generate this roster, I have opted to present here only an alphabetical listing of names and dates (when known) without a tedious recitation of the full supporting documentation.[3]

From its early years the membership of the St. Cecilia Society was limited to one hundred and twenty men. In a city the size of Charleston with a relatively small eligible population, the society may have determined that this number represented the point of balance between maintaining its social exclusivity and its fiscal health. Compared to subscription concert series in contemporary Britain, however, this number was rather low, less than half the subscription list of some London series.[4] The general character of the society's known members—their professions, educations, and affiliations—is comparable to that of similar organizations abroad.

The success of any eighteenth-century subscription concert organization, whether in Charleston or abroad, depended to a great degree on the existence of a network of relationships—both professional and social—among its members.[5] What is known of the early membership of Charleston's St. Cecilia Society clearly demonstrates that such a network existed. Through its members the society had ties to nearly every aspect of the region's social, civic, commercial, and artistic life. Extant evidence supports Charles Fraser's recollection that, during the concert era of the St.

Cecilia Society, its rolls included "the names of our most respectable citizens; and amongst its officers were always found some of the first men even of the State."[6]

The thirty-seven "original members," as listed in the notes of Wilmot Gibbes deSaussure and denoted with asterisks in the list below, were almost evenly divided between native-born Americans and British immigrants, with natives of Scotland composing about one-third of the first known members.[7] Roughly half these men had been educated at schools in England or Scotland, or both. If we expand the time frame of this pool of members to those who joined before 1780, the percentage of Scottish-descended members, as well as those educated abroad, increases dramatically. As far as can be determined, the median age of the thirty-seven founding members was in the early thirties. Some, such as Benjamin Huger and Charles Cotesworth Pinckney, had barely entered their twenties at the time of the society's founding in 1766. The majority of the early members were recently established professionals in the prime of their lives. In the context of this youthful assembly, therefore, it is perhaps no coincidence that John Moultrie, by far the eldest of the early members at sixty-four, was chosen as the society's first president.

A good number of the early members of the St. Cecilia Society were planters, an occupation considered the pinnacle of early South Carolina lowcountry society. Possessing large tracts of land and a labor force to work them, the most prosperous planters were able to eschew other business in favor of a more passive, leisurely existence. Many lowcountry lawyers, physicians, and merchants also acquired plantations and engaged in agricultural activities, but the title *planter* was usually reserved for those who had accumulated enough land and slaves to enable them to retire from other professional pursuits.

Many of the men included in this list were lawyers. During the period under study a number of young Charleston men were sent to London to study law, and some went to colleges in the northern states for their education. In the decades after the Revolution, however, it became more common for young legal scholars to serve a clerkship in the office of a local lawyer for several years before sitting for the bar examination.[8] In this fashion it appears that membership in the St. Cecilia Society was for many lawyers a kind of professional perquisite that signaled their entrance into Charleston's social and professional elite.

Physicians likewise formed a large portion of the early membership of the St. Cecilia Society, though at that time a specialized college education was more requisite in this profession than in the practice of the law. Most of the founding members of the Medical Society of South Carolina (now the South Carolina Medical Association), organized in Charleston in December 1789, were counted among the musical votaries on the St. Cecilia roll.[9]

The names accumulated from various extant sources indicate that many of the early members of the St. Cecilia Society were merchants. In the commercial environment of early Charleston, this title does not apply to modest shopkeepers; rather it represents those men involved in the larger business of shipping local agricultural products outward and/or receiving imported goods from abroad.[10] The port of Charleston was very active during the period in question, and vast amounts of money were made from the consignment of large shipments of raw materials and finished goods. By the turn of the nineteenth century, however, the number of merchants included among the society's membership was in decline. In his 1838 glance back toward Charleston of the late 1790s, Ebenezer Smith Thomas recalled "The door of the 'St. Cecilia Society' was shut to the plebeian and the man of business, with the two exceptions of Adam Tunno, king of the Scotch, and William Crafts, vice-king of the Yankees, under their legitimate head, Nathaniel Russel [Russell, of Rhode Island], than whom there was no better man."[11] Thomas was not privy to the society's roster, of course, and underestimated the number of businessmen among its ranks. As an adjunct to this professional class, a few of the names included among the society's early membership are identified in the newspapers and city directories of the period as *factors*, who functioned as middlemen between planters and exporters.

Beyond their professions, the members of the St. Cecilia Society also held other titles. The clergy, vestries, and wardens of the local Anglican (later Episcopal) churches were active in this musical society, and a few representatives from Charleston's Scots (First Presbyterian) Church and Congregational assembly were also included. St. Cecilia men were numbered among the officers of numerous other Charleston social organizations, such as the St. Andrew's Society, the Freemasons, the Library Society, and the Jockey Club. They formed the officers of the local military establishment, both in the nascent U.S. forces and in the state militia. Many of the managers of the St. Cecilia Society also served as trustees of the College of Charleston, chartered in 1785, the Charleston Orphan House, organized in 1790, and other municipal institutions.

Men from each of these professions were counted among those elected to hold political office in South Carolina between 1766 and 1820. The society's concerts at the South Carolina State House in 1784 and at Charleston's City Hall in the early 1790s underscore the degree of overlap between the society and the state and local government. Since only a fraction of its total membership has been identified, it is difficult to draw conclusions about the political ideologies that dominated the St. Cecilia Society during this era. Based on what is known of those positively identified as members, however, it appears that the conservative thought one would expect from men of financial means prevailed. During the Revolutionary War a majority of the society's members were active participants in the struggle for American freedom, but a number remained loyal to British authority. In the decades after the Revolution many of the St. Cecilia men were advocates of the Federalist Party, at both the local and national levels. An apparently smaller percentage of the membership sided with the rival Republican Party, however, no doubt causing some friction at the society's otherwise placid events.

The nexus of relationships that bound the members of the St. Cecilia Society together was further strengthened by intermarriage, for, as one historian of this era has adroitly described it, South Carolina's social and economic elite constituted "a vast cousinage."[12] The society's practice of allowing its members to introduce ladies at its concerts afforded ample opportunity for exclusive social intercourse and thus facilitated the formation of family alliances. While the present list of members during the society's first half century of activity represents only a fraction of its total membership during that era, the fact that many of the men included here were related by blood or by marriage suggests that much of the unknown portion of this membership might be deduced by following the branches of their family trees.

Bacot, Henry Harramond
   (1780–1834)
Bacot, Peter (1788–1836)
Bacot, Thomas Wright (1765–1834)
Bampfield, William (1731–1773)
Baron, Alexander, Jr. (1777–1842)
Bayly (Bailey), Benjamin (fl. 1791)
Bee, John Simmons (b. 1782)
*Bee, Thomas (1739–1812)
Bee, Thomas, Jr.
Bentham, Robert (1790–1843)
Beresford, Richard (1755–1803)
Bonneau, John Ewing (1786–1849)
Bonneau, Symes (Symmes)
   (1795–1852)
Bradley, Moses (1770–1812)
Brailsford, Edward
Brailsford, William (1753–1810)
Broun (Brown), Archibald
   (1752–1797)
*Bruce, Donald (d. 1792)
Bruckner, Daniel (ca. 1766–1832)
Buist, George (1770–1808)
Bullman, John (Reverend) (fl.
   1773–1775)
Butler, Pierce (1744–1822)
Calhoun, William (d. 1808)
Campbell, David (ca. 1760–1822)
*Carson, James
*Carson, William
Cave, Thomas (died ca. 1813)
Champneys, John (ca. 1743–1820)
Cheves, Langdon (1776–1857)
Cochran, Charles Burnham
   (1766–1833)
Cochran, Thomas (1780–1830)
Cogdell, John Stevens (1778–1847)

Cosslett, Charles Mathews (ca.
   1741–1776)
*Crabb, William
Crafts, William (1763–1820)
Crafts, William, Jr. (1787–1826)
*Crallan, James (d. 1768)
Cripps, John (1786–1817)
Cripps, John Splatt (1754–1811)
Cross, George Warren (1783–1836)
*Crosthwaite, William Ward
   (1743–1769)
Crouch, Abraham (ca. 1767–1826)
Darrell, Edward, [Jr.] (ca. 1770–1801)
Davis, John Norvelle (d. 1851)
Deas, David (1722–1775)
Deas, Henry (1770–1846)
*Deas, John (1735–1790)
Deas, Robert (1774–1839)
Deas, William Allen (1764–1820)
deSaussure, Henry Alexander
   (1788–1865)
deSaussure, Henry William
   (1763–1839)
Dickenson, Jeremiah (fl. 1823–1829)
Drayton, Charles (1743–1820)
Drayton, Glen (1752–1796)
Drayton, John (1766–1822)
Drayton, William (1776–1846)
*Drayton, William Henry (1742–1779)
Dulles, Joseph (1751–1818)
Edwards, Alexander (1767–1811)
*Elliott, Barnard (1740–1778)
Elliott, Charles (1788–1817)
Eveleigh, Thomas (1747–1816)
Farr, Joseph (1765–1804)
Fayssoux, Peter (1745–1795)
Ford, Timothy (1762–1830)

*Fraser, Alexander, [Sr.] (1722–1791)
Fraser, Alexander, [Jr.] (1750–1798)
Fraser, Charles (1782–1860)
Frost, Henry Rutledge (1795–1866)
Gadsden, John (1787–1831)
Gaillard, Samuel (1770–1795)
*Garden, Alexander (1728–1791)
Gilchrist, Adam (ca. 1760–1816)
Gilchrist, Robert Budd (1796–1856)
Glaze, John (d. 1818?)
Goodwin, Charles (ca. 1756–1827)
*Gordon, John (d. 1778)
Gordon, Thomas Knox (d. 1796)
Gough, John Parker (1778–1818)
Grimké, John (1785–1864)
Grimké, John Faucheraud
   (1752–1819)
Hall, Daniel (ca. 1750–1811)
*Hall, George Abbott (d. 1791)
Hamilton, James, Sr. (1750–1833)
Hamilton, James, Jr. (1786–1857)
Harper, Robert Goodloe (1765–1825)
Harris, Tucker (1747–1821)
Hasell, Andrew (d. 1821)
Hasell, William S. (ca. 1780–1815)
Haskell, Elnathan (ca. 1755–1825)
Heyward, Nathaniel, Jr. (1790–1819)
Heyward, Thomas, [Jr.] (1746–1809)
Holmes, John Bee (1760–1827)
*Huger, Benjamin (1746–1779)
Huger, Daniel Elliott (1779–1854)
*Huger, Isaac (1743–1797)
Inglis, Alexander, Sr. (d. 1791)
Inglis, Alexander, Jr. (ca. 1767–1814)
Izard, Henry (1771–1826)
Kinloch, Francis (1755–1826)
*L'Abbé, Anthony (Antoine Joseph)
   (ca. 1729–1798)
Ladson, James (1753–1812)
Ladson, William James (1793–1833)
Laurens, Henry, Sr. (1724–1792)
Laurens, Henry, Jr. (1763–1821)
Lee, James (d. 1810?)
*Lightwood, Edward, Jr. (1736–1797)

Logan, George (1778–1861)
Lowndes, James (1769–1839)
Lowndes, Rawlins (ca. 1721–1800)
Lowndes, Thomas (1766–1843)
Lowndes, William (1782–1822)
Macintosh (McIntosh), Simon (d.
   1806)
Manigault, Gabriel (1758–1809)
Manigault, Joseph (1763–1843)
Marshall, William (ca. 1770–1805)
*Mathews (Mathewes), John
   (1744–1802)
Mazyck, Philip Porcher (1792–1860)
McCall (M'Call), Hext (1784–1821)
McIntosh, Lachlan (ca. 1716–1789)
*Middleton, Arthur (1742–1787)
Middleton, Arthur (1785–1837)
Miller, George (ca. 1761–1805)
Miller, James (ca. 1748–1821)
Miller, William H. (d. 1830)
Mitchell, John (ca. 1741–1816)
Mitchell, John (ca. 1767–1808)
Montagu, Charles Greville
   (1741–1784)
*Motte, Isaac (1738–1795)
Moultrie, James (1766–1836)
*Moultrie, John (1702–1771)
*Moultrie, Thomas (1740–1780)
Nowell, Edward Broun (ca.
   1768–1801)
Ogier, John Martin (1794–1829)
*Oliphant (Olyphant), David (ca.
   1720–1805)
Owen, John (ca. 1737–1815)
Parker, John, Jr. (1759–1832)
Parker, Thomas, Jr. (1793–1844)
Parker, William Henry (1795–1828)
Peace, Joseph (1771–1826)
Penman, Edward (d. 1817)
*Peronneau, Henry (d. 1786)
Peronneau, Henry (ca. 1763–1823)
Philp, Robert (d. 1784)
*Pike, Thomas (ca. 1735–after 1787)
*Pillans, William (ca. 1744–1767)

Pinckney, Charles (1757–1824)
*Pinckney, Charles Cotesworth
  (1746–1825)
Pinckney, Thomas (1750–1828)
Pinckney, Thomas, Jr. (1780–1842)
Price, Thomas W. (d. 1827)
Pringle, Robert, [Jr.] (1755–1811)
Pringle, Robert (1793–1860)
Prioleau, Philip Gendron
  (1776–1844)
Prioleau, Samuel [III] (1784–1840)
Prioleau, Thomas Grimball
  (1786–1876)
Purcell, Henry (1742–1802)
Purcell, Robert (fl. 1773–1775)
Quash, Francis Dallas (1793–1857)
Ramsay, John (ca. 1768–1828)
Ravenel, John (1793–1862)
Read, Jacob (1752–1816)
Read, John Harleston (1788–1859)
Reid, George (ca. 1757–1810)
*Roberts, Owen (d. 1779)
Robertson, William (ca 1763–1832)
*Rose, Alexander (ca. 1730–1801)
Rose, Arthur Gordon (1798–1880)
Rose, Hugh (1756–1841)
Rose, James (1793–1869)
*Roupell, George (1727–1794)
Russell, Nathaniel (1738–1820)
Rutledge, Charles (1773–1821)
Rutledge, Edward (1749–1800)
Rutledge, Frederick (1769–1824)
Rutledge, Hugh (1745–1811)
Rutledge, John (1739–1800)
Rutledge, John, Jr. (1766–1819)
Rutledge, John, Jr. [III] (b. 1792)
*Shirley, Thomas (fl. 1762–1775)
Shubrick, Thomas, Jr. (1756–1810)
Simons, James (1761–1815)

Skirving, William, Jr. (ca. 1773–1805)
Smith, Benjamin Burgh (1776–1823)
Smith, John Rutledge (ca. 1774–1813)
Smith, O'Brien (1756–1811)
Smith, Robert (1732–1801)
Smith, Robert, Jr. (1786–1847)
*Smith, Roger (1745–1805)
Smith, Roger Moore (1770–1808)
*Smith, Thomas Loughton
  (1740–1773)
Smith, Thomas Rhett (1768–1829)
Smith, William Loughton
  (1758–1812)
Smith, William Mason (1788–1838)
Stevens, Jervis Henry (1750–1828)
Stewart, Thomas (d. 1806)
Teasdale, John, Jr. (ca. 1781–1826)
Theus, James (d. 1806)
Toomer, Joshua Washington
  (1789–1840)
Tunno, Adam (1753–1832)
Tunno, Thomas (ca. 1760–1818)
*Valton, Peter (ca. 1740–1784)
Vanderhorst, Arnoldus (1748–1815)
Waring, Daniel Jennings (1795–1832)
Waring, Thomas (b. 1799?)
Washington, William, Jr. (1785–1830)
Webb, Daniel Cannon (1782–1850)
White, James (fl. 1800)
Wilson, Samuel (1763–1827)
Winthrop, Augustus (1797–1844)
Winthrop, Frederick (1794–1851)
Winthrop, Joseph Augustus
  (1791–1864)
Wragg, William (ca. 1770–1803)
Wright, James Alexander (ca.
  1770–1800)
*Yarnold, Benjamin (ca. 1728–1787)

Notes

Abbreviations

CEG	*Charleston Evening Gazette*
CGDA	*City Gazette and Daily Advertiser* (Charleston)
CH	*Columbian Herald* (Charleston)
CMPDA	*Charleston Morning Post and Daily Advertiser*
GSSC	*Gazette of the State of South-Carolina*
RG	*Royal Gazette* (South Carolina)
RMC	Charleston County Register of Mesne Conveyance
RSCG	*Royal South-Carolina Gazette*
SCAGG	*South-Carolina and American General Gazette*
SCDAH	South Carolina Department of Archives and History, Columbia
SCG	*South-Carolina Gazette*
SCGCJ	*South-Carolina Gazette and Country Journal*
SCGGA	*South-Carolina Gazette and General Advertiser*
SCGPA	*South-Carolina Gazette and Public Advertiser*
SCHS	South Carolina Historical Society, Charleston
SCSG	*South-Carolina State-Gazette*
SCSGDA	*South Carolina State Gazette and Daily Advertiser*
SCSGGA	*South-Carolina State Gazette and General Advertiser*
SCWA	*South-Carolina Weekly Advertiser*
SCWG	*South-Carolina Weekly Gazette*
SGSC	*State Gazette of South-Carolina*
SPCA	*Southern Patriot and Commercial Advertiser*

Preface

1. Sonneck, *Early Concert-Life*, 8–41, was the first historian of American music to take notice of Charleston's early musical life and the St. Cecilia Society. Subsequent musicologists have almost uniformly repeated his findings for a century without additions or corrections.

2. Ibid., 8.

3. Eighteenth-century subscription concerts in New York, Philadelphia, and Boston are mentioned, but not explored, in Sonneck, *Early Concert-Life*; Gerson, *Music in Philadelphia*; Howard, *Our American Music*; Odell, *Annals of the New York Stage*; and Johnson, *Musical Interludes in Boston*.

4. Broyles, *"Music of the Highest Class,"* 91, proposes that the cultural and intellectual framework for the acceptance of orchestral music in mid-nineteenth-century Boston became the model for national acceptance by the end of the century. Without dismissing the entire breadth of that claim, I would argue that the experience of the "rise and fall" of the St. Cecilia Society retarded the acceptance of that model in Charleston.

5. This estimate of nearly four hundred concerts is based on a conservatively estimated average of eight or nine concerts per season over a period of forty-three active seasons. See appendix 1.

6. I would like to thank Prof. Thomas J. Mathiesen at Indiana University for his valuable insights on Latin spelling.

7. Following McCusker's directions, I have used the 2005 average consumer price index, as reported by the U.S. Department of Labor Bureau of Labor Statistics, to calculate dollar equivalents for 2005.

8. Edwards, *Ordinances of the City of Charleston,* 137–38.

Chapter 1

1. Rogers, *Charleston,* 3.

2. Edgar, *South Carolina,* 21–34.

3. Ibid., 35–46; Cheves, *Shaftesbury Papers,* 93–117.

4. Cheves, *Shaftesbury Papers,* 93–94.

5. Greene, "Colonial South Carolina," 193–95.

6. Edgar, *South Carolina,* 48–49.

7. Salley, *The Boundary Line between North Carolina and South Carolina,* 3.

8. Greene, "Colonial South Carolina," 193, 198.

9. Bowes, *The Culture of Early Charleston,* 93.

10. Sirmans, *Colonial South Carolina,* 231. Note that German-speaking Moravians settled in North Carolina, not in South Carolina.

11. Edgar, *South Carolina,* 50.

12. The name *deSaussure* frequently appears in printed sources as *Desaussure* or *DeSaussure.* Following the practice of the family in Charleston, however, my text adheres to the first spelling except in direct quotations taken from historic sources. I have added diacritical marks to the names *Hörrÿ, Hüger,* and *Mazÿck* to draw attention to their proper pronunciation.

13. Hagy, *This Happy Land,* 9–16.

14. The French name for this colony was Saint Domingue, but in this study I have elected to retain *St. Domingo,* the spelling used consistently in Charleston during the eighteenth and nineteenth centuries.

15. Hewatt, *Historical Account,* 2:127–28.

16. *SCG,* 2–9 March 1738.

17. Edgar, *South Carolina,* 67.

18. Wood, *Black Majority,* 152.

19. Hewatt, *Historical Account,* 2:291; Milligen-Johnston, *Short Description,* 109.

20. Edgar, *South Carolina,* 153.

21. Hewatt, *Historical Account,* 2:294.

22. Smyth, *A Tour in the United States,* 2:84.

23. Hewatt, *Historical Account,* 2:301.

24. The accumulation and conspicuous display of the material accoutrements of wealth in eighteenth-century Charleston is well documented by McInnis and Mack, *In Pursuit of Refinement*.

25. Fraser, *Reminiscences*, 57.

26. Kenney, "Alexander Garden and George Whitefield," 3.

27. St. John de Crèvecœur, *Letters from an American Farmer*, 158–59.

28. Barnwell, "Diary of Timothy Ford," 143.

29. Thomas, *Reminiscences*, 1:30–31.

30. Salley, "Diary of William Dillwyn," 6.

31. [Gordon], "Journal of an Officer," 397–98.

32. Ramsay, *The History of the Revolution of South Carolina*, 1:7.

33. Hewatt, *Historical Account*, 2:293–94.

34. Milligen-Johnston, *Short Description*, 149.

35. Drayton, *View of South Carolina*, 217.

36. Milligen-Johnston, *Short Description*, 134.

37. Hewatt, *Historical Account*, 2:297.

38. *SCG*, 1 March 1773.

39. Schoepf, *Travels in the Confederation*, 2:167–68.

40. Watson, *Men and Times of the Revolution*, 56.

41. Hume, *An Exhortation*, 33.

42. Hart, *Dancing Exploded*, 8.

43. Quincy, "Journal of Josiah Quincy, Junior, 1773," 455.

44. Merrens, "A View of Coastal South Carolina in 1778," 184.

45. *SCG*, 1 March 1773.

46. Schoff, *Life in the South 1778–1779*, 25.

47. Schoepf, *Travels in the Confederation*, 2:216.

48. Hewatt, *Historical Account*, 2:296.

49. Burke, *An Account of the European Settlements in America*, 2:258.

50. Lipscomb, *Battles, Skirmishes, and Actions*, 1–2.

51. Barnwell, "Diary of Timothy Ford," 202.

52. Ramsay, *History of South-Carolina*, 2:235–38.

53. Lockhart, "'Under the Wings of Columbia,'" 176–97; Severens, *Charleston*, 17.

54. Ramsay, *History of South-Carolina*, 2:105.

55. Drayton, *View of South Carolina*, 168; Ramsay, *History of South-Carolina*, 2:240.

56. Thomas, *Reminiscences*, 2:35–36.

57. Margaret W. Bowen in Charleston to Susan Bowen in Boston, 2 September 1806, Bowen-Cooke Papers, 11/78/10, SCHS.

58. Joseph Manigault to Gabriel Manigault, 28 July 1807, Gabriel Manigault Letters, 1805–8, 43/684, SCHS.

59. Ramsay, *History of South-Carolina*, 2:135–36.

60. Taussig, *The Tariff History of the United States*, 8–36.

61. Severens, *Charleston*, 27.

62. *CGDA*, 25 October 1815.

63. Cardozo, *Reminiscences*, 12–13.

64. Coker, *Charleston's Maritime Heritage*, 171–77.

65. Moffatt and Carrière, "A Frenchman Visits Charleston, 1817," 142. The editors identify the author as Baron Barthélemi Sernin Du Moulin de la Barthelle de Montlezun.

66. Rezneck, "Depression of 1819–1822," 29, 46.

67. Taussig, *The Tariff History of the United States,* 19–20.

68. Rezneck, "Depression of 1819–1822," 37.

69. *SPCA,* 4 December 1818.

70. *Courier,* 6 October 1819.

71. Charleston, S.C., City Council, *Census of the City of Charleston,* 10.

72. These quotations are from letters titled "The Hermit No. I" and "The Hermit No. II" in *SPCA,* 13 October 1821 and 16 October 1821.

73. Timothy Green to John Wroughton Mitchell, 4 December 1832. Mitchell Papers M-4282, Southern Historical Collection, University of North Carolina at Chapel Hill.

74. Rogers, *Charleston,* 3.

Chapter 2

1. McVeigh, *Concert Life,* xiv; Weber, "London," 294; Hawkins, *General History,* 4:382.

2. McVeigh, *Concert Life,* xiv.

3. McLamore, "Symphonic Conventions," 142; Sadie, "Concert Life in Eighteenth Century England," 17–30; Weber, "London," 301; McVeigh, *Concert Life,* 32; For an example of an Irish subscription concert series, see Boydell, *Rotunda Music.*

4. Excellent discussions of tavern life in eighteenth-century Britain may be found in Lillywhite, *London Coffee Houses,* 17–27; Barker-Benfield, *The Culture of Sensibility,* 50–52; and Clark, *British Clubs and Societies,* 6.

5. Weisberger, *Speculative Freemasonry;* Clark, *British Clubs and Societies,* 203, 229.

6. Rubin, *The English Glee,* 87–109.

7. Clark, *British Clubs and Societies,* 79–80.

8. Hawkins, *General History,* 5:128.

9. Weisberger, *Speculative Freemasonry,* 58.

10. Hawkins, *General History,* 5:123; McVeigh, *Concert Life,* 3; Weber, *The Rise of Musical Classics,* 56–73; Elkin, *The Old Concert Rooms of London,* 37; Timbs, *Club Life of London,* 2:179; Weisberger, *Speculative Freemasonry,* 38.

11. Weber, "London," 319.

12. Burchell, *Polite or Commercial Concerts,* 296.

13. McVeigh, *Concert Life,* 6.

14. Kierner, "Hospitality," 449–80; Rozbicki, *The Complete Colonial Gentleman,* 161–70.

15. McVeigh, *Concert Life,* 12.

16. Ibid., 4.

17. Kierner, "Hospitality," 459–60; Barker-Benfield, *The Culture of Sensibility,* 205–14, 249.

18. Burney, *Evelina,* letter 23. The concert in question took place at London's Pantheon. McVeigh, *Concert Life,* 60, describes the concert hall in Burney's time as "a principal venue for conversation and assignations."

19. Weber, "Did People Listen in the 18th Century?" 678–91; Weber, "Mass Culture," 5–21.

20. McVeigh, *Concert Life*, 54.

21. Ibid., 32, 93. I would like to thank Professor McVeigh for sharing with me further information regarding the St. Cæcilian Society from his "Calendar of London Concerts 1750–1800, Goldsmiths College, University of London."

22. Johnson, *Music and Society*, 37; Burchell, *Polite or Commercial*, 32–33.

23. Krauss, "Alexander Reinagle," 425–56.

24. Fraser Harris, *Saint Cecilia's Hall*; Johnson, *Music and Society*, 40–41; Burchell, *Polite or Commercial*, 35, 54–55.

25. Easterby, *History of the St. Andrew's Society*; Rogers, *Charleston*, 5–6; Calhoun, Zierden, and Paysinger, "The Geographic Spread of Charleston's Mercantile Community," 182–220.

26. Hyde, *History of Union Kilwinning Lodge*, 10–12, 56; Mackey, *The History of Freemasonry in South Carolina*, 537.

27. Easterby, *History of the St. Andrew's Society*, 45.

28. Fraser Harris, *St. Cecilia's Hall*, 290–99. Although not a member of the St. Cecilia Society until after the American Revolution, Charleston-born Francis Kinloch spent much of 1777–78 at the estate of his cousin, Sir David Kinloch of Gilmerton, fifth Baronet, who is included in Fraser Harris's membership list. According to Burchell, *Polite or Commercial*, 34, the second "governor" or president of the Edinburgh Musical Society (1731–35) was Thomas Pringle, who may have been a relative of Robert Pringle of Charleston. Edgar, "Robert Pringle's World," 9, states that Robert Pringle (1702–1776), a native of the County of Edinburgh, was made an honorary burgess and guild member of Edinburgh in September 1748. David Oliphant, a founding member of the St. Cecilia Society, was not only a Scottish-born physician but also the nephew to one Lord Olyphant of Scotland. See Bennet, "A Fleeting Show," 51–52.

29. Edgar, "The Libraries of Colonial South Carolina," 113–14.

30. In 1965–66 Alston Deas of Charleston communicated with the Scottish National Portrait Gallery about a possible family link between his eighteenth-century Scottish ancestors in the St. Cecilia Society and the Edinburgh Musical Society. The reply to Deas's query offered no insight beyond the agreement that there was a possible connection. See Basil C. Skinner, Edinburgh, Scotland, to Alston Deas, Charleston, S.C., 12 January 1966, St. Cecilia Society Collection, SCHS, 11/554/15.

31. Dawe, *Organists of the City of London 1666–1850*, 61, 159.

32. Daub, "Music at the Court of George II," 131–60, 356. Valton was a "Chapel Royal Child" until the spring of 1760. His age and the date of his admittance to the chapel are not recorded.

33. St. Philip's Church, vestry minutes, 29 October 1764. The full text of this quotation appears in Williams, "Eighteenth-Century Organists of St. Michael's," 212–13.

34. Hawkins, *General History*, 4:427; Daub, "Music at the Court of George II," 341, identifies Anthony L'Abbé as dancing master to the princesses, ca. 1714–40; L'Abbé, *A New Collection of Dances*; Sainsbury, "The French Protestants of Abbeville District, S.C.," 98.

35. One of many examples of this phenomenon, the Caecilian Society in London is described by Weber, "London," 321, as having been founded in 1785 for the purpose of singing hymns and anthems, "probably with a largely dissenting clientele."

36. Hawkins, *General History*, 4:502–3. Connolly, *Mourning into Joy*, explores the convoluted origins and early history of this saint but does not delve into her meaning to

musicians during the Renaissance and later periods. Luckett, "St. Cecilia and Music," is still the best treatment of the musical history of St. Cecilia. Both these sources provide convincing evidence to refute the widely accepted notion that St. Cecilia's connection to music is based on a late medieval misinterpretation of an antiphon written in her honor.

37. Husk, *An Account,* 204–5.

38. D'Urfey, *Songs Compleat,* 1:70.

39. Bray, "Dryden and Draghi in Harmony," 331.

40. Husk, *An Account,* 204–5.

41. Kinsley, *The Poems of John Dryden,* 3:1433. Whether or not Handel's music for *Alexander's Feast* was ever performed in Charleston is not known, but an intriguing clue appears in *SCSGDA,* 1 April 1785: "Any person possessing the Score of Alexander's Feast, and will either dispose of it, or accommodate a Gentleman with it for a week, will receive every suitable acknowledgement, by leaving it with Mrs. Timothy, or the Printer of this Gazette."

42. English Poetry Full-Text Database, accessed January 2004.

43. Husk, *An Account,* 168.

44. Thompson, *Poems on Several Occasions,* 16.

45. Ibid., 17–18.

46. English Poetry Full-Text Database, accessed January 2004.

47. Quoted from the printed text accompanying Boyce, *William Boyce: Ode for St. Cecilia's Day,* compact disc. See also Bartlett, "Boyce's Homage to St. Cecilia," 758–61.

48. Hopkins, "The London Odes on St. Cecilia's Day," 491.

49. The first edition of Laurens's *Extracts,* published in Philadelphia in November 1768, concerned only the seizure of his ship *Ann.* The second edition, published in Charleston in late February 1769, concerns six ships seized by the court of Vice-Admiralty. See *The Papers of Henry Laurens,* 6:430–32.

50. Leigh arrived from London in 1753 and accumulated several civic positions of rank in Charleston through the influence of his father, Peter Leigh, chief justice of South Carolina. See Krawczynski, *William Henry Drayton,* 80–83; and Calhoon and Weir, "The Scandalous History of Sir Egerton Leigh," 47–74.

51. *SCGCJ,* 4 April 1769.

52. William Shakespeare, *The Merchant of Venice,* 5.1.83–88.

53. In the years after Laurens's accusations, Sir Egerton Leigh was associated with two high-profile musical events in Charleston. *SCG,* 8 March 1770, reported the recent performance of an ode, set to music by Peter Valton, composed for Leigh's installation as grand master of the Free and Accepted Masons in the Province of South Carolina. The text, "composed by a Brother," is replete with Neoclassical praise for Leigh's worthiness for this position. The text of this ode was republished in Mackey, *The History of Freemasonry in South Carolina,* 44–45.Valton and Leigh collaborated on another Masonic ode, which was performed on 27 December 1772. The full text was printed in *SCG,* 31 December 1772. The republication of its text in Mackey, 46–48, includes several errors, and Mackey mistakenly states that it was performed in 1770.

54. Between 1762 and his death in 1793, Thomas Warren, the Catch Club's secretary, published thirty-three independently paginated collections of the club's vocal music. Publication dates do not appear on these books, but in his introduction to the facsimile edition of Warren's collections, Emanuel Rubin presents a speculative publication

chronology that places Warren's ninth collection, in which Valton's *Divine Cecilia* appears, in the year 1770. See Rubin's introduction to Warren, *A Collection of Catches Canons and Glees.*

55. A list of works composed by Valton appears in Williams, "Eighteenth-Century Organists of St. Michael's," 212–13. Note, however, that the dates of these compositions, as copied by Williams from the catalog of the music collection at the Boston Public Library, are not completely reliable. See also Williams, "Peter Valton's Hymns," 333. Valton, *The Reprisal.*

56. This text is the opening line of William Shakespeare's *Twelfth Night.*

57. Clingham, "Johnson's Criticism of Dryden's Odes in Praise of St. Cecilia," 167, citing Johnson's dedication to Charles Burney's *History of Music* (1776).

Chapter 3

1. Fraser, *Reminiscences,* 59.

2. The first advertisement for a concert, or "consort," in Charleston appeared in *SCG,* 8–15 April 1732: "On Wednesday next [19 April], will be a Consort of Musick at the Council Chamber, for the Benefit of Mr. Salter." The term *benefit* frequently referred to an extra performance outside a regular subscription series. McVeigh, *Concert Life,* 35–36, states that benefit concerts in eighteenth-century London were frequently the "offspring" of a more regular series and were "traditionally regarded as a public reward for long service." Thus it is possible that John Salter was allowed a benefit concert in April 1732 in appreciation of his efforts during the preceding season. In the following year the concert advertisements allude more directly to a series. After a pair of nonbenefit concerts in the autumn of 1732, *SCG,* 20–27 January 1733, included the notice of another performance billed as "the last Consort." After a pair of benefit concerts in the spring of 1733, *SCG,* 30 June 1733, announced another concert and noted, "This is the first time on the SUBSCRIPTION." *SCG* ceased publication for the next five months, so information about the rest of the series is not available. Sonneck, *Early Concert-Life,* 13, argues that these advertisements represent "the first effort [in British America] to establish a series of concerts at more or less regular intervals."

3. *SCG,* 29 October–5 November 1737: "At the New Theatre in Queen-street, on Tuesday the 22nd Instant being St. Cecilia's Day, will be performed a Concert of Vocal and Instrumental Musick, for the Benefit of Mr. Theodore Pachelbel, beginning precisely at 6 o'clock in the Evening. Tickets to be had at the house of the said Mr. Pachelbel, or at Mr. Shepheard's[,] Vintner. N.B. As this is the first time the said Mr. Pachelbel has attempted any thing of this kind in a Public Manner in this Province, he thinks it proper to give Notice that there will be sung a Cantata suitable to the Occasion."

4. Without citing supporting evidence, Ravenel, *Charleston,* 426, asserts that the society actually began after Pachelbel's concert on St. Cecilia's Day, 22 November 1737, but it was not formally organized until 1762. Sonneck, *Early Concert-Life,* 11–16, provides an overview of Charleston's colonial concerts.

5. McVeigh, *Concert Life,* 53.

6. Ramsay, *History of the Revolution of South Carolina,* 1:7.

7. Andrews, *The South-Carolina Almanack . . . 1763* and *The South-Carolina Almanack . . . 1765.*

8. Waring, *The South Carolina and Georgia Almanac . . . 1793,* [28].

9. *Courier,* 21 November 1853 and 21 November 1860.

10. Ibid., 20 November 1866.

11. Ibid., 24 October 1868. This series ran from 28 March 1868 to the end of October. The names of the founding members are given in appendix 4.

12. DeSaussure, "St. Cecilia Society," manuscript notes, ca. 1868. While it may be argued that deSaussure could have copied the text from this newspaper series into his notes, it is my conclusion that deSaussure's manuscript notes served as the basis for the newspaper series. This attribution is supported by the fact that the early "Charleston in Olden Times" columns borrow heavily from Fraser's *Reminiscences,* in which deSaussure bound his notes. In addition, the installment of "Charleston in Olden Times" in *Courier,* 29 August 1868—which discusses the names of old streets, wharves, and public buildings in Charleston—begins with and is dominated by a detailed description of deSaussure's own residence.

13. See Huguenot Society of South Carolina, *In Memoriam Wilmot Gibbes DeSaussure,* 9–13; and "Charleston a Century Ago," in Charleston, S.C., *Year Book 1881,* 378–79. Note also that his grandfather Henry William deSaussure was a president of the St. Cecilia Society.

14. My sincere thanks to Richard Hutson Jr. and the board of the St. Cecilia Society for permitting me to view the society's early minutes on 6 April 2006.

15. Mills, *Statistics of South Carolina,* 436.

16. Pike's concert was first advertised in *SCG,* 7–14 September 1765, for 25 September at the Orange Garden, but was postponed to 16 October and performed at the theater in Queen Street. The advertisement in *SCG,* 14–21 September 1765, notes that this concert will be performed "by the Gentlemen of the place." Valton's benefit concert was advertised in *SCG,* 19–31 October 1765, to take place on 13 November at the theater in Queen Street; the *SCG* was suspended after this issue because of the Stamp Act. L'Abbé's concert was advertised in *SCGCJ,* 21 January 1766, to take place at the theater on 3 February.

17. The program for Pike's concert, in *SCG,* 28 September–5 October 1765, includes no vocal music. The advertisement for Valton's concert states that "besides a Variety of Concertos, Overtures, Solos, &c.—there will be two Songs sung by Miss Wainwright, and two by Miss Hallam, who never appeared in Public. Likewise, a Concerto on the Harpsichord." L'Abbé's concert was advertised in *SCGCJ,* 21 January 1766, to include "a variety of Songs, Solos, Concertos, &c. &c." The songs at this concert were probably also performed by members of Douglass's theatrical company.

18. The concert was first advertised in the *SCGCJ,* 18 March 1766, and performed on 1 April at the theater in Queen Street. Churchwardens William Bampfield and Thomas Savage managed the subscription. See St. Michael's Church, vestry minutes, 4 September 1767. The case of this organ, which arrived in 1768, still stands in St. Michael's Church.

19. *SCGCJ,* 1 April 1766. The music for this work has not been found.

20. The existence of a subscription dancing assembly in colonial Charleston as early as the 1740s is mentioned in several contemporary sources. See, for example, Hume, *An Exhortation,* 33; Milligen-Johnston, *Short Description,* 135; Hewatt, *Historical Account,* 2:297; and Hart, *Dancing Exploded.* Dancing master Andrew Rutledge announced the commencement of "Public Nights at his long room once a fortnight" in *SCG,* 25 December 1762–1 January 1763.

21. At that time the *SCG* had temporarily ceased publication in protest over the Stamp Act; the *SCGCJ,* a new paper established in defiance of the Stamp Act, contains no mention of such an event. There are no extant copies of *SCAGG* between mid-1764 and late May 1766, but whether it was dormant in April 1766 or copies are simply lost is not known.

22. Elliott's marriage was noted in *SCGCJ,* 29 April 1766.

23. Fraser, *Reminiscences,* 59.

24. McVeigh, *Concert Life,* 59–60. Many non-St. Cecilia concert advertisements in Charleston—both before and after the founding of this society—testify to the customary pairing of the concert and ball. For example Edward Wallace's 1760 benefit concert (advertised in the *SCG,* 11–18 October 1760) stated that the performance would "conclude with a ball." The advertisements for Gaetano Franceschini's benefit concert on 12 April 1774, an event sponsored by the St. Cecilia Society, noted "after the Concert proper Music will be provided for Dancing" (see *SCG,* 28 March 1774). The flautist William Brown advertised his 1784 benefit concert (see *SCGPA,* 17–21 April 1784) with the notice "N.B. After the Concert, a ball." J. West's benefit concert in 1795 (see *CGDA,* 15 April 1795) gave notice that "after the concert the music [that is, the band of performers] will attend as usual to accommodate any parties who wish to dance."

25. Cometti, *Seeing America,* 55. This quotation is from the entry for Thursday, 11 December 1783.

26. *SCAGG,* 10–17 April 1771. This recruiting advertisement is discussed in detail in chapter 6.

27. See the discussion of Hartley in chapter 7.

28. *SCG,* 8 March 1773.

29. This number was fewer than some concert series, such as the Edinburgh Musical Society and the Rotunda Concert in Dublin, but not unusually low. Weber, "London," 310, reports that the fashionable Bach-Abel concerts in London presented only fifteen concerts each year.

30. Quincy, *Memoir of the Life of Josiah Quincy,* 5.

31. Quincy, "Journal," 441.

32. Ibid., 441–42.

33. Ibid., 442.

34. Ibid. In contemporary English usage, a *macaroni* was an Englishman affecting Continental (specifically French and Italian) fashions. Quincy is alluding to the styles of their perukes. The "bag" refers to an elongated silk pouch used to hold the hair (or to create the illusion of long hair) at the back of the neck; the "cue" or "queue" macaroni sported a braid of hair at the back of his neck.

35. Ibid.

36. *SCG,* 7 March 1774.

37. Library of Congress, *Journals of the Continental Congress,* 78.

38. Ramsay, *History of the Revolution of South Carolina,* 1:176–77.

39. Webber, "Order Book of John Faucheraud Grimké," 48. This order was copied into Grimké's book on 14 September 1778.

40. *GSSC,* 28 October 1777.

41. *SCAGG,* 6 November 1777.

42. Ibid., 19 February 1778.

43. Ibid., 6 August 1778.

44. This loan and other aspects of the society's finances are discussed in chapter 5.

45. *SCAGG,* 27 August 1778.

46. Ibid., 12 November 1778.

47. Ibid., 19 November 1779.

48. Ibid., 17 December 1779.

49. Ibid., 9 December 1780.

50. *SCWG,* 29 March 1783.

51. The society's incorporation is discussed in greater detail in chapter 5.

52. *CGDA,* 13 October 1788.

53. Ibid., 6 April 1791.

54. Ibid., 14 May 1791.

55. Ibid., 6 May 1791.

56. Jackson and Twohig, *The Diaries of George Washington,* 6:131.

57. *CGDA,* 24 November 1792.

58. Ibid., 16 July 1793.

59. Ibid., 19 August 1793. See chapter 8 for further discussion of this organization.

60. Sonneck, *Early Concert-Life,* 305, states that, for reasons not yet investigated, concert life in these northern cities was "at a very low ebb during the last years of the eighteenth century."

61. St. Michael's Church, vestry minutes, 10 October 1798. The men in attendance were Roger Smith, John Ward, Arnoldus Vanderhorst, Robert Hazlehurst, Daniel Hall, F. Bonneau, and John Huger, vestrymen; William Miller and George Reid, churchwardens.

62. Fraser, *Reminiscences,* 60.

63. Mason, *Extracts from A Diary,* 24.

64. *Times,* 5 September 1808.

65. Margaret Izard Manigault in Charleston to Charles J. Manigault in Philadelphia, Sunday, 15 February 1812, Manigault Family Papers, South Caroliniana Library. The "little doctor" could be Dr. Charles Drayton or, more likely, his physician son, Charles Jr. (1785–1844).

66. *Courier,* 7 October 1814.

67. *CGDA,* 28 February 1815.

68. *Courier,* 2 March 1815. The society may have been planning this concert since before the announcement of peace, as the advertisement (ibid., 13 February 1815) for its usual February general meeting (16 February) requested the punctual attendance of members "as business of importance will be laid before them."

69. Ibid., 30 March 1815; *CGDA,* 30 March 1815.

70. See, for example, two important early-twentieth-century publications on South Carolina history that clearly paraphrase Fraser: Wallace, *The History of South Carolina,* 2:363; and Ravenel, *Charleston,* 427.

71. Fraser, *Reminiscences,* 60.

72. Ibid., 60–61.

73. *Courier,* 6 February 1818.

74. Ibid., 3 May 1819. *Times,* 3 May 1819, reported that about two hundred ladies attended.

75. These performances, for which neither the content nor the performers are known, were held on Tuesday, 26 June 1827, and Wednesday, 9 February 1831, at St. Andrew's Hall in Broad Street (see *Courier*, 26 June 1827 and 9 February 1831). The society held its events at this venue, which was opened in late 1815, from February 1821 until the hall's destruction in the great fire of December 1861.

76. S[arah] Rutledge, to Elizabeth Lowndes, 6 April 1820, Harriott Hörrÿ Ravenel Papers, SCHS, 11/332A/5.

77. *Courier*, 28 February 1825.

Chapter 4

1. St. Cecilia Society, *Rules of the St. Coecilia Society . . . 1773*. References to this publication will hereafter be cited as *Rules 1773*.

2. See, for example, the extracts from the rules published in *CGDA*, 5 December 1792 and 12 January 1793.

3. *CGDA*, 6 February 1794.

4. "The 2d and last reading of a set of new rules" is mentioned in the notice for the anniversary meeting in ibid., 17 November 1802. A meeting notice in ibid., 27 January 1803, requests members to attend on 7 February "for the purpose of taking into consideration, and finally deciding on a set of new Rules, which were proposed and agreed to at the last Quarterly Meeting."

5. St. Cecilia Society, *Rules of the St. Cecilia Society. . . 1831*. References to this publication will hereafter be cited as *Rules 1831*.

6. St. Cecilia Society, *Rules of the St. Cecilia Society . . . 1843*. References to this publication will hereafter be cited as *Rules 1843*. A copy of this rare publication may be found at the Charleston Library Society.

7. *CGDA*, 20 March 1800.

8. Ibid., 15 March 1803.

9. *SCG*, 23–30 November 1767 (Monday): "At a meeting of the St. CECILIA SOCIETY on Tuesday last, Alexander Garden, Esq; was chosen President, David Oliphant, Esq; vice president, and Mr. Thomas Shirley, treasurer."

10. *SCAGG*, 3–10 June 1768, carried a notice of a meeting of the society on 16 June, but no purpose is stated. Like the usual general meetings, this meeting did fall on the third Thursday of the month, but June was very much outside the normal social season of that era. The timing of this meeting, however, coincided with the rather sudden departure for England of Benjamin Yarnold, one of the professional musicians among the founders of the society. The departure of the Yarnold family for London was noted in *SCG*, 13 June 1768. This extra meeting may have been called to discuss recruiting a replacement for Mr. Yarnold's services to the society's concerts.

11. See *SCGCJ*, 18 August 1772, for a notice of a quarterly meeting on 22 August.

12. St. Cecilia Society, *Rules 1831*, 3, also calls for three "general meetings," on the anniversary and on the third Thursdays of August and February. St. Cecilia Society, *Rules 1843*, 3, calls for just one "general meeting," on 22 November.

13. Published notices for seven extraordinary general meetings have been found. An extra meeting on 1 October 1787 (see *CH*, supplement to 25 September 1787) coincided with the arrival of violinist Alexander Juhan, who may have auditioned for a position in the society's orchestra. The extra meeting in August 1793, concerning the Benevolent

Society, is discussed in chapter 8. The extra meeting in March 1795 is discussed below. The extra meeting in August 1808, concerning arrears, is discussed in chapter 5. The two extra meetings called in September 1809, to discuss a "new Concert Hall," are discussed in chapter 6. The extra meeting in December 1817, concerning the prolonged absence of the society's professional musicians, is discussed in chapter 8.

14. St. Cecilia Society, *Rules 1773*, 4, 11. Rules 2 and 11 stipulate these times.

15. Ibid., rule 11. It should be noted that the form and value of currency used in Charleston changed several times in the decades after these 1773 rules, and the amounts levied against tardy or absent members were altered accordingly. Contrary to this rule, however, the wording of one of the society's newspaper notices (*CGDA*, 6 February 1794) suggests that such fines were not regularly enforced in the society's early decades. In calling its members to a quarterly meeting on 20 February, the society stated that "the rule relative to fines will in future be put in force against the members who may be absent at the annual or quarterly meetings of the society."

16. There were two exceptions to the 2 P.M. meeting time. In August 1805 and November 1806 the society's general meetings were advertised to begin at 1 P.M.

17. The meeting notice in *CGDA*, 28 April 1788, specifies dinner at "half past 3 o'clock."

18. Zaslaw, "Toward the Revival," 167; Sadie, "Concert Life in Eighteenth Century England," 29.

19. An exception to this pattern appears in *CGDA*, 13 October 1788, and is covered in chapter 5 under the discussion of arrears.

20. This notice, in ibid., 7 October 1791, is discussed in chapter 6.

21. The extra meeting on 17 October 1787 (see *CH,* 11 October 1787) was held "for the admission of members." An "adjourned meeting" of the managers was called for 27 October 1800 "on special and important business," though the topic of discussion is not clear (see *CGDA*, 27 October 1800). They may have been discussing the recently inaugurated lawsuits against members in arrears, contemplating the fate of the recently closed City Theatre, or debating the prospect of having concerts every week instead of every other week (see *CGDA*, 29 October 1800, and above). The last known mention of an extra meeting of the managers (*CGDA*, 2 April 1801) concerned an adjustment to the concert schedule on account of Passion Week.

22. For a list of these election returns, see note 1 to appendix 4.

23. *Courier,* 8 February 1810.

24. Ibid., 17 February 1810.

25. Ibid., 8 August 1810.

26. Ibid., 18 August 1810.

27. The society's election results for 1821 were published after the August general meeting (see *Courier,* 20 August 1821). Election results were not published in 1822 or 1823, but in 1824 and 1825 they were published after the November meeting. See ibid., 24 November 1824 and 25 November 1825. Rule 2 of St. Cecilia Society, *Rules 1831*, confirms that elections were to take place at the anniversary meeting. This final change of election date was probably owing to habitual low attendance at the society's August general meeting.

28. For a description of this organization and the traditions of Race Week, see Irving, *The South Carolina Jockey Club;* and Sparks, "Gentleman's Sport," 15–30.

29. For a demonstration of these scheduling anomalies, see appendix 1.

30. *CGDA,* 8 February 1797.

31. *Courier,* 13 January 1803.

32. St. Cecilia Society, *Rules 1773,* 10.

33. Burchell, *Polite or Commercial,* 34, 37.

34. George Abbott Hall, steward of the society, placed a notice for the 22 August meeting in *SCGCJ,* 18 August 1772.

35. As steward, Miller placed the notice for the society's 22 November meeting in *CGDA,* 15 November 1788. McVeigh, *Concert Life,* 59, states that at London concerts "it was customary for the organizer to provide light refreshments (with tea and coffee) in a side-room."

36. See also rule 2 of St. Cecilia Society, *Rules 1831.*

37. *Courier,* 23 February 1805; *Times,* 6 November 1805.

38. *CGDA,* 20 February 1808 and 18 February 1809.

39. The term *managers* first appears in an advertisement for a St. Cecilia concert in *SCG,* 22 February 1773, indicating that managers were chosen at the anniversary meeting in November 1772, if not earlier.

40. *CGDA,* 4 April 1792.

41. Burchell, *Polite or Commercial,* 256; Boydell, *Rotunda Music,* 129, 171.

42. This division of labor is first suggested by two November 1801 St. Cecilia concert advertisements, in which the managers are named: *CGDA,* 12 November 1801 (Thursday): "St. Cecilia Society. . . . Benj. B. Smith, Henry Deas, Acting Managers"; *CGDA,* 24 November 1801: "St. Cecilia Society. . . . J. Mitchell, W. Robertson, acting managers." Similarly each of the advertisements for the balls given during the 1820–21 season mentions one of the "acting managers." For example, the advertisement in *Courier,* 9 November 1820, names H. H. Bacot as "one of the acting Managers for the evening." The acting managers are mentioned several times in St. Cecilia Society, *Rules 1831* (see appendix 3).

43. Shanet, *Philharmonic,* 45–46, states that members of New York's first Philharmonic Society, ca. 1799, were required to wear silk "roses" on their breast to distinguish themselves from the rest of the company. Officers of the society also wore distinctive medals suspended around their necks by silk ribbons. Such emblems of distinction were no doubt common among social organizations of the period.

44. Thomas Waring, "A Quondam badge of Distinction," 1830, St. Cecilia Society Collection, SCHS, 11/554/13. Other ephemera included in this file confirm that Waring was secretary of the society in 1830, though he was apparently elected to that office some years earlier. The identity of this Thomas Waring is not entirely clear. See John Ball Waring, comp., "The Descendants of Benjamin Waring," 1997, vertical file collection, "Benjamin Waring," SCHS.

45. A complete list of these events is beyond the scope of the present project. Several examples of them are given in chapters 7 and 8.

46. *CGDA,* 28 December 1803 and 4 January 1804.

47. *SCG,* 3 December 1772.

48. Fraser Harris, *St. Cecilia's Hall,* 161–63; Burchell, *Polite or Commercial,* 35.

49. *SCG,* 6 December 1773. These parts must have been returned, for the anniversary concert performed on 23 November 1778 included much of this repertoire.

50. *CGDA,* 5 September 1788.

51. St. Michael's Church, vestry minutes, 5 June 1769. On this same day the vestry resolved to write to their representative Thomas Loughton Smith, then in London, regarding the recruitment of a suitable permanent organist.

52. St. Michael's Church, vestry minutes, 4 May 1772. For a summary of John Stevens's career, see Williams, "Eighteenth-Century Organists of St. Michael's," 150–52.

53. St. Michael's Church, vestry minutes, 22 June 1772.

54. Williams, *Jacob Eckhard's Choirmaster's Book of 1809,* 14–15.

55. For a summary of his career, see Stevens's obituary in *Courier,* 31 July 1828.

56. Although there is no proof that Stevens was paid for his duties as its librarian, the society may have given Stevens a stipend for his services. The Charleston Library Society, a subscription institution founded in 1748 by the same coterie of gentlemen who promoted the St. Cecilia Society, maintained a librarian on a salary from its earliest days.

57. St. Philip's Church, vestry minutes, 6 February 1753, citing the text of a letter to Benjamin Smith in London.

58. McVeigh, *Concert Life,* 3, 78.

59. Cometti, *Seeing America,* 58, quoting from a letter to his father dated "Charleston, South Carolina, December 2, 1783."

60. *SCSGDA,* 16 December 1784; *SCGPA,* 17 December 1785.

61. *CMPDA,* 5 December 1786.

62. Burchell, *Polite or Commercial,* 9.

63. Milligen-Johnston, *Short Description,* 135. Hewatt, *Historical Account,* 1:50. Schoepf, *Travels in the Confederation,* 2:172.

64. Bridenbaugh, "Colonial Newport as a Summer Resort," 2; Bridenbaugh, "Charlestonians at Newport, 1767–1775," 43–47; *SCAGG,* 30 May–8 June 1770. For more information on the residence patterns of early Charleston, see Brewster, *Summer Migrations and Resorts.*

65. [Gordon], "Journal of an Officer," 397.

66. Hewatt, *Historical Account,* 2:135.

67. Currie, *Historical Account,* 397, quoting from a letter from David Ramsay dated 17 March 1791.

68. William Ogilby, Diary, 1830, SCHS, 34/414.

69. Barnwell, ed., "Diary of Timothy Ford," 190.

70. Notices of the St. Cecilia concerts being suspended "until the second Thursday in January next" were published in *CGDA,* 9 December 1787, 12 November 1796, and 6 December 1798.

71. *CGDA,* 7 December 1793 and 7 December 1803.

72. William Ogilby, Diary, 1830, entry for December 24th, 1830 (Friday).

73. *CGDA,* 9 May 1795.

74. Margaret Izard Manigault, Charleston, to Alice Delancy Izard, New York, 5 March 1809, from the Izard Family Papers, Library of Congress.

75. Storer's activities in Charleston are discussed in chapter 7.

76. *CGDA,* 4 April 1792 and 17 March 1794.

77. Ibid., 27 February 1795, 30 October 1795, and 13 September 1796. See the calendar of concerts in appendix 1 for further discussion of this matter. Note also that this experimentation with a year-round schedule coincided with a change in the society's annual elections.

78. *CGDA,* 29 October 1800 (Wednesday).

79. The defendants whose suits, among the records of the Charleston District Court of Common Pleas at the SCDAH, specify weekly concerts are David Campbell, John Glaze, Charles Goodwin, James Hamilton Sr., Robert Goodloe Harper, William Marshall, John Mitchell, Charles Pinckney, John Ramsay, William Skirving Jr., Roger Moore Smith, and James Theus. See chapter 5.

80. Ravenel, *Charleston,* 426.

81. See appendix 1 for examples.

82. This starting time is stated in the society's very first advertisements (*SCAGG,* 3–10 October 1766; *SCG,* 6–13 October 1766; *SCGCJ,* 21 October 1766; *SCG,* 22 February 1773).

83. See *SCAGG,* 29 July–5 August 1774, and *SCWG,* 11 October 1783.

84. *SCGGA,* 17–20 April 1784; *SCSGDA,* 16 December 1784; *SCGPA,* 17 December 1785.

85. *CMPDA,* 5 December 1786; *CH,* 11 October 1787; *CGDA,* 12 March 1791, 7 October 1791, 9 November 1791, 28 November 1791, and 13 November 1792; *CH,* 5 September 1793 and 19 September 1793; *CGDA,* 14 November 1793, 8 January 1795, 13 January 1795, 7 September 1797, 16 November 1797, and 21 March 1804; *Courier,* 21 March 1804.

86. *CGDA,* 14 December 1799.

87. See John Cripps's statement in chapter 5.

88. *CGDA,* 14 February 1794.

89. McVeigh, *Concert Life,* 19.

90. For example "tickets for the season" are mentioned in St. Cecilia Society advertisements in *CGDA,* 13 December 1787; *CH,* 5 September 1793; *CGDA,* 29 October 1799, 24 October 1801, and 15 November 1803; and elsewhere.

91. St. Cecilia Society, season ticket, dated 1831, Hinson Clippings Collection, Charleston Library Society. The bearer of this ticket was "E. Milliken Esq." It is signed by the treasurer, G[eorge]. H. Ingraham, but the line for the signature of the president is left blank (contrary to the rules). Speaking of subscription concerts in London, McVeigh, *Concert Life,* 60, notes that "concert tickets were sometimes specially engraved; those designed by Cipriani and engraved by Bartolozzi for Giardini's benefits were regarded as minor art-works."

92. According to Margaret J. Abernethy Young, Shenfield, Essex, England, to Mrs. Granville T. [Mary Elizabeth] Prior, August 1967, vertical file collection, "Abernethie Family," SCHS. Thomas Abernethie came to Charleston around the time of the American Revolution and died on 20 August 1795. In the summer and autumn of 1785, he advertised his engraving and copper-plate-printing establishment in Broad Street. See, for example, *SGSC,* 20 October 1785. Abernethie is perhaps best remembered as the engraver of one of the first road maps printed in the United States, *Road to Watboo Bridge from Charleston* (Charleston, S.C.: Walker & Abernethie, 1787). He also engraved the several maps that accompanied David Ramsay's two-volume *History of the Revolution of South Carolina* (1785). Each of these items also bear the signature "Abernethie Sculpt. Charleston." In addition, Abernethie engraved paper money for the City of Charleston in 1786 and 1789.

93. For example the entrance for Thomas Pike's 1765 benefit concert in the Orange Garden was "two [Spanish] dollars for three tickets, to admit two ladies and a gentleman"

(*SCG*, 14–21 September 1765). Peter Valton's 1774 concert advertised "tickets to admit a Gentleman and two Ladies, at Five Pounds, and single Tickets, at Two Dollars" (*SCG*, 31 January 1774). The advertisements for Joseph Lafar's 1786 benefit concert listed "tickets at 3 *Dollars* each," and added "N.B. A Ticket is to admit two Ladies, or a Gentleman and a Lady" (*CH*, 30 January 1786). The promotional description of John Sollée's ephemeral "Anacreontic Concert" series, in *CGDA*, 19 January 1801, states "each subscriber shall have the right to bring two ladies with him."

94. *CEG*, 12 August 1785 (Friday).

95. *CGDA*, 2 March 1805.

96. The first St. Cecilia Society advertisement addressing this topic appeared in *SCAGG*, 7–14 November 1766, followed by others through 1767.

97. *CGDA*, 5 December 1792.

98. Hewatt, *Historical Account*, 2:294.

99. Quincy, "Journal," 441.

100. *SCSGDA*, 10 February 1785.

101. *SCGPA*, 17 December 1785.

102. *CGDA*, 24 November 1792.

103. Ibid., 26 October 1793.

104. James Brown IV Papers, MSS 310, box 1, folder 2, Rhode Island Historical Society.

105. See *Courier*, 25 November 1807; *Times*, 25 November 1807 and 19 October 1808.

106. Joseph Manigault, Charleston, S.C., to Gabriel Manigault, Philadelphia, 24 January 1807, Manigault Family Papers, SCHS, 11/277/2. It is unclear why Gabriel Manigault would have sent his letter of resignation through John Owen when William S. Hasell was secretary of the society at that time. Owen had been treasurer of the society in 1773–74 and was still active as a merchant in Charleston in the early years of the nineteenth century. Perhaps Owen simply acted as an agent who passed on Gabriel Manigault's resignation to the society's secretary. Gabriel Manigault did not live long enough to consider rejoining the society: he died in 1809.

Chapter 5

1. Henry Laurens, Account Book, 1766–73, Mss no. 27, Special Collections, College of Charleston. Laurens (or his bookkeeper) recorded a payment of £25 (current money of South Carolina) on 17 September "to the St. Cæcilian Society," under "sundry expenses" for the year 1766.

2. *SCG*, 31 January 1774.

3. McCusker, *Real Money*, 85–86. The entrance and subscription costs for the years after the Revolution are derived from the numerous lawsuits the society filed against members in arrears. The £10 "admission" or "entrance" fee was charged to Charles Goodwin in August 1785, John Ramsay in February 1794, and James Theus in November 1795. In the years after his election to the society in 1785, Charles Goodwin was charged £5 for his annual subscription. See *St. Cecilia Society vs. Charles Goodwin*, Charleston District Court of Common Pleas Judgment Roll, 1803, no. 291, SCDAH; *St. Cecilia Society vs. John Ramsay*, Charleston District Court of Common Pleas, Judgment Roll, 1802, no. 449, SCDAH; *St. Cecilia Society vs. James Theus*, Charleston District Court of Common Pleas, Judgment Roll, 1802, no. 537, SCDAH. In *CGDA*, 12 January 1793, the society published the full text of its revised sixth rule, which confirms that its members were to pay £5 for an annual subscription.

4. The society's lawsuits against David Campbell, Charles Goodwin, Charles Pinckney, John Rutledge Smith, and Roger Moore Smith all show that these gentlemen were charged £5.10.0 for a subscription in the spring of 1802 and possibly as early as the spring of 1801. See *St. Cecilia Society vs. David Campbell,* Charleston District Court of Common Pleas, Judgment Roll, 1804, no. 271, SCDAH; *St. Cecilia Society vs. Charles Goodwin,* 1803; *St. Cecilia Society vs. Charles Pinckney,* Charleston District Court of Common Pleas, Judgment Roll, 1807, no. 697, SCDAH; *St. Cecilia Society vs. John Rutledge Smith,* Charleston District Court of Common Pleas, Summary Process Roll, 1802, no. 95, SCDAH; *St. Cecilia Society vs. Roger Moore Smith,* Charleston District Court of Common Pleas, Judgment Roll, 1802, no. 518, SCDAH.

5. McCusker, *Real Money,* table A-1, 53.

6. *CGDA,* 10 August 1803, rule 3, section 1.

7. The extant papers of numerous lawsuits filed after 1803 corroborate this practice. During the 1806–7 season George Logan neglected to pay the requisite $10 at each of the general meetings in August, November, and February—representing an annual subscription fee of $30. A similar case against Henry Laurens Jr. demonstrates that the annual subscription was still $30 as late as 1819, when he was sued for failing to make the same $10 installment payments. See *St. Cecilia Society vs. George Logan,* Charleston District Court of Common Pleas, Summary Process Roll, 1809, no. 47, SCDAH; *St. Cecilia Society vs. Henry Laurens Jr.,* Charleston District Court of Common Pleas, Summary Process Roll, 1819, no. 30, SCDAH.

8. See appendix 3.

9. See McCusker, *Real Money,* table A-1, 53–54.

10. Fraser Harris, *St. Cecilia's Hall,* 276, says the annual fee for that series was one guinea in 1749, one and a half guineas in 1752, and two guineas in 1778. McVeigh, *Concert Life,* 13, says that the "typical" subscription fee in London during the second half of the eighteenth century was five guineas.

11. Rogers, *Charleston,* 15.

12. Hewatt, *Historical Account,* 2:299.

13. South Carolina Society, "Schedule of the Stock belonging to the South Carolina Society Easter 1790," South Carolina Society Records, SCHS, 11/482/1.

14. *SCAGG,* 6 November 1777.

15. Higgins, "The South Carolina Revolutionary Debt and Its Holders," 26. I have found no record of this bond being redeemed after the Revolution.

16. Ramsay, *History of South-Carolina,* 2:101.

17. Clark, *The History of the Banking Institutions Organized in South Carolina,* 6–12; Lesesne, *The Bank of the State of South Carolina,* 37–47.

18. *SCWG,* 29 March 1783.

19. The society's initial petition for incorporation is not extant. For the date of the petition's submission, see South Carolina, General Assembly, *Journals of the House of Representatives, 1783–1784,* 414. The names of the petitioners—Isaac Motte, John F. Grimké, Thomas Bee, and Thomas Shubrick, "and others"—appear in the unpublished Journal of the South Carolina Senate on 24 February 1784 (see Journal of the South Carolina Senate, 1783–85, 146, SCDAH).

20. This time line was constructed from information given in South Carolina, General Assembly, *Journals of the House of Representatives, 1783–1784,* 414, 422, 469, 476, 494, 506, 515, 539, and 542.

21. McCord, *Statutes at Large,* 8:124–25 (act no. 1199).

22. Ibid.

23. Joseph Farr to St. Cæcilia Society, Lease and Release by way of Mortgage, 29–31 August 1794, RMC, N6:197–204.

24. O'Brien Smith to St. Cæcilia Society, Lease and Release by way of Mortgage, 1–2 March 1795, RMC, N6:190–97. Bacot's note appears on 193.

25. Edinburgh Musical Society, Sederunt Books, Edinburgh Central Library, 3:32–33: "Accot. Betwixt the Governor & Directors of the Musical Society, and William Douglass their Treasurer from June 1769 to June 1770." My thanks to Mrs. Anne McClenny Krauss for sharing her photocopies of these records with me.

26. Quincy, "Journal," 441.

27. *Courier,* 7 January 1819.

28. Mason, *Extracts from A Diary,* 23. Mason is referring to the events of Tuesday, 12 February, and Thursday, 14 February 1805.

29. John Sollée, "Petition and supporting papers asking compensation for the use of the Concert Hall and other rooms in Charleston by a detachment of militia in October 1812," 8 December 1813, Petitions to the General Assembly, 1813, no. 115, SCDAH. The 2005 equivalent for this amount represents an average of the dollar values for 1813 and the "several years" leading up to it. In a similar petition, made in late 1807, Sollée sought compensation for the concert hall being used by the 28th and 29th regiments of the South Carolina militia on 3 January 1807. Sollée's petition mentions the inclusion of a certificate from Mr. [Daniel Cannon] Webb, treasurer of the St. Cecilia Society, testifying to the amount "customary to Societies who engage His Rooms," but this certificate is not extant. See John Sollée, "Petition asking compensation for the use of rooms by a detachment of militia," 30 November 1807, Petitions to the General Assembly, 1807, no. 136, SCDAH. The legislative committee assigned to review the petition, chaired by John Drayton, awarded Sollée $50 "for the use of his rooms, fire & candles." See South Carolina General Assembly, "Committee report on the petition of John Sollée concerning reimbursement for providing furnishings for military purposes," 11 December 1807, Committee Reports, 1807, no. 43, SCDAH. See chapter 6 for more information on the society's dealings with Sollée.

30. *SCAGG,* 14–21 November 1766.

31. *SCG,* 13 June 1774.

32. *SCWG,* 29 March 1783.

33. McCord, *Statutes at Large,* 8:124.

34. Pinckney, *Life of General Thomas Pinckney,* 143. *CGDA,* 21 April 1792, reported that Pinckney and his family sailed for Philadelphia on Thursday, 19 April, on their way to London. The author of this biography identifies Edward Penman as the secretary of the society (142), but no such office yet existed.

35. For a study of the Charleston Library Society's dealings with London booksellers, see Raven, *London Booksellers and American Customers.*

36. In *CGDA,* 12 January 1802, Thornhill, Wallis, and Company advertised the sale of a new shipment of "modern and fashionable Music" and "perfectly climate proof" instruments from London. Their instruments, especially the pianos, "are not made of those unseasoned materials which usually compose the cheap Piano Fortes made for exportation, and generally known by the name of *London runners.*"

37. *Courier,* Advertising Ledger, 1803–9, SCHS, 34/604 OvrSz, [38]–[39]. The society continued to advertise in the *Courier* after this time, but its subsequent advertisements are not included in this document. The least expensive advertisements in this account, single notices for concerts, cost $0.64, while the most expensive charge, a "Notice to Debtors" that appeared six times after 20 March 1805, cost $3.49.

38. *CMPDA,* 5 December 1786.

39. *SCG,* 6 February 1775. Similarly worded appeals are found in *SCGCJ,* 9 May 1775, and *CGDA,* 9 May 1793 and 19 March 1805.

40. Burchell, *Polite or Commercial,* 43.

41. McVeigh, *Concert Life,* 195; Rohr, *The Careers of British Musicians,* 155–57.

42. Boydell, *Rotunda Music,* 172–200. This concert series usually lasted about twenty-one weeks.

43. During the same period Charleston's St. Cecilia Society annually collected approximately £3,000 in South Carolina currency, or about £428 sterling, from its members in subscription money. This sum is derived from the figures specified in the St. Cecilia Society's 1773 rules: 120 members each paying £25 currency annually. Ten musicians with an average salary of £29 pounds sterling would have cost the society £290 sterling. This would have left the society with approximately £138 sterling to spend on other items, including additional musicians if it so wished. The statement that the society could afford to hire at least ten musicians is merely a suggestion meant to demonstrate that it could pay a respectable professional component of its orchestra without emptying its treasury.

44. Edinburgh Musical Society, Sederunt Books, Edinburgh Central Library, 3:32. Rohr, *The Careers of British Musicians,* 115, reports that the London violinist Giovanni Battista Viotti received 550 guineas for a season at Salomon's concert series in the 1790s, but this was a very unusual sum paid to the leader of one of the most prestigious orchestras in the world at the time.

45. Quincy, "Journal," 451, from the entry for 17 March 1773.

46. Barnwell, "George Harland Hartley's Claim," 50; *SCGCJ,* 19 January 1773. Thomas Pike made a similar claim to the British government, but he dated the beginning of his professional losses from the period commencing a year after his departure from Charleston in July 1774. See Cobau, "The Precarious Life of Thomas Pike," for details.

47. Mills, *Statistics of South Carolina,* 436.

48. *SCAGG,* 27 March–3 April 1767.

49. *SCG,* 10 May 1773.

50. See ibid., 31 January 1774; *SCAGG,* 26–29 April 1774; and below.

51. *SCAGG,* 8–15 July 1774.

52. *SCG,* 6 February 1775.

53. *SCGCJ,* 9 May 1775.

54. *GSSC,* 28 October 1777.

55. *SCAGG,* 6 November 1777.

56. Ibid.,19 February 1778.

57. Ibid., 27 August 1778 and 12 November 1778.

58. *SCGGA,* 10–12 February 1784.

59. Ibid., 6–9 November 1784.

60. *SCGPA,* 12–16 February 1785.

61. See the society's meeting advertisements in ibid., 11–14 May 1785, 13 August 1785, and 17 November 1785, and in *CH,* 30 January 1786.

62. *CMPDA,* 5 December 1786.

63. Ibid., 10 February 1787.

64. *CH,* 14 May 1787.

65. Francis Kinloch to Jacob Read, 3 August 1787, Francis Kinloch Papers, unbound correspondence, 1787–1804, South Caroliniana Library. The results of the St. Cecilia Society's November 1786 election were not published, but—in submitting such a writ, in accordance with the society's sixth rule—Read was undoubtedly its treasurer in 1787. The "installment act" refers to the statute allowing the satisfaction of debts in three annual installments. See act no. 1371, "An Act to Regulate the Recovery and Payment of Debts," ratified on 28 March 1787, in Cooper, *Statutes at Large,* 5:36.

66. *CGDA,* 13 October 1788.

67. Ibid., 15 November 1788.

68. The February 1802 lawsuit against Richard Beresford for his arrears to the society shows that he was charged for dinners only at the anniversary meetings in November 1788 and November 1789, not for concert subscriptions and dinners as he was in previous and in subsequent years. This matter is made clear in the society's June 1803 suit against Charles Goodwin, whose arrears due from the late 1780s show a similar pattern. On 22 November 1788 Goodwin was charged only £0.5.0 for "Dinner (Concerts discontinued)." On 22 November 1789 he was charged £0.5.0 for the same. On 22 November 1790, however, Goodwin was charged £1.5.0 for "a Quarters Subscription & dinner (concerts resumed)." See *St. Cecilia Society vs. Richard Beresford,* Charleston District Court of Common Pleas, Judgment Roll, 1802, no. 80, SCDAH; *St. Cecilia Society vs. Charles Goodwin,* 1803.

69. *CGDA,* 7 October 1791.

70. Ibid., 13 November 1792.

71. Ibid., 12 January 1793. According to rule 5, section 2 of St. Cecilia Society, *Rules 1831,* such defaulters were still liable for their arrears.

72. *CGDA,* 18 February 1793.

73. Ibid., 9 May 1793.

74. Ibid., 13 June 1793.

75. McCord, *Statutes at Large,* 8:125.

76. *CGDA,* 1 August 1793.

77. The resolutions of August 1795 and November 1797 were published in the notice for the February 1798 general meeting. See ibid., 7 February 1798.

78. Ibid., 6 August 1798.

79. Ibid., 29 October 1799 and 12 November 1799.

80. William Robertson served as solicitor in the society's suits against James Alexander Wright, David Campbell, John Mitchell, and John Ramsay. On the February 1802 judgment against Ramsay, however, the name Robertson is struck through and a note states that the solicitor was "changed to Peace & Cheves." *St. Cecilia Society vs. James Alexander Wright,* Charleston District Court of Common Pleas, Summary Process Roll, 1800, no. 72, SCDAH; *St. Cecilia Society vs. David Campbell,* 1804; *St. Cecilia Society vs. John Mitchell,* Charleston District Court of Common Pleas, Judgment Roll, 1802, no. 360, SCDAH; *St. Cecilia Society vs. John Ramsay,* 1802.

81. The defendants sued by the society between 1800 and 1829 include (in alphabetical order, with date of suit): Richard Beresford (1802), Moses Bradley (1809), Edward Brailsford (1805), William Brailsford (1802 and 1805), David Campbell (1804), Thomas Cave (1802), Thomas Cochran (1814), Abraham Crouch (1819), John N. Davis (1812 and 1820), Robert Deas (1803), Jeremiah Dickenson (1829), John Drayton (1806), John Glaze (1802), Charles Goodwin (1803), James Hamilton (1802 and 1807), Robert Goodloe Harper (1802), William James Ladson (1825), Henry Laurens Jr. (1819), James Lee (1806), George Logan (1809), William Marshall (1802), John Mitchell (1802), John Martin Ogier (1825), Charles Pinckney (1807 and 1809), Thomas W. Price (1805 and 1809), John Ramsay (1802 and 1807), James Simons (1809), William Skirving (1803), John Rutledge Smith (1802 and 1805), Roger Moore Smith (1802), John Teasdale Jr. (1818), James Theus (1802), and Alexander Wright (1800). The papers of these suits are among the records of the Charleston District Court of Common Pleas, SCDAH.

82. The society was also represented by Charles Fraser (against John N. Davis in 1812, Thomas Cochran in 1814, and John Teasdale Jr. in 1818), and the partnerships of Bentham & Parker (against Abraham Crouch and Henry Laurens Jr. in 1819 and John N. David in 1820), Bentham & Bentham (against John M. Ogier in 1825), and Bentham & Dunkin (against William James Ladson and John M. Ogier in 1825 and Jeremiah Dickenson in 1829).

83. *CGDA,* 29 October 1800.

84. Ibid., 24 October 1801.

85. Ibid., 10 August 1803.

86. Thomas W. Bacot to Alexander Inglis, receipt, 27 July 1801, Alexander Inglis Papers, SCHS, 28/678/17. This sum represented "his arrears due to the St. Cecilia Society [up to] 21 May last."

87. *CGDA,* 21 November 1803.

88. Ibid., 15 February 1805.

89. Ibid., 19 March 1805. According to Elizer, *A Directory for 1803,* Bruckner was the porter for South Carolina Bank, an institution for which many members of the St. Cecilia Society served as officers. In Negrin, *Negrin's Directory, and Almanac, for the Year 1806,* he is listed as a commission merchant. Burchell, *Polite or Commercial,* 45, notes that in 1777 the treasurer of the Edinburgh Musical Society requested the appointment of a "Collector to the Society."

90. *CGDA,* 8 August 1805.

91. *Courier,* 19 October 1807.

92. Ibid., 25 November 1807.

93. *CGDA,* 3 August 1808 and 11 August 1808.

94. *Times,* 14 November 1808.

95. *Courier,* 7 November 1809, and *CGDA,* 7 November 1809. Members were reminded of this regulation in the *Courier,* 13 November 1810 and 31 October 1811.

96. *St. Cecilia Society vs. Charles Goodwin,* 1803.

97. *St. Cecilia Society vs. James Hamilton,* Charleston District Court of Common Pleas, Judgment Roll, 1802, no. 297; *St. Cecilia Society vs. James Hamilton,* Charleston District Court of Common Pleas, Judgment Roll, 1807, no. 441, SCDAH. Note that Hamilton did not accumulate additional arrears between the two suits, a fact that suggests that his membership in the society was terminated after the first action in 1802.

98. *St. Cecilia Society vs. Charles Pinckney,* 1807; *St. Cecilia Society vs. Charles Pinckney,* Charleston District Court of Common Pleas, Summary Process Roll, 1809, no. 161, SCDAH. Of all extant records of the St. Cecilia Society's suits against members in arrears, the 1809 action against Pinckney is the only one to mention the defendant having been "read out." This fact should not be taken to mean that he was the only member to have been excluded, however, as the society's own record books would have surely named other, more egregious debtors, such as James Hamilton. It is not clear when this pencil notation was added to the court papers. It may have been made immediately after the suit in 1809, or perhaps at some time after 1817, when the case file was updated with Thomas Parker Jr.'s note acknowledging the satisfaction of the debt. The first possibility seems the more likely, as Pinckney does not seem to have accumulated any further debts to the society after 1809. If this is the case, then the society second suit against Pinckney also provides evidence that it pursued debts incurred by defaulters even after they had been read out of the society.

Chapter 6

1. For information on concert venues in eighteenth-century London, see Elkin, *The Old Concert Rooms of London,* and McLamore, "Symphonic Conventions."

2. Zaslaw, "Toward the Revival," 166.

3. Fraser Harris, *St. Cecilia's Hall,* 32; Weber, "London," 309; Zaslaw, "Toward the Revival," 166.

4. Zaslaw, "Toward the Revival," 166–67.

5. From 1732—when Charleston's first newspaper was established—through 1736, most concerts were held in the Council Chamber at the eastern terminus of Broad Street. The transferal of concerts to the tavern at the corner of Church and Broad streets in 1737 suggests that this was a relatively new venue, although its date of construction is not known.

6. The "Corner" is briefly mentioned in Fraser, *Reminiscences,* 34; Moultrie, *Memoirs of the American Revolution,* 1:10; Crouse, "The Letterbook of Peter Manigault," 90; and *CMPDA,* 6 February 1786.

7. William Nixon's advertisement to let this space in *CGDA,* 14 November 1794, includes a brief description its rooms.

8. John Webb to Martha Cannon, Lease and Release, 1–2 August 1787, RMC, A6:116–21. The plat appears between pages 117 and 118. It is difficult to determine the exact dimensions of the room because its depiction here is rather vague and not quite to scale. The focus of the plat is the property belonging to Miss Cannon, adjacent to the tavern's north side.

9. Zaslaw, "Toward the Revival," 164–65.

10. *SCAGG,* 10–17 September 1771.

11. See *SCG,* 5 September 1768, 9 August 1773, 9 August 1773, and 21 January 1774.

12. Ibid., 19 November 1772.

13. The St. Cecilia notice in ibid., 22 February 1773, confirms the location of the concert Quincy attended.

14. Pike's financial straits are described in Cobau, "Thomas Pike," 229–62.

15. *SCG,* 9 August 1773 and 15 November 1773.

16. Valk announced his tenancy in ibid., 27 June 1774. For sample sales advertisements, see *SCGCJ,* 26 July 1774 and 23 August 1774.

17. Cobau, "Thomas Pike," 252.

18. Schoepf, *Travels in the Confederation,* 2:168.

19. *SCAGG,* 29 July–5 August 1774; *GSSC,* 8 July 1778. From South Carolina's first proclamation of independence from Britain in March 1776, until February 1779, the chief executive of South Carolina was styled the "president" of the state.

20. The use of the State House for concerts and dancing assemblies during the British occupation of Charleston is demonstrated by a number of advertisements for individual events, as well as this notice in *RSCG,* 10 May 1781: "The Last Garrison Subscription Ball for this Season, will be held as usual, at the State-House, on Saturday the 12th instant, to commemorate the *reduction* of Charles-Town."

21. Harrison, *Journal of A Voyage from Philadelphia to Charlestown,* 4–5.

22. Lounsbury, *From Statehouse to Courthouse,* 37.

23. *RG,* 10–14 November 1781.

24. For more information about Douglass's theater, see Curtis, "Charles-Town's Church Street Theater," 149–54.

25. Eliza Wilkinson to "Miss M—— P——r," dated 6 March 1783, in Wauchope, *The Writers of South Carolina,* 408–9.

26. *SCWG,* 1 March 1783. The fact that this inventory was under, not inside, the Assembly Room is stated in the report of the fire in *SCWA,* 5 March 1783. Newspaper advertisements from the early days of the American Revolution in 1775 up to the British occupation in 1780 show that a number of pro-independence political meetings were held at the Assembly Rooms in Church Street, no doubt because they accommodated a larger crowd than the older State House and because that building was associated with British authority.

27. *SCGGA,* 13–16 September 1783. Following the opening of Pike's Assembly Room, the St. Cecilia Society held only three of its advertised meetings at this new venue: the quarterly meetings of 22 August 1772, 22 November 1772, and 18 February 1773. The only other advertised meeting that took place at a venue other than the City Tavern during the colonial period was the anniversary meeting of 22 November 1777, which was advertised to take place at Elisha Poinsett's Tavern in Elliott Street. The society's first advertised meeting after the Revolution (and the Assembly Room fire) took place on 10 April 1783 at Peter Lesesne's "house" at the corner of Meeting Street and Beresford's Alley (now Chalmers Street). In the spring of 1783 Lesesne's public house was briefly the site for the meetings of most of Charleston's elite organizations, including the Charleston Library Society (on 2 July 1783), the South Carolina Society (on 1 July 1783), and the Charleston Insurance Company (on 27 March 1783). Lesesne retired from this business in the autumn of 1789.

28. Cometti, *Seeing America,* 58.

29. *SCGGA,* 8–11 May 1784.

30. *SCGPA,* 22–25 September 1784.

31. Ibid., 6–10 March 1784.

32. The details of this incident are reported in a number of letters to the Republican *GSSC* throughout April 1784, and in South Carolina, General Assembly, *Journals of the House of Representatives, 1783–1784,* 578–85.

33. *GSSC,* 1 April 1784. Henry Peronneau Jr., secretary of the Marine Anti-Britannic Society, was the author of this statement. He was also a radical son of a founding member

of the St. Cecilia Society, Henry Peronneau Sr., who remained loyal to the British crown during the Revolution.

34. Ibid., 29 April 1784.

35. *SCGGA*, 20–23 March 1784. The overlapping management of the assemblies and the St. Cecilia Society is discussed in chapter 7.

36. Ibid., 8–10 April 1784.

37. The address and the governor's reply were printed in *GSSC*, 22 April 1784 and 6 May 1784. The Senate journal for the early months of 1784 yields no information about concerts or dancing assemblies in the State House, but it does confirm that on 26 March 1784, the final day of the spring session, John Lloyd was elected to participate in a bicameral committee to oversee repairs to the State House during the summer recess. See Journal of the South Carolina Senate, 1783–1785, 473–74, SCDAH.

38. *SCGGA*, 17–20 April 1784, 14–16 September 1784, and 16–19 October 1784.

39. *CEG*, 19 August 1785 (Friday), reporting on a trial that "came on yesterday in the Common Pleas." The text of this report is rendered in italics, with plain text serving for emphasis; I have reversed the format for ease of reading. The names of the plaintiffs are not known, for the court records from this period do not survive. The introduction to the report states only that the brawl took place "last winter," but Milligan's assault on the five musicians may have inspired the following notice in *SCGPA*, 29 January–2 February 1785: "At a Meeting of the Managers of the Dancing Assembly, Resolved, That Mr. [Thomas] Turner be appointed Master of the Ceremonies to the Dancing Assembly, and invested with full power and authority to conduct the etiquette of the same; that he be supported by the managers in maintaining good order, and carrying the rules into execution; and that the music shall receive directions from no person whatever but from him."

40. *CMPDA*, 5 July 1786.

41. *CH*, 24 March 1788, 18 August 1788, and 21 August 1788.

42. *CGDA*, 15 November 1788, 17 November 1788, and 13 January 1789.

43. The anniversary concert of 1788 was advertised to take place at the City Tavern, while the advertisements for the 1789 anniversary concert do not mention a venue. Beyond these annual events, there are no extant advertisements for a regular St. Cecilia concert until October 1791. It should be noted, however, that there are very few extant issues of *CH* between the autumn of 1788 and early 1793. There are many extant issues of *CGDA* for 1789 and 1791 but very few for 1790.

44. The managers of the St. Cecilia Society sponsored a concert at McCrady's on 18 March 1791 "for the benefit of a numerous family in distress" (*CGDA*, 16 March 1791). The first known advertisement of a St. Cecilia concert at McCrady's did not appear until February 1792.

45. In a notice for the city dancing assembly in ibid., 22 January 1789, the venue is described as McCrady's "new room."

46. John McCrady to Charles Snowden, Lease and Release, 27–28 April 1801, RMC, C7:386–98.

47. Lewis, "Archeological Investigations," 3. News of the St. Patrick's Day celebration at McCrady's mentions that after dinner "a band of music, placed in the orchestra, played some excellent Irish compositions between the toasts" (*CH*, 19 March 1791).

48. Sonneck, *Early Concert-Life*, 27–28; Willis, *The Charleston Stage*, 147–49.

49. *CGDA*, 5 May 1791 and 23 June 1792.

50. Naylor's plans for the Exchange are reproduced in Lipscomb, *South Carolina in 1791,* 25.

51. Quoted in Orr, "Rhode Islanders in Charleston, 181–82. The Mrs. Miller mentioned in this letter was probably related to either George Miller, who was elected a manager of the St. Cecilia Society in November 1791, or James Miller, a wine and liquor merchant who had served as steward of the society in 1787–88.

52. *CGDA,* 6 May 1791 and 14 May 1791.

53. St. Philip's Church, like St. Michael's, had recently established a boys' choir recruited from the city's new Orphan House. See Williams, *St. Michael's, Charleston,* 207–17.

54. *CGDA,* 7 October 1791.

55. Ibid., 11 October 1791.

56. Ibid., 9 November 1791 and 8 February 1792.

57. Ibid., 1 September 1792 and 7 November 1792. Harris's identity was revealed posthumously in a legal notice in *Courier,* 3 July 1823.

58. See, for example, *CGDA,* 9 January 1793, and *CH,* 1 August 1793.

59. *SCGPA,* 7 December 1785; *CH,* 26 July 1787. There is an old Charleston tradition that the house at no. 5 Bedon's Alley was used for the earliest St. Cecilia Society events. I have found no evidence whatsoever to support this story. Considering that no. 5 Bedon's Alley was once adjacent to the Carolina Coffee House, however, it seems likely that this tradition is derived from the society's concerts having been held at the coffeehouse for nine seasons, 1792–1801.

60. Birchin Lane is just south of the old Royal Exchange and east of St. Paul's Cathedral. See Lillywhite, *London Coffee Houses,* 147–49. The first known coffeehouse in Charleston, the Exchange Coffee House, was advertised in *SCG,* 26 November 1753.

61. *CGDA,* 1 November 1792 and 13 November 1792. Note that Charleston traffic followed British tradition of driving on the left side of the road until 1 January 1850. See *Times,* 23 October 1802, and Charleston City Council, *Ordinances of the City of Charleston, from the 19th of August 1844, to the 14th of September 1854,* 82.

62. *CGDA,* 24 August 1793; *CH,* 5 September 1793 and 19 September 1793.

63. *CGDA,* 19 November 1794.

64. See, for example, ibid., 21 March 1795, 26 March 1795, 7 November 1798, and 4 March 1800.

65. Ibid., 21 February 1799 and 16 April 1799.

66. Ibid., 29 October 1799; James Thompson advertised that he had taken control of the business from Mrs. Coates in *Times,* 5 March 1802.

67. *CGDA,* 12 August 1801 and 15 August 1801.

68. Ibid., 24 October 1801 and 12 November 1801.

69. Of the six performances advertised to take place at "St. Cecilia Society Concert Hall" (or some variation of that title), five were benefit concerts in which the performers had some relationship with the society. The use of this name may have been a public sign that the concert was to be performed under the aegis of the St. Cecilia Society, and would therefore be subject to its standards of decorous behavior, as well as upholding its reputation for excellence of performance and approved taste in musical selections. For Mr. Gallaher's benefit concert on 27 May 1812, the venue was styled "St. Cecilia Society Concert Hall." The title "St. Cecilia Hall" was used for Mr. Gallaher's benefit concerts on

30 March 1813 and 8 February 1814 and for Mrs. Sully's benefit on 7 March 1814. "St. Cecilia Concert Hall" was used for Mr. Gallaher's benefit concert on 2 May 1816 and for Mr. and Mrs. Ormsby's moral lectures on 22 June 1814.

70. Confusion about the history of the lot on which the Concert Hall was built dates back to 1819, in Shecut, *Shecut's Medical and Philosophical Essays*, 6.

71. "East-India Jugglers" are mentioned as performers at a benefit for the Charleston Orphan House in *Courier*, 24 February 1818.

72. See, for example, Seilhamer, *History of the American Theater*, 3:281–82; Willis, *The Charleston Stage*, 394–95; Hoole, *The Ante-Bellum Charleston Theater*, 3; Curtis, "Charles-Town's Church Street Theater," 154; Curtis, "John Joseph Stephen Leger Sollée and the Charleston Theater," 286; Porter, *With An Air Debonair*, 90.

73. Pike's Assembly Room, Douglass's theater, and Sollée's French Theater/Concert Hall were all constructed on lot no. 40 of the "Grand Model" of Charleston, which measured one hundred feet on the western side of Church Street, approximately midway between Broad and Tradd streets, and approximately two hundred and fifty feet in depth. According to the record of Benjamin Webb to Thomas Pike (Lease and Release, 27–28 August 1767, RMC, H3:39–46), Pike purchased the northern half of this lot. According to the record of Robert Wells et al. to David Douglass (Lease, 28 August 1773, RMC, C5:46–50), Douglass leased the southern half from a committee representing the Union Kilwinning Lodge. According to John Roberts to John Sollée (Lease and Release, 16–17 August 1795, RMC, S6:409–11), Sollée purchased the western end of the northern half of lot no. 40 from Roberts, who had acquired this property from the Reverend Robert Smith, who had in turn received it from Pike when he fled Charleston in 1774. The record of William Hasell Gibbes, Master in Equity, to William Grogan (Conveyance, 12 July 1814, RMC, P8:325–27), shows that this transaction took place in August 1793, not 1795. This earlier date is consistent with the chronology of the French Theater. It could be that in August 1793 Sollée leased the property from Roberts and then formally purchased it exactly two years later. Although Sollée did acquire a lease of the southern half of lot no. 40 from the Union Kilwinning Lodge (see William Calhoun and William Presstman to John Sollée, Assignment, 30 April 1794, RMC, M6:394–96), the French Theater and thus the subsequent Concert Hall were clearly built on the northern half of this lot. Many other RMC documents relating to the properties surrounding Sollée's theater confirm this fact.

74. Poston, *The Buildings of Charleston*, 79.

75. *CGDA*, 22 October 1792 and 12 November 1792.

76. Curtis, "John Stephen Leger Sollee and the Charleston Theater," 285, repeats the dubious genealogical information about Sollée found in the Sollée family vertical file at the South Carolina Historical Society, which states that he was a French protestant who fled Normandy in 1791. Both Sollée's marriage settlement (dated 9 October 1793) and obituary (*Courier*, 1 February 1820) confirm that he was a native of St. Domingo.

77. See the advertisement of M. Macarone (French confectioner Joseph Olman) in *CGDA*, 28 January 1795 (which appears without diacritical marks).

78. *SCSG*, 24 February 1794; *CGDA*, 10 April 1794.

79. A ca. 1800 plat of no. 3 (now no. 11) St. Michael's Alley, near the southwestern end of the alley, shows a portion of the land belonging to John Sollée on the northern half of lot no. 40. See Charleston County RMC, McCrady Plats, no. 519. In the upper right hand

corner of the plat is depicted the western end of a rectangular building approximately forty feet wide. A notation written on this structure reads "Building Two Stories partly Brick & partly wood." Thus Sollée's hall (alias French Theater, alias City Theater, alias Concert Hall, alias St. Cecilia Hall) was clearly built on the site of Pike's long room. The question raised by this plat is whether Sollée's building was two stories of wood above a brick foundation, or one story of brick and one of wood, or some other arrangement.

80. Fraser, *Reminiscences*, 44; *SCSG*, 26 April 1797.

81. *SCSG*, 28 April 1797 and 29 April 1797.

82. The width of the passageway is described in several documents concerning the land at the east end of lot no. 40, between Sollée's property and Church Street. See, for example, John Roberts to William Fiddy and Hugh Young, Lease and Release, 17–18 August 1795, RMC, P6:141–44; Anthony Bessiere to John and Harriett Sollée, Conveyance, 14 July 1800, RMC, I7:381.

83. *CGDA*, 21 July 1794. Note that this "Mme. Placide" was not Charlotte Wrighten, who married the theatrical manager Alexander Placide in August of 1796. Rather, this was Placide's mysterious consort, who advertised herself as the manager's wife from the time of his arrival in Charleston in 1793 until his marriage to Miss Wrighten.

84. Ibid., 18 January 1796. The gate is also mentioned in ibid., 12 March 1801.

85. Ibid., 6 March 1798.

86. See, for example, ibid., 16 November 1795 and 11 March 1799.

87. Ibid., 14 November 1799.

88. McCombs, *Letter-book of Mary Stead Pinckney*, 62.

89. *CGDA*, 13 February 1796.

90. Ibid., 25 March 1796 and 23 June 1796.

91. Ibid., 1 December 1798.

92. Ibid., 7 March 1798, 9 January 1799, 11 March 1799, and 12 March 1799.

93. Ibid., 29 March 1800 and 19 January 1801.

94. Ibid., 30 December 1800, 10 January 1801, and 16 January 1801.

95. Ibid., 19 January 1801. The name of Sollée's concert series is drawn from London's Anacreontic Club. The widespread popularity of John Stafford Smith's vocal glee "To Anacreon in Heaven," the tune of which now accompanies Francis Scott Key's poem "The Star-Spangled Banner" in the U.S. national anthem, caused a fashion for all things "anacreontic."

96. Ibid., 28 January 1801, 14 March 1801, and 27 March 1801.

97. Ibid., 20 November 1801.

98. Ibid., 24 November 1801. For other notices regarding Mrs. Daniel, see ibid., 11 April 1798 and 20 October 1801; *Times*, 24 March 1802 (concerning the estate of Mary Clodner Vesey); *CGDA*, 27 June 1803 and 10 September 1806; and her will, dated 23 December 1816 and proved on 9 October 1817, in which Daniel identifies herself as a "black woman." See Charleston County Will Book E (1807–18): 661, South Carolina Civil Works Administration transcription, vol. 33 (1807–18): 1306.

99. *CGDA*, 10 August 1803. During the intervening months, the society meetings were held at St. Mary's Hotel (ibid., 15 February 1802) and the Carolina Coffee House (ibid., 12 August 1802, 17 November 1802, and 12 February 1803).

100. Besides the meeting of August 1803, those of November 1803, February 1804, and August 1804 were held at Sollée's Long Room. See ibid., 15 November 1803, 13 February

1804, and 10 August 1804. The following meetings were held at the Carolina Coffee House: November 1804; February, August, and November 1805; and February and August 1806. See ibid., 16 November 1804, 15 February 1805, 8 August 1805, 18 November 1805, 15 February 1806, and 19 August 1806.

101. The four exceptions, all regularly scheduled meetings, were held at the Carolina Coffee House in February 1809, November 1810, February 1812, and November 1813. See *Courier,* 13 February 1809, 13 November 1810, 13 February 1812, and 18 November 1813.

102. See, for example, the auction advertisements in *CGDA,* 21 February 1803 and 7 March 1803; *Times,* 8 March 1806; and *CGDA,* 18 December 1807. Many similar advertisements appeared in ensuing years.

103. Moore, "The Abiel Abbot Journals," 68, entry for 21 November 1818. Note that Abbot's visit did not take place during a concert performance.

104. See, for example, the auction advertisements in *Times,* 11 May 1802 and 14 June 1802. The term *piazza*—used in Charleston to describe the porches or verandas common to the city's vernacular architecture since the early eighteenth century—may have in this case been synonymous with the "Terrace on each side of the Roof" that Sollée mentioned in *CGDA,* 9 January 1799, as being part of the "extensive alteration" to his theater. Because there are no references to a piazza after 1802, it appears that this feature of the building may have been removed in subsequent renovations.

105. *CGDA,* 20 December 1802.

106. *Times,* 7 November 1803.

107. *CGDA,* 4 January 1804.

108. *Courier,* 11 September 1809 and 26 September 1809. These meetings were scheduled for 14 and 28 September (both Thursdays).

109. Ibid., 7 November 1809; *CGDA,* 7 November 1809; *Courier,* 16 November 1809 and 21 November 1809.

110. *Courier,* 31 May 1813. This phrase appears in an advertisement for an exhibition of panoramic paintings at Concert Hall.

111. See 1814 plat in Charleston lot no. 40 Records, 1769–1833, 47/9, SCHS. All of these details are discussed in William Hasell Gibbes, Master in Equity, to William Grogan, Conveyance, 12 July 1814, RMC, P8:325–27. The adjoining lot to the south is the one John Sollée leased from the Union Kilwinning Lodge of Freemasons in May 1794, which was included in the purchase by Harriett Sollée in June 1816. The dimensions of Sollée's main structure, approximately 100 feet by 40 feet, are confirmed in *Courier,* 9 June 1825.

112. Union Kilwinning Lodge to William Grogan et al., trustees for Harriet Sollée, Lease and Release, 25–26 June 1816, RMC, P8:328–42. In this instrument Grogan is identified as both the seller and as the representative of Mrs. Sollée's family in England, suggesting that he had acted as her family's agent in the 1814 purchase.

113. RMC, P8:336.

114. *Courier,* 16 April 1813 and 29 September 1814.

115. The existence of a "New Upper Room" is first mentioned in an advertisement for Mr. Langdon's "Columbian Museum" in ibid., 20 December 1815.

116. *CGDA,* 26 October 1815; *Courier,* 26 October 1815. This announcement accompanies the program for the benefit concert of Virginia Bridon (also spelled *Breidon*), which was managed by John Rutledge, Joseph Manigault, Thomas Bee, George W. Cross,

and James Ferguson. The "certificate" testifying to the security of the venue was signed by Hume Greenhill, Walter Knox, Frederick Wesner, Jeremiah Shrewsbury, and John George Spidel.

117. *Courier*, 11 October 1816 and 28 October 1816.

118. Ibid., 8 May 1817.

119. Ibid., 4 November 1817.

120. Ibid., 21 November 1817 and 6 October 1819.

121. See the advertisement for Mrs. Giraud's concert and ball in ibid., 13 February 1823. Ibid., 27 April 1825, includes an advertisement for the second "exhibition" of "Songs, Recitations, and scenes from the most celebrated Tragedies" by Master Dixon at Concert Hall this evening.

122. See the notice of the auction on 13 June in ibid., 9 June 1825.

123. Ibid., 16 November 1816. There was one interesting exception to the relocation of the society's business meetings. Because of the popularity of the Carolina Coffee House as a meeting site, these events had to be scheduled well in advance. When the St. Cecilia Society called an extra meeting in December 1817 to discuss the absence of the theater musicians, therefore, it was forced to meet in an alternative venue. According to its advertisement in Ibid., 3 December 1817, the society was to meet on 8 December at the house of Sally Seymour. According to the city directories of this era, Seymour (d. 21 March 1823) was a free person of color who kept a pastry shop in Tradd Street.

124. Ibid., 8 October 1816 and 21 November 1817.

125. Ibid., 30 April 1819.

126. South Carolina Society, *Transactions of the South Carolina Society*, 16.

127. *Courier*, 3 May 1819.

128. In ibid., 3 August 1819, the property owner, Scottish merchant Adam Tunno, advertised that the "Carolina Coffee-Houses [note the use of the plural form] are for sale, lease, or to rent. Possession (with the Standing Furniture) will be given on the first of October next." Days later, in ibid., 9 August 1819, James Whitehurst asked his customers to pay their bills soon, "as his lease of that Establishment will terminate on the 30th of Sept." By October, R. Heriot was advertising that he had leased the coffeehouse (ibid., 4 October 1819 and 14 October 1819).

Chapter 7

1. Fraser, *Reminiscences*, 59.

2. Ibid.

3. Sadie, "Concert Life in Eighteenth Century England," 17.

4. Burchell, *Polite or Commercial*, 33.

5. Neal Zaslaw, "The Compleat Orchestral Musician," 57.

6. Fraser, *Reminiscences*, 59. Fraser's keyboard skills are mentioned in a letter from Charles Fraser, New Haven, Conn., to Ann Fraser, Charleston, S.C., 25 September 1806, Fraser-Winthrop Papers, on loan to the South Carolina Historical Society. See also Curtis, "Redating 'Sketches from Nature.'"

7. *SCG*, 19 March 1753 and 4–11 June 1754.

8. Ibid., 11–18 October 1760.

9. Milligen-Johnston, *Short Description*, 135.

10. *SCG*, 14–21 September 1765.

11. Ramsay, *History of South-Carolina*, 2:227.

12. *Courier*, 24 July 1805.

13. This fact does not confirm that they were musicians themselves, of course, as other members of the household could have used the instruments.

14. Zahniser, *Charles Cotesworth Pinckney*, 28, 66; Cross, "Letters of Thomas Pinckney," 146; "Money paid by James Glen Esq. on Acct of Mr. Drayton," [20 May 1762], James Glen Account Papers, South Caroliniana Library; Smith, Journals, 1781–82, William Loughton Smith Papers, SCHS, 11/476/5; Huff, *Langdon Cheves*, 44–45; Salley, "An All-Accomplished Man."

15. John Lenton (1657?–1719) is credited with composing a three-part catch titled "A Rebus to the Late H. Purcell's Name." This piece appears on the inside front cover of a manuscript music book produced in early-nineteenth-century Charleston. Here the title is paraphrased as "A Rebus on the name of the Late Henry Purcell, by John Lenton," and the text is somewhat altered from the original: "The Mate to a Cock, & Corn tall as Wheat, is his Christian name who in Musick's compleat. His Sir-name begins with a grace of a Cat, & concludes with the place a Hermit lives at." See Anonymous, "Instructions for the Kent Bugle," ca. 1813, SCHS, 34/124. Weber, *The Rise of Musical Classics*, 100, reproduces the original text and states that it was included in the 1760 edition of *The Catch Club, or Merry Companions*.

16. A perusal of the performers listed among the concert programs transcribed in Hindman, "Concert Life," demonstrates the validity of this statement.

17. *SCG*, 19 November 1772; *CGDA*, 5 September 1788; *Times*, 17 April 1806 and 13 April 1807; *Courier*, 10 March 1817, 3 May 1821, and 17 July 1823.

18. McVeigh, *Concert Life*, 86.

19. Milligen-Johnston, *Short Description*, 134; *SCG*, 21 January 1773; *SCAGG*, 21 February 1781; *RG*, 29 September–3 October 1781; *Times*, 13 April 1807; *Courier*, 26 March 1816. The managers for this 1816 event were Charles Fraser, Robert Bentham, and Thomas Parker Jr. It is not clear from the published program whether the vocal items were performed by the same person or by two separate lady amateurs.

20. McVeigh, *Concert Life*, 35.

21. Fraser, *Reminiscences*, 59.

22. See Daub, "Music at the Court of George II," 154–55; and Rohr, *The Careers of British Musicians*, 63–66.

23. See Pike's advertisements in *SCG*, 22–29 October 1764 and 14–21 September 1765.

24. L'Abbé is known to have given lessons on the citternlike English guitar (or "guittar"), but this is not an orchestral instrument. An advertisement for the sale of L'Abbé's personal property in *CGDA*, 23 February 1798, mentions "several Musical Instruments."

25. The names of such instrumental musicians include James McAlpine, Edward Wallace, John Speissegger, Frederick Hoff, Francisco Doracio, Mr. Blake, John Stevens, Jervis Henry Stevens, and Jacob Hood.

26. Little is known of the management of the dancing assemblies during the colonial era. The subscription dancing assemblies, such as the society's concerts, recommenced in the autumn of 1783. John Splatt Cripps is identified as the treasurer of the city's subscription dancing assemblies in *SCGGA*, 23–26 October 1784. A similar advertisement in *CH*, 9 November 1785, mentions that "the subscription list is lodged with the Treasurer, No.

87, Broad-street" (identified as Cripps's office in another advertisement in ibid., 23 January 1786). In *CH*, 2 November 1786, William Brailsford is named as the keeper of the subscription list (treasurer) of "the Dancing Assembly," as is James Miller in *CGDA*, 22 January 1789, and John Berney in *CGDA*, 21 December 1791. In *CGDA*, 11 October 1793, Thomas Simons, brother of a St. Cecilia Society officer, is named as treasurer of the "City Dancing Assembly." In *CGDA*, 23 October 1794, the treasurer of the "City Dancing Assembly" is identified as Thomas W. Bacot. Between January 1795 and November 1802 there is no information on the officers of these subscription assemblies. In an advertisement for "the Dancing Assemblies" in *Times*, 15 November 1802, the managers are given as William Allen Deas, Adam Tunno, Henry Izard, K. L. Simons, Dr. [William or Edward] Brailsford, and Charles Rutledge. In *Times*, 30 January 1804, the managers of "the Charleston Assemblies" are identified as Henry William deSaussure, E. Coffin, Charles Rutledge, Adam Tunno, and Benjamin Burgh Smith. In *Courier*, 12 December 1804, the managers of the "City Dancing Assemblies" are listed as H. W. deSaussure, Charles Rutledge, Adam Tunno, B. B. Smith, and P. G. Prioleau. In *Times*, 23 November 1805, the managers of the "Dancing Assemblies" are given as William Loughton Smith, Charles Rutledge, Adam Tunno, B. B. Smith, P. G. Prioleau, and John S. Bee. After this point, dancing assemblies began to proliferate and, after the War of 1812, individual dancing masters started having regular "cotillion parties" under their own management. I found no further evidence of an overlap between the management of the "city dancing assemblies" and that of the St. Cecilia Society after the 1805–6 season. While the management of these two organizations may have continued to overlap after 1806, no evidence to support this possiblity is found in the newspapers of the day.

27. Cobau, "Thomas Pike," 231–32.

28. This notice was repeated weekly in *SCAGG* through the issue of 1–8 July 1771; Sonneck, *Early Concert-Life*, 18.

29. Among the additional instrumental musicians known to have been active in Charleston after the 1771 advertisement are Ann Windsor, Shadrach Windsor, Robert Launce, John Mills, Philip Martunoz, James Juhan, George Christie, John William Beck, Louis Vidal, John Joseph Abercromby, Gaetano Franceschini, George Harland Hartley, and Peter Van Hagen.

30. Burchell, *Polite or Commercial*, 37.

31. Rogers, *Charleston*, 13–14; and Nash, "The Organization of Trade and Finance in the Atlantic Economy," 74–107.

32. Rohr, *The Careers of British Musicians*, 9.

33. Raven, *London Booksellers*, 91–92.

34. St. Philip's Church, vestry minutes, 6 March 1758 and 22 March 1758; Shaw, *The Succession of Organists*, 114.

35. St. Michael's Church, vestry minutes, 2 June 1768. Yarnold transferred to St. Michael's from St. Philip's on the arrival of Peter Valton in October 1764.

36. St. Michael's Church, vestry minutes, 31 December 1770. Thomas Loughton Smith was the son of Benjamin Smith, who, during his trips to London, had played an active part in recruiting Benjamin Yarnold and Peter Valton to Charleston.

37. Ibid., 24 December 1771, citing a letter from John Nutt.

38. Ibid., 31 December 1770. Butler, a major in the 29th Regiment of Foot, stationed in Boston, married Mary Middleton in Charleston in January 1771.

39. Ibid., 24 December 1771 and 28 December 1771.

40. Ibid., 22 June 1772, and copy of letter dated 20th July 1772. The text of the St. Cecilia Society's offer was not copied into the vestry minutes. Since the results of the society's annual elections were not published in November 1771, the identity of the society's president in the summer of 1772 is not known. Thomas Loughton Smith was named as vice president in the society's April 1771 recruitment advertisement, however, and he probably served as president during the 1771–72 season.

41. *SCG*, 21 January 1773. Barnwell, "George Harland Hartley's Claim for Losses as a Loyalist," 49, repeats a family tradition that Hartley was a native of the Orangeburg district of South Carolina. This claim, which has been repeated by other authors, is based on Hartley's 1787 self-identification as "a Native of America." The family lore cited by Barnwell is based on the flawed conflation of George Harland Hartley with one George Hartle, or Hartly, of Germanic descent in the rural Saxe Gotha area of colonial South Carolina. George Harland Hartley was more likely a native of Barbados. During the colonial era, the islands of the Caribbean were routinely included under the general geographical rubric "America."

42. The details of Abercromby's parentage were generously provided to me by Brenda Abercrombie Ledet. Abercromby's later connection to the Mitchell family of Charleston is described in Mitchell, *Mitchell Record*.

43. Quincy, "Journal," 441–42. English musician William Sampson Morgan arrived in Boston in late 1770 and advertised himself as a pupil of the Italian violinist Felice Giardini. William Turner Sr. was the impresario of Boston's Concert-Hall. John Turner was probably this man's son. See Colonial Society of Massachusetts, *Music in Colonial Massachusetts*, 2:1094–95.

44. *SCG*, 28 March 1774.

45. Gaetano Franceschini, *Opera 1*, performed by the Accademia della Magnifica Comunità, liner notes by Francesco Passadore.

46. *SCG*, 31 January 1774 and 28 March 1774.

47. This conclusion is strengthened by the fact that Douglass leased the property for this theater from the Union Kilwinning Lodge of Freemasons. See Curtis, "Charles-Town's Church Street Theater," 149–54. As mentioned in chapter 2, there was a great deal of overlap in the membership of the Union Kilwinning Lodge and the St. Cecilia Society.

48. *SCAGG*, 28 October–4 November 1774. Van Hagen's advertisement also appeared in *SCG*, 31 October 1774, and *SCGCJ*, 1 November 1774, with slightly different wording. According to Burney, *The Present State of Music in Germany, The Netherlands, and United Provinces*, 2:314–15, Van Hagen's father was a talented German organist and violinist working in Rotterdam. Burney also mentions a daughter, the sister of the Charleston immigrant, who was a fine singer. Sonneck, *Early Concert-Life*, 23, suggests that "Signora Castella" was the professional name of Peter Van Hagen's sister. Since Italian singers commanded the most attention and premium wages in eighteenth-century England, it was not unheard of for female vocalists in London to use Italian names for professional purposes.

49. *SCAGG*, 14–21 October 1774; *SCG*, 24 October 1774.

50. The estimate of twenty musicians in the orchestra is based on the similarities between Quincy's observation and that made by a German officer stationed in Charleston in 1782, described below.

51. Quincy, "Journal," 451.

52. At the event Quincy attended, reviewed in *SCG*, 22 March 1773, the following men were elected officers of that club: Thomas Knox Gordon, president; James Carson, vice president; Thomas Phepoe, treasurer and secretary; Macartan Campbell and Edward Rutledge, stewards. Newspaper notices of the activities of the Sons of St. Patrick in subsequent years further demonstrate that its membership overlapped with that of the St. Cecilia Society.

53. Sadie, "Concert Life in Eighteenth Century England," 29.

54. Burchell, *Polite or Commercial*, 36–37, 43, 103–4,197–98. Zaslaw, "Toward the Revival," 171–78, presents a table comparing the size of many European orchestras, 1774–1796.

55. *SCAGG*, 21–28 April 1775.

56. See *SCGCJ*, 26 July 1774; *SCG*, 25 July 1774; *SCAGG*, 23–30 September 1774, 14–21 October 1774, and 9–16 December 1774.

57. *The Papers of Henry Laurens*, 11:259.

58. Personal correspondence with several descendants of the Juhan family, autumn 2001.

59. It is likely the two performers advertised their imminent departure in late 1775 in newspapers now lost. Years later Van Hagen reappeared in Boston, where he enjoyed an active career.

60. According to St. Michael's Church, vestry minutes, 13 April 1776, all agents of the church were required to take an oath of allegiance to the state of South Carolina—just two weeks after the state had proclaimed its sovereignty in a new constitution. Hartley's refusal to take the oath and his dismal are recorded in the vestry minutes of 16 July 1776. He lingered in Charleston until August 1777.

61. According to the genealogical research of Brenda Abercrombie Ledet, Abercromby sailed for Europe soon after his marriage in January 1777. He returned to Charleston in July 1779 with the coat of arms he had registered at Edinburgh on 10 August 1778 that named his ancestors. John Joseph's father, Alexander Abercromby, Esquire, was apparently not the Alexander Abercrombie, Esquire, listed among the 1775 members of Edinburgh Musical Society in Fraser Harris, *St. Cecilia's Hall*, 291.

62. Levett, "Loyalism in Charleston."

63. See Simons, "Regimental Book of Captain James Bentham," 15, 230–31; and Moss, *Roster of South Carolina Patriots*, 547.

64. *SCAGG*, 19 November 1779, carried an advertisement seeking wagon drivers for Continental Service, signed "Andrew Rutledge, Deputy Wagon Master General." There were several men with this name in colonial South Carolina, but the dancing master and musician (apparently not related to the others) is the most likely candidate for this position. Andrew Rutledge, speaker of the Commons House of Assembly, died in 1755. His nephew of the same name lived 1740–1772. *RG*, 7–10 November 1781, mentions the death of one Andrew Rutledge, but gives no further details. According to the register of St. Philip's Church, Charleston, however, "Andrew Rutledge, dancing master," was buried on 31 October 1781. See Webber, "Dr. John Rutledge and His Decedents," 7.

65. *GSSC*, 8 July 1778; *SCAGG*, 7 February 1781; Palmer, *Biographical Sketches of the Loyalists*, 611.

66. Cobau, "Thomas Pike," 252.

67. *RSCG,* 10 May 1781; *RG,* 9–12 May 1781.

68. The first concert of this season took place on 8 October 1781. The final performance was Franceschini's benefit on 24 May 1782.

69. Sonneck, "A Contemporary Account of Music in Charleston, S.C., of the Year 1783," 96, 98. In this article Sonneck presents his translation of an anonymous letter titled "On Music in America principally at Charleston in South Carolina, in the years 1776 to 1783." This letter, dated 20 December 1783, is included in the first volume of *Musikalische Bibliothek,* published in 1784, under the heading *Auszüge von Briefen* on pp. 113–16. Coincidentally the program for Franceschini's benefit concert on 24 May 1782 states that one Mr. Smith would perform an oboe concerto by Fischer. See *RG,* 18–22 May 1782.

70. Franceschini advertised a concert in the *Royal Gazette* (New York), 31 May 1783. Palmer, *Biographical Sketches of the Loyalists,* 611, states that John Mills departed with the British in December 1782. Jacob Hood, whose gravestone is at St. John's Lutheran Church in Charleston, died on 20 October 1782, aged thirty-seven years.

71. Schoepf, *Travels in the Confederation,* 2:164. No public or benefit concerts were advertised during Schoepf's visit. Evidence suggests, however, that the unpublicized fortnightly concerts of the St. Cecilia Society continued throughout this period. See appendix 1.

72. For a brief discussion of this phenomenon in other American cities, see Porter, *With an Air Debonair,* 5–9.

73. The history of theater in Charleston during the 1780s is included in Curtis, "The Early Charleston Stage," 117–65.

74. Valton's obituary appears in *SCWG,* 13 February 1784.

75. Williams, "Early Organists at St. Philip's," 87, says Stevens was organist of St. Philip's "by 1785" until his retirement in 1815. St. Philip's vestry minutes for late April 1784 until late March 1785 are missing, so we cannot know the details of his appointment.

76. *CGDA,* 11 January 1798.

77. Abercromby appears to have departed Charleston by January 1791, when he remarried and moved northward. According to a notice in ibid., 6 September 1792, Abercromby had assigned all his property to a lawyer, Daniel deSaussure, for the benefit of his creditors. His subsequent performances in Charleston, in the summer of 1802 and again in the summer of 1804, were isolated visits. In *Times,* 23 June 1804, for example, Abercromby advertised himself as "having just arrived."

78. St. Michael's Church, vestry minutes, 16 January 1784. Yarnold's return is noted in *SCGPA,* 25–29 December 1784. Little is known of Yarnold's activities during his absence from Charleston. Dawe, *Organists of the City of London,* 22 and 159, mentions one Yarnold as an unsuccessful candidate for the position of organist at London's All Hallow's Barking by the Tower in 1770.

79. St. Michael's Church, vestry minutes, 3 December 1787. William Yarnold was in Charleston for at least a decade after his father's death. In Young, *Palladium of Knowledge,* [34], William Yarnold is listed as "assistant" at the Bank of South Carolina. He later appears as a music teacher in Boston in 1811–12. See Johnson, *Musical Interludes in Boston,* 292–94.

80. See Howard, *Our American Music,* 106; Keefer, *Baltimore's Music,* 31. Brown's first Charleston concert, on 29 April 1784, was announced in *SCGPA,* 17–21 April 1784 and 21–24 April 1784.

81. Howard, *Our American Music,* 106.

82. Lafar first advertised in Charleston in *SCAGG,* 13 March 1777. In 1784 he was elected a constable of the South Carolina Society (see *SCGGA,* 10–13 April 1784). No further mention of his music shop has been found beyond its initial advertisement in *SCGPA,* 17 November 1785.

83. See *CMPDA,* 13 November 1786. How the series fared is not clear, as no further advertisements appeared after December 1786.

84. Lafar's benefit was on 14 February 1786 (see *CH,* 30 January 1786). He advertised nonmusical business in ibid., 7 June 1787, and was named as a "Grand Steward" of a Masonic feast in *CGDA,* 22 November 1787.

85. See *CGDA,* 12 March 1791 and 16 March 1791.

86. Ibid., 10 June 1791.

87. Lafar's obituary appears in ibid., 12 February 1795. The advertisement for the posthumous benefit concert, in ibid., 6 March 1797, lists a number of the performers, all of whom are known to have performed at the St. Cecilia concerts: Messrs. Petit, Foucard, Daguetty, Brunet, Villars, DeVillers, Lecat, Eckhard, West, and Mrs. Placide, "&c. &c." Tickets for the concert were available at the post office, operated by long-time officer of the society, Thomas Wright Bacot.

88. Bradford's first advertisement, in ibid., 1 February 1788, offers repair of and instruction on "violin, tenor [viola], violincello, guittar, harpsichord, &c." His last known advertisement appears in ibid., 10 September 1802. In *Times,* 7 February 1804, his wife was advertising as the proprietor of his music store. In a *Times* report of the death of William Bradford in London in February 1807, his father is described as "the late Mr. Thomas Bradford, of this city" (see ibid., 15 April 1807). Mrs. Bradford advertised their music store as late as 1810, and Thomas Bradford Jr. advertised his own music store in Charleston in 1812.

89. St. Michael's Church, vestry minutes, 13 May 1783.

90. *SCGPA,* 7–11 May 1785.

91. See the advertisements for Alexander Juhan's benefits in *CH,* 1 October 1787, and *CGDA,* 13 May 1788. One William Franco, "Lately arrived from Europe," advertised in *SGSC,* 22 August 1785, as a flute teacher.

92. See Milligan, *The Charleston Directory, and Revenue System,* published in 1790. Cumin and also appears in the 1790 federal census as a resident of urban Charleston.

93. *CH,* 24 March 1785.

94. See appendix 1 for a calendar of these performances.

95. *SGSC,* 9 May 1785 and 16 May 1785.

96. *CH,* 17 June 1785 and 20 June 1785.

97. *SGSC,* 23 June 1785; *SCGPA,* 22–25 June 1785; St. Michael's Church, vestry minutes, 29 June 1785.

98. Warfel, *Noah Webster,* 123. Webster landed in Charleston on Sunday, 26 June 1785, and went to three churches that day: St. Michael's, the Independent Congregational Church, and the Methodist Church. After Storer's performance, Webster went to the "White Church" (the Independent Church) and heard New England–style psalm singing, of which he approved. After leaving Charleston a few days later, Webster went to Baltimore, where he lingered long enough to teach classes in sacred vocal music.

99. *SGSC,* 30 June 1785.

100. Storer's known appearances at St. Cecilia concerts follow a pattern of two-week intervals, suggesting that unadvertised concerts took place at regular intervals throughout the summer of 1785. See appendix 1 for more details.

101. *CEG*, 28 January 1786.

102. *SGSC*, 23 June 1785; *CEG*, 12 August 1785. The likelihood that Capron's stay in Charleston was influenced by an engagement with the St. Cecilia Society is increased by the fact there was no theatrical company in town at that time. Godwin's Harmony Hall did not open until the summer of 1786, by which time Capron may have been on his way back to Philadelphia.

103. *CH*, 22 August 1785, 2 January 1786, and 23 February 1786.

104. Capron returned to Philadelphia by the fall of 1786, for at that time he was comanaging a concert series with Alexander Juhan, Alexander Reinagle, and William Brown. See Howard, *Our American Music*, 76, and Krauss, "Alexander Reinagle," 237–38.

105. See, for example, Maurer, "The 'Professor of Musick' in Colonial America," 511–24; and Crawford, *Andrew Law*, xv.

106. The exact date of his return to Charleston is not known. Gerson, *Music in Philadelphia*, 38–39, states that George Washington attended Juhan's a benefit concert in Philadelphia on 29 May 1787. Juhan's first Charleston concert advertisement appeared in *CH*, 1 October 1787.

107. *CMPDA*, 6 July 1786, includes a long report of a "grand Concert of vocal and instrumental Music" in Philadelphia on 4 May 1786.

108. Juhan had benefit concerts on 11 October 1787 (see *CH*, 1 October 1787) and on 15 May 1788 (*CGDA*, 13 May 1788). He sold tickets for the Amateur Society's charity concert on 20 October 1791 (*CGDA*, 11 October 1791). In June 1792 he advertised "Proposals, For publishing by subscription, a set of Six Sonatas, for the Piano-Forte or Harpsichord; and a book of Twelve Songs, with an accompaniment for the same instrument, composed by Alexander Juhan" (*CGDA*, 12 June 1792). The first three of these sonatas were advertised for sale in ibid., 25 January 1793. The first six songs were advertised for sale in *CGDA*, 11 August 1794. No further advertisements for the remaining sonatas and songs have been found. Juhan was in Charleston at least as late as 1798, when he assisted in the settlement of the estate of Israel Bourdeaux (*CGDA*, 23 February 1798).

109. Juhan's marriage to Eliza Bourdeaux is noted in *CGDA*, 2 March 1792. The earliest newspaper advertisement placing Juhan outside Charleston appears in early 1804, when he was advertising as the executor of the estate of Nathaniel Bourdeaux (ibid., 10 February 1804).

110. These quotations and biographical data are taken from the tribute to Eckhard written by Martin Strobel, secretary of the German Friendly Society, and published in *Courier*, 15 November 1833.

111. The "requisition" could be a reference to Eckhard's 1809 move from organist of St. John's Lutheran Church to that of St. Michael's Episcopal Church. The fact that this move is explicitly addressed later in the tribute, however, suggests that the author is here referring to an earlier "requisition" of Eckhard's services. Although Eckhard never received a benefit concert in Charleston, he participated in nearly every benefit and charity concert presented in the city after his arrival, including those sponsored by the St. Cecilia Society. Furthermore he was for many years the conductor of musical celebrations of the anniversary of the 1794 opening of the Charleston Orphan House—a

civic institution governed by the city's elite gentlemen, many of whom also served as officers of the society.

112. Considering that his predecessor and successor as organist at St. Michael's were involved in the St. Cecilia concerts and that the rector and vestry of the church were members of the society, it seems likely that Rodgers was included in the society's concerts. In March 1800 Rodgers was also listed as a ticket seller for a charity concert for one Mr. Salter, which was performed "with the assistance of the performers of the St. Cecilia Society" (*CGDA*, 1 March 1800).

113. Henry Purcell, Charleston, S.C., to Samuel Rogers [*sic*], Montego Bay, Jamaica, 4 February 1789, St. Michael's Church Records, SCHS. Another letter dated Windsor, England, 14 September 1788, advised Rodgers to write to John F. Grimké and Henry Purcell in Charleston offering himself as organist for St. Michael's. The author of this letter, whose signature has unfortunately been torn or cut away, reminded Rodgers that "he may mention his having been formerly recommended by Dr. Cooke, who if written to on the Subject will be ready to confirm it." See anonymous, Windsor, England, to Samuel Rodgers, 14 September 1788, St. Michael's Church Records, SCHS.

114. Rodgers announced his willingness to teach these instruments in *CGDA*, 4 June 1789. For an example of Rodgers's piano imports, see ibid., 19 May 1800.

115. These biographical details of Poitiaux were generously provided to me by one of his descendant, Janet Tennent of Kensington, Maryland.

116. *CGDA*, 28 September 1792.

Chapter 8

1. Cooper, *Statutes at Large*, 5:195.

2. *CGDA*, 31 May 1792.

3. Fraser, *Reminiscences*, 26.

4. See *CGDA*, 17 July 1792, 1 August 1792, and 1, 4, and 9 January 1793.

5. Entr'acte music is mentioned in a card inserted in ibid., 22 March 1793.

6. The source for this information, ibid., 10 April 1794, is discussed below.

7. Other proprietors continued Vauxhall Garden for several seasons after Placide's death, but its activity was severely curtailed.

8. The overlap between the orchestra of the Charleston Theatre and that of the St. Cecilia Society is demonstrated in several ways, the most significant of which is the number of newspaper advertisements for concerts during this era. With very few exceptions, the advertisements for the St. Cecilia Society's regular concerts do not include the names of performers. Benefit concerts performed by vocal and instrumental musicians under the aegis of the local theater or Placide's Vauxhall Garden commonly named at least some of the players, as did advertisements for benefit and charity concerts sponsored by the St. Cecilia Society. An examination of these advertisements, too numerous to cite here, reveals there was little or no difference in the professional performing forces of the theater and the St. Cecilia Society's concerts. Taking into consideration the degree to which the personnel of these various events overlapped, therefore, any professional musician performing in Charleston between 1766 and 1820 may be counted as a candidate for having participated in the St. Cecilia concerts. Readers without easy access to the concert advertisements in Charleston newspapers of the years 1793–1820 can consider the concerts described in Sonneck, *Early Concert-Life*, 28–40, and Hindman, "Concert

Life," 289–391. While the data contained in these secondary sources is not complete, they provide more than enough evidence to support this point.

9. See Burchell, *Polite or Commercial,* 38, 55, 57; and Rohr, *The Careers of British Musicians,* 119–29. During the period under examination, there were several ephemeral Charleston musical organizations about which little or nothing is known: the Anacreontic Society, the Harmonic Society, and the Amateur Society, for example. More substantial data can be gleaned about the Philharmonic Society and the Union Harmonic Society.

10. The phrase "gentlemen of the Orchestra" appears in *CGDA,* 8 January 1802, but this advertisement specifically names only Mr. Story and "Signor Trajetta." The microfilmed copy of this paper has the name "Mr. Muck" (musician Philip Muck) written over the program for this concert, indicating that Muck had either brought the advertisement to the newspaper's office or had paid for its insertion. Muck was almost certainly part of that orchestra. The reference to the performance of Leaumont's "Grand Overture" at the St. Cecilia Society's anniversary concert appears in *Times,* 9 January 1802, and *CGDA,* 11 January 1802.

11. *CGDA,* 2 September 1805. The program is reproduced in Hindman, "Concert Life," 331.

12. See *Courier,* 21 March 1807 and 23 March 1807; and *Times,* 23 March 1807.

13. The obituary for French refugee musician Joseph Brunet (*Times,* 5 September 1808) states "The Orchestra of Charleston performed an elegant *Requiem* to his departed shade."

14. The veracity of this statement is demonstrated by the regular newspaper advertisements of Charleston's theatrical performances during the period in question. For a more expedient demonstration of this point, however, compare appendix 1 with the calendar of performances at Charleston's theaters in the 1790s in Willis, *The Charleston Stage.*

15. For information on theater management in Charleston between 1794 and 1825, see Sodders, "The Theatre Management of Alexandre Placide"; Stephenson, "The Charleston Theatre Management of Joseph George Holman" and "The Charleston Theatre Management of Charles Gilfert."

16. The subscribers to the loan to build the Charleston Theatre were the city's elite businessmen. These shareholders elected officers and received dividends from the profits of the theater. It is not surprising, then, that the list of theater shareholders overlapped with the membership and even the officers of the St. Cecilia Society. John Cripps, for example, served as secretary of both the society and of the proprietors of the theater. Stephenson, "Charles Gilfert," 44, mentions that one Stephen Cogdell held title to shares in the Charleston Theatre around 1814. This was actually John Stevens Cogdell, a manager of the St. Cecilia Society. The "Act to Incorporate the Proprietors of the Charleston Theatre," which was passed by the South Carolina legislature on 17 December 1817, named the following men: William Read, John Bay, William James Ladson, James Gilchrist, John B. Holmes, Abraham Motte, William Wightman, Thomas R. Smith, Timothy Ford, Robert Hazlehurst, William Broadfoot, John S. Cogdell, E. Mortemer, E. Blake, F. C. Mey, Adam Tunno, John Gordon, "and others" (see McCord, *Statutes at Large,* 8:288–90). The prosperous merchant Thomas Cochran not only served as an officer of the St. Cecilia Society and the theater's shareholders, he also imported pianos and was a close friend of theater manager Charles Gilfert. When Mr. Nicola (also spelled *Nicholas, Nicolai,* etc.), the leader of the Charleston Theatre's orchestra under Gilfert's

management, advertised to teach music in 1826, he directed prospective pupils to inquire "at the office of Mr. [Thomas] Cochran," who was then president of the theater's directors (see *Courier*, 22 February 1826).

17. In a provocative statement that may have been as true in Charleston as it was in Edinburgh, Burchell, *Polite or Commercial*, 57, states that "In some respects the theatre and assemblies seems to have acted as a training ground for the [Edinburgh] Musical Society."

18. Since no financial records for either institution have survived, it is not possible to determine the extent to which the personnel of these orchestras overlapped. Furthermore, in the absence of sufficiently accurate and detailed examinations of the professional musical communities in other American cities such as New York, Boston, Philadelphia, and Baltimore during the late eighteenth and early nineteenth centuries, it is not possible, at least at the present time, to identify positively some of these musicians and to determine the length of their tenure in Charleston.

19. Janson, *The Stranger in America*, table of contents.

20. Ibid., 254.

21. Mary Anne Pownall died on 11 August (see *CGDA*, 13 August 1796), and her daughter Mary Wrighten died on 24 August (see ibid., 25 August 1796). John Patterson, a theatrical dancer who "possessed considerable talents as a musical performer on wind instruments," died on 11 July at the age of thirty-two (see ibid., 13 July 1796). Had Benedict Bergman not died in Charleston that summer, he may have become a significant figure in the history of early American theater music. Since his death has not been reported in any other source, I include the entire obituary here: ibid., 27 July 1796 (Wednesday): "Died, last Monday morning, in the bloom of youth, Mr. *Benedicte Bergman*, age 26 years, Leader of the Orchestra in the Church-street theatre—a young gentleman whose abilities in the musical line were extensive. His death is much regretted by Amateurs, and his acquaintances in general. His remains were interred in St. Philip's church yard, attended by a few friends." Despite these losses, it should be noted that Graupner returned to Charleston in 1817. "Mr. Graupner, lately from Boston" performed a "Solo on the Oboe" at the benefit concert of theatrical singer Mrs. Waring. This concert, which took place at Concert Hall on Tuesday, 8 April 1817, was managed by H. B. Toomer, Thomas Parker Jr., James Rose, and John Rutledge Jr. Thus it was probably connected to the St. Cecilia Society to some extent. See *Courier*, 5 April 1817.

22. *CGDA*, 23 October 1805 and 13 August 1807. The "Theatre Picturesque and Mechanique" was held at Peter Fayolle's long room.

23. William Ogilby, Diary, 1830, SCHS, entry for 10 June 1830.

24. *CGDA*, 4 April 1793 (Thursday). In a performance of *The Beggar's Opera* the following week, Mr. Chambers sang the role of Macheath, while Mrs. Decker was Polly Peachum. See ibid., 13 April 1793.

25. Eliza Poe sang William Shield's "Whilst with village maids I stray" and James Hook's "When ruddy Aurora" at LeFolle's benefit (see *Courier*, 21 March 1811). Many other theatrical singers probably appeared at the regular concerts of the St. Cecilia Society. Evidence to support this assertion is drawn from those singers named in the advertisements for benefit concerts of other musicians known to have been affiliated with the society. Candidates include Mrs. Pick, Miss Mary Wrighten, Mrs. Pownall, Mrs. Chambers, Mrs. Marshall, Mr. West, Mr. Story, Mr. Sully, Mrs. French, and others.

26. *CGDA*, 12 November 1801. Broadhurst is mentioned in several studies of early American musical theater, but her first name, age, and untimely death less than a year

after this performance with the St. Cecilia Society have eluded scholars focusing on the northern theaters. Janson, *The Stranger in America*, 254, notes her death, but is mistaken about her tenure in Charleston. Her obituary is therefore offered in full: *CGDA*, 2 October 1802: "Died, yesterday morning, at 10 o'clock, Miss Dorothea Broadhurst, late of Philadelphia, aged 25 years. During life this young lady bore the most exalted character for upright behaviour and filial affection; by her own merit and abilities she has supported her mother since she was fourteen years of age, who is left to lament the loss of this most amiable and dutiful child. Her friends and acquaintances are invited to attend her funeral at her late dwelling in King-street, this morning at 10 o'clock." Miss Broadhurst was buried in the western cemetery of St. Philip's Church, where her gravestone states that she died at the age of twenty-eight years and six months and was a native of St. Mary Newington, Surrey, England. Broadhurst's untimely death was observed with great regret, and her mother was "induced" by "a number of respectable Ladies and Gentlemen" to present a subscription concert to help support herself. The concert was announced in *CGDA*, 5 February 1803: "*To the Friends of departed Merit.* Mrs. Broadhurst, (Mother of the late Miss Broadhurst, of the Theatre, who last summer fell a martyr to that dreadful fever which proves so fatal to strangers)," and took place on 19 February 1803.

27. *CGDA*, 24 November 1801 and 21 November 1803.

28. Charlotte Wrighten Placide and her sister Mary Wrighten were daughters of the renowned English theatrical singer Mrs. Pownall. These three women arrived in Charleston in the autumn of 1795. Charlotte Wrighten married Alexander Placide shortly before the deaths of Mrs. Pownall and Mary Wrighten in August 1796.

29. See *Courier*, 5 February 1813 and 8 February 1813; *CGDA*, 9 February 1813; and *Courier*, 16 February 1813. By April 1816 the widow Placide had settled in Philadelphia and married the violinist Jean-Claude LeFolle (see *CGDA*, 26 April 1816).

30. *Courier*, 2 October 1805. At least one of Hodgkinson's daughters was also known to the city's theatrical audiences. In ibid., 29 February 1804, "Thespis, No. XLIII," described John Hodgkinson's recent benefit at the Charleston Theatre: "The wonderful little sprite Miss Hodgkinson, was promised to the audience in one dance. . . . The enjoyment of the audience was not a little heightened by the anxiety displayed by her master, Mr. *Fayal* [dancing master Peter Fayolle], who stood playing the violin in the orchestra and expressed his enthusiastic admiration of his little scholar by motions so animated and expressive as to strike all the beholders."

31. Ibid., 10 October 1805. In ibid., 19 October 1805, the following sentence was inserted in the middle of this advertisement: "The Concert will conclude as usual, with Dancing."

32. Ibid., 16 October 1805; *CGDA*, 23 October 1805 and 29 October 1805.

33. *CGDA*, 29 October 1805. A similar story appears in *Courier*, 29 October 1805.

34. This anonymous promotional letter appeared in both the *Courier*, 29 October 1805, and *CGDA*, 29 October 1805.

35. *Courier*, 1 November 1805 (Friday). The precise identity of Mrs. Sully is unclear. See Biddle and Fielding, *The Life and Works of Thomas Sully*, 2.

36. *Times*, 6 November 1805 and 7 November 1805. The French musicians listed here will be described below. Like his father, Jacob Eckhard Jr. (1787–1832) was a professional musician. Philip Muck (d. 1824) was a German-born performer on violin, horn, and

trumpet who arrived in Charleston from northern theaters in 1799. William Stone (ca. 1756–1823) was a native of Massachusetts but a member of the orchestra of the Charleston Theatre for many years after his arrival ca. 1800. James Tomlins arrived in Charleston from London in the spring of 1804, but the date of his departure is not known.

37. *Courier,* 27 November 1805. Considering the ticket price of two dollars, the receipts from this benefit concert demonstrate that more than two hundred and fifty tickets were sold. The expenses for the concert presumably did not include the musicians' fees, as they had ostensibly volunteered for the occasion. The amount of the expenses is almost identical to that which the society paid to John Sollée in 1813 for each night it used Concert Hall (see chapter 6).

38. *Times,* 19 December 1805 (Thursday evening).

39. Fraser, *Reminiscences,* 39; Kennedy, "A French Jacobin Club in Charleston," 4–22.

40. Ott, *The Haitian Revolution,* 71.

41. *CGDA,* 20 September 1793, citing extracts from a letter dated Norfolk, Virginia, 30 August 1793.

42. Petit, Le Roy, Foucard, and Villars first advertised their benefit concert in *CGDA,* 12 December 1793. The program, first published in ibid., 14 December 1793, and reproduced in Sonneck, *Early Concert-Life,* 29, mentions a musician named "Poition." I am confident that the intended musician was M. B. Poitiaux, who participated with these same musicians in later events. This concert was performed on 17 December 1793. These same musicians, with the addition of Duport, "aged 13 years," was first advertised in *CGDA,* 1 January 1794, and performed on 9 January 1794.

43. *CGDA,* 16 July 1793. Ibid., 13 July 1793, includes a letter by St. Domingan planter James Delaire expressing gratitude to the Benevolent Society. He names Edward Penman, a St. Cecilia Society manager in the summer of 1793, as the "original proposer of the benefaction."

44. *CGDA,* 17 July 1793, lists the men collecting money for the Benevolent Society as Nathaniel Russell, Edward Penman, Joseph Vesey, Tucker Harris, James Gregory, Thomas Gaillard, John J. Pringle, Archibald Broun, Daniel deSaussure, Adam Tunno, Edward Rutledge, Edward Darrell, David Ramsay, Henry William deSaussure. The intendant (mayor), John Huger, was named as the chairman of the society.

45. *CGDA,* 19 August 1793.

46. See ibid., 25 February 1794 and 6 March 1794. The managers were probably not seated on the stage, but rather appeared on the stage occasionally during the concert to assist with logistical matters.

47. In his diary actor William Dunlap recorded his dealings with John Sollée in New York and Boston during the summer of 1797 and 1798. See Dunlap, *Diary of William Dunlap,* 1:107–328. Sollée's recruitment efforts are summarized in Curtis, "John Joseph Stephen Leger Sollée and the Charleston Theatre," 285–95.

48. *CGDA,* 10 April 1794. This letter is reproduced in its entirety in Willis, *The Charleston Stage,* 210–11.

49. *CGDA,* 9 April 1795 and 22 October 1795. Unlike Placide, who operated his Vauxhall Garden during the summer months from 1799 through 1812, Cornet presided over a year-round, indoor Vauxhall during 1795–96. The overlap between the orchestras of Cornet's Vauxhall, the French Theatre, and the St. Cecilia Society is demonstrated by schedule adjustments seen in extant newspaper advertisements. On the commencement

of the theatrical season in December 1795, Cornet's French musicians were pre-engaged at the City Theatre (formerly the French Theatre), and he was forced to give notice that "on account of the Comedians having changed their days of Representations," his Vauxhall entertainments would "in future take Place on Thursday Evening, of each week" (ibid., 17 December 1795). Cornet's performances continued on Thursday evenings through December, but once the St. Cecilia concerts recommenced in early January the schedule for the masked balls at his Vauxhall was again altered: for the subsequent duration of his establishment, which he continued to advertise through March 1796, Cornet's masked balls were held on Tuesday evenings during weeks in which a St. Cecilia concert was performed and on Thursday evenings in alternate weeks.

50. Ibid., 18 April 1796 and 2 July 1796. Unfortunately only four instrumentalists are identified in the advertisements for this festival: violinist Benedict Bergman (who performed a "solo"), violinist M. B. Poitiaux, Remy Victor Petit (identified as "leader of the concert"), and Louis DeVillers (identified as "organist").

51. This agreement was announced in ibid., 29 March 1800.

52. This concert was first announced in ibid., 28 December 1803. The named managers distributing the $5 (roughly $86 in 2005) tickets were Don Diego Morphy, Thomas Miller, Constant Boisgerard, and George Jouve. The next day the concert was postponed to 30 December, on account of the weather. Another concert, advertised in ibid., 4 January 1804, as a follow-up to that on 30 December also stated "the St. Cecilia Society's rules and decorum strictly observed." This concert was scheduled for 9 January, but later postponed to 17 January. *Times,* 11 January 1804, stated "The Vocal parts will be performed by two Young Ladies and by Signor Trajetta; and the instrumental parts by professors and many amateurs." The men who "cheerfully agreed to undertake the functions of managers" were Benjamin [Burgh] Smith, William S. Hasell, and John Stocks.

53. *CGDA,* 5 March 1804; ibid., 31 March 1804, citing extracts from the minutes of a meeting of City Council held on 20 March 1804. The French priest Rev. Le Mercier, secretary of the "Committee of Benevolence," apparently instigated the formation of this special "committee of subsistence." The City Council committee included Nathaniel Ingraham, George Chisolm, and John McCall Ward. The other men requested to assist in the distribution were Henry William deSaussure (then president of the St. Cecilia Society), Nathaniel Russell, John Parker, John Splatt Cripps, and Gabriel Manigault. This source does not identify these last-named men as representatives of the St. Cecilia Society, but they are acknowledged members of the society nonetheless.

54. *Courier,* 15 November 1804. That the *Courier's* correspondent was speaking of the ensemble and not the physical placement of the musicians is clarified in the continuation of the thought: The "enlargement . . . indicated an improvement in the Music, which was much wanting, the band having been last season [1803–4] extremely deficient; and gave promise of operas which by diversifying the performances will afford more amusement and satisfaction to the public."

55. This concert was first announced in *Times,* 5 January 1805, as a "Grand Concert of Vocal and Instrumental Music, for the benefit of the Gentlemen, Composing the Ochestra [*sic*], at the St. Cecilia Society's Concerts." A note published in *Times,* 7 January 1805, however, states that this announcement had been in error, and that the concert was in fact for "the benefit of the late sufferers from St. Domingo." The newspaper's confusion over the beneficiaries of the concert is easily understandable, however, because

the society's orchestra was at that time largely composed of refugees from St. Domingo. Besides the orchestra, the soloists for this concerts included Mrs. Sully on piano, "two Ladies" on harp and piano, and songs by Antoinette La Roque, John Hodgkinson, and "a Lady." The program for this concert, given on the day of performance in *CGDA*, 26 February 1805, is reproduced in Hindman, "Concert Life," 326.

56. *CGDA*, 13 February 1805 and 14 February 1805.

57. Ibid., 2 March 1805. The approximate number of guest is derived from the stated net proceeds. More than 320 tickets at $5 each must have been sold to achieve a net balance "upwards" of $1,600. Each ticket, according to ibid., 14 February 1805, admitted one gentleman "who can introduce as many Ladies as he may please." Calculating that each of the more than 320 ticket holders brought between one and three ladies (a normal range at the time), we arrive at a total in the neighborhood of 1,000.

58. Ibid., 26 July 1799: "*Remy Victor Petit*, master of music in the Concert of St. Cecilia, died on the 23d inst. after a long and painful illness. His rare talents, which have been displayed in the different countries of the continent, had acquired him the esteem and particular friendship of all who knew him; he has left them inconsolable for their loss."

59. Philip Villars is listed in the Charleston city directory as late as 1801 as a musician living in Church Street. See Nelson, *Nelson's Charleston Directory*. The 1807 directory lists a "Villers, Mrs." at 52 Queen Street. See Negrin, *Negrin's Directory for the Year 1807*. This was probably his widow, though no obituary has been found.

60. Foucard's obituary appeared in *Courier*, 3 March 1818.

61. *CGDA*, 25 September 1807: "Died on the 9th inst., Mr. J. B. Dacquety, one of the first [i.e., best] performers on the Violin, in South Carolina." *Times*, 25 September 1807, spelled his name "Bacquetty," while the *Courier*, 26 September 1807, spelled it "Dacquete," probably implying *Dacqueté*. The details of his identity have not yet been established.

62. DeVillers (also spelled *De Villers* and *Devilliers*) first appeared on the program for Mr. Le Roy's benefit concert on 17 December 1795. (The program for this event is given in Sonneck, *Early Concert-Life*, 32.) He began advertising music retail sales in 1799 and continued through the late 1820s.

63. Noel performed a concerto by Viotti on John Joseph Abercromby's benefit concert on 10 June 1802. Noel's death was briefly noted in *Times*, 10 November 1808.

64. See *Courier*, 3 April 1805; and his obituary in *CGDA*, 10 August 1814. According to Lesure, *Catalogue de la musique imprimée avant 1800*, 374, Robert de Leaumont published *Duo concertant pour le clavecin ou le forte-piano et violincelle* in Paris in 1786.

65. See the obituary for Arnold Remoussin in *SPCA*, 9 August 1820. There were at least two other Remoussin sons in Charleston, Henri and Pluton, about whom little is known.

66. *Courier*, 10 March 1809.

67. Holcomb, *South Carolina Naturalizations*, 99. His mother married the Chevalier Remoussin, and thus he was stepbrother to the above-mentioned brothers Remoussin. One "Mr. Piere" (no doubt Mr. Peire or Peyre) advertised a "Dancing Academy" in *CGDA*, 28 August 1801. A fractious incident between the Peire and Remoussin families and George Izard is described in Charlton deSaussure Jr., "Memoirs of General George Izard," 43–55.

68. *CGDA*, 6 September 1808.

69. Carrere was in Charleston by September 1793, when he buried an infant son at St. Mary's Catholic Church. See "Extrait des Registres de la Chancelerie du Consulat de

la Republique Françoise à Charleston," 26 September 1793, Carrere Family Papers, 1793–94, SCHS, 43/768. In a codicil to his will, dated 23 February 1826 and proved on 25 November 1829, Carrere instructed his family to attempt recovery of "a handsome property" he left behind in St. Domingo. See Charleston County Will Book G (1826–34): 368, South Carolina Civil Works Administration transcription, vol. 38 (1826–34): 654.

70. *Courier,* 15 November 1813. Heulan was the brother-in-law of violinist and dancing master Peter Fayolle and thus probably the "brother" who advertised with Fayolle in *CGDA,* 25 November 1794, to teach dancing, violin, and French.

71. Holcomb, *South Carolina Naturalizations,* 21. Miniere, "just arrived with his family," first advertised to teach singing, piano, and harp in *Times,* 16 June 1803.

72. The earliest clue to the identity of Mons. Labatut is the notice of his marriage in *CGDA,* 11 May 1798 (Friday): "Married, on Wednesday evening, by the Rev. Dr. Gallaher [of St. Mary's Catholic Church], Mr. Isador Labatut, son of Mr. Labatut, commander and owner of the island of Tortuga, to the most charming and accomplished Miss Remoussin, daughter of Mr. Remoussin, planter, of the island of St. Domingo."

73. Low, "Of Muslins and Merveilleuses," 51, citing a letter in English from Mrs. Manigault to Mrs. du Pont, dated Charleston, 22 December 1799. Josephine du Pont (1770–1837), wife of French diplomat Victor du Pont (1767–1827), arrived in Charleston in September 1795 and resided there for some time before her family moved northward. She and Margaret Izard Manigault (1768–1824) continued to correspond for many years after the removal of the du Ponts. According to ibid., 39, these letters are now at the Eleutherian Mills Historical Society, Greenville, Delaware. Madame Labatut was herself an accomplished vocalist. Both Mrs. Manigault and Mrs. du Pont must have heard this young lady perform sometime in Charleston, before her marriage in May 1798 when she was still known as Mlle. Remoussin. In a letter from Sullivan's Island, S.C., dated 24 July 1798, Mrs. Manigault asked Mrs. du Pont in Paris "Let me know when you hear a finer voice than Mlle. Remoussin's, and a more agreeable performer." See ibid., 48.

74. Ibid., 71–72, citing a letter in English from Mrs. Manigault to Mrs. du Pont, dated Charleston, 24 November 1800. Labatut continued to work as a professional musician and visual artist well into the nineteenth century.

75. The exact date of the La Roque family's arrival in Charleston is not known, but an 1804 reference to Antoinette La Roque's participation in concerts and oratorios, given below, suggests that she arrived several years before her name first appears in print in April 1804. Oratorio concerts were given in Charleston on 14 April 1802 and 6 April 1803, and thus her arrival probably predated these events. According to the published programs, no anonymous ladies performed songs at these events. Perhaps La Roque sang in the various choral excerpts included among the vocal solos and instrumental music.

76. See *Courier,* 2 April 1804 and 5 April 1804.

77. *CGDA,* 11 April 1805. The text regarding the ticket sellers reads as follows: "Tickets, at *a Dollar each,* may be had of the following gentlemen, viz. Henry W. Desaussure, Thomas Bee, jun. Thomas W. Bacot, John S. Cogdell, James Ladson, John Mitchell, Dr. James Moultrie, William L. Smith, Dr. Robert Pringle, Dr. Philip G. Prioleau, Timothy Ford, George Reid, Charles B. Cochran, William S. Hasell, Benjamin B. Smith, Dr. A. Baron, jun., *Officers and Managers of the St. Cecilia Society.* Also of Don Diego Morphy, J. F. Soult, I. E. A. Steinmetz, and Peter Freneau, Esquires; likewise, at the Post-Office [i.e., postmaster Thomas W. Bacot], and of Miss La Roque, No. 10, Liberty-street."

78. Ibid., 18 April 1805. The named overtures are discussed in chapter 9.

79. *Times,* 18 April 1805.

80. *Courier,* 24 April 1805.

81. Advertisements relating to Miss La Roque's benefit concerts of 1806 and 1807 are found in *Times,* 9 April 1806 and 17 April 1806; *Courier,* 9 April 1807; *Times,* 13 April 1807; and *Courier,* 16 April 1807.

82. The marriage announcement appears in *CGDA,* 21 April 1807. Mrs. Placide's benefit concert, at which Mrs. Robin appeared, was performed on 16 February 1813. She appears again in the city directories of 1819 and 1822 as the widow Antoinette Robin, but is missing from later directories.

83. Holcomb, *South Carolina Naturalizations,* 19. The 1816 Charleston city directory lists Andrew Labat, merchant, and Jane Labat, "Piano Forte Teacher," at 37 King Street. See Motte, *Charleston Directory and Stranger's Guide.* Various public records at SCDAH give his name as "André Labat."

84. See *Courier,* 7 March 1807; *CGDA,* 13 March 1807 and 11 March 1807. Tickets for this benefit concert, advertised at the uncommonly steep price of $5 each (roughly $84 in 2005) and admitting, as usual, "one gentleman and the ladies of his company," were available from the managers of the concert and ball, Robert Pringle, T. W. Bacot, Daniel C. Webb, Henry H. Bacot, Wm. Loughton Smith, Charles B. Cochran, Timothy Ford, and "the other managers of the St. Cecilia Society."

85. *CGDA,* 17 March 1807.

86. *Courier,* 21 March 1807. As in other references noted elsewhere in this study, the singular form *concert* was frequently used to refer to the St. Cecilia Society's concert series in general rather than to a single event.

87. The phrase "elegant talents" is taken from the program for the oratorio concert performed "for the benefit of the Gentlemen who compose the Orchestra of the St. Cecilia Society" at the Charleston Theatre on 25 March 1807 (see ibid., 23 March 1807). Madame Labat's talents were described as "well known" in a puff for Miss La Roque's benefit concert on 16 April 1807 in *Times,* 13 April 1807. The phrase "uncommon powers" is taken from a similar puff in *Courier,* 16 April 1807.

88. *Courier,* 17 April 1807.

89. Madame Labat advertised her continued availability to teach piano in ibid., 17 November 1807, after which her tenure in Charleston is not clear. In ibid., 27 June 1812, Labat announced: "Mrs. Labat, lately returned from London, having taken the determination of fixing her residence in this city, offers her services as a Teacher of Piano Forte and Vocal Music. The kind reception which she met with, on her former arrival here in 1807, she still remembers with gratitude."

90. Ursule Labat's benefit concert, on 3 March 1815, was managed by Thomas Parker Jr., Arthur Middleton, and Daniel Ravenel—all young managers of the St. Cecilia Society (see *CGDA,* 3 March 1815). For the many other concerts on which the Labats performed during the years 1812–17, see the listing of concert programs in Hindman, "Concert Life."

91. Act no. 1972, ratified on 20 December 1810, includes the names R[obert]. Leaumont, L[ouis]. D[e]. Villers, Charles Giffert [Gilfert], P[hilip]. C. Mack [Muck], Daniel Remoussin, E[ugene]. Guilbert, S. [Isadore] Labatut, Augustus Remoussin, and Arnold Remoussin. See McCord, *Statutes at Large,* 8:257–58.

92. During its several years of operations the Philharmonic Society published numerous concert advertisements and anniversary notices, which give the names of many of its officers.

93. This "rivalry" is discussed in chapter 10.

94. See Sodders, "Theatre Management of Alexandre Placide In Charleston"; and Chevalley, "The Death of Alexandre Placide," 63–66.

95. *Courier,* 11 January 1813.

96. The Philharmonic Society apparently continued to exist in some private form for several more years. An oratorio concert performed in Charleston on 8 February 1820 was advertised as a joint venture between the Union Harmonic Society and the Philharmonic Society.

97. Robinson, "Dr. Irving's Reminiscences of the Charleston Stage," 129, citing an article in *Courier,* 19 January 1858.

98. Ibid., quoting from *Courier,* 11 April 1870. Irving identifies the "'lads of the village,' as Gilfert called them; the two Remoussins—Jarvis, the painter, a man of rare amusing qualities, and inexhaustible spirits—Dr. [Henry] Farmer, the poet—Dr. [Isaac] Harby, a fine Belle Lettre scholar—Colleton Graves, an excellent classic, though eccentric—Thomas Cochrane; Wm. H. Miller; Samuel Lothrop; Charles Graham; R. W. Cogdell, (gentleman duck, by which appellation he was known to the whole town,)—and other jovial characters of Gilfert's liking, with all the stars that happened to be from time to time in Charleston, fulfilling an engagement."

99. This event was first advertised in *Times,* 16 January 1807, but not performed until 3 March 1807.

100. St. John's Lutheran Church, Charleston, S.C., vestry minutes, 4 December 1809. There was a vacancy at St. John's because Jacob Eckhard had just transferred to St. Michael's.

101. *Times,* 19 December 1810. Later advertisements indicate that Gilfert's business partner was the German musician Philip Muck.

102. According to the St. John's Lutheran Church, vestry minutes, 17 May 1811, Gilfert's place was declared vacant "in Consequence of the recent Conduct of the Organist Mr. Charles Gilfert in fighting a Duel, and of the Probability of his being absent from the State for some Time." The vestry received Gilfert's letter of resignation the following day.

103. The tickets for many concerts during the 1811–12 season were advertised to be sold at Gilfert & Co.'s music store, but this fact does not necessarily mean that Gilfert himself was present. *Times,* 24 June 1812, carried the news of the U.S. Senate's declaration of war against Britain on 18 June. (The *Courier* carried this same news the following morning.) No doubt in an effort to reduce political complications during wartime, Gilfert immediately took the oath of citizenship. According to Holcomb, *South Carolina Naturalizations,* 12, Federal records show that Charles Gilfert, age twenty-six, a musician from Hesse Cassel, Germany, was admitted to citizenship in Charleston on 26 June 1812.

104. Gilfert's career in New York during the War of 1812 is discussed in Stephenson, "The Charleston Theatre Management of Charles Gilfert," 38–51. His marriage was announced in Charleston in *Courier,* 9 March 1815.

105. Stephenson, "The Charleston Theatre Management of Charles Gilfert," 53–54, cites several sources that demonstrate Gilfert was in New York through the end of January 1816.

106. The program for Gilfert's benefit was given on the day of its performance, in *Courier,* 19 March 1816. The managers of the ball were Henry Manigault, James Ferguson, Dr. Warley, and Dr. Ferguson. Gilfert was assisted by the singer Mr. Taylor of the theater, the guitarist Mr. Thieneman, and Miss Labat. The postconcert review appeared in *CGDA,* 21 March 1816.

107. M. C. [Martha Coffin] Derby, Charleston, S.C., to Mrs. [Margaret Izard] Manigault, Philadelphia, 26 March 1816, Manigault Family Papers, South Caroliniana Library. Mrs. Derby's husband, Richard Derby, was a wealthy Massachusetts merchant. My thanks to Alice Skelsey and Robert Cuthbert for bringing this letter to my attention.

108. *CGDA,* 5 November 1816. The 1816 Charleston city directory lists "Gilfert, Charles, music master at the Theatre." See Motte, *Charleston Directory.*

109. *SPCA,* 9 November 1816.

110. See *CGDA,* 7 December 1801, and *Courier,* 25 January 1803.

111. Stephenson, "The Charleston Theatre Management of Charles Gilfert," 59.

112. Robinson, "Dr. Irving's Reminiscences of the Charleston Stage," 171, quoting from *Courier,* 21 March 1870. According to leases recorded among the Miscellaneous Records of the Secretary of State, now housed at SCDAH, the shareholders of the Charleston Theatre awarded Holman a seven-year lease in 1815. In April 1817 that lease was extended for three years beyond 1 July 1822. This lease was formally transferred to Gilfert in 1818.

113. Stephenson, "The Charleston Theatre Management of Charles Gilfert," 81.

114. Gilfert and his company were justified in their concert for their health. In autumn 1817 there was an especially severe outbreak of fevers, which resulted in many deaths.

115. *SPCA,* 9 October 1817; *Courier,* 20 November 1817.

116. *Courier,* 3 December 1817. According to the *Courier* ship news, many members of the theater company arrived by ship from Norfolk on 8 and 9 December 1817.

117. The St. Cecilia Society's concert for 29 January was first advertised in the *Courier* 24 January 1818. Stephenson, "The Charleston Theatre Management of Charles Gilfert," 158, points out that the Charleston newspapers did not take notice of the fact that Gilfert had sent half of the theater company out of town from mid-January to early April.

118. *Courier,* 6 February 1818. Note that this announcement appeared a year and a day earlier than stated in Fraser, *Reminiscences,* 60.

119. *Courier,* 9 February 1818.

120. Stephenson, "The Charleston Theatre Management of Charles Gilfert," 180.

121. Ibid., 240, 244; *Courier,* 4 November 1818, 10 November 1818 (Tuesday), and 3 May 1819.

122. Stephenson, "The Charleston Theatre Management of Charles Gilfert," 375; *Courier,* 6 October 1819.

123. Stephenson, "The Charleston Theatre Management of Charles Gilfert," 392, 494, 518–23; *SPCA,* 25 May 1822.

Chapter 9

1. Burney, *A General History of Music,* 4:673.

2. McVeigh, *Concert Life,* 121.

3. For information on the character and scope of the Classical style, see Blume, *Classic and Romantic Music;* Ratner, *Classic Music;* and Rosen, *The Classical Style.*

4. McVeigh, *Concert Life,* 121.

5. Webber, "Peter Manigault's Letters," 276, 278.

6. Ravenel, *Charleston,* 426; Deas, *The Correspondence of Mr. Ralph Izard,* vi; Cheves, "Izard of South Carolina," 205–40.

7. Deas, *The Correspondence of Mr. Ralph Izard,* 38. Music at Ralph Izard's home in 1783 is mentioned in Cometti, *Seeing America,* 55.

8. See, for example, *SCG,* 24 June–1 July 1756 and 2 November 1769; *SCGCJ,* 26 March 1771; *SCGPA,* 3–6 March 1784; *CGDA,* 6 February 1789.

9. *CGDA,* 1 February 1788, 14 November 1789, and 25 June 1792.

10. See, for example, Eckhard's advertisement in *Times,* 10 June 1806.

11. A complete discussion of locally composed music is not possible here. For a few references to such works, see Bagdon, "Musical Life in Charleston"; Hindman, "Concert Life"; Sonneck, *A Bibliography of Early Secular American Music;* and Wolfe, *Secular Music in America.*

12. McVeigh, *Concert Life,* xiii, 137.

13. See ibid., 35, and Burchell, *Polite or Commercial,* 49.

14. Sadie, "Concert Life in Eighteenth Century England," 27.

15. If we conservatively estimate that the society performed an average of 8 concerts per season (see appendix 1), then over the course of forty-three active seasons it would have performed about 350 concerts. If one handbill were printed for each member (known to be limited to 120 in 1774) for each concert, then as many as 42,000 programs may have been printed during the society's concert-giving era. If programs were also printed for ladies and strangers in attendance, this figure would be far greater.

16. Sadie, "Concert Life in Eighteenth Century England," 28; McVeigh, *Concert Life,* 101; Burchell, *Polite or Commercial,* 61, 204; Boydell, *Rotunda Music,* chapter 9.

17. Burchell, *Polite or Commercial,* 61, 205; McVeigh, *Concert Life,* 104.

18. Weber, "London," 312. McVeigh's *Concert Life* includes an appendix with sample programs from eighteenth-century subscription concerts in London.

19. Weber, "London," 312–13; McVeigh, *Concert Life,* 101.

20. *SCG,* 11 April 1774. See similar advertisements in ibid., 19–31 October 1765, and *SCGCJ,* 21 January 1766.

21. In *SCAGG,* 14–21 October 1774, Peter van Hagen advertised his benefit concert, sponsored by the St. Cecilia Society, as "Consisting of Three Acts." The extant St. Cecilia Society program of November 1778 is in three acts, each of which contains four items. The program of Franceschini's concert, in *RG,* 18–22 May 1782, was divided into three acts of three items each. The St. Cecilia Society's March 1794 charity concert was arranged in three acts, with five works in each of the first two parts and four in the last (*CGDA,* 6 March 1794).

22. A perusal of the concert programs transcribed in Hindman, "Concert Life," 289–391, will demonstrate this point. Note that Hindman included in this list the advertised programs of performances at Charleston's Vauxhall Garden. These events represent a different species of concert, however, and their programs follow a different format.

23. See Boydell, *Rotunda Music,* 129; Burchell, *Polite or Commercial,* 42, 296.

24. Burchell, *Polite or Commercial,* 296.

25. The names of the composers listed in these programs are often misspelled, no doubt because concert organizers or their agents submitted hand-written programs to

the newspaper office, where they were then set to type by nonmusical employees. Such misspellings can lead to confusion about the identities of the composers in question, but I have endeavored to be as accurate as possible in determining these identities based on extant primary sources and widely available secondary literature.

26. Zaslaw, "Toward the Revival," 168; Weber, "London," 312; Burchell, *Polite or Commercial*, xi.

27. McVeigh, *Concert Life*, 104.

28. For example "Roxelane, executed by [DeLarousserie] from Haydn," was performed at Mde. DeLarousserie's 1802 benefit (*CGDA*, 8 May 1802). Mr. Gallaher's 1812 benefit also included "Roxalane, Haydn" (*CGDA*, 27 May 1812). Whether this was meant to indicate Haydn's Symphony no. 63, which is subtitled "La Roxelane," in its entirety or just the second movement, which contains the "Roxelane" theme, is not known.

29. Yarnold, *Six Overtures for the Harpsichord of Piano Forte* (1780). An original imprint of this work is at the British Library, shelfmark g.79.l, and a microfilm copy of this publication exists at the New York Public Library.

30. Jones, "Robert Bremner," 64–65; Fiske, *English Theatre Music*, 287.

31. Harriott Pinckney (later Mrs. Daniel Hörry), Charleston, S.C., to Charles [Cotesworth] Pinckney, London, 3 March 1767, in Harriott Pinckney, Copy book, 1760–1769, on loan to the SCHS in 2003.

32. Weber, "London," 310.

33. This series includes works by Carl Friedrich Abel, Thomas Arne, J. C. Bach, Giovanni Gastone Boccherini, Christian Cannabich, Pietro Maria Crispi, Carl Ditters von Dittersdorf, Johann Anton Filtz, Ignaz Fränzl, Christoph Willibald Gluck, François-Joseph Gossec, Pietro Alessandro Guglielmi, Joseph Haydn, Michael Haydn, J. Herschel, Ignaz Holzbauer, Niccolò Jommelli, Thomas Erskine (Earl of Kelly), Niccolò Piccinni, Gaetano Pugnani, Francesco Pasquale Ricci, Franz Xavier Richter, Antonio Sacchini, Joseph Schmitt, Johann Schobert, Friedrich Schwindl, Johann Stamitz, and Johann Baptist Vanhal. See Jones, "Robert Bremner," 65; and Fiske, *English Theatre Music*, 287. The eight-part score was not the only orchestral texture known in Charleston during the early years of the St. Cecilia Society's activity, however. When Shad Windsor advertised musical scores for sale in *SCAGG*, 10 June 1771, he included "A Set for six Instruments by Hasse, Campioni, &c."

34. As with most European concerts in the eighteenth century, the St. Cecilia concerts included continuo accompaniment performed on a keyboard instrument. A harpsichord was used for this purpose in the society's early decades, but, as in contemporary Britain, that instrument was probably replaced by a piano around 1790. Continuo, also known as figured bass, was not exclusively a feature of any particular genre of music. It was employed in orchestral works, chamber music, concerti, and in the accompaniment of songs. It is not known when the society dispensed with keyboard continuo at its concerts, but it probably followed European musical conventions in abandoning the practice by the turn of the nineteenth century. See McVeigh, *Concert Life*, 215, 218.

35. *SCG*, 6 December 1773. This advertisement was repeated in ibid., 11 December 1773. The "overtures" by Martini probably refer to the four-part "sinfonias" of Bolognese priest Giovanni Battista Martini (1706–1784), who was so admired by Charles Burney and Wolfgang Mozart.

36. *RG*, 18–22 May 1782. The orchestral works in question were advertised as "Overture No. 3, Di Abel. . . . Sinfonia, No. 3, Di Swindell [Schwindl], Op. 1. . . . Overture No.

4, Di Mistieveeck [Myslivecek]. . . . Sinfonia Periodical, No. 30, Di Filz [Filtz]. . . . Overture N 6, Di Schwindel [Schwindl], Op. 1. . . . Sinfonia, No. 1, Di Mistieveeck [Myslivecek]."

37. McVeigh, *Concert Life,* 122, notes that Haydn's symphonies were not unknown in London during the 1770s, but not until the "astonishing success" of his Symphony no. 53 did Haydn became a preeminent composer.

38. Sonneck, "A Contemporary Account," 96–97.

39. *CH,* 11 October 1787 (Thursday). In contrast to this selection, an "overture" by William Boyce was played at Juhan's concert six months later (*CGDA,* 15 May 1788). This was probably one of the twelve three-movement overtures for oboes, strings, and continuo that Boyce published between 1760 and 1770, some of which were adaptations of earlier operatic and occasional overtures.

40. Among the concert programs published in the various Charleston newspapers from the late 1780s through 1820, there are at least sixty separate references to symphonic works by Haydn. The first reference to a symphony by Pleyel appeared in the advertisement for the 1793 "Public Concert" (*CGDA,* 19 February 1793), and more than forty references to such works appear by 1820. A "Grand Overture" by Mozart was first mentioned on a Charleston concert advertisement in March 1797 (ibid., 9 March 1797), and references to such works reappear about a dozen times over the next two decades. An "overture" by "Girovetz" (Gyrowetz) is mentioned in ibid., 26 March 1795, and about ten further references to this composer's symphonies are found through 1820. The earliest reference to the performance of a "Grand Sinfonia" by Krommer appears in *Courier,* 19 July 1810, which was followed by at least six further references in the subsequent decade.

41. Fraser, *Reminiscences,* 60.

42. A "Grand Simphonia" by Cimarosa is mentioned in *CGDA,* 14 December 1799. A reference to "Grand Overture (la Chasse), Gosset [Gossec]" appears in ibid., 6 March 1794. A "Simfonia, Guenin" is listed in ibid., 16 April 1795. Leaumont's "Grand Overture" was performed at the St. Cecilia Society's 1801 anniversary concert and at the 1802 benefit for the "gentlemen of the orchestra" (ibid., 11 January 1802). A "Simfonie, Massoneau" is mentioned in ibid., 9 March 1797. A "Grand Sinfonia" by "Trajetta" is mentioned in ibid., 26 February 1805, but whether this was a work of *père* or *fils* is not known. An "Overture" by Vanhal is mentioned in ibid., 8 November 1798, and *Courier,* 2 May 1816. There are references to an "Overture" by Winter in ibid., 11 March 1817, 8 April 1817, and 9 February 1819. An "Entire new Sinfonia, Scmitbaur" is mentioned in *CGDA,* 11 January 1802.

43. *Courier,* 10 April 1805 and 2 April 1806. The latter performance included both a "Grand Overture" and a "Finale" by Beethoven, but it is not clear whether these were two independent works or parts of the same composition.

44. *SCG,* 28 September–5 October 1765.

45. As a testament to the popularity of performing Handel's opera and oratorio overtures as independent concert music, John Walsh, the most prominent music publisher in mid-eighteenth-century London, published a collection of sixty Handel overtures around 1750. Copies of Walsh's collection may have been the object of the society's 1773 call for missing orchestral parts.

46. A reference to the overture to Handel's *Sampson* appears in *CGDA,* 3 March 1796. The overtures to *Messiah, Esther, Sampson,* and the *Occasional Oratorio* are all

mentioned in ibid., 24 March 1796. Overtures to the *Sampson* and the *Occasional Oratorio* are also mentioned in ibid., 14 April 1802.

47. For a survey of the English and French operas performed in Charleston from the 1760s through 1820, see Crain, "Music in the Colonial Charleston, South Carolina Theater"; Curtis, "The Early Charleston Stage"; Sodders, "The Theatre Management of Alexandre Placide In Charleston"; Stephenson, "The Charleston Theatre Management of Joseph George Holman" and "The Charleston Theatre Management of Charles Gilfert."

48. William Elliott to Ann Smith, 16 September 1816, transcribed in Scafidel, "Letters of William Elliott," 1:37–40. Ann Smith was the daughter of Thomas Rhett Smith, a manager of the St. Cecilia Society.

49. McVeigh, *Concert Life,* 126. For programs including the overture to *Henry IV,* see *CGDA,* 17 December 1793, 17 December 1795, 3 March 1796, 24 March 1796, and 6 July 1796; *Courier,* 7 August 1805, 26 August 1805, 25 March 1807, 27 August 1807, 19 January 1808, 21 August 1809, and 21 May 1812. In addition to these references, a number of concerts between 1787 and 1817 include an unspecified "Grand overture" by Martini. These items were probably references to J. P. G. Martini's overture to *Henry IV* rather than to the late Baroque string overtures of Giovanni Martini. See *CGDA,* 11 October 1787, 15 May 1788, 6 April 1803, 27 March 1804, and 10 April 1805; *Courier,* 2 April 1806 and 12 May 1817.

50. See *CGDA,* 28 February 1804, 27 March 1804, 11 April 1804, and 18 April 1805; *Courier,* 29 July 1805, 25 March 1807, 16 June 1807, 9 February 1808, 8 March 1808, 18 July 1809, 19 July 1810, 21 March 1811, 16 May 1812, 18 March 1814, 19 March 1816, and 12 May 1817. Stephen Storace adapted *Lodoiska* for the London stage in 1792 by using music from Kreutzer's and Cherubini's versions, both of which appeared nearly simultaneously in Paris in 1791. Fiske, *English Theatre Music,* 527, attributes the overture and the other three purely orchestral items of Storace's version to Kreutzer.

51. See *CGDA,* 24 March 1796, 6 July 1796, 9 March 1797, 14 April 1802, and 6 April 1803; *Courier,* 3 September 1805, 25 March 1807, 8 March 1808, and 19 February 1811.

52. The British reaction to French concert music of the 1780s and 1790s is discussed in McVeigh, *Concert Life,* 126.

53. For *Panurge,* see *Courier,* 7 June 1804, 18 July 1809, 21 August 1809, 20 November 1810, 29 April 1812, 6 May 1813, 15 March 1814, 5 December 1816, and 17 December 1816. For *La Caravane,* see *CGDA,* 17 December 1793, and *Courier,* 21 October 1816. An overture titled *L'épreuve de la Aillagoist,* probably a corruption of the title *L'épreuve villageoise* is mentioned in *Courier,* 24 August 1809. References to unspecified overtures by Grétry appear in *CGDA,* 17 December 1793 and 6 March 1794; and *Courier,* 26 March 1816.

54. For *Nina,* see *CGDA,* 18 April 1805; *Courier,* 9 May 1809, 24 August 1809, 19 July 1810, 19 February 1811, and 18 February 1817. For *La Soirée orageuse,* see *Courier,* 17 March 1807. For *Renaud d'Ast,* see ibid., 5 March 1811. For *Camille; ou, le Souterrain,* see ibid., 3 September 1805 and 18 February 1817. For *Les Deux Petits Savoyards,* see ibid., 5 August 1809 and 24 August 1809. On the day of Leaumont's benefit at the Charleston Theatre in 1805, the *Courier* carried a strong endorsement of the musician's talents and choice of repertoire. See ibid., 3 April 1805.

55. *CGDA,* 26 February 1805 and 18 April 1805; *Courier,* 3 September 1805, 25 March 1807, 5 July 1810, and 3 March 1812.

56. *Courier,* 21 October 1816 and 5 December 1816.

57. *Blaise et Babet* and *Blue Beard* are mentioned in *Courier,* 3 September 1805 and 16 June 1807. The overture to "La Marriage Secret" is mentioned in ibid., 9 May 1809 and 21 August 1809. A reference to the overture to *Le Petit matelot* appears in ibid., 18 July 1809. The overture to *Le Déserteur* is listed in ibid., 5 August 1809. Leaumont's overture to *The Forty Thieves* is mentioned in ibid., 4 December 1810. The "Overture (by desire), a Scotch medley, from the Opera of Love & Money, Arne [i.e., Arnold]," is listed in ibid., 5 July 1810. Hook's overture to *The Fortress* received two performances in 1811 (ibid., 5 March 1811 and 31 October 1811). Mozart's overture to "La Flute enchantée" was performed twice in 1819 (ibid., 2 November 1819 and 22 November 1819).

58. McVeigh, *Concert Life,* 106, 139.

59. A reference to "Sinfonie concertante of Davaux" appears in *CGDA,* 19 February 1793 and 14 December 1799. A "concertant symphony for two violins and a tenor [viola]" is mentioned in ibid., 17 December 1793. A "Sinfonie concertante" by Pleyel is mentioned in ibid., 3 March 1796 and 27 March 1804; *Courier,* 10 April 1805 and 2 April 1806 ("for Violin and Tenor [viola]"). A "Concertante for two Flutes" is mentioned in ibid., 9 February 1808. A "Symphony Concertante for two clarinets" is mentioned in *CGDA,* 27 August 1808. A "Grand Sinfonia for two violins, principals" is mentioned in *Courier,* 16 March 1813.

60. *SCG,* 28 September–5 October 1765. These items are listed in the published program as "French Horn Concerto, 2nd Concerto of Stanley . . . 5th Concerto of Stanley, Bassoon Concerto . . . Concerto on the Harpsichord, Bassoon Concerto . . . French Horn Concert of Hasse." The op. 2 concerti of John Stanley (1712–1786), published in London in 1742, clearly represent a Baroque idiom. They are scored for a concertino of two violins and cello and a four-part string ripieno.

61. Weber, "London," 317.

62. Sonneck, "A Contemporary Account," 98.

63. *CGDA,* 19 February 1793. The advertisement for this event, the first concert in Charleston to be specified as a "Public" event, mentions only the inclusion of a "Concerto grosso of Corelli" at the opening of the second act.

64. As an exception to this categorization, it should be noted that a few concerti for harp and orchestra were performed in the early nineteenth century. At each of these, the soloist was a lady. Miss La Roque's 1807 benefit included "a Lady, who will play a Concerto uon [upon] the Harp" (*Courier,* 16 April 1807). At her husband's 1816 concert, Mrs. Andral played a harp concerto by Eugène Guilbert (ibid., 21 October 1816). At Eugene Fayolle's 1819 concert, his sister, Mrs. Giraud, played a "Grand Concerto" on harp composed by Guilbert (ibid., 2 November 1819).

65. Mr. Le Roy played a "Concerto on the Basse" (that is, cello) by Pleyel at his 1795 concert (*CGDA,* 17 December 1795). "Mr. Dumarque, lately arrived from Philadelphia," played a cello concerto of his own composition at Mrs. Grattan's 1798 concert (ibid., 8 November 1798). Dumarque played an unspecified cello concerto at his own 1799 benefit (ibid., 5 March 1799). At his 1816 benefit, Mr. Gilles played a "Concerto on the Violencello [*sic*], composed and executed by Mr. Gilles" (*Courier,* 17 December 1816). Mr. Vandever, "lately arrived from France," played a cello concerto by Bergen (or Berges) at Mr. Andral's 1817 concert (ibid., 27 November 1817).

66. A double concerto for violin and violoncello by Stamitz (probably Carl Stamitz, 1745–1801) is mentioned in *CGDA*, 15 May 1788. A double concerto for violin and tenor (viola) by Pleyel is mentioned in *Courier*, 28 May 1818.

67. Franceschini played an unspecified violin concerto at his own concert on 12 April 1774 (*SCG*, 28 March 1774). Franceschini's concert on 24 May 1782 included Abercromby performing a violin concerto by "Giordini" [Felice Giardini] (*RG*, 18–22 May 1782).

68. Fiske, *English Theatre Music*, 284–85, identifies London's three most famous violinists as Giardini, Cramer, and Barthelemon.

69. For his benefit concert in June 1802, advertised first in *CGDA*, 10 June 1802, Abercromby performed "A Comic Pastorale, composed by Mr. Abercromby, and played by him on the Viol d'Amour; an instrument never performed on in Charleston, but by himself." This statement definitively identifies this John J. Abercromby as the man who performed with the St. Cecilia Society in the early 1770s and who probably performed a "Concerto on the Viol d'Amour" at Gaetano Franceschini's St. Cecilia–sponsored benefit concert in April 1774 (see *SCG*, 28 March 1774).

70. McVeigh, *Concert Life*, 145.

71. Unspecified violin concerti include those performed by Mr. Bergman, "Conductor of the Operas," at the City Theatre (*CGDA*, 26 April 1796); by Petit (ibid., 5 March 1799); by LeFolle (ibid., 25 May 1812); and by De Yonge [De Jonge] (ibid., 25 March 1816). LeFolle played a violin concerto by "Hook" at his own 1811 benefit (*Courier*, 21 March 1811). The intended composer in this advertisement may have been James Hook, though he is not known to have written any works for solo violin and orchestra.

72. Alexander Juhan played a violin concerto by Davaux (*CH*, 1 October 1787). The French youth Master Duport played a Lamotte concerto (*CGDA*, 26 March 1795).

73. There are references to violin concerti by "Giornovichi" in *CGDA*, 19 February 1793; by "Jarnowick" in ibid., 14 July 1794, and ibid., 19 May 1802; by "Jernovick" in ibid., 17 December 1795; by "Jarnovick" in ibid., 21 March 1796 and 9 March 1797, and *Courier*, 11 April 1804 and 4 December 1810; by "Jarnwick" in *CGDA*, 6 July 1796. De Jonge played a "Concerto on the Vielle" by "Ganieveck" (*Courier*, 5 December 1816); this may have been the work of Giornovichi or perhaps Feliks Janiewicz (1762–1848), a Polish violinist and composer active in London between 1792 and 1815.

74. Viotti's concerto with variations on "Marlborough" is mentioned in *CGDA*, 17 December 1793 and 21 March 179. Further Viotti performances are mentioned in ibid., 6 March 1794, 11 June 1802, and 3 March 1807; *Courier*, 26 October 1815; and *CGDA*, 2 May 1816.

75. Concerti by Rode are mentioned in *Courier*, 29 April 1812 and 21 May 1812; *CGDA*, 27 May 1812 and 30 March 1813; *Courier*, 21 October 1816 ("the 7th Concerto of Rode on the violin"), 27 November 1817, and 28 May 1818.

76. LeFolle's playing of Kreutzer's concerti is mentioned in *Courier*, 16 April 1811 and 16 February 1813.

77. A 2 February 1773 concert (probably Peter Valton's benefit, as he was the ticket seller) included "a Concerto on the Harpsichord, By a Lady, a Pupil of Mr. Valton's" (*SCG*, 21 January 1773). Valton's benefit concert on 15 February 1774 included "A Concerto on the Harpsichord by one of Mr. Valton's Pupils" (ibid., 31 January 1774).

78. Franceschini's benefit on 5 March 1781 included "a Harpsichord Concerto by a Lady" (*SCAGG*, 21 February 1781). Note that one week after this initial advertisement,

the *SCAGG* became the *RG*. A 1781 concert included "a Concerto Solo upon the Harpsichord, by a Lady" (*RG*, 29 September–3 October 1781).

79. McVeigh, *Concert Life*, 90.

80. Unidentified piano concerti are mentioned in *CGDA*, 24 March 1796, 5 March 1799, 26 February 1805, and 18 April 1805; *Courier*, 1 November 1805.

81. References to piano concerti include those by "Durham" (*CGDA*, 15 May 1788), by Hoffmeister (ibid., 19 February 1793), by Kozeluch (ibid., 17 December 1795), by Krumpholtz (ibid., 9 March 1797), by "Bertoni" (ibid., 21 March 1796). Bertoni may have been the Italian composer Ferdinando Gasparo Bertoni (1725–1813), who paid several visits to London.

82. McVeigh, *Concert Life*, 123, describes the "London piano-forte school," including Muzio Clementi, Dussek, J. B. Cramer, Steibelt, and John Field, as composers who were all were more or less influenced by Haydn.

83. References to piano concerti by Cramer appear in *Courier*, 11 April 1804, 10 April 1805, 9 May 1809, 5 July 1810, 5 March 1811, 16 April 1811, 3 March 1812 (a "Concerto and Variations"), and 16 February 1813; *CGDA*, 16 March 1813 ("the sixth of Cramer") and 30 March 1813; *Courier*, 17 February 1814; *CGDA*, 3 March 1815—a "Concerto on the Piano Forte, (Cramer) [followed] by a Spanish Air, with Variations, (Ste[ibelt)]"—and *CGDA*, 9 October 1815 (a "New Concerto on the Piano").

84. References to Dussek concerti appear in *Courier*, 6 April 1803; *CGDA*, 28 February 1804, 27 March 1804, 19 January 1808, and 2 April 1806; *Courier*, 21 March 1811 and 26 March 1812; *CGDA*, 27 May 1812; *Courier*, 29 November 1813, 9 February 1808, and 7 March 1814 ("never performed here").

85. References to Steibelt concerti appear in *Courier*, 25 March 1807 (concerto "with variations"), 19 July 1810, 20 November 1810 ("The Storm"), 23 February 1811; and 26 October 1815 ("Andante, with Variations, and the Storm").

86. References to Viotti piano concerti appear in *Courier*, 4 December 1810 and 21 May 1812; *CGDA*, 25 May 1812.

87. References to piano concerti include those by "Giarnovich" (*CGDA*, 5 January 1802, by "Jarnovick" (ibid., 19 February 1803), by Boieldieu in (ibid., 8 March 1808, and *Courier*, 18 March 1819), by Fodor (*CGDA*, 3 March 1807, and *Courier*, 2 February 1813), by Wölfl (*Courier*, 14 April 1813, and *CGDA*, 3 March 1815).

88. References to piano concerti include those by Mozart (*CGDA*, 14 April 1802), by "Guiliana" (ibid., 11 June 1802), by João Domingo Bontempo (1775–1842) "with variations" (ibid., 17 March 1807); by "Herman" (probably David Hermann, 1764–1852) (*Courier*, 31 October 1811).

89. An unspecified clarinet concerto is mentioned in *CGDA*, 17 December 1793.

90. Clarinet concerti by Michel are mentioned in *CGDA*, 21 March 1796, 8 November 1798, and 5 March 1799; *Courier*, 11 April 1804, 25 March 1807, 20 November 1810, 29 November 1813, and 9 February 1808; *CGDA*, 8 March 1808; *Courier*, 3 March 1812 and 18 April 1814; *CGDA*, 9 October 1815 (Michel's "Fourth Concerto"); *Courier*, 18 May 1812; *CGDA*, 27 May 1812 ("in the course of which he will introduce the favorite Irish air of 'Erin go Bragh'"); *Courier*, 2 February 1813; *CGDA*, 30 March 1813 ("Grand Military Concerto"); *Courier*, 14 April 1813, 21 May 1812, and 11 March 1817.

91. References to Vanderhagen clarinet concerti appear in *CGDA*, 14 December 1799 and 11 January 1802, and *Courier*, 9 May 1809. A Devienne concerto is mentioned

in *CGDA,* 19 February 1803. Concerti by Duvernoy are mentioned in *Courier,* 7 June 1804 and 5 December 1816 ("First Concerto"). References to concerti by Lefevre appear in *Courier,* 21 March 1811 and 31 October 1811. A clarinet concerto by "Soller" is mentioned in *Courier,* 16 April 1811; one by "Vogel" is mentioned in ibid., 8 February 1814; and there is a reference to one by "Dacosta"—probably Rodrigo Ferreira da Costa (1776–1825)—in *CGDA,* 25 March 1816.

92. A clarinet concerto "composed and performed by Mrs. [Mr.] Dubois" is mentioned in *CGDA,* 26 March 1795; the same paper mentions Dubois's performances of an unspecified clarinet concerto (16 April 1795) and others by Michel (19 January 1808 and 27 August 1808). This musician was perhaps Louis Dubois (1767–1828), a native of the Ath, Netherlands, who settled in Charleston by 1795. Mr. Gautier's playing of a "Grand Concerto" for clarinet by "Gautier" is mentioned in *Courier,* 18 February 1817. My thanks to Jane Ellsworth for sharing information about Gautier's career with me.

93. The anonymous flute concerto listed on the St. Cecilia Society's 1778 anniversary program was the only concerto in that concert. At his concert on 27 April 1784, William Brown played a "Solo Concerto on the German Flute, of a new construction" (*SCGPA,* 17–21 April 1784). Other references to flute concerti include those by Fischer (*CH,* 1 October 1787, and *CGDA,* 15 May 1788), by Pleyel (*Courier,* 16 February 1813), and by Devienne (*CGDA,* 14 April 1802, *Courier,* 6 April 1803, 21 March 1811, 26 March 1812, March 1814, and 5 December 1816).

94. Oboe concerti by Fischer are mentioned in *RG,* 18–22 May 1782, and *CGDA,* 21 March 1796. Gottlieb Graupner also played unspecified oboe concerti, which are mentioned in *CGDA,* 10 November 1795 and 24 March 1796. McVeigh, *Concert Life,* 81, discusses Fischer's importance.

95. One Mr. Passage played a bassoon concerto by "Oze" (probably Etienne Ozi, 1754–1813), *Courier,* 18 March 1819.

96. McVeigh, *Concert Life,* 104–5.

97. The subscription plan for Valton's music was advertised in *SCAGG,* 30 September–7 October 1768, but no extant copy of these works or proof that this plan was realized has ever been found.

98. Many of the chamber works for harp performed in Charleston during this era were the work of Spanish-born French composer Eugène André Louis Guilbert (1758–1839), who arrived in the city in 1798 and is buried at St. Mary's Church. Some of his works were undoubtedly played at the St. Cecilia concerts.

99. McVeigh, *Concert Life,* 105.

100. Many varieties of chamber music are mentioned in advertisements published by Charles Morgan in *SCGPA,* 3–6 March 1784; by W. P. Young in *CGDA,* 6 February 1789; by Thomas Bradford in ibid., 14 November 1789; and by Jacob Eckhard in *Times,* 10 June 1806. Quintets, though often included among the offerings of Charleston music and booksellers, do not appear in any extant concert programs of the period under study. The first known advertised concert performance of a quintet (and also for a wind divertimento) in Charleston appeared in late 1820, at the concert given by one Mrs. Knittel (*Courier,* 23 October 1820 and 6 November 1820).

101. For more information on this practice, see McVeigh, *Concert Life,* 104.

102. See references to a "Solo on the Violoncello" (*SCG,* 28 September–5 October 1765), a "Solo on the Violin" (ibid., 31 January 1774), and a "Solo and a Concerto on the

Violin" (ibid., 28 March 1774). The St. Cecilia Society's 1778 anniversary concert (see figure 9.2) included a "Solo on the Violin." A "Solo Violino" is mentioned in *RG*, 18–22 May 1782.

103. Mrs. Pick performed a "Pot Pouri on the Harmonica" (*CGDA*, 26 March 1795). A reference to "Solo Violincello, [performed and perhaps composed by] Mr. Dumarque" appears in ibid., 4 March 1800. Other solos mentioned are a "Comic Pastorale, composed by Mr. Abercromby, and played by him on the Viol d'Amour; an instrument never performed on in Charleston, but by himself" (ibid., 10 June 1802); a "Potpourri on the violin" by Kreutzer (*Courier*, 19 March 1811); "Variations on the Violin, (Hope told a flattering Tale), [by] Kreutzer" (ibid., 8 February 1813); Mr. Andral's performance of "Variations on the Clarionet" of his own composition (ibid., 8 March 1813); a performance by Mr. Brown, "lately arrived from Europe," of a "Solo on the French Horn, with accompaniments, in which will be introduced several original Irish Airs," (ibid., 3 December 1816); a "Solo on the Flute" by Hoffmeister (ibid., May 1816); "Variations on the Clarionet" by Dacosta and "Variations on the Violencello, composed and executed by Mr. Gilles, with accompaniments for the Piano Forte, by Miss Labat" (ibid., 14 December 1816); a "solo on the Violin" by Rode (ibid., 27 October 1818); a sonata for piano and violin by Pleyel (ibid., 25 March 1819).

104. For example *CGDA* mentions a "Duetto, violin and claronet [*sic*] of Michel" (15 February 1793) and a "Duo, Harp and Piano Forte, by two Ladies" by Krumpholtz (26 February 1805). In addition Eugène Guilbert's music for harp and other instruments was frequently heard in Charleston in the years after his arrival in 1798.

105. Note Josiah Quincy's complaint that the "capital defect" of the St. Cecilia concert he attended in March 1773 (cited in chapter 3) was the "want of an organ."

106. *SCG*, 28 September–5 October 1765.

107. *SCAGG*, 10 June 1771. To this list of trios could be added the works of Thomas Arne, Felice Giardini, and Johann Stamitz, which were then in currency. Windsor's advertisement also included "likewise Duets for two German flutes by Granom, Hasse, Martini, &c."

108. To date the best summary of this composer's career is presented in Gaetano Franceschini, *Opera I*, compact disc, biographical notes written by Francesco Passadore, translated by Candace Smith.

109. References to trios include: an "Extraordinary Trio, by three Clarionets" (*CGDA*, 9 October 1815); a "Trio for the Violencello [*sic*] principale, by Mr. Gilles, with the accompanyments [*sic*] of Violin and Violencello" by "Berges" (*Courier*, 14 December 1816); and a "Trio, (for flute, Guitar and Alto)" by "Cull," probably Leonhard von Call (1767–1815) (ibid., 15 February 1817).

110. A number of unspecified quartets were advertised in Charleston, including, for example, a "Quartetto Violin, [led by] Juhan" (*CGDA*, 15 May 1788); a "Flute Quatuor, [led] by Mr. Stone" (*Times*, 8 May 1802); a "Quartetto on the bassoon, [led] by Mr. Perossier" (*CGDA*, 27 August 1808); and a "Quartetto, on the Clarionet, [led] by Mr. Andral" (ibid., 3 March 1815).

111. Unspecified quartets led by clarinet are mentioned in *CGDA*, 14 December 1793 and 13 December 1799. References to unspecified quartets by Pleyel appear in ibid., 15 February 1793, 14 December 1793, and 26 March 1795. Pleyel quartets led by a flute are mentioned in ibid., 13 December 1799, and *Courier*, 15 April 1811. Pleyel quartets led by

a violin are mentioned in *CGDA,* 6 March 1794, 8 November 1798, 4 January 1802, and 27 May 1812.

112. Such references to quartets include one by Daveaux (*CGDA,* 16 April 1795); a "Quartetto, on the Clarinet, [led] by an Amateur, Furche [Fuchs]" (*Courier,* 28 February 1804); a "Quartetto, Concertante for a French Horn, Violin and two Violincellos, [performed] by Mr. Muck and Messrs. Remoussins, Punto" (*CGDA,* 3 July 1810); and Rode quartets led by a violin (ibid., 30 March 1813, and *Courier,* 1 November 1819).

113. Franceschini's April 1774 benefit included a "Sonata on the Harpsichord," and the St. Cecilia Society's 1778 anniversary concert included a "Harpsichord Sonata" in the middle of the second (central) act (see *SCG,* 28 March 1774, and the St. Cecilia Society handbill).

114. *CH,* 1 October 1787. Act 1 of this concert included a "Sonata Piano Forte, Mr. Juhan, Haydn," while act 2 included a "Sonata Piano Forte, Mr. Juhan, Juhan." James Juhan was known to be a keyboardist, but the sonata in question was probably composed by Alexander Juhan, for in June 1792 he advertised his intention to publish a set of six keyboard sonatas (*CGDA,* 12 June 1792). In ibid., 25 January 1793, Juhan announced "Just received and for sale . . . Three sonatas for the piano forte or harpsichord, one with an accompaniment for the flute or violin, and two without, composed by Alexander Juhan, being a part of his book of six sonatas, the three last of which will appear as soon as possible." No further information regarding these sonatas has been found.

115. For example Mrs. Sully, a regular concert soloist in Charleston from the mid-1790s through the early 1800s, performed a "Sonata Piano Forte" on the St. Cecilia Society's March 1794 concert to aid St. Domingan refugees and two unidentified sonatas on the "grand piano forte" at J. West's 1795 benefit (*CGDA,* 6 March 1794 and 16 April 1795).

116. References to sonatas include a Dussek sonata (ibid., 26 March 1795), Clementi sonatas (ibid., 8 November 1798, and *Courier,* 25 October 1815), and Cramer sonatas (*CGDA,* 13 December 1799, and *Courier,* 8 February 1814). Cramer's "Caledonian Air, with Variations" is mentioned in *CGDA,* 30 March 1813; *Courier,* 25 March 1814 and 6 May 1813. A "Chase" by Cramer and "Le Depart de Paris pour St. Petersburg" are mentioned in *CGDA,* 3 March 1815. A sonata by Valentino Nicolai and a "Sonata and Rondo on the Piano Forte" by "Dussek and Steibelt" are mentioned in ibid., 13 March 1807. Also mentioned are "An Air, with Variations on the Piano Forte" by Steibelt (*Courier,* 16 March 1813) and "The Belizaire, with variations," by Steibelt (*CGDA,* 6 October 1815).

117. A Pleyel sonata is mentioned in *CGDA,* 21 March 1796. An "Air, with Variations" by Steibelt and "a Fantasia, with variations" by Beethoven are mentioned in *Courier,* 16 March 1813. The variations "Life let us Cherish" by Wölfl are mentioned in ibid., 25 October 1815. A "Rondo, with variations" by Wölfl is mentioned in ibid., 18 March 1816 and 14 December 1816. Piano variations by Boieldieu are mentioned in ibid., 13 March 1819. A "Nocturne, on the Piano Forte, with an accompaniment on the French Horn," [composed by?] "Nodermand and F. Davernoy," is mentioned in ibid., 14 December 1816.

118. Johnson, *Musical Interludes in Boston,* 70, testifies to the popularity of this work at concerts in Boston. Gerson, *Music in Philadelphia,* 38, says that George Schetky orchestrated Koczwara's *Battle* in Philadelphia, ca. 1793. A letter from "An Old Batchelor [*sic*]" in *Times,* 1 August 1805, promoting Mr. Placide's upcoming benefit at Vauxhall Garden (performed on 21 August 1805), promises a performance of "the *Overture of the Battle of Prague:* by the intended addition of amateurs to the band—of itself excellent. I

have no doubt but that the audience will be enabled to have a just conception of this piece of music, so much admired in Europe." Other Vauxhall performances of this piece were advertised in *Courier,* 18 July 1809 (performed "by a full orchestra") and 24 August 1809 ("with a full orchestra").

119. "La Bataille de Trenton" is mentioned in *CGDA,* 5 March 1799.

120. Gilfert's 1816 benefit, for example, included his "Pot Pouri, for Piano Forte in which will be introduced Nina, with Variations" (*Courier,* 18 March 1816). Mr. Taylor's 1816 concert, the one mentioned by Mrs. Derby as being a competition between Madame Labat and Charles Gilfert, included Miss [Ursule] Labat playing Geleneck's "Valse, varia," Madame Labat playing a sonata by Dussek, and, "by Particular desire, Mrs. Labat will play the Spanish Air, with variations, which was received with so much applause at her Concert [last spring]." At that concert Gilfert performed his own "French Air [Nina, no doubt], with variations" (ibid., 25 March 1816). As a further example of local composition, Mrs. Placide's 1813 concert included Arnold Remoussin playing his own variations on "Oui j'aime a Boire moi" (ibid., 16 February 1813).

121. It is interesting that the only extant published concert program from this period in which no vocal music was included occurred during the British occupation of Charleston. See the advertisement for Franceschini's benefit in *RG,* 18–22 May 1782.

122. Burchell, *Polite or Commercial,* 61.

123. For a discussion of the vocal music and vocal styles performed in the United States between approximately 1785 and 1815, see Hamm, *Yesterdays,* 1–25, and Porter, *With An Air Debonair,* 305–60. Catches and glees, composed mostly for men to sing at their convivial gatherings, do not appear on the Charleston concert programs as their content would not have been appropriate for such serious, mixed-sex events. Burchell, *Polite or Commercial,* 61, states that the Edinburgh Musical Society practiced a similar censorship.

124. A complete examination of the composers, song titles, and vocal styles heard during this era is beyond the scope of the present project. Transcriptions of Charleston concert programs can be found in Sonneck, *Early Concert-Life* and *Early Opera in America;* and Hindman, "Concert Life in Ante Bellum Charleston."

125. Fiske, *English Theatre Music,* 269.

126. *SCG,* 28 September–5 October 1765 and 19–31 October 1765.

127. *SCAGG,* 13–20 June 1766, 20–27 November 1767, 6–13 May 1774. *The Summer's Tale* (1765) is a comedy by Richard Cumberland with music by Samuel Arnold, Arne, Abel, and others. *Daphne and Amintor* (1765) is a comic opera pastiche with text by Isaac Bickerstaff. Throughout the final years of the eighteenth century and through the War of 1812, emphasis was placed on following the latest musical fashions of London. Thomas Bradford, for example, advertised in 1793 the importation from London of the "songs sung this season at Vauxhall," and in 1800 "a large assortment of New Songs" (*CGDA,* 30 September 1793 and 25 October 1800). In 1802 Thornhill, Wallis, and Company announced the importation of "A variety of the last new Songs" (ibid., 12 January 1802). In 1804 Eckhard advertised an assortment of the "newest Operas, Songs, &c. (*Courier,* 10 May 1804) and in 1806 "the newest English Songs" (*Times,* 10 June 1806). In 1805 De-Villers sold "New English and French Songs" (ibid., 15 November 1805) and in 1811 "A Collection of the most fashionable Songs" (*Courier,* 26 March 1811).

128. Quoted in Sonneck, "A Contemporary Account," 98.

129. See *CH*, 1 October 1787.

130. *CGDA*, 12 May 1789 (Tuesday): "The truly musical song of 'The Lark's shrill notes invites [awakes] the moon [morn],' was sung on Saturday night by Miss Wall in a capital manner. With excellent musical accompaniments, this young lady gave even a novelty to repetition [that is, she embellished the repetitions], and infused into the enraptured auditors the soul of divine harmony."

131. Ibid., 4 March 1800.

132. See ibid., 5 January 1802 and 8 January 1802.

133. See ibid., 18 February 1803.

134. *Courier*, 5 April 1804.

135. *Times*, 2 April 1805.

136. *CGDA*, 3 March 1807.

137. *Courier*, 5 March 1811.

138. Ibid., 21 March 1811.

139. *Times*, 16 February 1813. Mrs. Waring sang a very similar song by Moore, "You tell me your heart is another's," at Mr. Gallaher's 1816 concert (*Courier*, 2 May 1816).

140. Ibid., 16 March 1813.

141. Ibid., 14 December 1816.

142. Ibid., 10 March 1817.

143. Ibid., 9 February 1817.

144. *SCGPA*, 3–6 March 1784.

145. *CH*, 9 May 1785.

146. Ibid., 1 July 1785.

147. Tommaso Giordani and Giusto Ferdinando Tenducci, *Queen Mary's Lamentation* (1782). The cited quotation appears on the title page of this edition. This song, which begins with the line "I sigh and lament me in vain," was published in score for voice, two violins, viola, and bass.

148. The "Giardini" mentioned in this review was probably Felice Giardini, who, though best remembered for his violin works, also composed Italian operas and English songs. Allowing for the possibility of a printer's error, however, the composer in question could also have been Tommaso Giordani or Giuseppe Giordani, who were both best known for their vocal music.

149. The diary of William Dunlap contains many references to Mrs. Oldmixon, who was also heard at theaters in Baltimore and in New York.

150. Italian songs by Paisiello are mentioned in *CGDA*, 4 January 1802; *Courier*, 27 April 1812; *CGDA*, 25 May 1812; *Courier*, 29 November 1813 ("Nel cor più no mi sento").

151. Madame DeLarousserie, "lately arrived from Germany, first singer of the Grand Opera, Pupil of Mengozy," sang a "Grand Arietto, sung in Italian" by Mozart (*CGDA*, 19 May 1802). Mozart's duet "The Manly Heart" (an adaptation of the duet "Bei Männern, welche Liebe fühlen" from *Die Zauberflöte*) is mentioned in ibid., 19 January 1808, and *Courier*, 10 March 1817. "Forget me not"—attributed to Mozart when published as "Vergiss mein nicht" by Clementi in London in 1799, but really the work of Georg Laurenz Schneider—is mentioned in *Courier*, 21 May 1812. Mozart's "'O dolce Contenti' with variations, arranged by the celebrated Signora Catalani" is mentioned in ibid., 26 October 1815 and 4 February 1819. This was an arrangement of "Das klinget so herrlich" from *Die Zauberflöte* with vocal variations by Italian soprano Angelica Catalani

(1780–1849), who made her London debut in 1806. A "Song, in the style of the celebrated Signora Catalani" is mentioned in ibid., 25 October 1815 and 25 March 1816.

152. Trajetta probably arrived in Charleston with other members of the theatrical company from Boston or New York in October 1801; see *Times*, 25 September 1801, and *CGDA*, 29 October 1801 and 1 January 1802. Over the next several years he appeared as vocal soloist, composer, instrumental performer, and conductor at a number of events. Announcing himself as "Master of Music and Composer, from Naples," on 5 January 1802 Trajetta sang an "Italian Song" by Paisiello, and with the assistance of Mr. Story sang a "French Duetto" identified only as by "Trajetta" (*CGDA*, 4 January 1802). Trajetta's own "Canzonetta Venetiana, accompanied on the Piano Forte," and a "Scena di Berenice" by his father are mentioned in ibid., 8 January 1802. An unspecified song by "Trajetta" is mentioned in ibid., 17 March 1807. The time of Trajetta's departure from Charleston is not certain, but Trajetta probably left the city after a publicized argument over the cancellation of his comic opera *Harlequin's Triumph in War and in Love* owing to insufficient rehearsals in March 1808. For more information on this event, see ibid., 15 March 1808; *Times*, 17 March 1808; *CGDA*, 18 March 1808; and *Times*, 18 March 1808.

153. Mr. Perossier, "lately from Havana," sang "An Italian Song" by "Piccini" [*sic*] at an 1808 concert (*CGDA*, 27 August 1808). *The Servant Mistress*, "translated from the Italian, by Pergoleze," was performed at the City Theatre in September 1796 and repeated at Mr. Lavalette's 1797 theatrical benefit (ibid., 15 September 1796 and 10 May 1797). Several sacred vocal pieces by Pergolesi were also heard at oratorio concerts in early-nineteenth-century Charleston. Madame DeLarousserie performed a "Grand Arietto de Ariane" in ibid., 19 May 1802. This could have been from the operatic setting of the story of Ariadne on Naxos by Signor Edelmann or Georg Benda or from Haydn's solo cantata on that subject. At his 1812 benefit Mr. Garelli, "first singer at the Opera Houses of London and Paris," sang an unidentified recitative and aria by Cimarosa, arias by Paisiello and Nicolini, and a comic song by Giovanni Liverati. With the assistance of Mrs. Placide, he sang a duet by "Andrevzai" (?). With Mrs. Placide and Miss Thomas, Garelli also sang an unidentified terzetto by Tritto (*Courier*, 2 March 1812). This was probably Tritto's work published in England as *The Favorite Terzetto as Performed . . . at the Kings Theatre Pantheon in the Opera of "La bella pescatrice"* (1791). At Cornelia Thomas's benefit concert in May 1812, Miss Thomas and Mrs. Placide sang a "duetto" entitled "Sweet is the breath of Morn" (*CGDA*, 25 May 1812). This was actually a English arrangement of John Milton's verse set to the Jommelli duet "Non dan pace." In addition several foreign musicians passed through Charleston in the years after the War of 1812 and performed Italian songs, but none lingered. For example: "Signior Granella, Italian, lately from Naples, a Member of the celebrated Musical Academy of the said city," performed a number of Italian arias at his concert in November 1818. See *Courier*, 3 November 1818.

154. For example the 1793 "Public Concert" included a "French song, accompanied by the guitar and violin" (*CGDA*, 15 February 1793). Mrs. Pownall sang a "French Song" at LeRoy's 1795 benefit and Messrs. Petit and Villars's 1796 benefit (ibid., 17 December 1795 and 3 March 1796).

155. Mrs. Marshall sang Thomas Linley's "O Richard, O My Love," an adaptation of a song from Grétry's 1785 opera *Richard Cœur-de-lion*, at the St. Cecilia Society's 1800 concert for the Salter family (ibid., 4 March 1800). In 1802 Madame DeLarousserie sang a "Grand Arietto" from Grétry's 1778 opera *Les fausses apparences, ou L'amant jaloux*

(ibid., 19 May 1802). Sophia Sully sang "Comme un éclair" from Grétry's *La fausse magie* (1775) at Miss Dupuy's 1811 benefit (*Courier*, 30 October 1811). Miss Sully sang "Richard Coeur de Lion" at the Philharmonic Society's 1814 anniversary concert (ibid., 17 February 1814). Constance Labat and "an Amateur" sang a duet from Grétry's *Zémire et Azor* (1771) at Ursule Labat's 1815 benefit (*CGDA*, 3 March 1815). At her own 1810 benefit and at Mr. LeFolle's 1812 benefit, Cornelia Thomas sang "Est il un Sort plus glorieux," identified as a work by Gluck and by Grétry in the respective programs (*Courier*, 3 December 1810 and 21 May 1812).

156. Antoinette La Roque sang "an ariette from the celebrated Opera of Nina" at the St. Cecilia Society's 1805 concert for Hodgkinson's orphans (*Courier*, 1 November 1805). *CGDA*, 23 July 1794, carried an advertisement for a performance of "the opera *Nina*" at the French Theatre. Considering that this was a French theater, the work in question was undoubtedly Dalayrac's 1786 work *Nina, ou, La folle par amour*. Nearly a decade later, however, the "Opera of Nina; Or, Love and Madness" was advertised for a performance at the Charleston Theatre in *Courier*, 3 April 1805, and described as "Never performed here. With the Original Music." Whether this was a performance of an English adaptation of Dalayrac's opera, or a similar adaptation of Giovanni Paisiello's 1789 opera entitled *Nina* is not clear. At Mrs. Placide's 1813 benefit sponsored by the St. Cecilia Society, however, Antoinette La Roque Robin sang "O ma Nina," a piece identified as a work by Dalayrac (*Courier*, 16 February 1813). Miss Labat sang unspecified songs from Boieldieu's *Le Calife de Bagdad* (see *CGDA*, 3 March 1815; *Courier*, 25 March 1816 and 14 December 1816). Although the title of this opera was advertised in English and in French on different occasions, the songs were probably sung in Miss Labat's native French.

157. References to a "Rondeau" and "a select Air and Rondeau called Enfant Cheri Des Dames" from Devienne's *Les Visitandines* appear in *CGDA*, 19 May 1802, and 22 May 1804. Devienne's "O toi dont ma memoire" is mentioned in ibid., 3 March 1807.

158. Trajetta's "Avec l'object de mes Amour" is mentioned in ibid., 23 June 1809 and 25 May 1812; and *Courier*, 29 January 1813. This last issue also mentions Trajetta's duet "Mon Coeur supire des L'Aurore."

159. A reference to a "French Song, Accompanied on the Harp" by Milico appears in *CGDA*, 8 November 1798. Méhul's "Quand le Guerrier vole aux Combats" (probably from *Le Jeune Henri*) and LeMoyne's "Palais des Dieux" are mentioned in ibid., 26 February 1805. A song from Kreutzer's *Lodoiska* is mentioned in *Courier*, 21 May 1812. A "French Song" by Berton is mentioned in ibid., 26 October 1815.

160. References to works by Sacchini include A "Bravura Song" (*CGDA*, 8 November 1798); "Dieu! Ce n'est pas pour moi" from *Oedipe a Colone*, and a Sacchini piece in translation ("Leave not the Man of Worth without a Friend") (ibid., 28 February 1804); "Le fils des Dieus" from *Oedipe* and "Ciel Injuste!" from *Renaud* (*Courier*, 5 April 1804); the "Grand Song from the Opera of Ranaud [*Renaud*], 'Deja la Trumpette Guerriere,' accompanied on the trumpet by Mr. Muck," the "Song, from the Opera of Chimene, 'Je vois dan mon Amant l'assassin, de mon Pere,'" and an unspecified duet from *Renaud* (ibid., 4 June 1804); "Leave not the Man of Worth without a Friend" (*CGDA*, 26 February 1805); "Pere Barbare" and the "Favorite Aria 'T'aresta Engrata'" (ibid., 3 March 1807); "A French Bravura Song" (ibid., 3 July 1810); "Ciel Injust" (*Courier*, 16 February 1813); and an ariette from *Oedipe à Colone* (*CGDA*, 3 March 1815).

161. Compare, for example, the above-mentioned musical repertoire with the "Cumulative index of orchestral repertoire by year and composer," 1750–99, in Burchell, *Polite or Commercial,* 303–77. This list was compiled from extant evidence of concerts in Bath, Edinburgh, Oxford, Manchester, and Newcastle.

Chapter 10

1. Fraser, *Reminiscences,* 60.

2. Farmer, *An Address,* 3.

3. Weber, *The Rise of Musical Classics in Eighteenth-Century England,* offers the best description of the origins of this phenomenon in England. Broyles, *"Music of the Highest Class,"* provides a strong description of the emphasis placed on the morality of music in early-nineteenth-century Boston. For further discussion of the rise of musical classics and democratically oriented choral societies in Europe, see also Raynor, *Music and Society since 1815,* 86–99; Fulcher, "The Orphéon Societies," 47–56; Dalhaus, *Nineteenth-Century Music,* 160–90. For a discussion of related phenomena in the United States, see Ahlquist, *Democracy at the Opera;* Levine, *Highbrow/Lowbrow;* Rasmussen, *Musical Taste as a Religious Question.*

4. Susannah Holmes, daughter of Union Harmonic Society president Charles Holmes, is described as a member of that society in the announcement of her funeral at the Baptist Church (*Courier,* 5 October 1822).

5. Ibid., 30 January 1821.

6. See Farmer, *An Address,* 5; Handel and Haydn Society, *History of the Handel and Haydn Society,* 1:39.

7. *Courier,* 8 April 1819.

8. Farmer, *An Address,* 4.

9. *Courier,* 24 October 1823.

10. Quincy, "Journal," 442.

11. Sonneck, "A Contemporary Account," 98.

12. *Courier,* 1 November 1805 (Friday). The context of Mrs. Oldmixon's performance and of this concert are discussed in chapter 8.

13. *Times,* 2 February 1811.

14. Ibid., 8 February 1811.

15. Ibid.

16. Weber, "Did People Listen in the 18th Century?" 689–90.

17. McInnis, *The Politics of Taste,* 284–86.

18. Weber, "Did People Listen in the 18th Century?" 681.

19. Rutledge, "Letters from Thomas Pinckney Jr. to Harriott Pinckney," 113, quoting a letter dated 2 February 1802. Despite the young Pinckney's animosity toward Smith, later that month Smith was elected a manager of the St. Cecilia Society.

20. *Times,* 5 September 1808; *Courier,* 20 March 1813, 1 February 1814, and 7 January 1819.

21. *Courier,* 14 December 1809, 26 March 1810, 16 April 1810, 19 April 1810, 3 January 1816, 10 February 1817, and 13 February 1817.

22. Ibid., 21 November 1817 and 10 March 1818.

23. See the letter from "Alcanor" in *Times,* 5 January 1809. Note that I have corrected the flawed wording of the original phrase "Northern named the Carolinians thermometer."

24. Margaret Izard Manigault, Charleston, S.C., to Alice Izard, Philadelphia, 10 March 1811, Izard Family Papers, Library of Congress: "Pray tell Tom [Smith?] that his friend le Folle is very much admired here—& is about to give a Concert next Thursday. All of our party are engaged to a Ball at Mrs. Gregories—but they have all taken tickets to Patronize this [missing word]. Our St. Cecilia Society concerts are sadly fallen off." I am greatly indebted to Alice Skelsey for bringing this letter to my attention. LeFolle's concert is noted in *Courier,* 21 March 1811, the day of performance.

25. Fraser, *Reminiscences,* 61.

26. The subjects are identified as James Rose, Arthur Middleton, John Rutledge, Henry Bounetheau, Henry Middleton, William Skirving Smith, Henry Mey, Charles Parker, Thomas Middleton, Frederick Kinloch, John H. Wilson, and Abraham Miller.

27. *Courier,* 26 June 1827.

28. Mills, *Statistics of South Carolina,* 436.

29. Charleston's transformation from energetic and cosmopolitan to passive and insular around the year 1820 is discussed in Rogers, *Charleston,* 141–66. The broader national significance of this process of transformation, or "changing of the guard," is discussed in Jaher, *The Urban Establishment,* 317–451.

Conclusion

1. Rath, *How Early America Sounded.*

2. See, for example, McCord, *Statutes at Large,* 7:410, article 36 of "An Act for the Better Ordering and Governing of Negroes," passed on 10 May 1740 in response to the Stono uprising; Hall, *Ordinances of the City Council of Charleston,* 49 and 111, "An Ordinance to prohibit the frequent beating of Drums," passed in 1787 and updated in 1794; Eckhard, *A Digest of the Ordinances of the City Council of Charleston,* 169–73, "An Ordinance for the Government of Negroes and other Persons of Color," passed in 1806.

3. Eighteenth-century subscription concerts in New York, Philadelphia, and Boston are mentioned, but not explored, in Sonneck, *Early Concert-Life;* Gerson, *Music in Philadelphia;* Howard, *Our American Music;* Odell, *Annals of the New York Stage;* and Johnson, *Musical Interludes in Boston.*

4. Pease and Pease, *The Web of Progress,* provides a valuable comparison of these two cities during the second quarter of the nineteenth century.

Appendix 1

1. See, for example, *CGDA,* 19 November 1791.

2. During the months of October, November, and December 1766, the society published ten known concert announcements in three separate newspapers. The first two notices, dated 8 October and published in *SCAGG,* 3–10 October 1766, and *SCG,* 6–13 October 1766, concern a concert performed on Tuesday, 14 October. Three subsequent advertisements, in *SCGCJ,* 21 October 1766, 28 October 1766, and 11 November 1766 (all Tuesdays), also bear the date 8 October, but refer vaguely to concerts "on Tuesday evening next." The remaining five concert notices published in 1766, in *SCAGG,* 7–14 November 1766; *SCG,* 10–17 November 1766; and *SCGCJ,* 18 November 1766, 25 November 1766, and 2 December 1766, all bear the date 13 November and refer to a concert on Tuesday, 25 November. On first examination it may appear that third, fourth, and fifth of these ten notices, dated 8 October, were intended to advertise the concert on 14

October but were mistakenly published after the concert had already taken place. The fact that they refer vaguely to concerts on "Tuesday evening next," suggests, however, that concerts may have taken place on 28 October and 11 November, thus creating a fortnightly schedule from 14 October. This possibility is strengthened by the fact that the next confirmed concert performance took place two weeks later, on 25 November. The last of these ten advertisements, published on 2 December, may have been intended to remind the members of a concert to be performed on 9 December, thus continuing the fortnightly schedule. Since the society's concert series may have been the first reoccurring social event in Charleston, it may have taken a few months to learn how to advertise its events in the most efficient manner. *SCAGG,* 29 December–2 January 1767 and 27 March–3 April 1767.

3. *SCG,* 28 September–5 October 1767. The society's unadvertised anniversary meeting was reviewed in ibid., 23–30 November 1767; a concert probably took place that evening. The concert performed on 10 May was originally scheduled (but not advertised) for 19 April but was postponed. See *SCGCJ,* 19 April 1768 and 26 April 1768.

4. The society's unadvertised anniversary meeting was reviewed in *SCGCJ,* 8 December 1772; a concert probably took place that evening. *SCG,* 22 February 1773 and 8 March 1773.

5. At its anniversary meeting on Monday, 22 November 1773, the society adopted a set of rules that mandated a concert on the anniversary. See *SCG,* 8 November 1773. As in subsequent years, the society's concert season presumably began around October and continued fortnightly into the spring of 1774.

6. *SCAGG,* 29 July–5 August 1774 and 14–21 October 1774. The assertion that the society's fortnightly concerts were continued through the spring of 1775 is supported by the advertisement for the quarterly meeting on 18 May 1775, which states that the performers' contracts were about to expire. See *SCGCJ,* 9 May 1775.

7. *SCGGA,* 11 October 1783; Cometti, *Seeing America,* 55; *SCGPA,* 6–10 March 1784 (a postconcert notice of performance at the State House); M. I. [Margaret Izard] to, Miss Stead, 30 March 1784, Manigault Family Papers, SCHS, 11/276/69: In a section dated "Thursday night" [1 April], "I am very much vex'd my dear Cousin, I have not been to the Concert on account of the Mau's [*sic*] insolent behaviour; Being the last I would be at for a long time, I wished vastly to go to it"; *SCGGA,* 17–20 April 1784.

8. *SCSGDA,* 16 December 1784 and 10 February 1785. In *CH,* 9 May 1785, a correspondent advised Storer "not to introduce any more Italian songs, at the St. Cecilia concert," probably referring to a performance on Thursday, 5 May; *CH,* 1 July 1785, said Maria Storer sang last night at the St. Cecilia concert. The concerts probably continued until Storer's departure in January 1786.

9. *CEG,* 12 August 1785, mentioned a St. Cecilia concert last night featuring Storer and Henri Capron; *SCGPA,* 17 December 1785 (Saturday), carried a notice from the managers of the St. Cecilia Society, dated 15 December, stating that the concerts "in future will begin at seven o'clock precisely."

10. *CMPDA,* 5 December 1786, announced a concert for 7 December, which "will be continued once a fortnight as usual"; *CMPDA,* 19 December 1786; *CH,* 25 December 1786 (Monday), carried an advertisement dated 19 December for a St. Cecilia concert "Thursday evening next" (28 December). This may have been a newspaper error.

11. *CH,* 11 October 1787 and 12 November 1787; *CGDA,* 13 December 1787 and 9 January 1788.

12. *CGDA,* 15 November 1788.

13. Ibid., 5 November 1789.

14. Very few Charleston newspapers survive from 1790. According to *CGDA,* 6 May 1791 (Friday), George Washington attended the society's concert at City Hall on 5 May. Calculating backward at two-week intervals leads to the second Thursday in January—the usual date for the recommencement of the society's spring concerts.

15. *CGDA,* 7 October 1791, 9 November 1791; 28 November 1791; and 8 February 1792. According to ibid., 4 April 1792, the society was to meet and discuss the possibility of holding summer concerts on 6 April 1792.

16. Ibid., 13 November 1792, 26 March 1793, and 15 May 1793.

17. *CH,* 5 September 1793, 19 September 1793, and 12 November 1793; *CGDA,* 14 November 1793, 27 November 1793, 7 December 1793, and 7 January 1794; James Brown's ticket, discussed in chapter 4, proves the concert on 23 January; *CGDA,* 25 February 1794 and 17 March 1794. The 7 December 1793 notice of a holiday recess marks the first public announcement of what was probably a regular feature of the society's earlier concert seasons and a practice that continued through the rest of its years of concert activity.

18. *CGDA,* 19 November 1794, 25 November 1794, 8 January 1795, 13 January 1795, 17 February 1795, and 27 February 1795.

19. It appears that all Charleston newspapers from the beginning of July 1795 through September are lost. It is therefore impossible to tell when the society's season began. On 6 October 1795 the managers resolved "to continue the concerts" until the anniversary (see ibid., 30 October 1795); ibid., 7 January 1796 and 18 February 1796.

20. Ibid., 13 September 1796, 12 November 1796, 7 January 1797, and 8 February 1797.

21. Ibid., 7 September 1797, 16 November 1797, 9 December 1797, 21 February 1798, and 26 April 1798.

22. Ibid., 3 October 1798, 15 November 1798, 6 December 1798, 8 January 1799, 24 January 1799, 21 February 1799, 13 March 1799, 28 March 1799, and 11 April 1799.

23. Ibid., 29 October 1799, 12 November 1799, 8 January 1800, 29 January 1800, 12 February 1800, 5 March 1800, 20 March 1800, 30 April 1800, and 9 May 1800.

24. Ibid., 29 October 1800, 14 November 1800, 29 December 1800, and 2 April 1801.

25. Ibid., 24 October 1801, 12 November 1801, 20 November 1801, 13 January 1802, 28 January 1802, and 11 February 1802; *Times,* 4 March 1802; *CGDA,* 18 March 1802.

26. *CGDA,* 21 October 1802, and 8 December 1802; *Courier,* 13 January 1803, 25 January 1803, and 3 February 1803; *CGDA,* 12 February 1803; *Courier,* 3 March 1803; *CGDA,* 15 March 1803 and 29 March 1803.

27. *CGDA,* 14 October 1803, 21 November 1803, 7 December 1803, 8 December 1803, 26 January 1804, 9 February 1804, 22 February 1804, 7 March 1804, and 21 March 1804.

28. Ibid., 16 October 1804, 7 November 1804, 16 November 1804, and 5 December 1804; *Courier,* 14 January 1805, 30 January 1805, 14 February 1805, 28 February 1805, and 13 March 1805.

29. *Courier,* 17 October 1805; *CGDA,* 7 November 1805; *Courier,* 18 November 1805, 5 December 1805, and 16 January 1806; *Times,* 30 January 1806 and 13 February 1806; *Courier,* 27 February 1806 and 12 March 1806.

30. *Courier,* 16 October 1806; *Times,* 5 November 1806; *Courier,* 17 November 1806; *Times,* 4 December 1806 and 14 January 1807; *CGDA,* 29 January 1807; *Courier,* 11 February 1807 and 18 March 1807.

31. *Courier,* 19 October 1807; *Times,* 27 October 1807; *Courier,* 12 November 1807; *Times,* 24 November 1807; *Courier,* 9 December 1807, 13 January 1808, 28 January 1808, 11 February 1808, and 25 February 1808; *Times,* 9 March 1808 and 22 March 1808.

32. *Times,* 19 October 1808 and 10 November 1808; *CGDA,* 23 November 1808; *Times,* 8 December 1808; *CGDA,* 21 January 1809; *Times,* 9 February 1809 and 21 February 1809; *Courier,* 9 March 1809 and 13 March 1809: the concert announced for 15 March, just six days after a regularly scheduled Thursday concert, may have been given in honor of General James Wilkinson, commander of the U. S. Army, who arrived in Charleston on 17 February 1809 (see *Courier,* 18 February 1809) and left very soon after this performance; *Courier,* 21 March 1809.

33. *Courier,* 7 November 1809, 16 November 1809, 21 November 1809, 6 December 1809, 20 December 1809, 10 January 1810, 23 January 1810, 8 February 1810, 21 February 1810, 7 March 1810, 20 March 1810, and 22 March 1810.

34. Ibid., 13 November 1810; *Times,* 21 November 1810; *Courier,* 5 December 1810, 9 January 1811, 15 January 1811, 29 January 1811; 13 February 1811, 6 March 1811, 26 March 1811, 9 April 1811, 11 April 1811, and 15 April 1811. With the exception of the first and last concerts, each of the St. Cecilia Society's performances during the 1810–11 season was advertised with ordinal numbers (such as "second concert," "third concert").

35. *Courier,* 31 October 1811, 15 November 1811, and 4 December 1811 (the society held a concert on Friday, 6 December, because City Council decreed 5 December a day of general thanksgiving); *Times,* 15 January 1812 and 28 January 1812; *Courier,* 13 February 1812; *Times,* 12 March 1812, 2 April 1812; *Courier,* 7 April 1812.

36. *Courier,* 17 January 1812, 5 January 1813, 19 January 1813, 4 February 1813, 19 February 1813, 10 March 1813, and 23 March 1813.

37. Ibid., 3 November 1813, 19 November 1813, 9 December 1813, 20 January 1814, and 18 February 1814. The last concert was probably on a Tuesday because the "Annual Races" commenced on Wednesday, 23 February, according to ibid., 23 February 1814.

38. Ibid., 2 March 1815.

39. Ibid., 13 November 1815, 5 December 1815, 13 January 1816, and 3 February 1816. In ibid., 5 March 1816, a St. Cecilia concert was advertised for Thursday, 7 March, but ibid., 7 March 1816, carried a notice that "The Concert is postponed until further notice." No further notice appeared, and thus the concert was effectively cancelled. Complications arising from the unsettled ownership of Concert Hall may have played a part in this confusion.

40. Ibid., 14 November 1816, 23 November 1816, 7 December 1816, 10 January 1817, 27 January 1817, 8 February 1817, 25 February 1817, and 14 March 1817.

41. Commencement of the season was delayed by the absence of the musicians with the Charleston Theatre company. Ibid., 24 January 1818, 6 February 1818, 21 February 1818, 6 March 1818, and 20 March 1818.

42. Ibid., 10 November 1818, 20 November 1818, and 7 January 1819; the performance on 28 January was announced in ibid., 21 January 1819, as a "concert" and then changed to a "ball" in ibid., 28 January 1819; ibid., 18 February 1819; the concert on 1 May was given for President Monroe (see ibid., 30 April 1819).

43. Ibid., 11 December 1819, 14 January 1820, 10 February 1820, 14 February 1820, 19 February 1820, and 9 March 1820.

Appendix 4

1. The St. Cecilia Society's election returns, which list the names and titles of its officers, were published in *SCG*, 23–30 November 1767, 3 December 1772, 6 December 1773; *SCWG*, 28 November 1783; *SCSGGA*, 20–23 November 1784; *CGDA*, 23 November 1791, 24 November 1792, 27 November 1793, 24 November 1794, 27 February 1796, 24 February 1800, and 20 February 1802; *Courier*, 23 February 1803, 18 February 1804, and 23 February 1805; *Times*, 21 February 1806; *Courier*, 20 February 1807; *CGDA*, 20 February 1808 and 18 February 1809; *Courier*, 17 February 1810 (at which time all the 1809 officers were re-elected), 18 August 1810, 17 August 1811, 25 August 1812, 21 August 1813, 21 August 1815, 6 September 1817, 25 August 1818, 19 August 1820, 20 August 1821, 24 November 1824, and 25 November 1825. In many cases only the initials of the given names of the officers were published in the election returns. In this appendix I have expanded those names when the identity is clear. In cases where there is some ambiguity about the identity of the officer in question, I have provided the name as published in the newspaper.

2. The extant papers of the court cases generally include a receipt showing the breakdown of the defendant's debt, a copy of the writ served to the defendant, the plaintiff's complaint (a legal argument with little or no case-specific data), and the judgment against the defendant.

3. Readers curious about the sources behind this list and biographical details about the men are encouraged to consult Nicholas Michael Butler, "Votaries of Apollo," 449–517.

4. McVeigh, *Concert Life*, 20, states that a "typical" subscription from the 1760s to the early 1790s was five hundred people.

5. Weber, "London," 299.

6. Fraser, *Reminiscences*, 59.

7. According to the manuscript notes of Wilmot Gibbes deSaussure: "The Society was formed 28 April 1766, and the officers elected were John Moultrie, President, Alexander Garden, Vice President, Isaac Motte, Treasurer. The original members, 37 in number, were John Moultrie, Alexander Garden, Isaac Motte, David Oliphant, John Gordon, William Pillans, Benjamin Yarnold, Donald Bruce, Thomas Bee, Henry Peronneau, Owen Roberts, James Crallon [Crallan], Thomas Loughton Smith, Edward Lightwood Jr., Thomas Moultrie, Roger Smith, George Roupell, Anthony L. Labbe [L'Abbé], Alexander Rose, Thomas Shirley, William Carson, Isaac Huger, John Deas, W. W. Crosthwaite, Thomas Pike, Alexander Fraser, William H. Drayton, George Abbott Hall, James Carson, Peter Valton, John Matthews [Mathews], William Crabb, Lachlan McIntosh, Barnard Elliott, Arthur Middleton, Benjamin Huger, Charles Cotesworth Pinckney" (Wilmot Gibbes deSaussure, "St. Cecilia Society," manuscript notes, ca. 1868, 206). The same names are given in the same sequence in "Charleston In Olden Times," *Courier*, 24 October 1768.

8. See Canaday, *Gentlemen of the Bar*, and Rogers, *Generations of Lawyers*.

9. See Waring, *A Brief History of the South Carolina Medical Association* and *A History of Medicine in South Carolina*.

10. For a list of Charleston's colonial merchants and craftsmen, see Calhoun, Zierden, and Paysinger, "The Geographic Spread of Charleston's Mercantile Community."

11. Thomas, *Reminiscences*, 1:33–34.

12. Edgar, *South Carolina*, 123.

Bibliography

Archives and Collections

Bowen-Cooke Papers, South Carolina Historical Society, Charleston.

James Brown IV Papers, MSS 310, Rhode Island Historical Society, Providence

Carrere Family Papers, 1793–94. South Carolina Historical Society, Charleston.

Charleston County, S.C. Miscellaneous records. South Carolina Civil Works Administration transcriptions.

Charleston County, S.C. Property records, Register of Mesne Conveyance Office.

Charleston County, S.C. Wills, Probate Office. South Carolina Civil Works Administration transcriptions.

Charleston Courier. Advertising Ledger, 1803–9. South Carolina Historical Society, Charleston.

Charleston Lot No. 40 Records, 1769–1833. South Carolina Historical Society, Charleston.

Court of Common Pleas, Charleston County, S.C. Judgment Rolls, 1800–1830. South Carolina Department of Archives and History, Columbia.

Court of Common Pleas, Charleston County, S.C. Petitions and Decrees in Summary Process, 1800–1830. South Carolina Department of Archives and History, Columbia.

Drayton Family Papers. Drayton Hall, National Trust, Charleston, S.C.

Edinburgh Musical Society, Sederunt Books, Edinburgh Central Library.

Fraser-Winthrop Papers, Gibbes Museum of Art, Charleston, S.C., on loan to the South Carolina Historical Society, Charleston.

James Glen Papers, 1738–77. South Caroliniana Library, University of South Carolina, Columbia.

Hinson Clippings Collection, Charleston Library Society, Charleston, S.C.

Alexander Inglis Papers, 1782–1811. South Carolina Historical Society, Charleston.

Ralph Izard Family Papers, 1778–1826. Library of Congress, Washington, D.C.

Francis Kinloch Papers, 1787–1804. South Caroliniana Library, University of South Carolina, Columbia.

Manigault Family Papers, 1685–1971. South Carolina Historical Society, Charleston.

Manigault Family Papers, 1750–1900. South Caroliniana Library, University of South Carolina, Columbia.

Mitchell Papers, M-4282, Southern Historical Collection, University of North Carolina at Chapel Hill.

Harriott Hörrÿ Ravenel Papers, 1694–ca. 1935. South Carolina Historical Society, Charleston.

St. Cecilia Society Collection, 1830–2004. South Carolina Historical Society, Charleston.

St. John's Lutheran Church, Charleston, S.C. Vestry minutes (microfilm).

St. Michael's Episcopal Church, Charleston, S.C. Records. South Carolina Historical Society, Charleston. ·

St. Philip's Episcopal Church, Charleston, S.C. Vestry minutes (microfiche).

William Loughton Smith Papers, 1774–1834. South Carolina Historical Society, Charleston.

South Carolina General Assembly. Committee Reports. South Carolina Department of Archives and History, Columbia.

South Carolina General Assembly. Journals of the South Carolina Senate. South Carolina Department of Archives and History, Columbia.

South Carolina General Assembly. Petitions to the General Assembly. South Carolina Department of Archives and History, Columbia.

South Carolina Society Records, 1790–1890. South Carolina Historical Society, Charleston.

Unpublished Manuscripts

Anonymous. "Instructions for the Kent Bugle." Ca. 1813. South Carolina Historical Society, Charleston.

Bennet, Silvia S. "A Fleeting Show: A Group of Perthshire Families in the West Indies." Typescript, 1982. South Carolina Historical Society, Charleston.

DeSaussure, Wilmot Gibbes. "St. Cecilia Society," ca. 1868, bound with a copy of Charles Fraser's *Reminiscences of Charleston* (1854). Hinson Collection, Charleston Library Society, Charleston, S.C.

Laurens, Henry. Account book, 1766–73. Special Collections, College of Charleston.

Manigault, Gabriel. Journal, 1774–84. South Carolina Historical Society, Charleston.

————. Letters, 1805–8, South Carolina Historical Society, Charleston.

Ogilby, William. Diary, 1830. South Carolina Historical Society, Charleston.

Pinckney, Harriott. Copy book, 1760–69. On loan from the estate of the late Henry Buist Smythe of Charleston to the South Carolina Historical Society, Charleston.

Young, Margaret J. Abernethy, Shenfield, Essex, England, to Mrs. Granville T. [Mary Elizabeth] Prior, Charleston, S.C., August 1967. Vertical file collection, "Abernethie Family," South Carolina Historical Society, Charleston.

Newspapers

Charleston Courier, January 1803–December 1831.

Charleston Evening Gazette, July 1785–October 1786.

Charleston Mercury, January 1822–December 1831.

Charleston Morning Post and Daily Advertiser, January 1786–November 1787

Charlestown Gazette, November 1778–1779.

City Gazette and Daily Advertiser (Charleston), November 1787–December 1831.

Columbian Herald (Charleston), November 1784–December 1796.

Gazette of the State of South-Carolina, April 1777–March 1785.

Royal Gazette (South Carolina), March 1781–September 1782.

Royal South-Carolina Gazette, June 1780–September 1782.

South-Carolina and American General Gazette, April 1764–February 1781.

South-Carolina Gazette, January 1732–December 1775.

South-Carolina Gazette and Country Journal, December 1765–August 1775.

South-Carolina Gazette and General Advertiser, March 1783–October 1784.

South-Carolina Gazette and Public Advertiser, March 1784–January 1786.

South-Carolina State-Gazette, January 1794–September 1802.

South Carolina State Gazette and Daily Advertiser, December 1784–August 1785.

South-Carolina State Gazette and General Advertiser, October 1784–November 1784.

South-Carolina Weekly Advertiser, February 1783–April 1783.

South-Carolina Weekly Gazette, 1758–March 1764.

South-Carolina Weekly Gazette, February 1783–February 1784.

Southern Patriot and Commercial Advertiser, July 1814–December 1831.

State Gazette of South-Carolina, March 1785–December 1793.

Times (Charleston), October 1800–July 1821.

Published Materials

Ahlquist, Karen. *Democracy at the Opera: Music, Theater, and Culture in New York City, 1815–60.* Urbana: University of Illinois Press, 1997.

Andrews, George. *The South-Carolina Almanack and Register for the Year of Our Lord 1763.* Charleston, S.C.: Robert Wells, 1763.

———. *The South-Carolina Almanack and Register for the Year of Our Lord 1765.* Charleston, S.C.: Robert Wells, 1765.

Barker-Benfield, G. J. *The Culture of Sensibility: Sex and Society in Eighteenth-Century Britain.* Chicago: University of Chicago Press, 1992.

Barnwell, Joseph Walker, ed. "Diary of Timothy Ford, 1785–1786." *South Carolina Historical Magazine* 13 (July 1912): 132–47; (October 1912): 181–204.

Barnwell, Robert Woodward, Jr., ed. "George Harland Hartley's Claim for Losses As A Loyalist." *South Carolina Historical Magazine* 51 (January 1950): 45–50.

Bartlett, Ian. "Boyce's Homage to St. Cecilia." *Musical Times* 123 (November 1982): 758–61.

Biddle, Edward, and Mantle Fielding. *The Life and Works of Thomas Sully.* Philadelphia, 1921. Reprint, New York: Da Capo Press, 1970.

Blume, Friedrich. *Classic and Romantic Music: A Comprehensive Survey.* Translated by M. D. Herter Norton. New York: Norton, 1970.

Bowes, Frederick P. *The Culture of Early Charleston.* Chapel Hill: University of North Carolina Press, 1942.

Boyce, William. *William Boyce: Ode for St. Cecilia's Day.* Compact disc. ASV CD GAU 200, 2000.

Boydell, Brian. *Rotunda Music in Eighteenth-Century Dublin.* Dublin: Irish Academic Press, 1992.

Bray, Roger, "Dryden and Draghi in Harmony in the 1687 'Song for St. Cecilia's Day.'" *Music & Letters* 78 (August 1997): 319–36.

Bremner, Robert, ed. *The Periodical Overtures in 8 parts.* 60 issues. London: Robert Bremner, 1763–83.

Brewster, Lawrence Fay. *Summer Migrations and Resorts of South Carolina Low-Country Planters.* Durham: Duke University Press, 1947.

Bridenbaugh, Carl. "Charlestonians at Newport, 1767–1775." *South Carolina Historical Magazine* 41 (April 1940): 43–47.

———. "Colonial Newport as a Summer Resort." *Rhode Island Historical Society Collections* 26 (January 1933): 1–23.

Broyles, Michael. *"Music of the Highest Class": Elitism and Populism in Antebellum Boston.* New Haven: Yale University Press, 1992.

Burchell, Jenny. *Polite or Commercial Concerts?: Concert Management and Orchestral Repertoire In Edinburgh, Bath, Oxford, Manchester, and Newcastle, 1730–1799.* New York: Garland, 1996.

Burke, Edmund. *An Account of the European Settlements in America.* 2 vols. London: J. Dodsley, 1777.

Burney, Charles. *A General History of Music, from the Earliest Ages to the Present Period, to which is prefixed, A Dissertation on the Music of the Ancients.* 4 vols. London, 1776–89.

———. *The Present State of Music in Germany, The Netherlands, and United Provinces, or The Journal of a Tour through Those Countries, Undertaken to Collect Material for a General History of Music.* 2 vols. London: T. Becket, 1773.

Burney, Fanny. *Evelina, or The History of a Young Lady's Entrance Into the World.* London, 1778; New York: Signet Classic, 1992.

Calhoon, Robert M., and Robert M. Weir. "The Scandalous History of Sir Egerton Leigh." *William and Mary Quarterly,* 3rd ser., 26 (January 1969): 47–74.

Calhoun, Jeane A., Martha A. Zierden, and Elizabeth A. Paysinger. "The Geographic Spread of Charleston's Mercantile Community, 1732–1767." *South Carolina Historical Magazine* 86 (July 1985): 182–220.

Canaday, Hoyt Paul. *Gentlemen of the Bar: Lawyers in Colonial South Carolina.* New York: Garland, 1987.

Cardozo, Jacob Newton. *Reminiscences of Charleston.* Charleston, S.C.: Joseph Walker, 1866.

Charleston, S.C. *Year Book, Charleston, S.C., 1881.* Charleston, S.C.: News and Courier Book Presses, 1882.

Charleston, S.C., City Council. *Census of the City of Charleston, South Carolina.* Charleston, S.C.: J. B. Nixon, 1849.

———. *Ordinances of the City of Charleston, from the 19th of August 1844, to the 14th of September 1854.* Charleston, S.C.: A. E. Miller, 1854.

Chevalley, Sylvie. "The Death of Alexandre Placide." *South Carolina Historical Magazine* 58 (January 1957): 63–66.

Cheves, Langdon, "Izard of South Carolina." *South Carolina Historical Magazine* 2 (July 1901): 205–40.

———. ed. *The Shaftesbury Papers.* Charleston: South Carolina Historical Society, 1897. Reprint, Charleston: South Carolina Historical Society, 2000.

Clark, Peter. *British Clubs and Societies, 1580–1800: The Origins of an Associational World.* New York: Oxford University Press, 2000.

Clark, W. A. *The History of the Banking Institutions Organized in South Carolina Prior to 1860.* Columbia, S.C.: State Company for the South Carolina Historical Commission, 1922.

Clingham, Gregory J. "Johnson's Criticism of Dryden's Odes in Praise of St. Cecilia." *Modern Language Studies* 18 (Winter 1988): 165–80.

Cobau, Judith. "The Precarious Life of Thomas Pike, A Colonial Dancing Master in Charleston and Philadelphia." *Dance Chronicle* 17, no. 3 (1994): 229–62.

Coker, P. C., III. *Charleston's Maritime Heritage, 1670–1865*. Charleston, S.C.: Cokercraft Press, 1987.

Colonial Society of Massachusetts. *Music in Colonial Massachusetts, 1630–1820: A Conference Held by the Colonial Society of Massachusetts, May 17 and 18, 1973*. 2 vols. Boston: Colonial Society of Massachusetts, 1980.

Cometti, Elizabeth, ed. and trans. *Seeing America and Its Great Men: The Journal and Letters of Count Francesco dal Verme, 1783–1784*. Charlottesville: University Press of Virginia, 1969.

Connolly, Thomas. *Mourning into Joy: Music, Raphael, and Saint Cecilia*. New Haven: Yale University Press, 1994.

Cooper, Thomas, ed. *The Statutes at Large of South Carolina*. Vol. 5. Columbia, S.C.: A. S. Johnston, 1839.

Crawford, Richard. *Andrew Law, American Psalmodist*. Evanston: Northwestern University Press, 1968.

Cross, Jack L., ed. "Letters of Thomas Pinckney, 1775–1780." *South Carolina Historical Magazine* 58 (January 1957): 19–33; (July 1957): 145–62.

Crouse, Maurice A. "The Letterbook of Peter Manigault, 1763–1773." *South Carolina Historical Magazine* 70 (April 1969): 79–96; (July 1969): 177–95.

Currie, William. *An Historical Account of the Climates and Diseases of the United States of America*. Philadelphia: T. Dobson, 1792. Reprint, New York: Arno Press, 1972.

Curtis, [Mary] Julia. "Charles-Town's Church Street Theater." *South Carolina Historical Magazine* 70 (July 1969): 149–54.

———. "John Joseph Stephen Leger Sollée and the Charleston Theatre." *Educational Theater Journal* 21 (October 1969): 285–98.

———. "Redating Sketches from Nature by A. Fraser and C. Fraser." *South Carolina Historical Magazine* 93 (January 1992): 51–62.

Dalhaus, Carl. *Nineteenth-Century Music*. Translated by J. Bradford Robinson. California Studies in 19th Century Music, no. 5. Berkeley: University of California Press, 1989.

Davis, Nora Marshall. "The French Settlement at New Bourdeaux." *Transactions of the Huguenot Society of South Carolina* 56 (1951): 28–57.

Dawe, Donovan. *Organists of the City of London, 1666–1850: A Record of One Thousand Organists, with an Annotated Index*. Purley, U.K.: D. Dawe, 1983.

Deas, Anne Izard, ed. *The Correspondence of Mr. Ralph Izard of South Carolina*. New York: Charles S. Francis, 1844.

DeSaussure, Charlton, Jr. "Memoirs of General George Izard." *South Carolina Historical Magazine,* 78 (January 1977): 43–55.

Drayton, John. *A View of South Carolina, as Respects Her Natural and Civil Concerns*. Charleston, S.C.: W. P. Young, 1802. Reprint, Spartanburg, S.C.: Reprint Company, 1972.

Dunlap, William. *Diary of William Dunlap (1766–1839)*. 3 vols. New York: New York Historical Society, 1930.

D'Urfey, Thomas. *Songs Compleat, Pleasant and Divertive*. 6 vols. London.: J. Tonson, 1719–20.

Easterby, J. H. *History of the St. Andrew's Society of Charleston, South Carolina, 1729–1929*. Charleston, S.C.: Privately printed, 1929.

Eckhard, George B. *A Digest of the Ordinances of the City Council of Charleston, from the Year 1783 to Oct. 1844*. Charleston, S.C.: Walker & Burke, 1844.

Edgar, Walter B. "Robert Pringle's World." *South Carolina Historical Magazine* 76 (January 1975): 1–11.

———. *South Carolina: A History.* Columbia: University of South Carolina Press, 1998.

Edwards, Alexander, comp. *Ordinances of the City of Charleston.* Charleston, S.C.: W. P. Young, 1802.

Elizer, Eleazer. *A Directory for 1803: Containing the Names of All the House-Keepers and Traders in the City of Charleston, Alphabetically Arranged, Their Particular Professions, and Their Residence.* Charleston, S.C.: W. P. Young, 1803.

Elkin, Robert. *The Old Concert Rooms of London.* London: Arnold, 1955.

English Poetry Full-Text Database, Copyright © 1992–1995 Chadwyck-Healey Ltd. http://bert.lib.indiana.edu:2140/epd/, accessed January 2004.

Farmer, Henry T. *An Address, Pronounced before the Union Harmonic Society of Charleston, S.C. on the 30th Day of January 1821.* Charleston, S.C.: T. B. Stephens, 1821.

Fiske, Roger, *English Theatre Music in the Eighteenth Century,* 2nd ed. New York: Oxford University Press, 1986.

Franceschini, Gaetano. *Opera I.* Accademia della Magnifica Comunità. Compact disc. Tactus TC 730601, 1998.

Fraser, Charles. *Reminiscences of Charleston.* Charleston, S.C.: John Russell, 1854. Reprint, Charleston, S.C.: Garnier, 1969.

Fraser Harris, David. *Saint Cecilia's Hall in the Niddry Wynd: A Chapter in the History of the Music of the Past in Edinburgh,* 2nd ed. Edinburgh: Oliphant, Anderson & Ferrier, 1911. Reprint, New York: Da Capo Press, 1984.

Fulcher, Jane. "The Orphéon Societies: 'Music for the Workers' In Second-Empire France." *International Review of the Aesthetics and Sociology of Music* 10 (June 1979): 47–56.

Gerson, Robert A. *Music in Philadelphia.* Philadelphia: Theodore Presser, 1940.

Giordani, Tommaso, and Giusto Ferdinando Tenducci, *Queen Mary's Lamentation.* London: John Preston, 1782.

[Gordon, Lord Adam]. "Journal of an Officer who Traveled in America and the West Indies in 1764 and 1765." In *Travels in the American Colonies, 1690–1783,* ed. Newton D. Mereness, 365–453. New York: Macmillan, 1916.

Greene, Jack P. "Colonial South Carolina and the Caribbean Connection." *South Carolina Historical Magazine* 88 (October 1987): 192–210.

Hagy, James W. *This Happy Land: The Jews of Colonial and Antebellum Charleston.* Tuscaloosa: University of Alabama Press, 1993.

Hall, Dominick Augustin, ed. *Ordinances of the City Council of Charleston, in the State of South Carolina.* Charleston: John MacIver, 1796.

Hamm, Charles. *Yesterdays: Popular Song in America.* New York: Norton, 1979.

Handel and Haydn Society. *History of the Handel and Haydn Society, of Boston, Massachusetts.* 2 vols. Boston, A. Mudge, 1882–1913. Reprint, New York: Da Capo Press, 1977–79.

Harrison, T. P. ed. *Journal of A Voyage from Philadelphia to Charlestown In So. Carolina by Pelatiah Webster In 1765.* Reprinted from the *Publications of the Southern History Association,* April 1898. Charleston: South Carolina Historical Society, 1898.

Hart, Oliver. *Dancing Exploded. A Sermon, Shewing the Unlawfulness, Sinfulness, and Bad Consequences of Balls, Assemblies, and Dances in General. Delivered in Charlestown, South-Carolina, March 22, 1778.* Charleston, S.C.: David Bruce, 1778.

Hawkins, John. *A General History of the Science and Practice of Music.* 5 vols. London: T. Payne & Sons, 1776.

Hewatt, Alexander. *An Historical Account of the Rise and Progress of the Colonies of South Carolina and Georgia.* 2 vols. London: Alexander Donaldson, 1779.

Higgins, W. Robert. "The South Carolina Revolutionary Debt and Its Holders, 1776–1780." *South Carolina Historical Magazine* 72 (January 1971): 15–29.

Holcomb, Brent, comp. *South Carolina Naturalizations 1783–1850.* Baltimore: Genealogical Publishing, 1985.

Hoole, W. Stanley. *The Ante-Bellum Charleston Theater.* Tuscaloosa: University of Alabama Press, 1946.

Hopkins, David. "The London Odes on St. Cecilia's Day for 1686, 1695, and 1696." *Review of English Studies,* n.s., 45 (November 1994): 486–95.

Howard, John Tasker. *Our American Music: Three Hundred Years of It.* New York: Crowell, 1931.

Huff, Archie Vernon. *Langdon Cheves of South Carolina.* Columbia: University of South Carolina Press for the South Carolina Tricentennial Commission, 1977.

Huguenot Society of South Carolina. *In Memoriam Wilmot Gibbes DeSaussure.* Charleston, S.C.: Lucas & Richardson, 1886.

Hume, Sophia. *An Exhortation to the Inhabitants of the Province of South-Carolina, to Bring their Deeds to the Light of Christ, in Their Consciences.* Philadelphia: Leeds, 1752.

Husk, William Henry. *An Account of the Musical Celebrations on St. Cecilia's Day in the Sixteenth, Seventeenth and Eighteenth Centuries.* London: Bell & Daldy, 1857.

Hyde, Joseph Bell. *History of Union Kilwinning Lodge No. 4, A. F. M.* Charleston, S.C., 1930.

Irving, John Beaufain. *The South Carolina Jockey Club.* Charleston, S.C.: Russell & Jones, 1857.

Jackson, Donald, and Dorothy Twohig, eds. *The Diaries of George Washington.* Vol. 6: January 1790–December 1799. Charlottesville: University Press of Virginia, 1979.

Jaher, Frederic Cople. *The Urban Establishment: Upper Strata in Boston, New York, Charleston, Chicago, and Los Angeles.* Urbana & Chicago: University of Illinois Press, 1982.

Janson, Charles William. *The Stranger in America: Containing the Observations Made During A Long Residence in That Country.* London: Albion Press, 1807.

Johnson, David. *Music and Society in Lowland Scotland in the Eighteenth Century.* London: Oxford University Press, 1972.

Johnson, Harold Earle. *Musical Interludes in Boston, 1795–1830.* Columbia University Studies in Musicology, no. 5. New York: Columbia University Press, 1943.

Jones, David Wyn. "Robert Bremner and the Periodical Overture." *Soundings* 7 (1978): 62–84.

Keefer, Lubov Breit. *Baltimore's Music: The Haven of the American Composer.* Baltimore, 1962.

Kennedy, Michael L. "A French Jacobin Club in Charleston, South Carolina, 1792–1795." *South Carolina Historical Magazine* 91 (January 1990): 4–22.

Kenney, William Howland. "Alexander Garden and George Whitefield: The Significance of Revivalism in South Carolina, 1738–1741." *South Carolina Historical Magazine* 71 (January 1970): 1–16.

Kierner, Cynthia A. "Hospitality, Sociability, and Gender in the Southern Colonies." *Journal of Southern History* 62 (August 1996): 449–80.

Kinsley, James, ed. *The Poems of John Dryden.* 6 vols. Oxford: Clarendon Press, 1958.

Krauss, Anne McClenny. "Alexander Reinagle, His Family Background and Early Professional Career." *American Music* 4 (Winter 1986): 425–56.

Krawczynski, Keith. *William Henry Drayton: South Carolina Revolutionary Patriot.* Baton Rouge: Louisiana State University Press, 2001.

L'Abbé, Anthony. *A New Collection of Dance.* London: F. Le Roussau, 1725. Facsimile ed. *Music for London entertainment 1660–1800.* Series D. With an introduction by Carol Marsh. London: Stainer & Bell, 1991.

Laurens, Henry. *The Papers of Henry Laurens.* Edited by Philip M. Hamer, George C. Rogers, David R. Chesnutt, and C. James Taylor. 16 vols. Columbia: University of South Carolina Press for the South Carolina Historical Society, 1968–2003.

Lesesne, J. Mauldin. *The Bank of the State of South Carolina: A General and Political History.* Columbia: University of South Carolina Press, 1970.

Lesure, François ed. *Catalogue de la musique imprimée avant 1800: conservée dans les bibliothèques publiques de Paris.* Paris: Bibliothèque Nationale, 1981.

Levett, Ella Pettit. "Loyalism in Charleston, 1761–1784." *Proceedings of the South Carolina Historical Association* (1936): 3–17; (1939): 44.

Levine, Lawrence. *Highbrow/Lowbrow: The Emergence of Cultural Hierarchy in America.* Cambridge, Mass.: Harvard University Press, 1988.

Lewis, Kenneth E. "Archeological Investigations in the Interior of McCrady's Longroom, 38CH559, Charleston, South Carolina." *Institute of Archeology and Anthropology Notebook* 15 (September–December 1983): 1–14.

Library of Congress, *Journals of the Continental Congress 1774–1789. Vol. 1, 1774.* Washington, D.C.: U.S. Government Printing Office, 1904.

Lillywhite, Bryant. *London Coffee Houses: A Reference Book of Coffee Houses of the Seventeenth, Eighteenth, and Nineteenth Centuries.* London: Allen & Unwin, 1963.

Lipscomb, Terry. *Battles, Skirmishes, and Actions of the American Revolution in South Carolina.* Columbia: South Carolina Department of Archives and History, 1991.

———. *South Carolina in 1791: George Washington's Southern Tour.* Columbia: South Carolina Department of Archives and History, 1993.

Lockhart, Matthew A. "'Under the Wings of Columbia': John Lewis Gervais as Architect of South Carolina's 1786 Capital Relocation Legislation." *South Carolina Historical Magazine* 104 (July 2003): 176–97.

Lounsbury, Carl R. *From Statehouse to Courthouse: An Architectural History of South Carolina's Colonial Capitol and Charleston County Courthouse.* Columbia: University of South Carolina Press, 2001.

Low, Betty-Bright P. "Of Muslins and Merveilleuses: Excerpts from the Letters of Josephine du Pont and Margaret Manigault." *Winterthur Portfolio* 9 (1974): 29–75.

Luckett, Richard. "St. Cecilia and Music." *Proceedings of the Royal Musical Association* 99 (1972–73): 15–30.

Mackey, Albert G. *The History of Freemasonry in South Carolina.* Columbia: South Carolina Steam Power Press, 1861.

Mason, Jonathan. *Extracts from A Diary Kept by the Hon. Jonathan Mason of A Journey from Boston to Savannah In the Year 1804.* Reprinted from the *Proceedings of the*

Massachusetts Historical Society, 1885. Cambridge, Mass.: John Wilson & Son, University Press, 1885.

Maurer, Maurer. "The 'Professor of Musick' in Colonial America." *Musical Quarterly* 36 (October 1950): 511–24.

McCombs, Charles F. *Letter-book of Mary Stead Pinckney (November 14th, 1796 to August 29th, 1797).* New York: Grolier, 1946.

McCord, David J. ed., *The Statutes at Large of South Carolina. Vol. 7.* Columbia, S.C.: A. S. Johnston, 1840.

———. *The Statutes at Large of South Carolina. Vol. 8, Acts Relating to Corporations and the Militia.* Columbia, S.C.: A. S. Johnston, 1840.

McCusker, John J. *How Much Is That In Real Money? A Historical Commodity Price Index for Use as a Deflator of Money Values In the Economy of the United States,* 2nd ed. Worcester, Mass.: American Antiquarian Society, 2001.

McInnis, Maurie D. *The Politics of Taste in Antebellum Charleston.* Chapel Hill: University of North Carolina Press, 2005.

McInnis, Maurie D., and Angela D. Mack, eds. *In Pursuit of Refinement: Charlestonians Abroad, 1740–1860.* Columbia: University of South Carolina Press, 1999.

McVeigh, Simon. *Concert Life in London from Mozart to Haydn.* Cambridge: Cambridge University Press, 1993.

Merrens, H. Roy, ed. "A View of Coastal South Carolina in 1778: The Journal of Ebenezer Hazard." *South Carolina Historical Magazine* 73 (October 1972): 177–93.

Milligan, Jacob. *The Charleston Directory, and Revenue System.* Charleston, S.C.: T. B. Bowen, 1790.

Milligen-Johnston, George. *A Short Description of the Province of South-Carolina, with an Account of the Air, Weather, and Diseases, at Charles-town, Written in the Year 1763.* London: John Hinton, 1770. Republished in *Colonial South Carolina: Two Contemporary Descriptions by Governor James Glen and Doctor George Milligen-Johnston,* ed. Chapman Milling, 105–206. Columbia: University of South Carolina Press, 1951.

Mills, Robert. *Statistics of South Carolina.* Charleston, S.C.: Hurlbut & Lloyd, 1826.

Mitchell, Clarence Blair. *Mitchell Record.* Princeton, N.J.: By the Author, 1926.

Moffatt, Lucius Gaston, and Joseph Médard Carrière, eds. "A Frenchman Visits Charleston, 1817." *South Carolina Historical Magazine* 49 (July 1948): 131–54.

Moore, John Hammond, ed. "The Abiel Abbot Journals: A Yankee Preacher in Charleston Society, 1818–1827." *South Carolina Historical Magazine* 68 (April 1967): 51–73; (July 1967): 116–39; (October 1967): 232–54.

Moss, Bobby Gilmer. *Roster of South Carolina Patriots in the American Revolution.* Baltimore: Genealogical Publishing, 1983.

Motte, Abraham. *Charleston Directory and Stranger's Guide, for the Year 1816; Including the Neck to Six Mile House.* Charleston, S.C.: Printed for the Publisher, 1816.

Moultrie, William. *Memoirs of the American Revolution, So Far as It Related to the States of North and South Carolina, and Georgia.* 2 vols. New York: David Longworth, 1802.

Nadelhaft, Jerome J. *The Disorders of War: The Revolution in South Carolina.* Orono: University of Maine at Orono Press, 1981.

Nash, R. C. "The Organization of Trade and Finance in the Atlantic Economy: Britain and South Carolina, 1670–1775." In *Money, Trade, and Power: The Evolution of Colonial*

South Carolina's Plantation Society, ed. Jack P. Greene, Rosemary Brana-Shute, and Randy J. Sparks, 74–107. Columbia: University of South Carolina Press, 2001.

Negrin, J. J. *Negrin's Directory, and Almanac, for the Year 1806: Containing Every Article of Utility.* Charleston, S.C.: J. J. Negrin, 1806.

———. *Negrin's Directory for the Year 1807: Containing Every Article of Utility.* Charleston, S.C.: J. J. Negrin, 1807.

Nelson, John Nixon. *Nelson's Charleston Directory, and Strangers Guide, for the Year of Our Lord 1801.* Charleston, S.C.: John Nixon Nelson, 1801.

Odell, George C. D. *Annals of the New York Stage. Vol. 1, To 1798.* New York: Columbia University Press, 1927. Reprint, New York: AMS Press, 1970.

Orr, Joseph K. "Rhode Islanders in Charleston: Social Notes." *South Carolina Historical Magazine* 75 (July 1974): 180–83.

Ott, Thomas O. *The Haitian Revolution, 1789–1804.* Knoxville: University of Tennessee Press, 1973.

Palmer, Gregory. *Biographical Sketches of Loyalists of the American Revolution.* Westport, Conn.: Meckler, 1984.

Pease, William H., and Jane H. Pease. *The Web of Progress: Private Values and Public Styles in Boston and Charleston, 1828–1843.* New York: Oxford University Press, 1985. Reprint, Athens: University of Georgia Press, 1991.

Pinckney, Rev. Charles Cotesworth. *Life of General Thomas Pinckney.* Boston & New York: Houghton, Mifflin, 1895.

Porter, Susan L. *With An Air Debonair: Musical Theatre in America 1785–1815.* Washington, D.C.: Smithsonian Institution Press, 1991.

Poston, Jonathan H. *The Buildings of Charleston: A Guide to the City's Architecture.* Columbia: University of South Carolina Press, 1997.

Quincy, Eliza Susan, ed. *Memoir of the Life of Josiah Quincy, Junior, of Massachusetts Bay: 1744–1775.* 3rd ed. Boston: Little, Brown, 1875.

Quincy, Josiah, Jr. "Journal of Josiah Quincy, Junior, 1773." *Proceedings of the Massachusetts Historical Society* 49 (June 1916): 424–81.

Ramsay, David. *The History of South-Carolina, from Its First Settlement in 1670, to the Year 1808.* 2 vols. Charleston, S.C.: David Longworth, 1809. Reprint, Newberry, S.C.: W. J. Duffie, 1858.

———. *The History of the Revolution of South Carolina from a British Province to an Independent State.* 2 vols. Trenton, N.J.: Isaac Collins, 1785.

Rasmussen, Jane. *Musical Taste as a Religious Question in Nineteenth-Century America.* Studies in American Religion, vol. 20. Lewiston, N.Y.: Edwin Mellen, 1986.

Rath, Richard Cullen. *How Early America Sounded.* Ithaca, N.Y.: Cornell University Press, 2003.

Ratner, Leonard G. *Classic Music: Expression, Form, and Style.* New York: Schirmer, 1980.

Ratzlaff, Robert K. *John Rutledge Jr.: South Carolina Federalist, 1766–1819.* New York: Arno Press, 1982.

Raven, James. *London Booksellers and American Customers: Transatlantic Literary Community and the Charleston Library Society, 1748–1811.* Columbia: University of South Carolina Press, 2002.

Ravenel, Mrs. St. Julien [Harriott Hörrÿ Rutledge]. *Charleston: The Place and the People.* New York: Macmillan, 1906.

Raynor, Henry. *Music and Society since 1815.* New York: Schocken, 1976.

Rezneck, Samuel. "The Depression of 1819–1822, A Social History." *American Historical Review* 39 (October 1933): 28–47.

Robinson, Emmett, ed. "Dr. Irving's Reminiscences of the Charleston Stage." *South Carolina Historical Magazine* 51 (July 1950): 125–31; (October 1950): 195–215; 52 (January 1951): 26–33; (April 1951): 93–106; (July 1951): 166–79; (October 1951): 225–32; 53 (January 1952): 37–47.

Rogers, George C., Jr. *Charleston in the Age of the Pinckneys.* Norman: University of Oklahoma Press, 1969. Reprint, Columbia: University of South Carolina Press, 1980.

———. *Generations of Lawyers: A History of the South Carolina Bar.* Columbia: University of South Carolina Press, 1992.

Rohr, Deborah. *The Careers of British Musicians, 1750–1850: A Profession of Artisans.* New York: Cambridge University Press, 2001.

Rosen, Charles. *The Classical Style: Haydn, Mozart, Beethoven.* New York: Norton, 1972.

Rousseau, Jean-Jacques. *The Cunning Man, A Musical Entertainment, in Two Acts, Taken from the Devin du Village of J. J. Rousseau, and Adapted to His Original Music by C. Burney.* London: R. Bremner, 1766.

Rozbicki, Michal J. *The Complete Colonial Gentleman: Cultural Legitimacy in Plantation America.* Charlottesville: University Press of Virginia, 1998.

Rubin, Emanuel. *The English Glee in the Reign of George III: Participatory Art Music for an Urban Society.* Detroit Monographs in Musicology/Studies in Music, no. 38. Warren, Mich.: Harmonie Park Press, 2003.

Rutledge, Anna Wells, ed. "Letters from Thomas Pinckney Jr. to Harriott Pinckney." *South Carolina Historical Magazine* 41 (July 1940): 99–116.

Sadie, Stanley. "Concert Life in Eighteenth Century England." *Proceedings of the Royal Musical Association* 85 (1958–59): 17–30.

Sainsbury, W. Noel, comp. "The French Protestants of Abbeville District, S.C. 1761–1765." *Collections of the South Carolina Historical Society* 2 (1858): 75–103.

St. Cecilia Society. *Rules of the St. Cecilia Society: Adopted 17th February, 1831.* Charleston, S.C.: A. E. Miller, 1831.

———. *Rules of the St. Cœcilia Society: Agreed upon and Finally Confirmed, November 22d, 1773.* Charleston, S.C.: Robert Wells, 1774.

———. *Rules of the St. Cecilia Society, Revised and Adopted 10th Jan. 1843.* Charleston, S.C.: S. S. Miller, 1843.

St. John de Crèvecœur, J. Hector. *Letters from an American Farmer.* London: Thomas Davies, 1782. Reprint, New York: Dutton, 1912.

Salley, A. S., Jr. "An All-Accomplished Man. John S. Cogdell Lawyer, Banker, Artist and Musician." Charleston *News & Courier,* 14 July 1901.

———. *The Boundary Line between North Carolina and South Carolina.* Bulletins of the Historical Commission of South Carolina, no. 10. Columbia, S.C.: State Company, 1929.

———, ed. "Diary of William Dillwyn during a Visit to Charles Town in 1772." *South Carolina Historical Magazine* 36 (January 1935): 1–6.

Schoepf, Johann David. *Travels in the Confederation 1783–84.* Translated by Alfred J. Morrison. 2 vols. Philadelphia: William J. Campbell, 1911.

Schoff, James S., ed. *Life in the South 1778–1779: The Letters of Benjamin West.* Ann Arbor: Williams L. Clements Library, 1963.

Seilhamer, George O. *History of the American Theatre.* 3 vols. Philadelphia: Globe Printing House, 1888–91. Reprint, New York: B. Blom, 1968.

Severens, Kenneth. *Charleston: Antebellum Architecture and Civic Destiny.* Knoxville: University of Tennessee Press, 1988.

Shanet, Howard. *Philharmonic: A History of New York's Orchestra.* New York: Doubleday, 1975.

Shaw, Watkins. *The Succession of Organists of the Chapel Royal and the Cathedrals of England and Wales from c. 1538.* Oxford: Clarendon Press, 1991.

Shecut, John Linnaeus Edward Whitridge. *Shecut's Medical and Philosophical Essays.* Charleston, S.C.: A. E. Miller, 1819.

Simons, Elizabeth P. *Music in Charleston from 1732–1919.* Charleston, S.C.: J. J. Furlong & Son, 1927.

Simons, Robert Bentham. "Regimental Book of Captain James Bentham, 1778–1780." *South Carolina Historical Magazine* 53 (January 1952): 13–18; (April 1952): 101–12; (July 1952): 161–71; (October 1952): 230–40.

Sirmans, M. Eugene. *Colonial South Carolina: A Political History, 1663–1763.* Chapel Hill: University of North Carolina Press, for the Institute of Early American History and Culture, Williamsburg, Va., 1966.

Smyth, John Ferdinand Dalziel. *A Tour in the United States of America.* London: G. Robinson, 1784.

Sonneck, Oscar G. *A Bibliography of Early Secular American Music, 18th Century.* Revised and enlarged by William Treat Upton. Washington, D.C.: Library of Congress, Music Division, 1945. Reprint, New York: Da Capo Press, 1964.

————. "A Contemporary Account of Music in Charleston, S.C., of the Year 1783." *New Music Review and Church Music Review* 11 (August 1912): 373–76. Republished in *Oscar Sonneck and American Music,* ed. William Lichtenwanger, 92–99. Urbana & Chicago: University of Illinois Press, 1983.

————. *Early Concert-Life in America 1730–1800.* Leipzig: Breitkopf & Härtel, 1907. Reprint, Wiesbaden: M. Sandig, 1969.

————. *Early Opera in America.* New York: Schirmer, 1915.

South Carolina, General Assembly. *Journals of the House of Representatives, 1783–1784.* Ed. Theodora J. Thompson. Columbia: University of South Carolina Press for the South Carolina Department of Archives and History, 1977.

South Carolina Society. *Transactions of the South Carolina Society upon the Occasion of the Centennial Celebration, July 25, 1904, of the Occupancy of the Society's Hall on the East Side of Meeting Street between St. Michael's Alley and Tradd Street in the City of Charleston, S.C.* Charleston, S.C.: Evans, Walker & Cogswell, 1905.

Sparks, Randy J. "Gentleman's Sport: Horse Racing in Antebellum Charleston." *South Carolina Historical Magazine* 93 (January 1992): 15–30.

Taussig, F. W. *The Tariff History of the United States.* New York: Putnam, 1888.

Thomas, Ebenezer S. *Reminiscences of the Last Sixty-Five Years, Commencing with the Battle of Lexington: Also, Sketches of His Life and Times.* 2 vols. Hartford, Conn.: By the Author, 1840.

Thompson, William. *Poems on Several Occasions.* Oxford, 1757.

Timbs, John. *Club Life of London, with Anecdotes of the Clubs, Coffee-Houses, and Taverns of the Metropolis during the 17th, 18th, and 19th Centuries.* 2 vols. London: Richard Bentley, 1866.

Tritto, Giacomo. *The Favorite Terzetto as Performed . . . at the Kings Theatre Pantheon in the Opera of "La bella pescatrice."* London: Goulding & Skillern, 1791.

Valton, Peter. *The Reprisal. . . . the words by Mr. Lockman. Sung at Marylebone Gardens by Mr. Lowe.* London: Welker, 1765.

Wallace, David Duncan. *The History of South Carolina.* 4 vols. New York: American Historical Society, 1934.

Warfel, Harry R. *Noah Webster, Schoolmaster to America.* New York: Octagon Books, 1966.

Waring, Joseph Ioor. *A Brief History of the South Carolina Medical Association.* Charleston: South Carolina Medical Association, 1948.

———. *A History of Medicine in South Carolina.* Vol. 1: 1670–1825. Charleston: South Carolina Medical Association, 1964.

Waring, William. *The South Carolina and Georgia Almanac for the Year of Our Lord 1793.* Charleston, S.C.: Markland & M'Iver, 1792.

Warren, Thomas, comp. *A Collection of Catches Canons and Glees.* Facsimile ed. With an introduction by Emanuel Rubin. 4 vols. Wilmington, Del.: Mellifont Press, 1970.

Watson, Elkanah. *Men and Times of the Revolution; or Memoir of Elkanah Watson, including Journals of Travels in Europe and America from 1777 to 1842.* Ed. Winslow C. Watson. New York: Dana, 1856.

Wauchope, George Armstrong. *The Writers of South Carolina.* Columbia, S.C.: State Company, 1910.

Webber, Mabel L. "Dr. John Rutledge and His Descendants." *South Carolina Historical Magazine* 31 (January 1930): 7–25.

———, ed. "Order Book of John Faucheraud Grimké." *South Carolina Historical Magazine* 13 (January 1912): 42–55; (April 1912): 89–103; (July 1912): 148–53; (October 1912): 205–12.

———, ed. "Peter Manigault's Letters." *South Carolina Historical Magazine* 32 (October 1931): 270–80.

Weber, William. "Did People Listen in the 18th Century?" *Early Music* 25 (November 1994): 678–91.

———. "London: A City of Unrivalled Riches." In *The Classical Era: From the 1740s to the End of the 18th Century,* 293–326. Man & Music Series. Englewood Cliffs, N.J.: Prentice Hall, 1989.

———. "Mass Culture and the Reshaping of European Musical Taste, 1770–1870." *International Review of the Aesthetics and Sociology of Music* 8 (January 1977): 5–21.

———. *The Rise of Musical Classics in Eighteenth-Century England: A Study in Canon, Ritual, and Ideology.* Oxford: Clarendon Press, 1992.

Weisberger, R. William. *Speculative Freemasonry and the Enlightenment: A Study of the Craft in London, Paris, Prague, and Vienna.* Boulder: East European Monographs, 1993.

Williams, George W. "Early Organists at St. Philip's, Charleston." *South Carolina Historical Magazine* 54 (April 1953): 83–87.

———. "Eighteenth-Century Organists of St. Michael's, Charleston." *South Carolina Historical Magazine* 53 (July 1952): 146–54; (October 1952): 212–22.

———. *Jacob Eckhard's Choirmaster's Book of 1809: A Facsimile with Introduction and Notes.* Columbia: University of South Carolina Press, 1971.

———. "Peter Valton's Hymns." *South Carolina Historical Magazine* 97 (October 1996): 332–33.

———. *St. Michael's, Charleston, 1751–1951.* Columbia: University of South Carolina Press, 1951.

Willis, Eola. *The Charleston Stage in the XVIII Century.* Columbia, S.C.: State Company, 1924.

Wolfe, Richard J. *Secular Music in America 1801–1825.* 3 vols. New York: New York Public Library, 1964.

Wood, Peter H. *Black Majority: Negroes in Colonial South Carolina from 1676 through the Stono Rebellion.* New York: Knopf, 1974.

Yarnold, B. *Six Overtures for the Harpsichord of Piano Forte.* London: Stafford Smith, [1780].

Young, William P. *The Palladium of Knowledge: or, The Carolina and Georgia Almanac, for the Year of our Lord, 1796.* Charleston, S.C.: W. P. Young, 1796.

Zahniser, Marvin R. *Charles Cotesworth Pinckney: Founding Father.* Chapel Hill: University of North Carolina Press for the Institute of Early American History and Culture, Williamsburg, Va., 1967.

Zaslaw, Neal. "The Compleat Orchestral Musician." *Early Music* 7 (January 1979): 46–57.

———. "Toward the Revival of the Classical Orchestra." *Proceedings of the Royal Musical Association* 103 (1976–77): 158–87.

Dissertations and Theses

Bagdon, Robert Joseph. "Musical Life in Charleston, South Carolina, from 1732 to 1776 As Recorded In Colonial Sources." Ph.D. diss., University of Miami, 1978.

Butler, Nicholas Michael. "Votaries of Apollo: The St. Cecilia Society and the Patronage of Concert Music in Charleston, South Carolina, 1766–1820." Ph.D. diss., Indiana University, 2004.

Coker, John W. "Charleston, South Carolina: A Century of Music, 1732–1833." M.M. thesis, Cincinnati Conservatory, 1955.

Crain, Timothy Mark. "Music in the Colonial Charleston, South Carolina Theater: 1732–1781." Ph.D. diss., Florida State University, 2002.

Curtis, [Mary] Julia. "The Early Charleston Stage: 1703–1798." Ph.D. diss., Indiana University, 1968.

Daub, Peggy Ellen. "Music at the Court of George II, 1727–1760." Ph.D. diss., Cornell University, 1985.

Edgar, Walter B. "The Libraries of Colonial South Carolina." Ph.D. diss., University of South Carolina, 1969.

Hindman, John Joseph. "Concert Life in Ante Bellum Charleston." Ph.D. diss., University of North Carolina at Chapel Hill, 1971.

McLamore, Laura Alyson. "Symphonic Conventions in London's Concert Rooms, circa 1755–1790." Ph.D. diss., University of California Los Angeles, 1991.

Scafidel, Beverly Robinson. "Letters of William Elliott." 2 vols. Ph.D. diss., University of South Carolina, 1978.

Sodders, Richard Phillip. "The Theatre Management of Alexandre Placide In Charleston, 1794–1812." Ph.D. diss., Louisiana State University Agricultural and Mechanical College, 1983.

Stephenson, Nan Louise. "The Charleston Theatre Management of Charles Gilfert, 1817 to 1822." Ph.D. diss., University of Nebraska at Lincoln, 1988.

———. "The Charleston Theatre Management of Joseph George Holman, 1815 to 1817." M.A. thesis, Louisiana State University, 1976.

Index

About the Author

NICHOLAS MICHAEL BUTLER is a musicologist, historian, archivist, and musician immersed in the study of Charleston during the colonial and early republic eras. Formerly the archivist for the South Carolina Historical Society, he has taught at the University of South Carolina, the College of Charleston, and Indiana University. Butler is special collections manager at the Charleston County Public Library.